ISSUES IN SOCIOLOGICAL THEORY

Another Look at the "Old Masters"

James T. Duke

Brigham Young University

UNIVERSITY
PRESS OF
AMERICA

LANHAM • NEW YORK • LONDON

Copyright © 1983 by

University Press of America,™ Inc.

4720 Boston Way
Lanham, MD 20706

3 Henrietta Street
London WC2E 8LU England

Printed in the United States of America

ISBN (Perfect): 0-8191-3456-2
ISBN   (Cloth): 0-8191-3455-4

To

Ruth, Jim, Shari, Dave,
Steve, Rich, Kathy,
Jeff, Angela, and Lisa

PERMISSIONS

Quotations from <u>Foundations</u> <u>of</u> <u>Sociology</u>, Revised Edition, by George A. Lundberg. Copyright 1964 by Longman Inc. Reprinted by permission of Longman Inc.

Quotations reprinted with permission of Macmillan Publishing Company from <u>The</u> <u>Methodology</u> <u>of</u> <u>the</u> <u>Social</u> <u>Sciences</u>, by Max Weber, translated by Edward A. Shils and Henry Finch. Copyright 1949 by The Free Press, renewed 1977 by Edward A. Shils.

Quotations reprinted with permission of Macmillan Publishing Company from <u>The</u> <u>Sociology</u> <u>of</u> <u>Georg</u> <u>Simmel</u>, translated and edited by Kurt H. Wolff. Copyright 1950, renewed 1978 by The Free Press, a Division of Macmillan Publishing Company.

Quotations from <u>Social</u> <u>Behavior</u> <u>and</u> <u>Personality</u>: <u>Contributions</u> <u>of</u> <u>W.I.</u> <u>Thomas</u> <u>to</u> <u>Theory</u> <u>and</u> <u>Social</u> <u>Research</u>, edited by Edmund H. Volkart. Copyright 1951 by the Social Science Research Council, reprinted by permission of the Social Science Research Council.

Quotations from <u>The</u> <u>Protestant</u> <u>Ethic</u> <u>and</u> <u>the</u> <u>Spirit</u> <u>of</u> <u>Capitalism</u>, by Max Weber, translated by Talcott Parsons (New York: Charles Scribner's Sons, 1930) reprinted by permission of Charles Scribner's Sons.

Quotations from <u>Human</u> <u>Nature</u> <u>and</u> <u>the</u> <u>Social</u> <u>Order</u>, by Charles Horton Cooley (New York: Charles Scribner's Sons, 1902, 1922) reprinted by permission of Charles Scribner's Sons.

Quotations from <u>Mind</u>, <u>Self</u>, <u>and</u> <u>Society</u>, by George H. Mead, edited by Charles W. Morris (Chicago: University of Chicago Press, 1934) reprinted by permission of The University of Chicago Press.

ACKNOWLEDGEMENTS

I wish to acknowledge my intellectual debt to the following people who influenced my appreciation and understanding of theory: Henry H. Frost, Ted C. Smith, Max L. Carruth, and Robert M. Gray of the University of Utah; Richard J. Hill, Melvin Seeman, Ralph H. Turner, Wendell Bell, Raymond J. Murphy, and Richard J. Morris at U.C.L.A.; and my colleagues in the Department of Sociology at Brigham Young University who are too numerous to mention.

Of course, my deepest intellectual debt is to the theorists whose works are examined here. I have learned much by debating the ghostly presences of theorists like Emile Durkheim and Max Weber.

My fellow students at U.C.L.A. and my own students at Brigham Young University and elsewhere have been a great stimulus to me. One learns quickly which theoretical ideas can be taught and justified easily and which have little validity. Having to express my ideas in interaction with students has disciplined my mind and stimulated me to deeper reflection on the issues presented here.

My love for the gospel of Jesus Christ is deep and personally rewarding, and I have often pondered the relationship between these spiritual principles and sociological theories. Each has given me deeper insight into the other.

I am especially grateful to Dean Martin B. Hickman of the College of Family, Home, and Social Sciences and to the department chairmen, Bruce Chadwick and Spencer J. Condie, who have supported my research efforts. The department, college, and university officers have been extremely supportive of me and my academic pursuits, and have created a climate in which scholarship is valued and encouraged.

Thanks also should be expressed to Marilyn Webb, Jennifer Everette, and Gail Cozzens and to all the personnel of the Faculty Support Center of the college for their excellent work and pleasant disposition during the difficult task of preparation of the manuscript. Thanks also to Sherilyn Snow, Barbara Jenkins, and Alison Mueller for excellent secretarial assistance and other help in numerous ways.

Finally, my love and appreciation for my wife and children, my parents, and brothers and sisters, are beyond expression. I have learned more about sociology and personal relationships from them than from all of the books I have read. My family has always been the laboratory within which I have practiced and applied the principles of human relationships which I study and teach.

TABLE OF CONTENTS

CHAPTER ONE

ALTERNATIVE PERSPECTIVES IN SOCIOLOGICAL THEORY

What can the modern student of sociological theory learn from the "Old Masters"? The contemporary sociological literature is full of references to Durkheim, Weber, Marx, Simmel, Pareto and others of the "classical" theorists, and the Old Masters have maintained a remarkably influential place in the training and functioning of contemporary sociologists.[1]

Our explanation of the continuing influence of the Old Masters is simple: <u>the major contribution of the Old Masters to contemporary sociology is found in the fact that they demarcated and defined the broad orientations which have since governed sociological work</u>. The Old Masters provided the foundations for contemporary sociology by developing a number of alternative theoretical orientations. Contemporary sociologists base their own work upon orienting assumptions and assertions initially developed by the great theorists of the past. It therefore becomes a relatively easy task to show that a given sociologist's work is in the Durkheimian tradition, while another is essentially an intellectual descendant of Marx or Weber, of Cooley or Pareto.

SOCIOLOGICAL THEORY AS ORIENTATION

One of the chief functions of sociological theory is to direct the attention of the sociologist toward certain kinds of phenomena. It gives him or her a peculiar way of looking at these phenomena. It limits his range of vision, but helps him focus more clearly upon certain kinds of phenomena and certain kinds of relationships among these phenomena. According to Merton, such orientations include broad postulates about the nature of the social world.[2] Further, they include a series of concepts or variables which orient the sociologist to a specific manner of conceptualizing and examining the social world. General sociological orientations provide the context within which sociological inquiry and research are pursued.

Merton gives as examples of such sociological orientations (1) Durkheim's assertion that a social fact can only be explained by reference to sociological (not biological nor psychological) facts which precede it as causes, (2) the Paretian notion that society is a system of interrelated parts, and (3) the Weberian assertion as to the importance of individualistic subjective and volitional components of social action.[3] In each case these broad general orientations provide a framework which sensitizes the investigator to the presence of important aspects of social life.

Utilizing a given sociological orientation often can lead a researcher to important breakthroughs in the explanation of specific facts. Merton points to Malinowski's seminal research on Trobriand family organization which led him to a reinterpretation of Freudian psychology and the Opedipal Complex.[4] Beginning with a Durkheimian orientation to social causation rather than a Freudian orientation to deep-seated psychological drives, Malinowski was able to re-examine the intimate relations between males and females, and between parents and children. He said that the intimate ties between male children and their mothers and fathers are due to the manner in which authority relations are structured rather than to sexual drives. The acceptance of a given theoretical orientation was the key factor in leading Malinowski to a new insight and explanation of these data.

Merton's hope is that contemporary sociologists will direct more attention to the development of specific generalizations which express determinate relationships along clearly defined variables. Indeed, this is probably the most significant thrust of contemporary sociology. Yet Merton recognizes that such specific hypotheses and generalizations have a less lasting influence upon the direction and development of a scientific discipline than do general orientations. A new orientation often is the means by which a science changes direction and discovers new paths leading to substantial advances in its sophistication and explanatory ability.

ORIENTATIONS AS ASSUMPTIONS

General sociological orientations represent weltanschauung or "worldviews" which serve to guide the thinking of those who hold them. They contain assumptions which are held unconsciously rather than consciously. Such orientations are taught "by

2

osmosis" so to speak rather than directly. They are seldom questioned precisely because they seem so basic and self-evident that they do not come to the attention of the scientist.

What makes this point so significant is that sociological researchers almost invariably base their research on certain theoretical assumptions which are either unexamined or unexaminable. These assumptions exert their influence upon every aspect of the investigation, from the choice of methodology to the choice of concepts to the conclusions which are derived from the data gathered. As Arnold M. Rose expressed it, "many social science researches do not test the theory, or the hypothesis associated with the theory, they are intended to test. Rather, the researches are self-fulfilling results of the applications or assumptions that are a part of their original ingredients."[5] The results of such investigations are pre-determined by the nature of the implicit assumptions assumed by the investigator.

Rose argued, for example, that if the researcher assumes the stimulus-response model of social behavior to be correct, he will choose an experimental method of research which will lead him to only those kinds of data which are consistent with his initial assumptions. If instead he accepts a Freudian orientation, his research will include deep analysis which can only confirm his initial orientation. Stimulus-response theorists do not use deep analysis, and Freudian theorists do not use experimental methods. The research they each pursue may be able to test specific hypotheses derived from their theoretical orientation, but cannot make any test of the strength of this theoretical orientation vis-a-vis another one. Many researches in the social sciences thus become "self-fulfilling prophecies" which go unrecognized as such. No matter how sophisticated the research design, how extensive or representative the sample, how careful the interviewing and coding, or how powerful the statistical methods employed, the theoretical assumptions underlying the investigation remain untested and largely unrecognized.

A major change in both the thinking and behavior of sociological researchers is clearly needed. And the kind of change is just as clearly indicated, although it is not easily brought about. Sociological investigators must be made aware of the theoretical

3

orientations which serve as unrecognized assumptions underlying their investigations. These orientations must be stated as extensively and explicitly as possible. Further, alternative orientations must also be identified and explicated. Research projects must then be formulated which bring data to bear not only upon the specific hypotheses derived from the theory but upon the alternative orientations themselves. Only if this latter step is accomplished can it be said that the theory has been tested and the conclusions validly drawn.

ALTERNATIVE PERSPECTIVES IN SOCIOLOGICAL THEORY

The major intent of this book is to discuss the various alternative theoretical orientations developed by the Old Masters and to show their application to contemporary sociology. Rather than focus upon the life and times of specific theorists, we will devote our attention to the theoretical issues to which important theorists have addressed themselves and to the broad sociological orientations which they developed in the course of their work.[6] Some of the theorists whose work is to be discussed herein were not themselves fully aware of the orientational assumptions contained in their work. Many did not fully comprehend how drastically their orientation differed from those of others. Most, however, were successful precisely because they recognized the importance of setting forth clearly the assumptions upon which their work was based. They took polemic stances in presenting their own orientations and rejecting alternative ones.

Because they recognized the importance of explicating their own orientations, and because they developed theoretical orientations in opposition to those of others, the theorists to be discussed in the chapters to follow have had a lasting influence on the direction of sociological development. Their influence upon contemporary sociology is still clearly felt precisely because contemporary sociologists base their work upon one or another of the major orientations developed by the Old Masters. Modern sociologists who ignore the works of Marx, Durkheim, Weber and the like do so at their own peril because they will almost certainly fail to recognize the foundations of their own work. The modern student of suicide can sometimes ignore Durkheim's data on suicide and many of the specific explanations given by

4

Durkheim for the relationships he found. However, Durkheim's underlying orientation, his mode of thought and analysis, his assertions about the nature of social organization and social processes, cannot be ignored. They provide the foundation for much of contemporary research in a number of fields widely different from that of deviant behavior.

The sociologist who carefully studies the works of the Old Masters with an eye turned to the perception of theoretical orientations, develops a foundation for his own later work which cannot be matched. It is for this reason--the practical experience that most sociologists have had that a close study of the works of the Old Masters gives one a mode of reasoning and analysis, a manner of thought and practice, which can be obtained in no other way--that the "greats" of sociological theory have retained their influence through the decades. It is for this reason that we approach the study of classical issues in sociological theory in the chapters to follow.

TYPES OF WORLD-VIEWS

Before we begin our more extensive investigations, it is well to summarize, however briefly, the major theoretical issues to be discussed. Each of the orientations which we will examine tends to be opposed by an alternative orientation. Each of these orientations involves an alternative manner of viewing social life. Indeed, each orientation was developed, at least in part, in opposition to another competing orientation. And each orientation tends to be centered around some one or two central issues in sociological theory. In working out the opposing sides of each issue, the Old Masters collectively developed a series of alternative world-views which today define the boundaries within which contemporary sociologists operate.

Theoretical orientations or world-views can be of many different types. Llewellyn Gross has identified many of the most important of these world-views in the course of world history. These include (1) the belief in the dominance and influence of great leaders, (2) the belief in the divine intervention of God to direct the course of history, (3) the balance between freedom and control, (4) the belief in the perfectability of man, (5) the struggle for existence

5

and evolutionary process of development, (6) the conflict between pleasure and pain, and (7) the belief in the cyclical growth and decline of empires.[7] Each of these general orientations tends to direct not only the thoughts but also the behavior of those who accept them; they influence both the nature of social organization which is developed and also the very course of history of the peoples involved.

Such broad world-views, of course, tend to be incorporated into the culture and ethos of a given people. They strongly influence the types of modal personalities and indeed all aspects of social life found in such societies. Robin Williams' widely-read analysis of the culture of the United States presents a detailed description of some of the most widely accepted values of American culture. These include achievement and success, activity and work, moralistic and humanitarian orientation, efficiency and practicality, belief in progress, material comfort, equality, freedom and democracy, external conformity, nationalism and patriotism, scientific rationality, individualism, and racism and ethnocentric superiority themes.[8] While any list of characteristics and values such as this one cannot fully express the ethos of a country as large and complex as the United States, it does give us an indication of the kinds of orientations which we might expect most Americans to take on most issues. There is a characteristic mode of thinking and behaving, a peculiar style of life and belief, that sets the American citizen apart from those of other nations and allows him to be identified rather easily as an American if he travels beyond his own borders.

This American ethos, through the process of sociological forces quite well understood by sociologists, has had its expected effect upon American sociology. Even for a sociologist it is difficult to divorce oneself from a manner of thought and action to which one has been socialized and which one has fully if unconsciously internalized. The sociology practiced by Americans at the turn of the century was as characteristically American as the different brand of sociology found in Germany was characteristically German.

It is not our intent in this book to investigate sociological and historical foundations for the theoretical orientations to be discussed. This is a

6

book on sociological issues, not a book on the sociology of sociology. It is beyond the scope of the present investigation to delve deeply into the social conditions in specific nations which produced the theoretical orientations of their major sociologists. Such analyses are being pursued with increasing emphasis. Several important works of this kind have recently been published.[9]

Our intent is different if no less modest. It is to demarcate clearly the major issues which have been addressed by sociological theorists and the theoretical orientations which they have arrived at in their attempts to confront these issues. It is our feeling that such an approach has more practical and immediate relevance to contemporary sociology and to the average student. Certainly the two approaches are not mutually exclusive, but the size of the task tends to limit the scope of any investigation. Thus, while we recognize the importance of identifying the social and historical roots of the theoretical orientations which we will discuss, and hope that the student may avail himself of such information, we will content ourselves in this volume with delving more deeply into the issues and orientations themselves.

THE ISSUES INTRODUCED

In the chapters to follow, we will discuss three major issues in the development of sociological theory.[10] Each of these issues has proved to be a long-standing one; it was important enough to be addressed by the classical theorists as well as being relevant to contemporary theory.

The Structural vs. the Subjective Approach

This issue addresses itself to the comparative importance of "structure" and "ideas" in the determination of social life. The structural approach focuses upon social organization and social structure as the major feature of social life, and tends to use it as the causal factor in explaining other aspects of social life. Events and conditions in the history of a nation are explained as being due to the particular features of social structure found in that group. The attitudes and behavior of an individual social actor are explained as being due to his structural position or status in some social organization.

7

On the other hand, the subjective approach identifies ideas as the major feature of social life. Man is assumed to possess intelligence and the capacity to think about and reflect upon his own behavior. Subjective thought processes are identified as the major causes of behavior, and therefore of historical events. Individual subjective orientations tend to become embodied in the cultural or normative systems of a society. Sociological explanation involves the process of identifying the subjective aspects of social life and of individual actors and in demonstrating how particular events and conditions were produced by these subjective aspects.

Cause vs. System

Causal theorists tend to assume that two or more events are linked together in a temporal and causal sequence. Those who accept this orientation tend to assume the presence of invariant or probabilistic relations among phenomena such that the first can be said to be the cause of the second. For such theorists, sociological explanation consists primarily of identifying the cause or causes of a particular event or condition. The thrust of their investigations is directed to discovering and laying bare the causal connections among social phenomena.

Systems theorists emphasize the interdependence of sociological units. They conceive of social life as a multiplicity of factors which are mutually dependent upon each other, and that each exercises an influence upon all others. Analysis tends to be directed toward identifying the units of the system and demonstrating their interrelatedness. Multidimensional influence rather than single-directional influence is the essence of such an orientation. The language of causation is replaced by the terminology of systems, including such concepts as equilibrium, feedback, loops, boundary maintenance, etc.

Determinism vs. Individualism

Determinists assume an orderly social world governed by a set of social laws which are determinate and natural. They assume that what occurs in a social group is caused; it occurs because of the workings of social forces or causes which are determinate and law-like. Nothing is due to pure chance. Social life

8

is repetitive, and can be reduced eventually to a set of sociological generalizations through proper scientific investigation. Determinists tend to play down the influence which individual people can exert upon social life. They view history as the working out of the potentialities inherent in social laws rather than as the actions of individuals.

Individualists begin from different premises. They assert that humans are fundamentally thinking, willing, acting beings who are capable of directing the course of their own actions and ultimately the course of history. They tend to begin their sociological investigation from the point of view of the individual actor, and treat such phenomena as group formation, group processes and social history as due to the choices and actions of individuals. Determinists are more likely to seek to generalize their findings to all peoples in all places, while individualists tend to take a relativistic perspective.

THE IDEAL-TYPE NATURE OF THE ISSUES

These issues should be viewed as ideal types which have been developed largly for comparative purposes, since few theorists ever have taken an extreme position on any of these issues. The major sociological theorists whose works we shall study can fruitfully be classified as taking a position on many or all of these issues. Frequently they sought to make their theoretical position contrast clearly with that of some other theorists, and tended to overemphasize certain theoretical assertions in order to make this contrast visible. Yet the great theorists typically do not fit perfectly in any classification scheme, and rarely take an unequivocal position on the major issues of sociological theory.

The three issues to be discussed here, together with the conflict vs. integration issue discussed in Conflict and Power in Social Life,[11] are the most significant issues addressed by sociological theorists during the course of the development of sociology. These issues define the boundaries within which sociological perspectives have developed and encompass the varying alternative theoretical orientations which have become the true legacy of the classical theorists.

The issues thus provide the theoretical springboard which allows us to identify and explore the major orientations in classical sociological theory as well as the development and contemporary relevance of these orientations in modern sociology. As we address each issue in turn, we shall first discuss the classical development of each alternative position on the issue discussed by delving deeply into the works of the classical theorists. Once the alternative orientations have been identified, once we have sorted out the major assertions and implications of each perspective, we shall turn to an examination of contemporary sociology and sociological theorists to see how the classical sociological orientations have been utilized in contemporary sociology.

We believe it is characteristic of contemporary sociology that it tends to hold tightly to its roots in classical theory. Weber, Durkheim, Marx, Simmel, and Pareto, to name the most important, carry as much prestige and influence--and often more--than they did during their own lifetimes. Most sociologists do not consider themselves well trained until they have gained at least an introductory knowledge of the works of the classical theorists.

In contrast, however, it seems equally true of contemporary sociologists that they tend to exhibit some notable theoretical blind-spots, some rather amazing atheoretical tendencies--amazing because of the high regard they give to the classical theorists. The survey researcher, for example, can become the "grubby fact finder," the abstracted empiricist,[12] without ever explicating the structural and positivistic roots of his own orientation or coming to grips with the central issues of sociological theory. He can rather naively take a side on the most important of these theoretical issues without even recognizing that he is doing so.[13] Such actions tend to lead to "self-fulfilling" research rather than to cumulative empirical tests of crucial theoretical positions which ultimately result in the acceptance of one and the rejection of its opposite.

It is our firm belief that the theoretical issues to which the classical theorists addressed themselves are still vitally important to contemporary sociology, and that the failure to recognize these issues and address them directly has resulted in the production of a multitude of theoretically meaningless studies and the slower development of theoretical sociology than its precursors had hoped for. Only by dealing directly with the meaningful issues of classical sociological theory can sociology attain the promise for which both its former and current practitioners optimistically hope.

FOOTNOTES

[1]Compare Robert K. Merton, Social Theory and Social Structure (Glencoe: Free Press), 1957, pp. 4-5 with his later comments in "Foreword," in Lewis A. Coser, Masters of Sociological Thought (New York: Harcourt), 1971, pp. vii-viii. Lewis A. Coser, "The Uses of Classical Sociological Theory," in Buford Rhea (ed.), The Future of the Sociological Classics (London: Allen & Unwin), 1981, pp. 170-182.

[2]Robert K. Merton, "The Bearing of Sociological Theory on Empirical Research," in Social Theory and Social Structure, pp. 87-89. See also William J. Goode and Paul K. Hatt, Methods in Social Research (New York: McGraw-Hill), 1952, pp. 9-12.

[3]Merton, Social Theory and Social Structure, p. 88.

[4]Ibid., pp. 88-89. See Bronislaw Malinowski, Sex and Repression in Savage Society (London: Routledge and Kegan Paul), 1927.

[5]Arnold M. Rose, "The Relation of Theory and Method," in Llewellyn Gross, editor, Sociological Theory: Inquiries and Paradigms (New York: Harper), 1967, p. 213.

[6]The literature on theoretical issues is broad and varied, but the following are especially notable: Irving Louis Horowitz, "Mainliners and Marginals: The Human Shape of Sociological Theory," in Llewellyn Gross, op cit., pp. 358-383; Alvin Boskoff, Theory in American Sociology (New York: Crowell), 1969, especially Chapter One; James T. Duke, "Theoretical Alternatives and Sociological Research," Social Forces, 45 (June 1967), pp. 571-582; Otis Dudley Duncan and Leo F. Schnore, "Cultural, Behavioral, and Ecological Perspectives in the Study of Social Organization," American Journal of Sociology, 65 (1959), pp. 132-146; Reinhard Bendix, "The Image of

Man in the Social Sciences: The Basic Assumptions of Present-Day Research," in Seymour M. Lipset and Neil J. Smelser, editors, Sociology: The Progress of a Decade (Englewood Cliffs, NJ: Prentice-Hall), 1961; Nelson J. Foote, et al., "Alternative Assumptions in Stratification Research," Transactions of the Second World Congress of Sociology (London: International Sociological Association), 1954; Walter L. Wallace, editor, Sociological Theory (Chicago: Aldine), 1969, Part I; and Helmut R. Wagner, "Types of Sociological Theory: Towards A System of Classification," American Sociological Review, 28 (October 1963), pp. 735-742.

[7] Llewellyn Gross, "Sociological Theory: Questions and Problems," in Gross, op. cit., pp. 23-24.

[8] Robin M. Williams, Jr., American Society (New York: Knopf), 1960, pp. 415-468.

[9] See especially Coser, Masters of Sociological Thought, op. cit.

[10] A fourth issue has been explored extensively by the author in a previous work. See James T. Duke, Conflict and Power in Social Life (Provo: Brigham Young University Press), 1976.

[11] Ibid.

[12] C. Wright Mills, The Sociological Imagination (New York: Grove Press), 1961, especially pp. 50-75.

[13] Duke, "Theoretical Alternatives and Social Research," op. cit.

CHAPTER TWO

CLASSICAL STRUCTURALISM: MARX AND ENGELS[1]

Few persons in history have caused as much intellectual ferment as Karl Marx and Friedrich Engels, and few have had such a profound effect on human history. Marx's influence upon 19th century sociology is immeasureable. Gradually, his influence upon sociology declined, reaching a low point in the 1950s at the heyday of functionalism. Since 1960, however, there has been an increased interest in the sociological aspects of Marxist theory, especially in the United States.

Because of Marx's and Engel's extensive writings on a great variety of subjects--for both scientific and propagandistic purposes--it is natural that many interpretations of Marxism have developed. This should be noted at the beginning of any study of Marx and his writings. Marx is much more consistent than many of his critics give him credit, but it is possible to find passages in his writings which support almost any interpretation or any theoretical point of view.

However, certain constant tendencies emerge from Marx's writings. First, he consistently used Hegelian dialectics in his writing and in his thinking. Second, Marx was a materialist (especially in his later writings), giving first priority as causal agents to material--i.e. economic--forces. Third, he consistently advocated revolutionary methods for achieving a destruction of the capitalistic system, which was to be replaced by a communistic economic system. And fourth, he uniformly emphasized the causal priority of the social structure in determining subjective states of mind.

HISTORICAL MATERIALISM

Marx was extremely impressed by Hegelian philosophy in his university days. He accepted wholeheartedly the notion of the dialectic[2] and used it throughout his life. Together with the other "Young Hegelians" in Berlin he sought to meliorate the authoritarianism of the Prussian Government and "free" it from the influence of religion.

13

Moreover, Marx at first accepted Hegel's idealism --his assertion that the ultimate reality was found in ideas. According to Hegel, the State was the embodiment of the "idea" of the state in its pure or ideal form. A leading Hegelian, Ludwig Feuerbach, rejected this doctrine in his book The Essence of Christianity,[3] arguing instead for the importance of materialistic factors in influencing ideas. This had a profound effect on Marx, Engels, and other Hegelians who quickly came to accept Feuerbach's point of view. Up until about 1844, Marx had been concerned primarily with philosophy and humanism. The changes he advocated were largely political and religious. After 1844, he and Engels increasingly emphasized economic production. Economics became more important in their studies than philosophy, and the changes they advocated in society were largely economic in nature.[4]

According to Marx and Engels, the mode of production is the key to understanding social institutions. Economic production can be organized in several different ways, or modes. Each mode of production is associated with a distinct pattern of thought and action on the part of individuals who are influenced by the positions they hold in the mode of production. All social relations and all ideas found in a society are simply reflections or effects of the organization of production.

People must produce to live; they soon learn that in order to survive they must produce the means of existence. In order to produce the means of existence most effectively, people enter into social relations with others--they cooperate together. All social relations depend ultimately upon the need for people to associate with others in order to produce the means of existence.[5] The need to cooperate leads to the division of labor and to increased specialization. To put it simply, the need for economic production leads to the creation and perpetuation of society.

It is important to note Marx's use of the terms "structure" and "superstructure" in his writings, especially in the Preface to the Critique of Political Economy.[6]

In the social production which men carry on they enter into definite relations that are indispensable and independent of their will; these relations of production

14

correspond to a definite stage of development of their material powers of production. The sum total of these relations of production constitutes the economic structure of society --the real foundation, on which rise legal and political superstructures and to which correspond definite forms of social consciousness. The mode of production in material life determines the general character of the social, political and spiritual processes of life. It is not the consciousness of men that determines their existence, but, on the contrary, their social existence determines their consciousness.[6]

The foundation of all social life is the economic structure (or substructure), which is the sum total of the forces and relations of production. The rest of society and its institutions (the superstructure) are built upon this structure.

Economic production, which Marx called the "substructure" of society, is subdivided into two elements. The first is called the "forces of production," which include the natural resources, the physical equipment, the people, the division of labor, and the scientific and engineering technology which are present in the economy. The second element is called the "relations of production." These consist of the social definitions of the relations between economic groups (e.g. between capitalists and laborers), the social norms governing the economy (such as ownership of private property), and the patterns of behavior found among economic groups.

Economic production is the major causal factor in social life. All ideas, attitudes, institutions and behavior patterns are dependent upon--that is, effects of--the organization of production. The "superstructure" of society, which is built upon the foundation of economic production, includes all these other aspects of social life. Other major institutions of society, including the government, religion, education and the family, are part of the superstructure. Individual attitudes, perceptions and emotions, all patterns of behavior, and the normative and cultural systems of society as well, are dependent upon the mode of production in the society.

As a simple illustration, Marx wrote in The German Ideology[7] of the need to produce children in order to perpetuate the existence of society. Such production obviously involves social relations among men and women. While Marx's notion of the origin of family life was extremely simplistic, the illustration is clear: social relations depend directly upon the need for production.

One of the crucial experiences in Marx's life was his move from Cologne to Paris in 1843.[8] Marx was struck with the extensive differences between France and Germany at that time. France was undergoing a rapid industrial transformation following the French Revolution. The social and intellectual climate in Paris, which Marx attributed to this economic transformation, was exhilarating to him. In contrast, Germany was still largely feudalistic, both economically and politically. The major differences between Germany and France were not abstract elements of culture, religion or ideology, but of economic production. A more developed mode of production had caused the differential development of these other ideational factors such as religion and culture. Marx came to realize that the Young Hegelians' original radical efforts in Germany were doomed to failure because Germany had not developed economically to the point where a revolution was possible. Historically significant events could be explained by reference to the mode of production which provided a framework upon which these events occurred and took on meaning.

Let us illustrate Marx's historical materialism by two further examples drawn from his works. Marx's opposition to religion is well known.[9] He thought of religion as an opiate--a drug which is given to people to keep them happy and encourage them to remain in their economic positions. Marx believed that religious organizations and religious values are controlled and influenced by those groups that control the economy. Sermons which are given from the pulpit almost invariably support the economic position of the owners and are utilized for the exploitation of the workers.

For example, the basic themes of religious teachings during the nineteenth century were hard work and traditional acceptance of one's position. The workers (Proletariat) were taught to work hard and to love their neighbors, including the capitalists (bourgeoisie), and to be happy with the social position which they occupied. Churches taught that God did not reward men for their righteousness in this life. Rather, men should look forward to a future heaven for their rewards for good service. Both hard work and discipline were encouraged. Working men were not to create a revolution. They were not to be violent, but were to look forward eventually to receiving just rewards for their labors. These rewards did not come in this life and did not come through their labors in the economy. Workers may not be paid sufficiently by the owners; however, they would eventually receive just compensation in an after-life.

Rather than praising the beneficial effects of religion, Marx was frustrated that the religious beliefs of the Proletariat kept them from being more revolutionary. And rather than being concerned with the theological aspects of religion, Marx cared only for the social ramifications of religious beliefs and practices.

Marx, therefore, believed that economic organizations influence religious bodies, much of the time indirectly. Religion makes people happy and draws away from their revolutionary spirit. In any confrontation between labor and management, the churches almost invariably side with the businessmen.

A second illustration of Marx's economic determinism is found in his analysis of the relationship of the economy to the government.[10] Previous political economists had taken the state as given (as cause), and had sought to derive the nature of economy from it (as effect). State regulation to these theorists determined the form of the economy.[11] In his <u>Preface to the Critique of Political Economy</u> Marx took the opposite point of view. To him, the form of the government is dependent upon the development and organization of the economy. Those social groups which control the economy also exercise control over the government. The sole purpose of government is as an exploitative force to keep the workers in line. In the stage of capitalism, the bourgeoisie use the government to exploit and control the behavior of the proletariat. No other purpose for government is identified. Marx believed that if economic exploitation were not present, that is, if there were no social classes within a society, the government would

17

eventually wither away and die. He believed that once communism was achieved, the economy would be controlled through natural and self-regulating means. No government would be necessary to maintain conformity.

Even under a supposedly democratic type of government, as found in England, Marx believed that the bourgeoisie were able to control the legislation and the other aspects of government. They exert influence on government officials through bribery or other forms of influence and are able to veto any government proposals which are decidedly contrary to their own interests. The actions of government are in almost every case determined by the interests of the owners and are for the benefit of such owners. The result is the political as well as economic exploitation of those who have little power--that is, the workers.

MODES OF PRODUCTION AND HISTORICAL STAGES

According to Marx, history can be divided into five distinct historical stages. Each stage is characterized by a separate mode of production. Each mode of production, in turn, can be characterized by a distinct type of ownership of the means of production.[12]

The first stage of human history is that of primitive production. In this stage, all property, including all means of production, is communally owned. All members of the tribe or group share the land, the waterways with their fish, and the animals-- either domestic or wild--upon which the group depends for its existence. As the society grows in size (both through natural increase and unity with other tribes), "state" ownership develops. Ownership is still held by the group, but since the group is larger and has a more formal political structure, the nature of ownership is different. This second stage is characterized by slavery as the common form of both servitude and production. In this stage, private property gradually develops, especially with relation to "immovable" objects and land.

The third stage of ownership is "feudal or estate-property." Slavery is replaced by serfdom. The serfs, who are the primary producing class, have certain traditional rights but no formal ownership of property. Here, the institution of private property has been considerably developed over the previous

18

stage, but the group still holds an important interest in such property. Cities also develop, and with them a small class of artisans, who in turn depend upon the labor of journeymen.

Capitalism represents the fourth stage of production. This mode of production is extensively analyzed in Capital. Marx devoted a great deal of his time in the later part of his life to examining and explaining the workings of capitalism as an economic system. In capitalism, private ownership of property reaches its zenith. Production is accomplished by the Proletariat, a class of supposedly "free" laborers who sell their labor to the capitalists. The Proletariat have no traditional ties to the land nor any traditional economic and political rights as the serfs did. Most importantly, they do not own the means of production, but are hired by the owners to run the factories and till the land owned by others.

According to Marx, the fifth and final stage in human history will be communism, which will supplant capitalism. Communism is characterized by communal ownership of the means of production. In a sense, ownership of the means of production has come full circle, and most closely approximates ownership in the first stage. However, the economy of communism is based on industrial production rather than hunting and gathering. Class divisions are destroyed in the communist stage, resulting in a single class of workers who share the fruits of production equally. Significantly, Marx devoted an extremely small part of his writings to an examination of the nature of communism and social conditions in this stage. Some few predictions are made in the Manifesto and in some of his correspondence. Marx, however, was a scientist, not a prophet. His sociological contributions are found primarily in his analyses of the economy and society of his day--in the workings of the capitalistic system of production and its influence upon other aspects of social life.

IDEOLOGY AND REVOLUTION

Marx's historical materialism was consistently applied in his theories of ideology and revolution. In The German Ideology[13] Marx and Engels developed a cogent theory of the promulgation of ideology. They argued that the ideology of a society originates in the ruling class and is proclaimed by the ruling class

19

to the rest of society. Control over the production
of goods is the major factor in allowing the ruling
class to control the production of ideas.

Education is differentially distributed among the
population, with only members of the ruling class able
to gain the education needed to manipulate ideas
successfully. (This analysis applies better to the
1840s than to the contemporary era, although there is
still an important correlation between social class
origin and education received.) Members of the ruling
class have great power, and have many means at their
disposal to motivate and otherwise influence the
masses to accept the ideology which they promulgate.

The major purpose of the ideology is to give a
justification for the status quo. That is, the ideology must explain why it is necessary that some people
be members of a ruling class while others remain in
poverty, why some people are able to control the
actions of others. By legitimizing the rule of the
ruling class, the ideology influences the masses to
accept their place in life and their inferior position
in relation to the ruling class. While the ideology
benefits only the ruling class, it often is accepted
by all other classes.

Marx and Engels argued that the masses accept
this ideology for two reasons. First, they lack
economic power, and are coerced by economic and political sanctions to accept the ideology of the ruling
class. Second, they lack the education and other
means to produce an ideology of their own to counter
that of the ruling class. This is why it is necessary
that a group of intellectuals join the working class
before the revolution of the masses against the ruling
class can occur.[14]

Material conditions always determine the ideas
which are accepted in a society. That is why ideology
always represents the interests of the ruling class.
How, then, can a revolution occur? According to Marx,
no change in the mode of economic production, no
change in political structure, no new way of life can
be achieved by peacefully preaching new ideas. Such
new ideas would come in conflict with the present mode
of economic production, and would be rejected or
suppressed. One cannot change social and economic
conditions through words.

In order to institute a new social order it is necessary that a complete change be made in the mode of economic production. Only when a new economic system has been founded can a new ideological system be promulgated. According to Marx and Engels, as capitalism matures the proletariat gradually becomes economically indispensable and the bourgeoisie lose control of the economy.[15] Labor becomes the most important aspect of capitalistic production, and management, especially absentee management, becomes less and less necessary. Eventually, therefore, the proletariat gain de facto control of the economy, while the bourgeoisie still have de jure control of the economy, the government and other ideological and institutional features of the society. At this point, a revolution is necessary to reestablish the connection between economic production and other features of the society. The changes which first occur in the economy must lead to changes in other aspects of the society. As the proletariat gradually become indispensable for economic production, they develop an ideology which justifies a revolution and the control of the economy by the workers. Only through a revolutionary change in who controls economic power can a new set of social ideas become institutionalized.

IS MARXISM A MONISTIC THEORY?

Most interpretations of Marxism (especially by its critics) have treated it as a consistent monistic theory, with economic production viewed as the cause of other social phenomena. Marx certainly was very much conditioned by the monistic orientation of most of science during his time. Many Marxists have argued, however, that ideas are significant factors in social life and have an independent existence apart from productive forces. They point to Marx's use of the word wechselwirken as implying the notion of reciprocity between productive forces and ideas. Causation can move in both directions, they argue. Certainly there are many passages in Marx's writings that can be so interpreted.[16]

For example, in The German Ideology, Marx foresaw a kind of culture lag in which ideas do not keep pace with economic developments. Thus a condition arises where the proletariat have become economically indispensable and where economic conditions are conducive to a major change in the society, but the culture and personality patterns remain unchanged. The revolution, then, is necessary to reestablish the continuity and the balance between economic conditions and the ideational phenomena which depend on these conditions.

The point we wish to make here is that Marx recognized that the relationship between structure and ideas is not automatic or completely in balance. Social structure is the ultimate cause of ideas, but there may be some time lapse between cause and effect. Further, revolution is sometimes necessary as an intervening variable between the economic conditions (structure) and the ideas (culture) of the society.[17]

Engels in his later writings also seemed to take a more moderate position on historical determinism. In his famous letter to Bloch,[18] Engels argued that economic production is the ultimate, the primary cause of other aspects of social life. But the link between cause and effect may be mediated by many other cultural and/or ideational factors. Further, Engels rejected materialism as the "sole" cause of social phenomena, thereby rejecting a monistic interpretation of Marxian theory. Many other factors in the superstructure also influence the course of history. Reciprocity rather than inflexible causal relations is characteristic of social life. But ultimately, the economic substructure "asserts itself" as the major cause of social phenomena.

However, it is important to note that both Marx and Engels were highly critical of any socialists who did not take a relatively extreme position as materialists and monistics. They constantly opposed idealism and all its ramifications. Engel's book Anti-Duhring is notable as an example. V. I. Lenin, who became their chief interpreter in the early 20th Century and who created the revolution which established communism in Russia, interpreted Marxism in this strictly materialistic way.[19]

Many modern critics have also taken this point of view.[20] I am in substantial agreement with this interpretation. Few can read Marx at any length without grasping the force of his realism and materialism. While it may be granted that he allowed some independence to other factors, it is clear that the major, the "essential" causes were economic. To interpret Marx otherwise is to transform Marx from a passionate revolutionary promoting the class struggle to a calm professor attempting to specify all the

22

qualifications to his theory. The latter he was not, however scientific he may have been. Therefore, while one should not classify Marx as an extreme determinist, one must recognize that Marx thought of production as much more important in determining historical stages and determining the occurrences in history than any other aspect of social life.

More consistently than almost anyone else, Marx took a monistic structural point of view in the explanation of social life. This essential insight is one of Marx's greatest contributions to our understanding of social life. The structural approach to the explanation of social phenomena is one of the most important theoretical models utilized by sociologists.

THE STRUCTURAL APPROACH

We are now in a position to discuss more clearly the basic principles of what we shall call "the structural approach." This approach owes its initial and most significant development to Marx. However, we wish to emphasize at this point that the structural approach as we shall develop it is broader than Marx's historical materialism. We consider historical materialism to be one kind of structuralism. Marx's theories provide us with a springboard for a more general theoretical discussion of structuralism.

The structural approach may be summarized in the following propositions:

(1) With regard to society, the manner in which a society is structured or organized is the major feature of social life; social structure determines or influences all other elements of a society.

(2) With regard to the individual, the position which an individual holds in a social structure is the major factor in determining all other social aspects of the individual's life.

SOCIETAL ORGANIZATION

The first proposition implies that the cultural and normative systems of the society, the patterns of behavior, the historical events which occur, and the personalities and attitudes of individuals are all largely influenced by the particular pattern of social organization found in the society. While social structure may be described in different ways, it is usually looked at as a system of statuses organized in such a way that the relationships among statuses are formalized. Each position in the structure is defined vis a vis other statuses. The total configuration of the social structure, and the relationships of all statuses to all other statuses, is stabilized and patterned.

Structural explanations take the following form. First, different types of social structures are distinguished and classified. Second, a theoretical or empirical argument demonstrates that one type of social structure results in different effects than another type. The structure is treated as the causal or independent variable. The dependent variables may include any relevant sociological factors, including patterns of behavior, cultural norms and values, specific personality traits, or attitudinal uniformities.

For example, Marx distinguished five types of economic organization--primitive production, slavery, feudalism, capitalism, and communism. He then sought to demonstrate the causal relationship between the type of economic organization present and other effects, such as political organization, religious teachings, revolution, etc.

Examples of structural explanations drawn from contemporary sociology include the following. Societies with a high degree of economic development are more conducive to a democratic governmental organization than societies with a lower level of development.[21] A group with a democratic pattern of social organization produces happier and more well adjusted personalities than autocratically organized groups.[22] A society with a large lower class is more conducive to emotionally-oriented religious beliefs and rites than a society with a large middle class.[23]

INDIVIDUAL POSITION

The second proposition is concerned with individual rather than group behavior. Here again, the way the group is structured is central to the explanation. The position the individual holds in a social structure is identified and categorized. This position or status is then viewed as a major determinant of other social aspects of the individual's social life, including his personality, attitudes and behavior. This position may be obtained through either ascription or achievement. The position is seen as placing limitations upon the individual and constraining him to act in conformity to the position.

Examples of this approach drawn from contemporary sociology include the following. An individual who occupies a lower class position is more likely to vote for liberal political parties than a member of the middle class.[24] A member of a minority group is more likely to become mentally ill than a member of the dominant group.[25] A couple from the middle class are more likely to have a stable marriage than a couple from the lower class.[26] Women are more likely to attend church than men.[27]

Explanations based on social class position or ethnic status are most likely to take this approach. However, any reference to organizational position rather than to specific cultural values or other ideational variables is assumed to be a structural explanation.[28]

SUMMARY

In this chapter Marx's and Engel's theory of historical materialism has been summarized. Marx and Engels clearly argued for the causal priority of economic organization in influencing ideas, historical events (such as revolutions) and all other social manifestations. The structural approach, which received its most extreme development in Marxism, was then discussed. The structural approach was illustrated with brief examples drawn from contemporary sociological research. In the next chapter, Durkheim's contribution to structuralism, which in large measure developed independently of Marxian theory, will be discussed.

FOOTNOTES

[1]It has become an impossible task to include the names of both Marx and Engels through the whole chapter. Therefore, we have resorted to the usual expedient of using only Marx's name in most references to their works. This is unfair to Engels, whose lifelong collaboration with Marx influenced him greatly. Perhaps nowhere in intellectual history is

there a better example of two men working more closely and effectively together in an intellectual enterprise. Engel's contributions to what has come to be called Marxism cannot be separated from those of Marx. In almost every respect, this theory is a joint enterprise.

[2]For a more extensive discussion of the dialect, economic determinism, and Marx's conflict theory, see James T. Duke, _Conflict and Power in Social Life_. Provo, Utah: Brigham Young University Press, 1976, Chapter 2.

[3]Ludwig A. Feuerbach, _The Essence of Christianity_. New York: F. Ungar Publishing Company, 1957.

[4]Louis Dupre, _The Philosophical Foundations of Marxism_. New York: Harcourt, 1966, p. 172. See also Robert Freedman (ed.), _Marxist Social Thought_. (New York: Harcourt), 1968; Robert C. Tucker (ed.), _The Marx-Engels Reader_, 2nd. Ed., (New York: Norton), 1978; and Alvin W. Gouldner, _The Two Marxisms_. (New York: Oxford University Press), 1980.

[5]Karl Marx and Friedrich Engels, _The German Ideology_. New York: International Publishers, 1947, pp. 8-18.

[6]Karl Marx, _Preface to A Contribution to the Critique of Political Economy_. Chicago: Kerr, 1904, pp. 11-12.

[7]Op. _cit_., pp. 13-14.

[8]For a good biography of Marx's life, see Robert Payne, _Marx_. New York: Simon and Schuster, 1968.

[9]Karl Marx and Friedrich Engels, _Manifesto of the Communist Party_. Chicago: Charles H. Kerr, 1904, pp. 39-40; Karl Marx, _Towards a Critique of the Hegelian Theory of Law_.

[10]_Manifesto_, especially page 15; Karl Marx, _The Poverty of Philosophy_. New York: International Publishers, 1963; I have been heavily influenced here, as elsewhere, by C. Wright Mills's cogent interpretation. See _The Marxists_. New York: Dell, pp. 88-89, 115-119.

[11]Henri Lefebvre, The Sociology of Marx. New York: Random House, 1968, especially pp. 126ff.

[12]Karl Marx and Friedrich Engels, The German Ideology. New York: International Publishers, 1947, pp. 10ff.

[13]Ibid.

[14]Manifesto, p. 26.

[15]The Poverty of Philosophy, pp. 120-123; Mills, The Marxists, pp. 88-89, 115-119; Duke, Conflict and Power, pp. 22-30.

[16]See for example Robert Tucker, Philosophy and Myth in Karl Marx. Cambridge, England: University Press, 1961. However, Lenin's book Materialism and Empirico-Criticism (Moscow: Foreign Languages Publishing House, 1947) was specifically written to rebut a group of Russian "revisionists" who were interpreting Marx in this way.

[17]See especially The German Ideology, p. 72.

[18]Friedrich Engels, "Letter to Joseph Bloch," in Robert C. Tucker, ed., The Marx-Engels Reader. New York: Norton, 1978, pp. 760-765.

[19]Lenin, Materialism and Empirico-Criticism; V. I. Lenin, Marx-Engels-Marxism. Moscow: Foreign Languages Publishing House, 1947, especially pp. 15-49, 84-98, 153-163.

[20]Emile Burns, What Is Marxism? New York: International Publishers, 1957, pp. 150-162, and Mills, The Marxists, pp. 91-93.

[21]Gabriel Almond and James S. Coleman, editors, The Politics of the Developing Areas. Princeton, N.J.: Princeton University Press, 1960, pp. 559-576, and Seymour Martin Lipset, Political Man. Garden City, N.Y.: Doubleday, 1960, pp. 27-63.

[22]Ronald Lippitt, "An Experimental Study of the Effect of Democratic and Authoritarian Group Atmospheres," Studies in Child Welfare (University of Iowa), Volume 16 (February 1940), pp. 43-195.

[23]Liston Pope, Millhands and Preachers. New Haven: Yale University Press, 1942, Vittorio Lanternari, The Religions of the Oppressed. New York: Knopf, 1963.

[24]Paul F. Lazarsfeld, Bernard Berelson and Hazel Gaudet, The People's Choice. New York: Duell, Sloan and Pearce, 1944, and Lipset, Political Man, pp. 230-331.

[25]August B. Hollingshead and Frederick Redlich, Social Class and Mental Illness. New York: Wiley, 1958.

[26]Julius Roth and R. F. Peck, "Social Class and Social Mobility Factors Related to Marital Adjustment," American Sociological Review, 16 (August 1951), pp. 478-487.

[27]Bernard Berelson and Gary A. Steiner, Human Behavior. New York: Harcourt, 1964, p. 392.

[28]James T. Duke, "Theoretical Alternatives and Social Research," Social Forces 45 (June 1967), pp. 571-582.

CHAPTER THREE

CLASSIC STRUCTURALISM: EMILE DURKHEIM

Emile Durkheim's eminence among sociological theorists is unsurpassed. While Auguste Comte originated sociology in France, it was Durkheim who established sociology in France and made it a respectable science. His great study of suicide is generally regarded as one of the most important classics of sociological literature and has provided the paradigm for later macrosociological research. He made important contributions to sociological methodology and statistics, as well as to the sociology of religion, education and deviant behavior. Most importantly, Durkheim provided the basic arguments for the establishment of sociology as a separate discipline which have been used ever since by sociologists to justify their work.

Like Marx, Durkheim was a structuralist in his approach to the explanation of social phenomena. However, his structualism was of a decidedly different sort than Marx's. Marx started with the organization of the economy, and analyzed the causal significance of economic organization in determining cultural values and norms. Durkheim seldom made mention of the economy. Instead, he assigned a central role to the importance of religion, ethics, and morality to society. Marx dismissed religion as "the opiate of the people." Durkheim devoted years of his life to the study of religious phenomena. If religion is an opiate, Durkheim was addicted--not to religious principles but to a scientific examination of the social significance of religion. Among the classic theorists, only Weber may be credited with more extensive studies of religion from a sociological point of view.

Why do people act the way they do? Like other classic theorists, Durkheim was interested in understanding and explaining human social behavior. In seeking for an answer, Durkheim was impressed by the influence of moral precepts and rules of conduct upon human behavior. These "collective representations" were the essence of religion and morality to Durkheim. While Durkheim's understanding of norms was not as clear as Sumner's, he fully appreciated the crucial role which moral standards of conduct play in bringing individuals into conformity with the social group and establishing such individuals as "social" beings.

SOCIAL FACTS AS THINGS: SOCIOLOGICAL POSITIVISM

Durkheim's methodological position is consistent with his structural emphasis. Social structure rather than ideas is the most important aspect of social life. Sociological methodology must recognize this, and place its emphasis upon structural realities, not ideas.

In The Rules of Sociological Method Durkheim developed his famous rule: "consider social facts as things."   According to him, most sociologists treat social facts as if they are ideas, not things. Instead of observing social facts as they would an object, they seek to manipulate them in their minds as they would an idea.   Comte and Spencer were criticized because they treated social facts as if they have a "reality only in and through the ideas which are their germ, and the ideas, therefore, become the proper subject matter of sociology."[1]

To treat social facts as things is to treat them as external occurrences, not as ideas. They cannot be modified by thought processes or human will. They must be studied from the point of view of an external observer, not the point of view of the actor. Durkheim specifically rejected introspection or subjective methods as proper to the study of social facts.[2] The use of introspection (or verstehen) had been advocated by many, and was later strongly supported by Max Weber. Durkheim believed that the use of introspection created a tendency to seek "the verities" or the essence of truth a priori. It led its user away from careful observation, description and analysis. For example, introspection might lead a sociologist to the conclusion that suicide is an individualistic phenomenon caused by such things as rejection by a loved one, financial failure, etc. It would be almost impossible for someone using introspection to discover variations in suicide rates among nations or social groups, to correlate them with social conditions, and arrive at scientific conclusions about the social causes of suicide.

Like most modern sociologists, Durkheim thought of moral precepts and norms as part of culture, and specifically as "ideas" which are part of the subjective realm of social life. Such ideas may be seen as causes of human behavior, and no sociologist can understand human behavior unless he understands the causal priority of these moral elements. But Durkheim did not stop his causal investigations at this point. Instead, he sought to investigate the antecedents of moral precepts and norms. These collective representations, Durkheim discovered, were "reflections" of the underlying social structure of a society. Thus, Durkheim became a staunch proponent of structuralism because he consistently treated ideas as dependent variables which were caused by patterns of social structure.

In most of his major works, Durkheim sought to explain sentiments--that is, broad cultural values and norms--and the customs and usages derived from these sentiments. These moral sentiments included religious beliefs (explored in the Elementary Forms), systems of ethics (explored in Moral Education), solidarity (a sentiment explored in the Division of Labor) and collective orientations toward deviance (explored in Suicide and the Rules).[3] Moral "ideas" were dependent variables in nearly all of Durkheim's works. Just as consistently, the independent variable was some form of social organization. His thought may be diagrammed as follows:

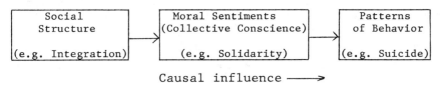

Social Structure		Moral Sentiments (Collective Conscience)		Patterns of Behavior
(e.g. Integration)	→	(e.g. Solidarity)	→	(e.g. Suicide)

Causal influence ⟶

COLLECTIVE CONSCIENCE

Durkheim began with the assumption that people are conscious beings. They are able to think, choose and create. Their perception of the world is of a subjective nature, since they use ideas and language to categorize objective reality. Objective reality is "represented" or "reflected" in the mind of human beings. This is not an automatic process, but is influenced by both the nature of objective reality and that of the individual actor. The ideas which are present in the mind of the individual are labelled by Durkheim as "individual representations." Durkheim conceded that people can think about the world and that this thought process often precedes behavior.[4]

31

Durkheim was not content to stop at this point. Individual's ideas are not random. They do not all originate in the mind of the particular individual. In addition to individual ideas, there is another category of ideas pertaining to the group as a whole. This is the "collective conscience" of a society, which Durkheim defined as follows:

> The totality of beliefs and sentiments common to average citizens of the same society forms a determinate system which has its own life; one may call it the <u>collective</u> or common conscience. [5]

The collective conscience is composed of "beliefs and sentiments," in short, of ideas. The collective conscience represents those subjective or ideational factors which are shared by many or most people in the society. It contains those values, norms and orienting assumptions that are common to the group and which define the nature of the social world to the individual group member.

Durkheim sought to emphasize the stability and durability of the collective conscience. It exists prior in time to the individual and continues to exist after the death of the individual. People from many walks of life and from many distinct social groups may share a single collective conscience.

The collective conscience has a separate existence apart from individual consciences. It is external to the individual. In addition, the collective conscience constrains the individual to bring his own thought processes in line with it. Individuals by taking thought can have little if any influence upon the collective conscience. Conversely, the collective conscience exerts great influence upon individual consciences.

Collective representations, unlike individual ones, are almost always general. General ideas--the idea of <u>all</u>--could not have come from any individual mind. They come from society, because society by its very nature is general. "The concept of totality is only the abstract form of the concept of society: it is the whole which includes all things."[6] General and permanent qualities, rather than unique and variable qualities, are of interest to society and to the sociologist.

SOCIAL STRUCTURE

Social structure was to Durkheim both "a way of existing" and "a way of acting." In many of his most important writings, he spoke of social structure as consisting of durable patterns of association or social interaction--much as Simmel did. However, structure is also something more than interaction.

> Structure of organisms is not only a way of acting; it is a way of existing that necessitates a certain way of acting. It implies not only a certain manner of vibrating, special to molecules, but an arrangement of the latter which makes any other kind of vibration almost impossible.[7]

Perhaps Durkheim's best discussion of the nature of social structure and the relationship between structure and ideas is contained in his essay "Sociology and Its Scientific Field."[8] In this essay, Durkheim first summarized Simmel's classic distinction between the form of association (patterns of interaction) and the content of such interaction (the ideas associated with the interaction).[9] However, he rejected Simmel's notion that only the forms of association have sociological significance, and instead argued that "ideas" are what "pre-eminently constitute the sociological phenomenon."[10]

Durkheim then distinguished between the "structure" or "substratum" of society and the culture (ideas) which is built upon this structure. These are "realities of two kinds" which are distinctly different and which must be studied by different methods.[11] He then set forth an explicit paradigm of those factors which are included in the social substratum of society and those which develop out of the substratum.

The social structure or substratum of society is analogous to physical organization, as studied by anatomy or morphology.

> The social substratum must, above all, be determined in its external form. This external form is chiefly defined by (1) the size of the territory; (2) the space which the society occupies. . . and (3) the form of its frontiers.[12]

33

Also included in this substratum is the "content" of society. This involves three aspects. First, "the total mass of population in its numerical size and density" is part of the substratum. Second, "secondary groupings which have a material basis, such as villages, cities, districts, and provinces of varying importance" are included. This encompasses "extensions of habitations, size of cities and villages, water courses, external enclosures, size and density of population, and so on." Third, "every group. . . makes use. . . of the soil or that part of it that it occupies. Nations surround themselves with fortresses or fortified cities, and roads for communication are constructed." This includes "the disposition of streets and squares, the architecture of the houses, and the structure of things made . . . ."[13]

In contradistinction to these structural elements are the "social modes of doing"--the "functional or physiological phenomena." These "latter must be more numerous than the former, for the vital manifestations are by far more varied and complex."[14] Durkheim then specified the criterion for determining "social phenomena of a physiological nature."[15] This criterion is that the phenomena must be both external and constraining. The phenomena which fit this criterion best are moral directives, which are not material, but ideational. Language, religious rites, legal moral maxims, and traditional usages are examples given by Durkheim of these moral forces.

> In short, social life is nothing but the moral milieu that surrounds the individual--or, to be more accurate, it is the sum of the moral milieus that surround the individual. By calling them moral we mean that they are made up of ideas.[16]

Durkheim further extended the definition of these "physiological" phenomena which make up the superstructure[17] of society to include "social practices." In essence, both moral norms and social practices are seen as aspects of the same thing--ideational factors which develop and grow through social interaction.

> It is these impersonal norms of thought and action that pre-eminently constitute the sociological phenomenon. They stand in

34

relation to society as the vital functions
do in relation to the organism.[18]

There is no question that Durkheim was much more
interested in these latter phenomena. He consistently
devoted himself to an understanding and an explanation
of moral norms and social practices. Just as
consistently he traced the causes of these phenomena to
social organizations. Both are important aspects of
social reality. Both must be studied in order to
achieve a full comprehension of the nature of social
phenomena. Ideational phenomena are more complex and
more diversified than structural phenomena, but they
depend upon and are ultimately determined by these
structural factors. Durkheim devoted his intellectual
life to a study of moral and ideational factors which
he believed had a strong influence on the individual.
But when he undertook to give a causal explanation for
the existence of ideational factors, he consistently
took a structural approach.

We now turn to an examination of a number of
Durkheim's works to see how he developed his structural
theory.

THE BACKGROUND: SAINT-SIMON AND COMTE

For Henri de Saint-Simon and Auguste Comte, as for
most French writers of the 19th century, the French
Revolution provided the central focus of their ideas.
They observed that the French Revolution and the
industrial revolution out of which it developed had
transformed France. The foundations of feudalism in
France had been weakened by the industrial revolution
and destroyed by the political revolution. Democratic
and individualistic doctrines and policies then were
introduced into French society.

Both Saint-Simon and Comte observed the
disorganization which resulted from these changes. The
former culture and traditions of France were being
replaced by new ones more in keeping with the economic
and political changes which had occurred. But the
process of transition was not an easy one. They
therefore collaborated in developing a plan for the
total reorganization of society.[19] A new moral order
based upon science, industry and the social relations
found in an industrial society was to be instituted.
Traditional economic and political systems had already
been destroyed. They were to be replaced by an

35

industrial factory system and a governmental system based upon scientific principles to be enunciated by social scientists and largely staffed by persons scientifically trained to understand the underlying social laws upon which social organization was based. Traditional religious and moral ideas were to be replaced by a secular and humanistically-oriented value system consistent with the values of science.

To state the point another way (anticipating Ogburn), technology and social structure change more rapidly than the normative system of society. This is a proof of the causal priority of social structure over ideas. The result of these differential rates of change is an imbalance, a culture lag.[20] According to Saint-Simon and Comte, people must consciously undertake to bring unity to the social and moral orders by developing a new moral system, a secular religion, based on the new social conditions.

In his book Socialism and Saint-Simon,[21] Durkheim examined these ideas in an amazingly (for him) dispassionate manner, and seemed to accept the basic theoretical argument of Saint-Simon and Comte while rejecting many of their socialistic conclusions. Durkheim found convincing the idea that the social structure of a society determines its religious and cultural belief systems.

SOCIAL STRUCTURE AND THE DIVISION OF LABOR

Durkheim's structural theory was well worked out by the time he wrote his first major work, The Division of Labor in Society, and was carried through consistently in his other works. Durkheim attempted to describe the evolution of society in terms of the continual increase in the division of labor and to analyze the basic causes of evolutionary changes. For the purposes of his analysis, he distinguished two types of social organization. The first, found in "lower" societies, is based on the similarity of homogeneous units or individuals who are tied together by a common set of cultural beliefs. Such a society is said to have mechanical integration. The second, found in modern societies, is characterized by "a system of different organs each of which has a special role, and which are themselves formed of differentiated parts."[22] Such a society has functional unity or what is called organic integration.

36

Human society is evolving from simple to complex, from homogeneous to heterogeneous, or as Durkheim would prefer, from a low division of labor to a high division of labor. Primitive or simple societies are characterized by mechanical integration. Modern industrialized societies possess organic integration. A description of the changes in the division of labor provides a broad framework in which to view the progress of social evolution and indeed all human history. From a sociological point of view, Durkheim argued that the most significant trend in human history is the long-range change from a low division of labor to a high division of labor.

But what is the underlying cause of the changes in the division of labor itself? Durkheim first postulated a steady if gradual increase in population (which he called physical density). Second, the increase in population leads to the increased concentration of the population, and eventually the formation of cities. Increased population density leads to greater communication among individuals. The total effect of these changes is to produce what Durkheim called an increasing "moral (or dynamic) density." Men are tied more closely together. They not only have more ties to other members of the society, but their ties are qualitatively stronger or more "dense."

An increase in physical and moral density naturally leads to greater competition over the available resources of the society. To maintain their existence, individuals are forced to specialize in order to increase production and their ability to compete. An increase in specialization of the members of a society is, by definition, an increase in the division of labor. The cause of the evolution of the division of labor is an increase in physical and moral density, with the competitive struggle being an intervening variable.

The changes in the division of labor also cause major changes in other features of social life--in law, religion, economic and political organization, etc. For example, ideas change only as social conditions change. The ideational system found in a particular society is always adapted to the kind of social structure found in that society. The cultural values, including the system of ethics, found in a society reflect the kind of social structure possessed by that society. Ethics, as a system of ideas, always is dependent upon social conditions.[23] There is little question here that Durkheim gave causal priority to "the structure of societies" rather than to ideas. Customs are ideas which reflect the established patterns of social structure. In analyzing social change, a scientist first should seek to understand the changes which have occurred in social structure, rather than look for changes in ideas or in the way individuals think.

Durkheim criticized his former mentor, Fustel de Coulanges, for "setting up the religious idea" and then deducing from it social arrangements.[24] That is, after noting that primitive societies always have family organizations which have a religious base, de Coulanges presumed that religious ideas are the cause of familial organizational arrangements within the group. Durkheim took the opposite point of view. Social organization was seen by him as causal, while religious beliefs were treated as effects. "Because all social masses have been formed from homogeneous elements . . . it was inevitable that the whole psychic life of society should take on a religious character."[25]

Durkheim observed a natural opposition between (a) the strength of the collective conscience and (b) the progress of the division of labor. He argued that these are two opposing conditions, and that one necessarily hinders the development of the other. Thus, where the division of labor is undeveloped, the collective conscience is strong and exercises firm control over the individuals in the society. However, as the division of labor progresses, the collective conscience becomes "weaker and vaguer."[26] Increased size of the social group causes competition over resources. This results in an increased division of labor, which in turn results in a weakening of the collective conscience and the force of tradition.

Durkheim noted a number of "secondary" factors which accompany the division of labor and which operate to weaken the collective conscience. Among these are (1) the tendency over time for religion to become more general and universal, accompanied by a decline of "formalism" in religion, (2) a tendency toward universalism in both law and morality, accompanied by a breakdown of the traditional multiplicity of rules governing behavior, and (3) a tendency toward rationality among men. All these factors represent a tendency toward universalism, to see things in broader and more general scope. Cultural universalism is in turn caused by the increase in size of social units necessitated by the progress in the division of labor.

The division of labor is a structural characteristic of society in Durkheim's view. It represents a special pattern of social organization. The division of labor and the collective conscience are closely correlated, and what affects one also affects the other. Although one might make the case that there is reciprocity between the two, it seems clear throughout the discussion that Durkheim saw the progress of the division of labor as the causal factor and the diminution of the collective conscience as an effect. Ideas are very important variables in Durkheim's explanation of the workings of society, but they clearly are caused by structural factors.

INTEGRATION AS THE CAUSE OF SUICIDE

Durkheim's classic study Suicide is generally regarded as the first major statistical study in sociology. Its contribution to the development of sociology can hardly be overestimated. Even today, it serves as a model of how a sophisticated sociologist can reach a scientific conclusion through the extensive analysis of available data.[27]

Suicide will be more thoroughly discussed in the chapter on determinism (Chapter 10). We shall restrict ourselves here to a brief summary of the major points made in the book. Durkheim first argued that suicide is a social fact, though it seems to be an individualistic act, because suicide rates are stable over time and change only at times of major social changes. Further, suicide rates for different groups vary widely, thereby demonstrating the strong influence of social groups upon suicide. After rejecting previous theories to explain suicide, Durkheim examined the influence of various social conditions on the suicide rate. After extensive examination of data from a variety of sources, including a study of 25,000 cases of suicide in France in the years 1889-1891 which Durkheim undertook himself, he made several important conclusions. First, Catholics have a lower rate of suicide than Protestants. Second, married persons have a lower rate of suicide than unmarried persons. Third, the suicide rate is lower in times of political crisis than in times of peace.

To explain these findings, Durkheim developed a theory of "egoistic" suicide. He argued that Catholics and married persons have higher degrees of social integration than Protestants and unmarried persons. Further, in times of political crisis, the integration of the society increases as a reaction to the crisis. In each case, the suicide rate varies inversely with the degree of social integration. Durkheim concluded, therefore, that variations in the degree of social integration cause the variations in the suicide rate.

This theory does not explain all variations in the suicide rate, however. Durkheim next turned to a discussion of "altruistic" suicide. He noted that in many primitive societies suicide occurs frequently. When the degree of integration in a social group is so high that the individual tends to lose his separate identity--when the society is all-important and the individual has little importance--the individual is likely to commit suicide if his society requires it of him. Instances of altruistic suicide include suicide of aged persons, women upon the death of their husbands, and servants upon the death of their masters,[28] as well as the high rate of suicide (or voluntary death in battle) of officers as compared to enlisted soldiers.

Durkheim developed a third type of suicide to explain the high rate of suicide in times of economic instability and among divorcees. Here, suicide occurs because of a breakdown of the stability of the society and its normative system, or because of a change in status of a person such that he loses his customary place in the established order of society. Durkheim called suicide of this kind "anomic" suicide, or suicide resulting from normlessness-a type of malintegration.

As Durkheim used it, integration is a characteristic of social organization, not a feature of the normative or ideational system of a society. Integration refers to the degree to which units in a system are related to each other. One individual who is isolated from other individuals cannot be integrated, by definition. But an individual in interaction with others may be a unit who is integrated into the social group. The word "integration" then is usable only in a social context. It is a term par excellence of social structure.

Durkheim's explanation of suicide is a structural explanation. If a society is well organized, the suicide rate remains low. If there is a change in social structure, the suicide rate also changes. Individual ideas and attitudes may reflect this organization or lack of it. People may feel frustration, or they may feel secure. But the root cause of these individual ideas, and of the behavior which results from the ideas, is the degree of integration of the social organization.

Several places in Suicide, Durkheim specifically rejected the subjective approach, and opted instead for a structural theory. For example, in his discussion of altruistic suicide, Durkheim noted that altruistic suicide is frequently found among Asian people with a pantheistic religious philosophy.[29] However, pantheism is not a cause of suicide. Rather, both pantheism and suicide are "reflections" of the underlying pattern of social structure found in the society. Social structure is the root cause of both religion and suicide.

Durkheim's use of the word "reflection" is similar to that of Marx. Ideas, and the words which give them form, are representations or reflections of reality. Social structure, not ideas, is the true reality of social life. Just as a reflection in a mirror is not the true essence of the individual being, the ideas in the minds of men are not the true essence of social life. Ideas only reflect the relations among men, the patterns of behavior, the social organization of social groups which are the true, the "real," essence of social life. These are structural in nature.

STRUCTURE AS THE DETERMINANT OF MORALITY

One of Durkheim's strongest statements supporting structuralism is found in his seminal work Moral Education.[30] His intention in this work was to show the social nature of morality and to develop a practical set of ethics based on sociological principles. This work is in the Saint Simon-Comte tradition. Durkheim observed the continual evolution of French society toward complexity and industrialization. He also observed that the system of morals of a society tended to be resistant to change. He argued that men must consciously attempt to develop and promulgate moral and ethical norms which are consistent with the social conditions of the times. If

41

a system of morals is developed which is not congruent with the social structure, any attempt to promulgate or practice this system would be fruitless. The principle underlying this argument is clearly stated: the system of morality practiced by a society is dependent upon--that is, caused by--the social structure of that society.

The moral system of a society may be used as an indicator of the pattern of social organization found therein because of the causal connection between the two. For example, Durkheim identified two broad moral orientations correlated to individual personality types.[31] The first is a disciplined type of morality which involves acceptance of and conformity to an established set of rules or moral imperatives. This type of morality is found in stable societies with a low degree of social change. The second type is much more emotional and outgoing. Morality is based on dedication to a cause and on humanistic love for other people. According to Durkheim, this passionate type of morality is difficult to regulate. Persons of this type are capable of great deeds, but do not have the same self-discipline found in the first type. Of course, the emotional type of morality is found in rapidly changing social structures where the systems of norms are constantly being challenged and replaced by others.

The degree of societal integration, which Durkheim identified as a characteristic of social structure, is viewed here as a causal determinant of both (1) the type of personality found in the society, and (2) a cultural norm, e.g. the spirit of discipline. Well-integrated societies are characterized by traditional norms, a strong sense of discipline, and traditional or rational personality types which exhibit consistent and disciplined behavior. Rapidly changing societies with a lesser degree of social integration are characterized by flexible and conflicting norms, a weak sense of discipline, and emotional and impulsive personality types. Subjective variables, i.e. cultural norms and individual personality types, are determined by structural variables, i.e. the degree of social integration.

THE SOCIAL NATURE OF RELIGIOUS PHENOMENA

Durkheim developed this point more fully in his last great work The Elementary Forms of the Religious Life. In this study he sought to discover and examine the "essential" or "elementary" aspects of all religion.[32] It is not possible to study all facts relating to all religious behavior throughout the world. Instead, he sought to discover those "crucial and decisive" facts which would help him short-circuit the long trial and error process of science and lead him to immediate conclusions about the nature of religious phenomena.

To discover these crucial and decisive facts, Durkheim reasoned that if he studied the simplest society in existence--one which contained the simplest form of religion--he could most easily observe the elementary or basic aspects of all religion. Through an examination of ethnographic accounts contained in the libraries of Paris, he decided that the simplest form of religion was found in Central Australia. The form of religion practiced was called totemism.

Durkheim first defined religion as "a unified system of beliefs and practices relative to sacred things" whose effect is to unite a group of people together into "a single moral community."[33] He drew the conclusion that the essence of religion is a normative distinction which the group draws between that which is "sacred" and that which is "profane." In two long sections of the book he analyzed (1) religious beliefs, and (2) religious practices. The religious beliefs of a society are derived from and symbolize the pattern of social structure found in the society. For example, most religions contain some idea of "the soul."[34] Men believe that they possess souls which are immortal--that exist after the death of their physical bodies. According to Durkheim, the idea of the soul is social in origin, and derives from the realization by men that the social group has a durability beyond that of any of its members. The group existed before the individual was born and will continue after his death. The social reality of the perpetuity of the life of the group is expressed by men in the belief in the immortality of the soul--in the perpetuity of the lives of individual group members.

Religious rituals have as their basic object the symbolization of social organization of the group.

43

Rituals involve behavior, but both beliefs and rituals are essentially symbolic in nature and are founded upon social structure. One extremely important aspect of religious rituals is that they contribute to the integration of the social group. Commemorative rites, for example, help the group members to remember important events in the history of the group, thus uniting them more closely together. Funeral rites have the function of giving the dead person a status within the group and providing group support (both physical and emotional) to the relatives of the deceased.

The major point which Durkheim made in this book is again evident. Religion as a system of ideas and practices doesn't spring forth from the minds of men without cause. Instead, religion symbolizes the life of the group. Groups come into existence and become structured. Later they develop religious beliefs and rituals to symbolize the social structure. Religion becomes an important--perhaps the most important--contributor to the maintenance of the integration of the social group. But religion could not exist, and would have no meaning, unless the group first were structured in a definite manner. Religious phenomena are almost always consistent with social structure because social structure is the determinant of religion.

In summary, Durkheim believed that religion is a social institution by means of which society is integrated and individuals are tied more closely to the social group. Religious beliefs and rituals come into existence only after a group is formed. Religion as a set of symbolic ideas reflects the organization of the social group from which it springs. In short, social structure determines ideational factors.

Durkheim did not grapple with the theological question of the existence of God, nor the even more difficult question concerning God's dealings with His children on earth. Had he done so, he might have arrived at different conclusions than he did by examining only the sociological question concerning the diversity of religious behavior throughout the cultures of the world. If God exists and if He deals frequently with his children, at least some religious phenomena must be explained from this perspective and not as being due to social responses to structural conditions. But even those of us who accept the theological position of the existence of God must also recognize that much of what is called religion is far removed from worship of God and is due to "the traditions of men."[35]

Durkheim did not dispute the ideational character of many social facts. But his methodological rule was clear-cut. One should treat social facts as things, not ideas. Later sociologists, most notably the behaviorists, have built upon this argument.

DURKHEIM AND MARX

Obviously there are many similarities between Durkheim's structural approach and that of Marx. Both theorists gave causal priority to structural factors, although they differ in their identification of those structural factors which are most important. Marx emphasized economic forces and economic organization, while Durkheim placed greatest weight upon community organization and interaction. Marx combined sociology with economics, Durkheim combined sociology with anthropology.

Both theorists were interested in religious phenomena. But Marx' interest was largely negative: religion serves to divert individuals from their true economic interests. Durkheim more clearly saw the important functional and integrative contributions which religious phenomena make to social life. Marx viewed ideology as a means by which a social group symbolizes its economic interests. Durkheim viewed religion and morality as means by which a social group symbolizes its social organization and achieves further integration. Ideational factors were of greater interest to Durkheim that Marx, and his analysis of them was more extensive.

However, both theorists recognized that, once a normative or ideological system is established, it is resistant to social change. If social organization changes, the normative system changes too, but this change is not automatic. Often a significant time lag occurs between the time the social structure changes and the time the normative system changes. This results in a lessening of social integration. Marx believed that this leads to open social conflict, to revolution and the establishment of a new social order. The major effects of such malintegration for Durkheim are higher rates of suicide and crime. He further believed in a more gradual and peaceful adjustment and reorganization than did Marx.

Taken together, the arguments of Marx and Durkheim provide a strong support for a structural theory of social life. Structuralism is also an important feature of Simmel's sociology, which will be examined in the next chapter. They stand in sharp contrast to the theories of Weber and the symbolic interactionists, whose subjective approach we shall discuss in chapters 5 and 7.

FOOTNOTES

[1]Emile Durkheim, The Rules of Sociological Method. (Glencoe: The Free Press), 1950, pp. 14-18. See also Anthony Giddens, Emile Durkheim. (New York: Penguin), 1978; and Steven Lukes, Emile Durkheim: His Life and Work. (New York: Penguin), 1973.

[2]Ibid., pp. xliii-xlv.

[3]Emile Durkheim, The Elementary Forms of the Religious Life. (Glencoe: Free Press), 1915; Moral Education. (New York: Free Press of Glencoe), 1961; The Division of Labor in Society. (New York: Free Press of Glencoe), 1933; and Suicide. (Glencoe: Free Press), 1951.

[4]Elementary Forms, p. 75; Emile Durkheim, "Pragmatism and Sociology," in Emile Durkheim, et. al., Essays on Sociology and Philosophy, Edited by Kurt H. Wolff (New York: Harper, 1964), pp. 414-415.

[5]The Division of Labor, p. 79. Italics are Durkheims's.

[6]Ibid., p. 442. See also Rules, pp. 3-13.

[7]The Division of Labor, p. 333; Suicide, p. 321.

[8]Emile Durkheim, "Sociology and Its Scientific Field," in Emile Durkheim, et. al., Essays on Sociology and Philosophy, Edited by Kurt H. Wolff (New York: Harper, 1964), pp. 354-375.

[9]See Chapter four for a discussion of Simmel's use of these terms.

[10]"Sociology and Its Scientific Field," p. 369.

[11]Ibid., p. 360.

[12]Loc. cit.

[13]Ibid., p. 361.

[14]Ibid., p. 362.

[15]Ibid., p. 364.

[16]Ibid., p. 367. Italics are mine.

[17]Durkheim didn't use the word "superstructure" although he frequently used its opposite--"Substratum."

[18]"Sociology and Its Scientific Field," p. 369.

[19]Henri de Saint-Simon and Auguste Comte, Plan of the Scientific Operations Necessary for the Reorganization of Society, 1822.

[20]William F. Ogburn, Social Change With Respect to Cultural and Original Nature, (New York: Dell, 1966), pp. 200-280.

[21]Emile Durkheim, Socialism and Saint-Simon, (New York: Antioch Press, 1958).

[22]The Division of Labor, p. 181.

[23]Ibid., pp. 285-290.

[24]The Division of Labor, p. 179.

[25]Loc. cit.

[26]Ibid., p. 283.

[27]For a good discussion of Durkheim's methodology, see Hanan C. Selvin, "Durkheim's Suicide and Problems of Empirical Research," American Journal of Sociology, 63 (May, 1958), pp. 607-619.

[28]Suicide, p. 219.

[29]Ibid., pp. 226-227.

[30]Emile Durkheim, Moral Education. New York: The Free Press of Glencoe, 1961.

[31]Ibid., pp. 99-101.

[32]The Rules of Sociological Method, pp. 78-81.

[33]Elementary Forms, p. 47.

[34]Ibid., pp. 240-272.

[35]Doctrine and Covenants 93:29; James T. Duke, "The Traditions of Their Fathers," The Ensign, 2 (November, 1972), pp. 39-41.

CHAPTER FOUR

CLASSICAL STRUCTURALISM: GEORG SIMMEL

Georg Simmel's theory of social structure as patterns of interaction differs significantly from those of Marx and Durkheim. The latter two theorists made a clear distinction between between social structure and ideas. Both argued for the causal priority of social structure in influencing social life. However, neither clearly distinguished between actual patterns of behavior and normative definitions of how individuals should act. Simmel's great contribution to structuralism was to focus directly on actual behavior as it became patterned through social interaction. He developed the theoretical insight that what constitutes social structure is actual behavior--not expected behavior. Many later sociologists have followed his lead in exploring social interaction but unfortunately few if any have treated social interaction as the main feature of social structure.

Simmel's Soziologie[1] began with the assertion that interaction between two or more people is the essential aspect of social life. Individuals who momentarily look at each other, who speak to each other or otherwise demonstrate their awareness of each other, are interacting with each other.[2] Simmel provides no definition of his key concepts "interaction" and "sociation," but their meaning is contextually clear. Persons who take each other into account, who alter their behavior to adjust to that of the other person, are interacting with each other. More significantly, much of the time people move past the mere awareness of others to a more intensive interest in them. Interaction becomes "more frequent and intensive." A pattern develops in the interaction, so that the behavior each person is engaging in becomes regularized or standardized. Simmel spoke of such patterns of interaction as "crystallized (into) definable, consistent structures."[3]

Large institutional structures such as the family, the state and the church are complex patterns of interaction. If human interaction is sufficiently patterned and stable that large numbers of people consistently act in the same way, a social institution can be said to exist. That is, the existence of the institution is dependent upon, and in fact defined in terms of, the patterns of interaction which exist among individuals.

Simmel fully understood that not all interactions attain this kind of fixity. The patterning of interaction is a matter of degree. However, it is normal that individuals should seek to bring their interaction into conformity with the expectations of those with whom they are interacting.

Interaction, then, is the most important concept used by Simmel to describe and analyze social life. It is the essence of social life. Any attempts to develop a science of social life must begin with interaction. The analysis of interaction is the most important task which the sociologist can perform. And the most important single conclusion which a sociologist can make about social interaction is that it tends to be patterned--to be organized.

THE FORMS OF INTERACTION

Following this insight, Simmel devoted much of his sociological work to an analysis of the "forms" of interaction.[4] He accepted the commonly held scientific notion that regularities exist in nature, and the chief aim of science is to explore and describe these regularities. Simmel sought to show that there were definite and regular patterns of interaction which could be found in all groups and among all people who were interacting with each other. If it were possible to develop a classification of the forms of interaction, one might be able to demonstrate that each form of interaction is causally related to other aspects of social life. For example, certain forms of interaction might lead to the formation of particular normative systems. Or certain personality types might be associated with certain typical forms of interaction.

Much of this theoretical orientation is implicit in Simmel's writings, rather than clearly spelled out. Simmel's great strength as a sociologist was in developing classification schemes, in showing the distinctions between different types of phenomena. His weakness--a very significant one--was that he seldom made clear-cut statements explicating the causal relationships among the concepts he developed. Simmel distinguished several different forms of interaction, but provided few details about how these forums

50

differed in their influence upon other sociological phenomena.

Simmel contrasted _form_ with _content_ in his discussion of interaction. He believed that the content of interaction is exceedingly variable. Yet he argued that a science of society is possible because forms of interaction are patterned and repetitive--that is, general and universal. Sociology must devote itself to a study of those aspects of social life that are patterned and general--to forms of interaction. Not only does the behavior of specific individuals become patterned as they interact with other individuals; in addition, certain forms of interaction are found among many different individuals under widely different circumstances.

The form of interaction, although never explicitly defined by Simmel, refers to the objectively observable pattern of behavior in which two individuals engage. For example, one individual may act in a way which suggests that he is the superior in the relationship, while the other acts in a subordinate manner. Superordination--subordination, as a form of interaction, is found in many groups and in a wide variety of circumstances.

The _content_ of interaction, while explicitly defined by Simmel, is not clearly distinguishable in many cases from the _form_ of interaction.

> Everything present in the individuals (who are the immediate, concrete data of all historical reality) in the form of drive, interest, purpose, inclination, psychic state, movement--everything that is present in them in such a way as to engender or mediate effects upon others or to receive such effects, I designate as the _content_, as the _material_, as it were, of sociation.[5]

The content of interaction, then, includes the nature of the individual and the specific subject and purpose of the interaction. The form of interaction includes those aspects of behavior which are patterned and which serve to organize the interaction in a structured way.

51

SUPERORDINATION AND SUBORDINATION

Simmel's best discussion of a form of interaction is found in his analysis of superordination.[6] He noted that dominance of one individual by another is a frequent phenomenon in social life. In almost every group there are some individuals who possess authority, prestige or other personal qualities which place them in a superordinate position over others. Equality of two individuals is usually found only in a situation where each is subordinate to a third party. There are very few situations which individuals face which do not place them in either a superordinate or a subordinate position relative to other individuals who are participating in the interaction.

Simmel took pains to note that the superordinate-subordinate relationship is one of interaction, that is, of reciprocity. No matter how powerful the superior in such a relationship, he still requires some behavior or reaction on the part of the subordinate, even if this behavior is obeisance. The subordinate therefore has some latitude or freedom of behavior. He may choose to react as expected, or he may choose to withhold his obeisance. In the latter case, he knows he will receive punishment for his behavior, and therefore is likely to refrain from choosing to deviate from the expectations of the superordinate. This does not negate the fact that he does have some latitude of behavior, and therefore some choice as to how he will act in relation to the superordinate individual.

SUBORDINATION TO AN INDIVIDUAL

Simmel discussed three types of subordination: to a single person, to a plurality, and to a principle or an objective force.[7] He noted that subordination under an individual almost always results in the unification of the group. This is accomplished either in unity with the superordinate, who becomes the direct expression of the group's interests or characteristics, or in opposition to the leader, who then becomes the object of hatred by his followers. These two expressions of unity under a leader are complementary, since they are often found together. Simmel also discussed (1) the effects of the homogeneity of the group, (2) the kind of stratification system present in the group, (3) the presence of a "higher tribunal" to mediate conflicts, and (4) the status of the leader as

52

a member or outsider. Each of these is significant in influencing the relationship of the superordinate to the subordinate in this form of interaction.

SUBORDINATION TO A PLURALITY

Subordination to a plurality possesses different characteristics than subordination to an individual. Simmel noted that most subordinates prefer to be under the control of a large organization such as a state or a business enterprise, rather than under the control of a single individual. Larger organizations generally act with more consistency, justice and restraint than does a single individual, and the subordinate is usually required to perform fewer services in a large organization. However, Simmel observed that there are exceptions to this, especially when the superordinate plurality is a crowd or other group of people who are physically present together. The Roman coliseum audiences were infinitely more cruel than a single ruler would have been.

SUBORDINATION TO A PRINCIPLE

The third form of subordination is that which is given to a principle or ideal. Simmel argued that in modern society, men prefer to be subordinated to an objective set of laws or principles rather than to people. Personal service is thought to be more degrading than service to a collectivity or to a principle. Laws which define acceptable behavior are thought to bring dignity to the person who conforms to them, whereas conformity to the commands of a ruler diminishes the dignity of him who conforms. The individual incorporates the group's moral principles into his own moral code and regards them as his own personal possession. The subordination to these principles is no less real than subordination to a person, but the individual does not feel the restraint and coercion in the same way. Since he almost always conforms to the moral principles of the group, he seldom faces the possibility of being sanctioned by a specific individual or plurality for his behavior.

Simmel pointed out that most relations of superordination-subordination "develop out of very real, personal power relations."[8] However, once established, such relations tend to become regularized or "spiritualized," so that the superordinate "exerts his power merely in the capacity of the closest representative of this ideal, objective force."[9] An ideology or normative system is developed which justifies and supports the superordinate-subordinate relationships. The subordinate benefits from this, since he suffers less degradation if he feels that he is subordinated to a system of principles or laws rather than to a person. This also benefits the superordinate, since his rule is more effective if his subordinates do not suffer psychologically from their subordination. The subordinates are also more likely to conform to the ruler's commands if these commands are legitimized by the normative system of the group.

Simmel's discussion of superordination-subordination is somewhat disappointing to one who seeks generalizations regarding the effects of different forms of interaction. He did not clearly show how the form of interaction can be used as an independent variable in the explanation of other kinds of behavior. However, if one reads Simmel's discussion for information about stratification systems and the processes which are found in them, he finds a rich store of insights and illustrations. Seldom has any social theorist written a more fruitful general statement of the effects of inequality in social relations than is found in Simmel's discussion of superordination and subordination.

THE SIZE AND STRUCTURE OF THE GROUP

While focusing on small-group interaction, Simmel also developed some key generalizations regarding the influence of group size and structure upon the behavior of individuals in those groups. Specifically, Simmel addressed the quantitative aspects of group life and their effects upon qualitative aspects. In addition, one of Simmel's most significant contributions to sociology was his discussion of "the significance of numbers," and of the dyad and triad. His analysis is one of the most familiar in the sociological literature.

THE SIGNIFICANCE OF NUMBERS

The size of a group, according to Simmel, has a significant influence upon its social structure and social processes. Certain types of interaction can take place only in small groups. Conversely, certain forms of social organization are appropriate to large groups but not to smaller ones.

It will immediately be conceded on the basis of everyday experiences that a group upon reaching a certain size must develop forms and organs which serve its maintenance and promotion, but which a smaller group does not need. On the other hand, it will also be admitted that smaller groups have qualities, including types of interaction among their members, which inevitably disappear when the groups grow larger.[10]

Simmel gave as examples of this principle: (1) socialism, which is well adapted to groups with small size, but which cannot be effectively practiced in a large group with a necessarily highly developed division of labor; (2) extreme religious sects with certain kinds of doctrines (such as restrictions on military service) "whose social structure makes it impossible for them to support a large membership;"[11] and (3) aristocracies, whose effectiveness in ruling a nation depends upon restricting the members of the aristocracy to a certain size. Masses are susceptible only to simple ideas, whereas smaller groups can deal with more complex ideas and ideologies.

The significance of certain social roles (e.g., a millionaire) differs with the size of the group in which the role is found. Likewise, the significance of radical elements in the group is influenced (1) by their own size in the group (as the number of radicals increases, their program becomes moderated) and (2) by the size of the total group (radical programs are more easily accomplished in larger groups). Simmel built example upon example to demonstrate the importance of the size of the group in determining the kinds of structure and activities found in the group.

THE DYAD[12]

This leads to Simmel's discussion of the "simplest sociological formation," that of the dyad. This is a union of two, and only two, elements. It is a particular form or structure of sociation, or interaction. Certain kinds of interaction can take place only in a dyad. Further, it "contains the scheme, germ and material of innumerable more complex forms."[13] A dyad normally results from the interaction of two individuals. However, Simmel notes that it is also possible to examine and describe the relations between two groups by reference to the dyad.

The most significant feature of the dyad is that the two members of the dyad confront each other directly, not through intermediaries. It follows from this that the relationship can be broken by the withdrawal of either party.

> Although, for the outsider, the group consisting of two may function as an autonomous, super-individual unit, it usually does not do so for its participants. Rather, each of the two feels himself confronted only by the other, not by a collectivity above him. The social structure here rests immediately on the one and on the other of the two, and the succession of either would destroy the whole. The dyad, therefore, does not attain the super-personal life which the individual feels to be independent of himself.[14]

The duration of the relationship is therefore directly subject to the wishes of the interacting partners. If either partner chooses to withdraw, the dyad ceases to exist. This tenuous duration is one of the significant characteristics of the dyad, and influences the thinking of the individuals who are members of it.

Simmel discussed several other significant characteristics of a dyad. Perhaps the most important is the high level of intimacy which is almost invariably found in the dyad. In fact, Simmel argued that intimacy naturally follows from dyadic organization. For example, a business partnership takes on the characteristics of intimacy because of the sharing of many activities and accomplishments by two individuals. The addition of a third party generally tends to reduce the level of intimacy present among the two original participants.

Simmel also spoke of "triviality" as a characteristic of a dyad. He argued that when two people interact intimately, they often do so because of the rare or peculiar qualities which the other possesses or which are developed in the interaction of the two. Dyadic relationships tend to emphasize these "trivial" characteristics rather than the general characteristics which the two individuals share with many others.

56

A further important characteristic of a dyad is the lack of "the delegation of duties and responsibilities to the impersonal group structure."[15] In larger groups, it is possible to expect certain things of the collectivity as such. Expectations are made of the group as a whole, rather than of individual members. If such expectations are not fulfilled, no one individual receives the blame for this failure. In a dyad, expectations are more direct, and failure to fulfill expectations can harm the existence of the relationship.

> . . . (T)he decisive characteristic of the dyad is that each of the two must actually accomplish something, and that in case of failure only the other remains--not a super-individual force, as prevails in a group even of three. . . . Precisely the fact that each of the two knows that he can depend only upon the other and on nobody else, gives the dyad a special consecration . . . the dyadic element is much more frequently confronted with All or Nothing than is the member of the large group.[16]

Dyadic relationships also encourage more individuality among its members than larger groups. In a dyad, the individual cannot be "overruled by a majority." The individual's wishes, then, become much more important in such relationships. A person is more frequently able to express his or her total personality in the presence of one other person. Larger groups require more conformity and subjugation of individual desires and characteristics. This does not mean that superordinate-subordinate relationships do not exist in a dyad. But individuals are more likely to regard each other as equals[17] in a dyad, since either party can sanction the other by withdrawing from the relationship.

THE TRIAD

A triad is composed of three individuals (or parties) who interact with each other in a more or less stable relationship. When a third person is added to a dyad to create a triad, the direct reciprocity and interdependence found in the dyad are mitigated. A third individual in the relationship creates the

possibility of mediation between the original two
members.

> . . . (A)mong three elements, each one
> operates as an intermediary between the
> other two. . . . Where three elements, A,
> B, C, constitute a group, there is, in
> addition to the direct relationship between
> A and B, for instance, their indirect one,
> which is derived from their common relation
> to C. The fact that two elements are each
> connected not only by a straight line--the
> shortest--but also by a broken line, as it
> were, is an enrichment from a formal
> sociological standpoint. Points that cannot
> be contacted by the straight line are
> connected by the third element, which offers
> a different side to each of the other two,
> and yet fuses these different sides in the
> unity of its own personality.[18]

In the dyad, no third party is present to mediate
the relationships between the two parties. They
confront each other directly. With the addition of a
third party in a triad, mediation becomes possible.
The third party can serve as an intermediary between
the other two parties either to create conflicts
between them or to remedy the conflicts present. This
possibility of a third party influencing the
relationship between the first two parties was called
the "principle of mediation" by Simmel. The principle
of mediation is never possible in a dyad, and is always
present in a triad.

> . . . (T)he principle (of mediation) itself
> changes the configuration radically, and
> always _emerges_ and operates when a third
> party is added.[19]

New social possibilities--for new social roles and new
social behavior--have been added. The addition of a
third party to a relationship is especially significant
sociologically, because this addition creates new
social possibilities. The _emergence_ of these new
possibilities has profound sociological significance.

THE PRINCIPLE OF EMERGENCE

The major sociological difference between the triad and the dyad as forms of interaction is that social roles not possible in a dyad emerge as soon as a third party is added. A dyad contains only one relationship, between person A and person B. In a triad, three relationships exist: between A and B, A and C, and B and C. The addition of one person necessitates the addition of two relationships. The size of the group grows arithmetically, while the number of relationships grows geometrically.[20]

Simmel was quick to point out, however, that sociologically the addition of a fourth person to a triad is not nearly as significant as the addition of a third person to a dyad. In the latter case, emergence of new social roles takes place. This does not occur with the addition of a fourth person. However, Simmel recognized that other social conditions may emerge as the size of the group grows, depending upon other conditions. Size of the group is a contributory factor in the emergence of other sociological phenomena.

Simmel's discussion of triad was devoted primarily to a discussion of three social roles which emerge upon the creation of a triad, and which are never found in a dyad. These three are discussed below.

THE MEDIATOR

Perhaps the most important role which is played by a third party in a social group is that of mediator. Simmel noted that in any group, conflict or dissent occurs from time to time between any two of the parties in the group. These conflicts may be serious, or they may be insignificant.

> The situation does not have to involve a real conflict or fight. It is rather the thousand insignificant differences of opinion, the allusions to an antagonism of personalities, the emergence of quiet momentary contrasts of interest or feeling, which continuously color the fluctuating forms of all living together. . . .[21]

Whenever such conflict occurs, according to Simmel, a third party usually seeks to mediate the conflict. He attempts to bring the parties together, to unify them.

> From the conversation among three persons that lasts only an hour, to the permanent family of three, there is no triad in which a dissent between any two elements does not occur from time to time . . . and in which the third member does not play a mediating role. This happens innumerable times in a very rudimentary and inarticulate manner, mixed with other actions and interactions, from which the purely mediating function cannot be isolated.[22]

The bond between the two conflicting parties is strengthened in several ways, according to Simmel. The mediator "may directly start or strengthen the union of the two,"[23] or he may work more indirectly to unite them through his own person. In the latter case, the bond of union is indirect, through the third party. Simmel mentioned the example of a child born to a couple who by his presence strengthens the bond between husband and wife. He suggested that the presence of the child is a strong influence on keeping the relationship between the husband and wife strong and viable.

A significant kind of mediation is that accomplished by what Simmel called a "non-partisan." This non-partisan third party may "stand above" the two conflicting parties, or he may be equally interested in both. In either case, the non-partisan may exert a strong unifying influence by helping the conflicting parties to come together. By serving as an objective link between the two the non-partisan mediator is able to reduce the emotion present in their conflict, encourage them to use reason in the presentation of their opposing arguments, and help them to consider the other's claim and arguments.

An extreme form of mediation is arbitration, in which the two conflicting parties voluntarily bind themselves to accept the decision of the arbitrator. Such a case exemplifies the great confidence both parties may have in a third party. Simmel noted that arbitration is most common between capitalists and workers, but also may be effectively used in relations among nations.

The great significance of this discussion, both to Simmel and to contemporary sociology, is that the expansion of a dyad to a triad by the addition of a third party creates the possibility of new social roles, new expectations for behavior, and new behavior patterns, and changes the nature of the social structure of the group.

> It is important for the analysis of social life to realize clearly that the constellation thus characterized (mediation) constantly _emerges_ in all groups of more than two elements.[24]

This emergence of mediation gives the triad a new character which is attributable to the group structure rather than to the personalities of the individuals who compose the group. One cannot understand or explain the behavior which occurs in a group merely by reference to the characteristic of the individuals who compose the group. For the behavior which occurs in a dyad is significantly different from that which occurs in a triad. This difference is due to the size of the group and the group organization which results from the addition of a third person. The emergence of mediation in a triad is the single most significant feature of such social organization.

THE TERTIUS GAUDENS

Mediation produces unity among the parties in a triad. Simmel recognized, however, that the third party can often produce conflict and disunity rather than harmony between the other two parties. The third party may either benefit from the conflicts between the other two parties (_Tertius gaudens_--"The third who enjoys"), or he may actively seek to divide the two in order to rule them (_divide et impera_--divide and rule).

In the emergent form of interaction labelled by Simmel as _tertius gaudens_, the third party uses the conflict existing between the other two parties "for purely egoistic interests."[25] The two parties may compete for the favors which the third party can bestow, thus giving the third party some measure of power over them. Simmel illustrated this with the example of two suitors actively courting a person of the opposite sex. The competition between the two gives the person courted certain advantages which he or she would not otherwise be able to obtain. Likewise,

61

the consumer in a capitalistic economy with free competition benefits from the competition of producers for his business.

A third party may also benefit from the conflict between the other two parties in additional ways. A weak third party may escape from exploitation by the other parties if such parties are equally matched and if their competition with each other leaves them no opportunity for exploitation of the third party. Further, a weak third party may throw his weight to one or the other of the conflicting parties, thus giving their combination an advantage.[26] According to Simmel, this explains the great influence of certain small political parties in a parliamentary political system.

Again, the point to be emphasized is that such an organizational structure of interaction, and the behavior which results from it are not possible in a dyad. They become possible only when a third party is added. The tertius gaudens emerges as a possible sociological form of interaction whenever the group adds a third party.

DIVIDE ET IMPERA

The other form of interaction resulting from the conflict between two parties in a triad is "divide and rule." In this case, "the third element intentionally produces the conflict in order to gain a dominating position."[27] Simmel discussed three kinds of this form of interaction.

The first occurs when a superior seeks to prevent the unification of two or more weaker parties. A government may prevent revolutionary movements from gaining success by preventing them from uniting together. An employer may prevent the unification of his employees against him. In this form, the third party maintains a superior position not by creating conflict, but by preventing the unification of the other two parties, which in turn would result in conflict between the superior party and the other two.

The second form of "divide and rule" is more active, according to Simmel. In this form, the third party creates jealousy or hard feelings among the other two parties, thus preventing them from uniting against him. Any means of provoking distrust or jealousy may be useful, especially an unequal distribution of rewards.

Finally, the third party may provoke or otherwise cause open conflict between the other two parties. Simmel described this as an art which is unfortunately possessed by many individuals and organizations. The key to this form of behavior is to provoke the conflict while remaining out of it oneself. This is done either by creating conflict over real differences of interests between the two parties, or by getting them to displace their aggression against each other.

The third party benefits in several ways. He may gain certain objective rewards, such as financial benefit, from the conflict between the two parties. He may gain a position of power or status that would not otherwise be his if the conflicting parties were not in conflict. Or he may gain psychologically from the conflict between the other two parties.

Superordination can certainly be achieved in a dyad, although equality of status is more likely in a dyad. However, only in a triad (or a more complex structure) is it possible to divide and rule. In such a case, the ability to rule depends largely upon the nature of the interaction between the other two parties. Such rule is significantly different from superordination which is achieved in a dyad.

THE SOCIOLOGICAL SIGNIFICANCE OF EMERGENCE

Simmel's discussion of the differences between the dyad and the triad is especially significant in its recognition of emergent forms of social interaction and social organization. By demonstrating that new social roles are possible in a triad, Simmel argued forcefully for the necessity of using sociological phenomena in the explanation of human behavior. The structure of the group creates possibilities for behavior which are not given in the makeup of the individual. One cannot use a reductionist explanation of group processes. That is, one cannot explain what happens in a group solely by reference to the characteristics of individuals. The size of the group, and the social structure which is dependent upon that size, are important variables in the explanation of human behavior. The emergence of the group (i.e., the triad) necessitates a new or emergent level of analysis of

63

human behavior. In reference to Simmel's analysis, Coser remarks that

> One cannot but be convinced that it
> constitutes one of the most persuasive
> demonstrations of the power of
> sociological analysis. Simmel reveals
> the sterility of psychological
> reductionism by demonstrating how the
> apparently peripheral fact that a third
> member has been added to a group of two
> opens up possibilities for actions and
> processes that could not otherwise have
> come into existence. He thereby
> underlines the new properties that
> emerge from the forms of association
> among individuals. The triadic group
> form provides new avenues of social
> action at the same time that it
> restricts other opportunities--such as
> the expression of individuality--which
> were available in the dyadic group.[28]

CONCLUSION

According to Simmel, social structure is achieved when the interactions among individuals become patterned and repetitive. Certain patterns of behavior, which Simmel called forms of interaction, can be identified in social life. Social structure can best be described in terms of these forms of interaction. Further, the most fruitful and effective generalizations regarding social life can be made by using the form of interaction as the independent variable in explaining other social phenomena. This is Simmel's significant insight, and the basis of his contributions, including his analysis of conflict[29] nd the significance of the number of persons in a social group, all derived from his emphasis on patterns of interaction.

THE LOGIC OF THE STRUCTURAL APPROACH

In the last three chapters, we have analyzed the structural theories of Marx and Engels, Durkheim and Simmel. The typical logic or manner of approaching the study of social phenomena which are characteristic of the structural approach of all three theorists may be outlined as follows.

First, a conceptual distinction is made between two or more types of social structures or patterns of social organization. (For example, Marx distinguished between feudalistic, capitalistic, and communistic modes of production; Durkheim distinguished highly integrated social groups from poorly integrated groups; Simmel distinguished between superordinate and subordinate forms of interaction.)

Second, an analysis is made of the relationship of each type of social structure to other important sociological phenomena. (For example, Marx argued that capitalism was associated with competitive attitudes and behaviors, while communism would be associated with cooperative attitudes and behaviors; Durkheim demonstrated a relationship between religious affiliation and suicide rates, and further argued for a relationship between the degree of integration and the suicide rate; Simmel argued that superordination and subordination lead to different behaviors and consequences, but failed to spell these relationships out adequately.)

Third, a further exploration is made of the causal connection between the type of social structure and other variables. Structuralists treat the type of social structure as the causal variable, and seek to show how this type of social structure has produced the observed consequences in other variables. The causal mechanism is detailed. (For example, Marx tried to show through exhaustive analysis of particular historical events how the capitalist mode of production produced specific historical events; Durkheim sought to show through both logic and further statistical proofs, that the structural variable (integration) was the only possible variable which might have produced the observed effects (suicide rate). There is little in Simmel's writings of this kind of analysis.

Fourth, a formal theory, consisting of concepts and propositional statements, is developed which explicates the causal connections between the social structure and the other variables analyzed. None of the three theorists we have been discussing stated their theories in this formal way.

65

FOOTNOTES

[1]Kurt H. Wolff, The Sociology of Georg Simmel (Glencoe, Illinois: The Free Press, 1950).

[2]Ibid., p. 9.

[3]Ibid.

[4]Ibid., pp. 21-23, 181-303.

[5]Ibid., pp. 40-41.

[6]Ibid., pp. 181-303.

[7]Ibid., pp. 190-267.

[8]Ibid., p. 261.

[9]Ibid.

[10]Ibid., p. 87.

[11]Ibid., p. 89.

[12]The term "dyad" has become identified with Simmel's work. Kurt Wolff, the translator of much of Simmel's work, including the section on the dyad, notes that Simmel himself never used this term. Simmel used several different terms (e.g., Zweierverbindung) whose meaning is expressed by "the shorter and more convenient" term dyad (Ibid., p. 123). Likewise, the term "triad" is a simplified expression of Simmel's terminology, including Verbindung zu dreien (p. 135).

[13]Ibid., p. 122.

[14]Ibid., p. 123.

[15]Ibid., p. 133.

[16]Ibid., pp. 134-135.

[17]Equality in the dyad is partly a function of Simmel's definition of the dyad; whenever a third party is involved, even if the third party is society, the relationship ceases to have a purely dyadic character. Thus, a marriage of two individuals which is sanctioned and regulated by society, is not a pure dyad. The best example of a dyad is found in a peer group of two friends, who voluntarily interact and who are free to

66

withdraw from the relationship without sanctions from a third party.

[18]Ibid., p. 135.

[19]Ibid., p. 144, italics added.

[20]The formula for the number of relationships in the group is expressed as $\dfrac{N\ (N-1)}{2}$.

[21]Ibid., p. 149.

[22]Ibid., pp. 148-149.

[23]Ibid., p. 146.

[24]Ibid., p. 148, italics added.

[25]Ibid., p. 154.

[26]Theodore Caplow built a theory of coalition formation largely upon this insight by Simmel. See Caplow, Two Against One: Coalitions in Triads (Englewood Cliffs, New Jersey: Prentice-Hall, 1968).

[27]Wolff, The Sociology of Georg Simmel, p. 162.

[28]Lewis A. Coser, ed., Georg Simmel (Englewood Cliffs, New Jersey: Prentice-Hall), 1965, p. 16.

[29]James T. Duke, Conflict and Power in Social Life (Provo: Brigham Young University Press, 1976), pp. 97-116.

CHAPTER FIVE

THE DEVELOPMENT OF STRUCTURALISM:
NEO-POSITIVISM, BEHAVIORISM AND SURVEY RESEARCH

Through much of the Twentieth Century, the structural orientation in sociology has been expressed most forcefully by a group of people usually labeled "neo-positivists." While the roots of positivism in sociology go back to Auguste Comte and beyond, the positivistic orientation in sociology gained strength only this century.[1] Behaviorism as an extreme form of positivism was developed by John B. Watson, and while its influence was felt first in psychology, it inevitably has had an impact upon sociology. George Lundberg was the strongest advocate of the positivistic approach in sociology for over thirty years. The impact of positivism upon sociology was magnified by the development of the techniques of public opinion polling and sampling associated with the title of "survey research." This chapter will be devoted to an examination of these influences upon the development of the structural orientation in sociology.

EARLY INFLUENCES:
WATSON AND BEHAVIORISM

Most historians of social ideas date the beginning of psychological behaviorism with John B. Watson. Watson was an experimental psychologist who did his early work with laboratory animals. After some years of extensive research, he rejected the psychological and philosophical theories of his day and developed his own explanation of human behavior.

The psychology of the early 1900's was introspectionist in method. It assumed that ideas or "consciousness" was the characteristic which distinguished human beings from other biological and physiological phenomena. The subject matter of psychology, then, was consciousness.[2]

In his studies of learning in animals, Watson became disconcerted with attempting to "intuit" the thoughts of the animals he observed. What did the rat think when he turned right at a certain point in a maze? Watson wondered whether such questions had any meaning. He quite suddenly came to the realization that he could explain the behavior of animals without reference to concepts like "mind," "consciousness,"

69

"thought," etc. If an animal had been trained through the presentation of a proper stimulus and reward to act in a certain way, its behavior became predictable. That is, all one needed to take into account in the explanation of behavior was the relationship between a stimulus (presented under certain specified conditions) and the behavioral response.

Watson generalized this principle to include human behavior. He reasoned that if it were possible to explain human behavior (response) as being due to the adjustment of the organism to certain external conditions (stimuli), no concept of mind or consciousness need be employed. Behavior, rather than consciousness, would become the subject matter of psychology. This would enable psychology to utilize the scientific methods of experimentation and observation rather than introspection or other subjectively oriented methods.

> Behaviorism . . . holds that the subject matter of human psychology is the behavior of the human being. Behaviorism claims that consciousness is neither a definite nor a usable concept. The behaviorist, who has been trained always as an experimentalist, holds, further, that belief in the existence of consciousness goes back to the ancient days of superstition and magic.[3]

The consequences of this position, generally well spelled out in Watson's writings, are the following:

(1) Only that which is observable, i.e., behavior, is the object of psychological investigation. No "inward" or "mental" states of the organism can be used in scientific investigations, except as they can be measured in terms of psychological responses.

(2) Strictly objective and scientific methods, especially the controlled experiment, are to be used. Introspection or other subjective methods are not scientific because they are not subject to verification by other qualified observers.

(3) The establishment of scientifically verified laws of human behavior, expressed in terms of probability, is the aim of all sciences, including the social sciences.

(4) Psychological laws, and thus psychological explanation, take the form of demonstrating a probable relationship between the presentation of a stimulus and the behavior (response) of the organism. Once such laws have been established, the psychologist can predict human behavior. Given a certain stimulus (often under the control of the psychologist), a given response will follow. Or, given an observed response, the psychologist can predict what stimulus provoked or caused it.[4]

Seldom is a social situation as simple as the S-R model would indicate. In almost every case, the organism is confronted with a multitude of stimuli. Some of these he perceives, others are not within his realm of perception. Whether he perceives a stimulus or not depends both upon his physiological capacities and his previous learning. According to Watson, the task of the researcher is to determine through experimentation the nature and types of stimuli which affect a particular organism. He then correlates the response (or responses) of the organism with the stimuli. However, it usually is advantageous to isolate a single response and study the stimuli which bring it about, rather than attempt to deal with the complexity of responses made by an organism.

Watson's behaviorism immediately provoked considerable controversy in psychology. Perhaps the most telling criticism of Watson's relatively simplistic stimulus-response model was that the response often does not follow the stimulus immediately, but may be delayed until a later time. (George H. Mead strongly held to this argument.) Watson's somewhat unsatisfactory answer to this question demonstrates a weakness of behavioristic theory and research. Watson argued that the response indeed followed the stimulus--automatically. The individual responds to the stimulus, but frequently the response is nothing more than a change at the "molecular" level in the individual's brain. The individual retains the stimulus, and is able to "reapply" the stimulus later in order to respond more fully to it. For Watson, the "essential" responses are molecular--that is, at the physiological level.

Behaviorism has undergone extensive development in psychology, especially experimental psychology. Watson's stimulus-response model has been replaced by much more complicated and sophisticated models which take into account the past learning of the organism, as well as such important influences as perception, motivation, etc. B. F. Skinner's studies of "operant conditioning" have led to a significant reorientation in psychological behaviorism. And Albert Bandura's work has led to the reintroduction of consciousness and agency into the working vocabulary of behaviorists.

Extensive research has been done upon "molecular" responses in organisms. Much more is now known about the brain and nervous system, and many believe that eventually it will be possible to correlate a pattern of external behavior with certain physiological and chemical phenomena within the body. However, most behaviorists have been content to work at the "molar" level, correlating stimuli with responses of a broader and more general nature, such as gestures, verbal responses, etc.

LUNDBERG'S STRUCTURAL ORIENTATION

Watson's effect upon psychology and social psychology was marked. His strongly held and well-developed theoretical position, combined with the scientifically rigorous and fruitful research studies which were produced by behaviorists, gave a great impetus to scientific psychology. Eventually this influence was felt in sociology, primarily through its link with social psychology. George A. Lundberg, more than any other sociologist, championed the behavioristic approach in sociology. We now turn to an examination of Lundberg's writings to explicate the sociological implications of behavioristic structuralism.

Like Watson, Lundberg rejected the widely held distinction between the social and the natural sciences. Instead he asserted that social life could be studied in the same manner, and with the same scientific objectivity as the natural sciences. What he described as the "natural science method" would permit the description and explanation of social life if properly used in sociology. Many sociologists, like Cooley and Mead, had accepted the dualistic nature of the world, i.e., Cartesian dualism.[5] They assumed a qualitative difference between the social world and the physical world.

In one of his earliest publications,[6] Lundberg discussed three ways in which social phenomena were

72

alleged to be different from physical phenomena: tangibility, complexity and variability, and volitionality. In each case, Lundberg rejected the difference, and argued that both physical and social phenomena are fundamentally the same.

Tangibility. Many sociologists had asserted that social phenomena were essentially subjective in nature. They believed that social phenomena could not be observed in the same manner as physical phenomena. One can touch an apple, an ocean, a field of wheat. These phenomena are "real" and easily experienced with the senses. In contrast, a social norm, a society, or the role of father are not tangible in the same sense. One cannot point to a norm as an object and demonstrate its existence.

Lundberg's rejection of this notion took several forms. First, many of the most important kinds of physical phenomena are not tangible in the sense implied. Physicists are still debating the nature of light. Gravity, subatomic particles and many other physical phenomena are less tangible than these simplistic assumptions would imply. Second, all physical phenomena must be "known" through the mechanism of symbols or language by which they are described and analyzed. The scientist manipulates symbols which stand for the phenomena he is studying. Third, the physical scientists have developed better ways of observing physical phenomena, and thus are better able to describe and analyze their nature. The social scientists are far behind in the development of scientific methods of observing their data. This is why they support the argument that social phenomena are less tangible. When social science methodology is developed further, this argument will be discarded.

Complexity and variability. Another alleged difference between social and physical phenomena is in complexity. Social scientists have long argued that social phenomena are more complex. They vary within wider limits. Lundberg replied that physical scientists have abstracted out certain characteristics of physical phenomena for study. Water as the common man knows it may include an extremely complex mixture of different substances. Physicists have abstracted out the chemical substance H_2O which they then analyze scientifically. That is, they find those common elements which form the "essence" of water and ignore the other complexities of this substance. Only certain

73

properties of minerals are important to geologists, while other complex properties are not analyzed. In short, the physical phenomena with which physical scientists deal are infinitely complex. Physical scientists have been able to abstract out certain properties for study. They simplify reality, rather than dealing with it in all its complexity. This same process must be followed by the social sciences. When this is done, the social scientist will find that his data can be as easily studied as physical phenomena.

This is related to the idea of consistency or changeability. Some argue that such physical entities as light, minerals and gravity do not change. But norms and societies do change, and social phenomena are more changeable than physical environment. Lundberg did not address this directly, but his answer was implied in his discussion of complexity and variability. Physical scientists have taken account of the changeability of their phenomena. They have abstracted out those stable elements, ignoring the unstable or variable ones. The simplicity of physical phenomena is "of our own making." By dealing with such characteristics as color, size, density or atomic weight, physical scientists can handle the stable elements of physical phenomena. This allows them to ignore the less stable and more variable elements.[7]

Volitionality. Perhaps the most important difference between physical and social phenomena, according to the dualists, is that the human being is "conscious," while physical elements are not. The power to think and to will, to choose our behavior, to act or not to act as we ourselves decide, sets people apart from molecules of water or revolving moons or fields of wheat.

> By virtue of his 'consciousness,' man is alleged to be subject to unaccountable whims and notions, which precludes the possibility of predicting his behavior by application of the scientific method.[8]

Lundberg argued that this assumption, too, is fallacious. Through scientific observations, behaviorists have shown that they can explain the behavior of human beings without reference to this conscious aspect. Under certain conditions or stimuli, the individual will respond or behave in specified and highly predictable ways. Lundberg argued that death is generally not considered to be volitional, whereas marriage almost always is. Yet sociologists can accurately predict both death and marriage rates. Both are determined by given social conditions which can be scientifically studied. Volition on the part of human beings need not be a deterrent to the development of an objective social science.

Symbols as Data

The debate over the "reality" of social phenomena masks a fundamental aspect of all science, according to Lundberg. All scientists, not just social scientists, deal with symbols. The world can only be known through our symbolic representations of it. There is no such thing as "direct" knowledge. All knowledge is filtered through our perceptual and conceptual processes.

Philosophical assumptions that physical objects are "objective" by nature while social facts are "subjective" by nature are invalid. Objectivity is not a quality of a fact, but a quality of mind. All scientific data are symbolic in nature, and can only be known through the subjective process.[9]

Behavior as Data

Having asserted that all scientific facts are known "subjectively," Lundberg made it clear that this does not mean that the most suitable methods for the study of social facts are "subjective." Intuition and introspection are not acceptable scientific methods.

The behavior of people provides the data for the social sciences. The task of the sociologist is to observe the behavior of people, conceptualize it symbolically, and develop scientific laws which explain it. Observation is improved to the extent to which unbiased, reliable and valid instruments can be developed to measure behavior.

The meaning of phenomena has to be inferred from the behavior of people toward whatever excites their behavior, whether this stimulus be people in uniforms, graven images in stone, totem poles, or words. The objectivity of phenomena is postulated from the degree to which observers agree in their reactions. This agreement, of course, is determined from their ability to communicate

their responses. <u>Symbols representing these</u>
<u>meanings of societal behavior as inferred</u>
<u>from behavior are what sociological science</u>
<u>deals with</u>.[10]

Sociologists must study actual behavior. Only
that which can be observed can form the domain of a
science. The sociologist cannot observe thought,
dreams or other subjective states of people. He can
observe behavior. Behavior, then, must serve as the
indicator of these subjective states. Scientists must
approach the study of behavior objectively, using
scientific detachment rather than subjective intuition.

Words are a form of behavior, according to
Lundberg. When a person speaks, the words he uses can
be observed, as can the inflection in his voice and
other behavior he engages in while speaking. Verbal
responses, then, are an important datum for sociology.
The sociologist should study verbal behavior as well as
other kinds of behavior, i.e., physical gestures. He
must attempt to determine the conditions under which
verbal behavior and overt behavior are parallel or
dissimilar.[11]

The Stimulus-Response Model

Lundberg accepted the Watsonian stimulus-response
model, which we discussed earlier. However, generally
Lundberg sought to work on a more macroscopic level
than do the behavioristic psychologists. He desired to
demonstrate that given social conditions tend to
produce determinate patterns of behavior. The social
condition is viewed as a causal agent, the behavior
pattern as a result or effect.

Social   Behavior
Conditions ──────────⟶ Patterns

These sociological patterns are ultimately
reducible to psychologically conditioned tendencies to
act, and perhaps ultimately even to physiological
neuromuscular sets. After having reemphasized his
contention that symbols are the immediate data of
science, Lundberg asserted:

These symbols correspond to
neuro-muscular sets or covert neural
behavior of some kind in the human organism.
The sets have been formed as a result of

76

responses to situations. The symbols subsequently serve as substitute stimuli for these situations. When these sets, namely our verbal mechanism and symbols, correspond closely to the conditions to which we must adjust, they greatly facilitate our adjustments.[12]

The sociologist, however, is most frequently concerned with the large-scale social manifestations of behavior. The psychologist, in the scientific division of labor, studies the psychological and physiological aspects of individual behavior.

Mind as an Intervening Variable

Lundberg was somewhat inconsistent in his treatment of such concepts as "mind," "thought," etc. He wrote of behavior as the external manifestation of inner subjective states of the human being, and frequently implied the existence of these internal states. However, in several places in his writings he took pains to reject concepts of subjective states as useless.

According to Lundberg, if the sociologist intends to be scientific, he cannot assume the existence of any internal or "intervening" variables between causal conditions and the behavior effects. Only variables subject to observation, that is, behavioral variables, can furnish the data of science. If one can conceptualize the external cause and effect in behavioral terms, one need never utilize any intervening subjective variables to "explain" behavior. In one's explanation of behavior patterns, one should seek to obtain observational data for the social conditions or stimuli which preceded the behavior. Extensive and often painstaking research will enable the sociologist to explain the behavior by reference to antecedent conditions rather than using any intervening concepts of mind or thought. Like phlogiston, concepts which refer to the subjective states of the individual will eventually be discarded. Rather than treating this subjective state as a "reality," we should look to the behavior or activities which the individual exhibits.[13] Lundberg said we should look for verbs, not nouns.[13]

Introspection as a Scientific Method

Sociologists who advocate introspection or other intuitive procedures to study social phenomena were castigated by Lundberg.[14] They fail to realize that insight on the part of the scientist is the goal toward which he strives, not a process of explaining social phenomena.

To have scientific value, a scientific fact must be subject to replication. That is, another trained scientist must be able to perform the same operations and observe the same data as the first scientist. Lundberg argued that the subjectivists have failed to provide a description of "understanding" or "introspection" which will enable one scientist to replicate the methods of another. An operational definition of insight is needed if it is to be used as a scientific methodological tool.[15] He strongly implied that because of the subjective and unique nature of the method of introspection, it can never be replicated. It therefore should be rejected by sociology, since sociology is a scientific discipline.

Those who use introspective methods usually are not well enough trained in more objective techniques to use the latter. It is much easier to sit in one's study thinking about social life than to go out and observe it, or especially to devise valid measures for certain social phenomena. Lundberg strongly implied that introspection is a method for lazy sociologists.

Sociology aspires to be a science. To be a science, it must utilize objective methods to gain valid and verifiable data regarding social phenomena. This cannot be achieved as long as sociologists adhere to theoretical postulates regarding the subjectivity of sociological phenomena and seek to study these using subjective and instrospective techniques. Lundberg referred to Heisenberg's assertions that "every fundamental advance in science involves the abandonment of hope for certain types of explanation.[16] Sociology must abandon hope for subjective explanations, and should seek instead to use the methods of the natural sciences to discover the laws of human behavior.

Behaviorism as a Structural Approach

As we have previously emphasized, Lundberg accepted as his fundamental explanatory model the stimulus-response model of John B. Watson. Lundberg asserted that the individual human being is constantly engaged in a process of adjustment to his environment. This process of adjustment is the major subject matter of sociology. Each individual is faced with a variety of situations. In order to adjust to a situation, he develops a "definition of the situation."[17]

According to Lundberg, the individual's definition of the situation is determined by several factors. First, the physiological tensions or what Lundberg calls "adjustment needs" of the individual strongly influence his definition of the situation and his actual adjustment to it. Second, the previous experience of the individual is important. Each individual is conditioned by his social group to respond in certain ways to certain stimuli. Norms, ideologies and customs all represent conditioned patterns of behavior. Each situation presents the individual with a problem of adjustment. He draws upon his past conditioned responses to enable him to adjust to the present situation. By studying the stimuli which have been presented to the individual as well as his past conditioning, the researcher can predict and explain his behavior. The term "definition of the situation" is therefore simply a term to express this complex state of conditioned habits and behavior sets which the individual brings into a particular situation. It is a representation not of a subjective inner state of the individual but of previous external conditioning stimuli which the individual has been taught to respond to. However, the temptation to speak of "internalization" of this response set is difficult to avoid. For Lundberg, the process of learning is a process of conditioning. Once the scientist has studied the previous stimuli to which the individual learned to respond, he can predict and explain the individual's present behavior without reference to any subjective or internal state.[18]

According to Lundberg, each society "structures" the social conditions in that society. Structure is achieved through organized habit patterns and through the consistent use of specific verbal terms to refer to external stimuli. The structuring to which Lundberg referred is a social psychological process of selection and organization by which individuals learn to "pattern" their responses to given situations. Each society achieves social organization through relating or structuring various aspects of society into a unified whole. This organizational pattern is then symbolized through the use of language. If the language used by members of the society communicates to them the relations of the various aspects of their society, then their society is "structured" in their minds.[19]

Lundberg's behaviorism is thus consistent with Both Marx' and Durkheim's structuralism. For each of these three theorists, structural or organizational patterns lead directly to specific patterns of behavior. While the role of subjective elements varies in the theories of these sociologists, the fundamental position which each takes is that the social structure is the determinant of behavior patterns. Social structure is the major causal element in any sociological explanation.

Each of these three has rejected subjective or ideational variables as causal. Lundberg argued that sociology will be able to develop as a science only insofar as it gives up assumptions that social phenomena are qualitatively different from those of other sciences, as well as the intuitive techniques which it has used to try to study subjective phenomena.

SURVEY RESEARCH AND STRUCTURALISM

The data gathering techniques encompassed by the term "survey research" have had a great influence upon sociology. Questionnaires and interviews gave sociologists the tools they needed to gain scientific respectability. Both scientists and laymen today recognize the influence these powerful techniques have on their societies.

Up to the 1920's, most sociological research studies were subjective and impressionistic.[20] They depended upon the acuity of observation of the sociologist. Some studies utilizing demographic data and data gathered from public records were made. However, observation by a sensitive analyst was still the method used by the great majority of sociologists.

Gradually during the 1920's and 1930's the use of questionnaires and interviews expanded. During this period, the research projects using these techniques were small and limited in scope. Samples of respondents were poorly drawn. Little use of statistics other than percentages was made. Bogardus's social distance test, Thurstone's techniques of scale construction, and other developments gradually had an impact upon sociology. Impressionistic observational studies lost favor and were replaced by survey research.

Lazarsfeld, Berelson and Gaudet's[21] study of voting in the election of 1940 gave both social scientists and politicians added respect for the power of survey research. During World War II, questionnaire and interview studies were carried on extensively in the American armed forces, and published in the influential American Soldier[22] series. Public opinion polling received a blow in its failure to predict Truman's victory in the 1948 election. By 1950, however, survey research techniques of gathering data were widely used not only by social scientists but by many other persons. Business organizations frequently used survey research in consumer research--probably its most extensively utilized application. Political parties and candidates found public opinion polling absolutely necessary in an effective campaign. Eventually, sociological methodology became almost synonymous with techniques of questionnaire construction, sampling, and statistical analysis of questionnaire data. Only since the middle 1960's have strong movements toward other kinds of techniques and data been felt in sociology.[23]

THE LOGIC OF SURVEY RESEARCH

Since survey research techniques involve asking questions of a sample or respondents, the data gathered by these techniques are almost exclusively concerned with opinions, attitudes and other verbal expressions of how individuals think. Typically, the survey researcher begins with a subject (or dependent variable) he wishes to study. For example, he may be interested in how people voted or plan to vote in an election, the sexual behavior of males, attitudes toward dating, opinions about how well the President is performing his job, whether clean restrooms or lower prices are more effective in enticing customers to service stations, or attitudes toward religion, racial questions, etc. Since the researcher cannot accompany the respondent into the voting booth or to office, he substitutes a series of questions for a direct observation of the subject's behavior. The data gathered represent verbal responses or checks on a questionnaire in which respondents tell about their behavior. Few survey researchers take the care to gather independent data on actual behavior by which to check their survey data. Behavior is therefore not studied directly, but indirectly through the verbal descriptions of the respondents.

Even more frequently, questions posed to respondents are concerned with their opinions and attitudes, not their behavior. How people think and feel about questions of the day become the subject of investigations. Attitudes are substituted for behavior as the subject of sociological research.

Some survey research studies are purely descriptive. They begin and end with a description of how the respondents think about a given subject. However, many survey researchers are interested in explanation as well as description. They therefore include on their questionnaires and interview schedules some questions which elicit information on "social background" characteristics of the respondents. Early studies utilizing survey research as well as demographic studies had demonstrated the importance of a number of background variables, including sex, age, income, occupation, education, race and nationality, religion, and urban-rural residence. These variables frequently were found to be correlated with other variables in which researchers were interested. It therefore became common in every questionnaire or interview to ask the respondent to give information on these variables.

In explaining the specific dependent variables which the research is studying, social background variables are consistently used as independent or causal variables.

Cause	Effect
Social Background Variables: Age, Sex, Income, Occupation, Education, Race, Religion, Urban-Rural Residence	Attitudinal Variables: Political Party Preferences, Attitudes Toward Race Relations, etc.

Social background factors are treated as causes and attitudes are treated as effects for at least two good reasons: time and manipulability.[24] In point of time, a person usually gains his sex, race, religion, urban-rural residence, and social class before his specific attitudes on many vital questions are developed. In addition, social background factors are less changeable or manipulable than attitudes. Suppose a correlation is found between race and political liberalism. It is easy to conceptualize race as the cause of liberalism, but very difficult to conceptualize liberalism as the cause of race. Changing a person's attitudes usually does not result in a change of social background characteristics. However, frequently a change of social background characteristics is followed by a change of attitudes.

STRUCTURAL IMPLICATIONS OF SURVEY RESEARCH

The findings of survey research are almost always utilized in a structural manner. The social background variables are treated as statuses in specified social structures. These are conceptualized as causes of ideational factors--attitudes, opinions, expressions of behavior. By locating an individual's position in a social structure, it is possible to predict and explain his opinions about an extremely wide variety of attitudinal questions.

We do not believe, however, that survey research need always involve structural orientations. Two major tendencies on the part of survey researchers have contributed to their structuralism. First, the researcher almost always conceptualizes social background variables as social statuses, rather than as indicators of cultural or ideational factors. Social class, as indicated by income, occupation, education, etc., can be conceptualized as a structural position a la Marx, or as a constellation of normative and cultural values a la Weber. Survey researchers almost invariably take the structural rather than the subjective alternative.

Second, few researchers gather data on the broad cultural values of a society and use these data as causal variables to explain the specific attitudes they are studying. Attitudes are treated as dependent variables. In the absence of any data on other subjective variables, the social background variables are treated as causal structural variables.

83

Occasionally the researcher may feel the need to "sketch in" some historical or cultural details. These are drawn from impressionistic observations rather than data explicitly gathered for the purposes of the study. Seldom are they given great weight as causal variables.

In conclusion, survey research is almost always used in a structural manner. Statuses like social class, race, urban-rural residence, etc., are treated as positions in social structures. These positions are utilized as independent variables to explain attitudinal and ideational variables. Frequently the structural implications of survey research are only tacitly recognized. Since the great majority of research done by sociologists in the recent past has been survey research, the predominant theoretical orientation in contemporary sociology is structural.

FOOTNOTES

[1] For an introduction to this literature, see the following: A. J. Ayer, editor, _Logical Positivism_, Glencoe: The Free Press, 1959; Gustav Bergmann, _The Metaphysics of Logical Positivism_, New York: Longmans, Green, 1954; Abraham Kaplan, _The Conduct of Inquiry: Methodology for Behavioral Science_, San Francisco: Chandler, 1964; Victor Kraft, _The Vienna Circle: The Origin of Neo-positivism_, New York: Philosophical Library, 1953; and Karl Pearson, _The Grammar of Science_, New York: Macmillan, 1892.

[2] John B. Watson, _Behaviorism_ (Revised edition), New York: Norton, 1930, p. 2. See also John B. Watson, "Psychology as a Behaviorist Views It," _Psychological Review_, 20 (1913), pp. 158-177; John B. Watson, _Behavior_, New York: Holt, 1914; John B. Watson, _Psychology from the Standpoint of a Behaviorist_, Philadelphia: Lippincott, 1919.

[3] _Behaviorism_, p. 2.

[4] See Arnold S. Kaufman, "Behaviorism," _The Encyclopedia of Philosophy_, New York: Macmillan, 1967, Volume 1, p. 271 for another propositional statement of behaviorism.

[5] This is often spoken of as "Cartesian dualism," or as the "mind-body problem" discussed by Descartes. For Lundberg's discussion of dualism, see George A.

Lundberg, Foundations of Sociology, New York: McKay, 1964 (originally published in 1939 by Macmillan), pp. 35-37; George A. Lundberg, "Contemporary Positivism in Sociology," American Sociological Review, 4 (1939), p. 45; George A. Lundberg, "Operational Definitions in the Social Sciences," American Journal of Sociology, 47 (1941-42), p. 736.

[6]George A. Lundberg, "The Logic of Sociology and Social Research," in George A. Lundberg, Read Bain and Nels Anderson, editors, Trends in American Sociology, New York: Harper, 1929, pp. 395-399.

[7]Ibid., p. 398.

[8]Ibid., pp. 398-399.

[9]"Contemporary Positivism," p. 48.

[10]Ibid., p. 49.

[11]Ibid., pp. 46-49; Foundations of Sociology, pp. 13-15, 25-26, 114; "Operational Definitions," p. 740; George A. Lundberg, "The Natural Science Trend in Sociology," American Journal of Sociology, 61 (1955), pp. 194-199.

[12]Foundations of Sociology, p. 54.

[13]Ibid., p. 7; George A. Lundberg, Can Science Save Us? New York: Longmans, Green, 1947, pp. 22-24.

[14]"Contemporary Positivism," p. 47; "The Natural Science Trend in Sociology," pp. 195, 200.

[15]Foundations of Sociology, p. 62.

[16]"Operational Definitions," p. 736.

[17]Here Lundberg used the term which was developed by W. I. Thomas (see the discussion in Chapter 8) and which generally has been used by subjectivists to refer to an inner state of mind or consciousness. See Lundberg's Foundations of Sociology, p. 101.

[18]Ibid., pp. 98-101.

[19]Ibid., p. 116.

[20]A quick perusal of such journals as the American Journal of Sociology is a good way to compare the kinds of research reported at different time periods.

[21]Paul F. Lazarsfeld, Bernard Berelson and Hazel Gaudet, The People's Choice, New York: Duell, Sloan and Pearce, 1944.

[22]Samuel Stouffer, et al., The American Soldier (4 volumes), Princeton: Princeton University Press, 1949.

[23]See for example Eugene J. Webb, Donald T. Campbell, Richard D. Schwartz and Lee Sechrest, Unobtrusive Measures: Nonreactive Research into the Social Sciences, Chicago: Rand McNally, 1966.

[24]Morris Rosenberg, The Logic of Survey Analysis, New York: Basic Books, 1968, pp. 11-12.

CHAPTER SIX

CLASSICAL SUBJECTIVISM: MAX WEBER

Max Weber is generally considered to be one of the most influential sociologists who ever lived.[1] Weber's writings range over a broad spectrum of sociological subjects, including religion, politics, economic life, law, urbanization, social change and sociological methodology. Unlike other great theorists of his time, his writings have a distinctly modern flavor to them. He anticipated many of the changes taking place in modern society and analyzed them insightfully. More importantly, he anticipated many of the significant theoretical questions raised by contemporary theorists. His answers to these questions are both sophisticated and complex. His writings are so important and so fruitful that few sociologists would claim to be well trained in their chosen discipline without a strong grounding in the Weberian literature. This is true despite the fact that Weber's works seldom have been read in the original German, and their translation into English has been inconsistent and incomplete.[2]

Despite this, Weber's basic approach to the study of social phenomena has generally not been adopted by contemporary sociologists. Survey research methodology and attitudinal research have been in vogue for the last thirty years, and are just now beginning to be supplemented by more subjective techniques. Further, Weber's historical approach has had little influence on several generations of sociologists who have had little interest or training in history.

Weber's influence, then, is felt primarily through the wealth of significant insights he developed. His writings often provide the starting point to any investigation of sociological phenomena with which he dealt. His insights were developed through a penetrating and consistent use of a subjective approach to the study of social phenomena. It is ironic that contemporary sociology has neglected his approach but voraciously used the principles and insights which he achieved through the use of this approach.

THE GERMAN BACKGROUND[3]

During the latter part of the Nineteenth Century, German philosophy made a distinction between the natural sciences and the "cultural" sciences. The natural sciences were thought to deal with definite and distinct natural phenomena, governed by determinist natural laws. The province of science was thought to be the discovery of these natural laws.

Social phenomena were thought to be of a different order of reality. People were assumed to be capable of independent thought, action and choice. They acted subjectively and unpredictably. Their behavior was not governed by natural law. Because of this, scientific methodology could not be used fruitfully in the study of man and his behavior. The assertion that no science of social phenomena was possible was commonly accepted.

WEBER AND CULTURE

Weber accepted this dichotomy between the physical and social sciences, as well as the assertion that human beings are of a different order of reality than natural phenomena. However, he did believe that a science of social phenomena is possible, and that this science should be built precisely upon the differences found between the natural and the social sciences. Weber accepted the subjective point of view, since it was self-evident to him that people are subjective creatures.

Weber reasoned that no science of social life is possible without an understanding of the subjective state of mind of the individual. The researcher must take the point of view of the actor. This means that he must understand the "social action" of an individual, including his goals, his choice of means, his values and his total subjective orientation to a situation. Every actor has complex motives. Likewise, every actor adheres to a relatively complex but integrated normative system. The sociological researcher must understand both the individual motives and the total normative system, and must utilize this understanding in his explanation of social reality.

Weber observed that there is a tendency for individuals within the same society, or the same social group, to hold common values and common motives. These uniformities are explainable by the existence of a normative system which pervades a culture and to which the individual is socialized. Weber's subjectivism thus emphasizes broad cultural values and orienting social norms--it is macrosociological. His subjective point of view is significantly different from that of the symbolic interactionists whose focus is on interpersonal interaction at the microsociological level.

THE FUNDAMENTAL CONCEPTS OF SOCIOLOGY

Weber's subjective approach is nowhere more apparent than in the introductory essay to his major work Economy and Society,[4] entitled "The Fundamental Concepts of Sociology." This was written near the end of his life and represents Weber's most systematic attempt to provide the foundation for a subjective theory of sociology. As the title implies, this section is devoted to the definition and elaboration of sociological concepts. Here, Weber attempted to develop a system of concepts which fit together in an orderly and progressive pattern.

According to Weber, sociology strives to arrive at an "understanding" of social action. The methodological process which the science of sociology uses is called "verstehen," i.e., understanding. The prime subject matter of sociology is "social action." By this term, Weber meant individual behavior which is subjectively oriented to the behavior of other individuals. Social action is action with a subjective content. Any other behavior is not "social," since it is not subjective. Thus Weber specified both the content and the scientific method of sociology as strictly subjective. Let us follow his argument closely as it proceeds.

THE METHOD OF VERSTEHEN[5]

Weber assumed that man's subjective nature provides the theoretical starting point for an explanation of his behavior. The methodology used to gain information about man must likewise be a subjective one--the method of verstehen (understanding). The sociologist must first seek to "understand" social behavior in terms of its meaningfulness to the actor. Once he understands how the actor thinks about his own behavior, he will be able to "explain" this behavior scientifically.

The subject matter of sociology is human conduct or behavior. Individuals usually do not act unless they have previously thought about their action. In order for the sociologist to explain such action, he must first understand the thought processes of the individual. Only in this way is the behavior "meaningful." An understanding of social action can be achieved through either of two ways: (1) rational thought processes, or (2) empathic emotion.

RATIONAL UNDERSTANDING

Rational understanding takes place when the actor is oriented toward a goal which is known to the observer and when the actor chooses means to reach that goal which are most effective.[6] The individual thinks about various alternative means and then rationally chooses to use that means which is "correct." Correct means can either be: (1) most effective in reaching the goal, or (2) normatively prescribed as the correct means. If both the goal and the means are clearly "right" in the sense that they are prescribed by the culture, and if the observer knows of these prescriptions, then "the highest degree of verifiable certainty" may be achieved.[7]

The best method of gaining rational understanding is to assume that all behavior is rational and to develop "ideal type" concepts and explanations based on this assumption. One can then analyze the extent to which actual behavior departs from this "ideal" type of behavior. Any "errors" in behavior can then be investigated. Such errors result either from errors in logic made by the actor or from emotional factors present in the individual. The latter factors can be understood by empathic understanding.

Weber was careful to point out that this method of treating behavior as if it were rational does not necessitate the additional premise that all individuals act rationally. It is merely a "methodological device" which is useful to achieve understanding. "It certainly does not involve a belief in the actual predominance of rational elements in human life."[8]

EMPATHIC UNDERSTANDING

Empathic understanding occurs when the actor and the observer share the same subjective orientation to a given situation. We emphathize with another person if we have experienced the same emotional feelings, the same thoughts and attitudes, that he has. The closer two persons are in their personal value system, emotional orientations and previous experiences, the easier it is for one to empathize with and understand the other. Weber clearly believed that "empathic understanding" can be most successfully achieved by observers whose status and experience are most closely related to those of the actor.

Understanding, therefore, is a supremely human characteristic. We are able to understand others because--and to the extend to which--we understand ourselves. We understand the emotions of others because we have behaved in the same way, or at least have thought about the possibility of so acting.

UNDERSTANDING AND MOTIVATION

Empathic understanding is achieved by imagining the motivation of the actor and by "placing the act in an intelligible and more inclusive context of meaning."[9] Additional information is needed to achieve this kind of understanding. One needs to know something of the actor, his relationships with other people, and his previous behavior in order to attribute a certain motivation to him. A person may chop wood to earn money, to provide himself with firewood, or for recreation. Simply observing the act of chopping wood gives no clue as to which motivation is used by the particular actor.

In making a causal assessment of the subjective motivation of a given actor in behaving in a given way, one "attempts to attain clarity and certainty," but no explanation is ever final.[10] It remains a "plausible hypothesis" rather than a certain interpretation. This is true because (1) the actor may have subconscious motives which are concealed, (2) motivation in any actor is extremely complex, and (3) "the actors in any given situation are often subject to opposing and conflicting impulses. . . ."[11] Thus, subjective understanding itself is not sufficient.

> . . . verification of subjective interpretation by comparison with the concrete course of events is, as in the case of all hypotheses, indispensable.[12]

Verstehen never stands by itself. It must be verified by other observations. Weber specifically mentioned in this regard psychological experiments, statistical generalizations, and comparison of the "largest possible number of historical and contemporary" events.[13] Even the "imaginary experiment" is useful where other scientific observations cannot be made.

The process of verstehen is complete when one can "adequately" relate the motivation to the behavior observed.

A correct causal interpretation of a concrete course of action is arrived at when the overt action and the motives have both been correctly apprehended and at the same time their relation has become meaningfully comprehensible.[14]

"Adequacy" is judged on two levels. On the level of meaning, an explanation is adequate if it conforms to our "habitual modes of thought." Simply put, it is easily understood. Secondly, an interpretation is "causally adequate in so far as . . . there is a probability that it will always actually occur in the same way."[15] Whether a given interpretation is adequate is relative to (1) the purposes of the scientist, (2) the historical epoch in which the behavior is observed, and (3) the future predictability of the behavior.

UNDERSTANDING DIFFERENT CULTURES

This does not mean that a social scientist can study only those individuals or groups with which he is already familiar. Weber's own studies dealt with an amazing variety of cultures and historical time periods. One is constantly amazed by the depth of his insights into these cultures.

. . . (T)he ability to imagine one's self performing a similar action is not a necessary prerequisite to understanding; 'one need not have been Caesar in order to understand Caesar.' For the verifiable accuracy of interpretation of the meaning of a phenomenon, it is a great help to be able to put one's self imaginatively in the place of the actor and thus sympathetically to participate in his experiences, but this is not an essential condition of meaningful interpretation.[16]

How does one go about studying behavior or cultures with which he is not familiar? One answer is

92

that given previously: one reduces the action to its ideal-typical rational aspects, and then analyzes the extent to which the behavior approaches this rational ideal. A second answer is that one observes and analyzes the "non-understandable" components of social life. This second answer is only alluded to by Weber, but is is clear in his own historical investigations that he attempted to take nonsubjective elements into account in his explanations.

What are these "processes and phenomena which are devoid of subjective meaning?" Weber did not attempt to make an exhaustive list. He specifically mentioned "certain psychic or psycho-physical phenomena such as fatigue, habituation, memory, etc." as well as biological, geographical and physical conditions.[17] Such phenomena may well influence behavior, but Weber accords them a place secondary to "meaningful" elements.

It is altogether possible that future research may be able to discover non-understandable uniformities underlying what has appeared to be specifically meaningful action, thought little has been accomplished in this direction thus far.[18]

Weber's approach is a practical one. He chose the subjective approach because to him it offered greater insights and better explanations of human behavior. If further developments in sociology demonstrate that better explanations can be arrived at by dealing with nonsubjective uniformities, Weber would be willing at that time to accept this alternative orientation.

It should be noted here that Weber's subjective approach was not a return to mysticism. Weber was a scientist. He wanted to make objective and empirical investigations and observations. He sought to free himself from his own cultural biases and describe the world in scientific terms. But he believed this could be done only by accepting rather than rejecting the subjective approach, including the reliance on ideas as the basic social phenomenon and the use of the method of verstehen to study these ideas.

SOCIAL ACTION

Social action or behavior for Weber was by definition subjective, in that one actor takes account of the behavior of the other. Weber distinguished this from (1) behavior which is not subjectively oriented, such as the unplanned collision of two cyclists, (2) similar actions by groups of people who are oriented to external stimuli rather than the behavior of other people, such as the collective putting up of umbrellas at the onset of rain, and (3) imitative behavior which is purely mechanical or "reactive" rather than meaningfully oriented.[19]

A "social relationship" is said to exist if two or more persons mutually take into account the behavior of the other.[20] The meaning for one actor may not be identical to that of the other actor--it need not be "reciprocal." The parties to a relationship may reach agreement on meaning by discussion, or they may orient their behavior to normative "maxims" which either they or others have formulated.

Uniformities of behavior result from social relationships, since individuals expect and depend upon a certain kind of behavior from others.

Social order results from interaction because of (1) uniformities in behavior, but more importantly (2) because individuals in the process of interaction develop normative rules which they believe to be valid. These rules are given legitimacy in the minds of the actors, who have a tendency to conform to them habitually. A rule is said to be a "law" when defiance to it is sanctioned by explicit punishments applied by a group especially designated to apply these sanctions.

These distinctions are extremely important, for they enabled Weber to (1) develop a matrix of definitions which are tied closely together, and (2) develop a classificatory scheme for types of social action.

TYPES OF SOCIAL ACTION

Weber's classification of types of social action (conduct) is rightly famous, yet very simple. It is a fourfold scheme, two of which are rational types and

the other two nonrational. These are ideal types which
attempt to classify the various ways in which human
actors orient themselves subjectively to the social
world and, on the basis of these orientations, choose
how to act.

    1. <u>Purpose-rational action</u>.[21] In this type of
action, the individual has a number of discrete ends he
wishes to attain. There are several means by which
each end may be attained. Further, other conditions
are present which must be considered in choosing among
both ends and means. The individual must take into
account all ends, means and conditions. He then
rationally chooses which end to seek and which means to
use to achieve it. The calculation is primarily in
terms of the benefit derived versus the costs suffered
in attaining the end.

    2. <u>Value-rational action</u>. Here the individual
holds some absolute end, usually of a religious or
ethical character. He then seeks to achieve this
single end rationally buy the utilization of the most
efficient means available. There is a decided absence
of calculation of cost here. Since the achievement of
the single goal is of overriding importance, it is
sought by the most efficient means.

    3. <u>Traditional action</u>. This is action which
follows the "habituation of long practice."[22] Again,
there is no calculation. Rather, the individual
blindly follows tradition and acts as he is expected to
act. Such action, Weber admitted, falls close to the
borderline between meaningful and nonmeaningful action.

    4. <u>Affectual action</u>. This is action which is
determined by the emotional state of the actor. It is
neither rational nor traditional. The meaning present
in the actor's mind is emotional in nature. The
individual acts almost instinctively, rather than in a
calculated manner. Again, this falls close to the
borderline of nonsubjective action.

    Each of these definitions is couched in terms of
the orientation of the individual actor. Weber made
use of these distinctions frequently in his historical
studies, even though the exact formulation of these
types came after his historical writings. However, he
did little to develop empirical generalizations using
these concepts. We have little to tell us which type
is most prevalent in a particular group, what social

conditions lead to one rather than the other type of social action, etc.

IDEAL TYPES[23]

One of the most difficult social phenomena with which to deal concretely is the broad cultural "orienting" norm or value. Such subjective ideas are important precisely because they are widely held by the members of a given society. Orienting norms such as the Protestant Ethic, which we shall discuss later in this chapter, may become important cultural ideas in a number of different societies. The social scientist who wishes to describe, analyze and explain these societal ideas must find some methodology to do so. He faces the problems of observing the content and the extent of such norms and or conceptualizing them in some meaningful way.

Many theorists previous to Weber had faced the same problem. Weber built upon the methods used by these previous theorists to explicate the process by which a social scientist is able to abstract out the important elements of the culture of a society and utilize them in the explanation of historical events. Weber developed what he called the "ideal type" as the conceptual tool by which an adequate scientific investigation can be pursued using the subjective approach.

An ideal type is developed by abstracting out certain subjective elements of the society. These elements may generally be treated as variables, although this is not absolutely necessary. The observer then conceptualizes each extreme of the variable--that is, each end of the continuum. This is a "one-sided" accentuation of which Weber speaks.[24] The ideal type is formed by a combination of a number of subjective variables, each of which is taken in an extreme form.

Weber's use of the ideal type in his conceptualization of a capitalistic economy will be used to illustrate how this is done. Several conditions which are important to distinguish a capitalistic economy from other types of economic organization are (a) extensive private investment of capital, (b) free competition, and (c) rational conduct toward making a profit. Each of these may be conceptualized as a variable, as follows:

96

Extensive		None
	Private investment of capital	

Free		Restricted
	Competition	

Rational		Irrational
	Rational Conduct	

The extremes of these three variables (again, extensive private investment of capital, free competition, and rational conduct) are taken as the constituent elements of the ideal type of a capitalist economy. These constituent elements are the defining characteristics of the ideal type. When one wishes to give a definition of "capitalist economy," he simply lists these three defining characteristics.

Several important points should be noted. First, Weber always used subjective cultural elements as the defining characteristics of his important ideal types. Second, Weber seldom used the other end of his variables in developing ideal types. For example, he did not combine (a) lack of investment of private capital, (b) restricted competition, and (c) irrational conduct to form an ideal type as the direct opposite of capitalism. Instead, he contrasted capitalism with other forms of economic organization, such as a handicraft economy, which has totally different defining characteristics.

It is important to note that the various elements which are used in the ideal type are combined to form a unity. Because of particular historical and cultural conditions, these ideas have "come together" in a certain place and time. They are found combined in the minds of the majority of members of a society. The sociologist therefore, needs only to observe and understand the subjective unity which these elements possess. There is present in Weber's formulation both the assumption and the observation that the ideas used to compose an ideal type do actually exist together at a particular time period in the minds of the members of the society. Such a condition is never one of perfection. Not all members possess each idea. Nor is there a perfect unity of these ideas in each individual's mind. Just as the scientist abstracts these elements from reality, so do the actors. One should not think of these ideal-types as "real" in the sense that they fully reflect objective reality or that

97

they are found in their pure form anywhere in any actual society. Like any concept, they accentuate certain aspects of reality and ignore others.

Ideal-types are used for comparative purposes. Once an ideal-type has been developed, the sociologist can use it to compare any two or more cases which he has observed. For example, he may compare the economies of France and Italy with regard to the extent to which they are capitalistic. If he finds that private investment is more extensive in one nation than the other, or that exchanges are less free or less rational in one than the other, he may conclude that the economy of that nation is less capitalistic than the other. An ideal-type concept is used in the same way as any other concept.

RELIGION AND THE ECONOMY

Weber's subjective approach to the study of social phenomena is applied in his studies of religion. Weber's work in the sociology of religion represents perhaps the most extensive comprehensive series of investigations of religion as a sociological phenomenon ever undertaken. While Durkheim's Elementary Forms of the Religious Life[25] is often regarded as the most important single work in the sociology of religion, Weber's studies covered more of the world religions and more points of sociological relevance than did Durkheim's.

Weber's interest in religion as a sociological phenomena developed only after he was a well-trained economist. Weber made it very clear that he was not interested in all aspects of religion, but only those that had implications for economic theory. His studies of the major religions of the world were conceived as part of a larger study by a number of investigators on the social foundations of the economy.

Weber's initial study of the relationship between religion and economics is found in his essays on the influence of the Protestant Reformation on the development of capitalism. This is designed as a refutation of Marx's theory that the economy is the major cause of religious phenomena. Weber, instead, sought to show that religion is at least partially independent of economic influences, and that often in concrete historical cases the nature of religious development has a causal influence on the course of

98

economic development. Much of Weber's work, especially his religious studies, has been correctly interpreted as a "debate with Marx's ghost."

The Protestant Ethic and the Spirit of Capitalism,[26] published in two parts in 1904-05, immediately provoked a heated intellectual exchange. His thesis that the ideas developed during the Reformation helped to bring about a rationalistic capitalistic development in Western Europe, was widely debated. This debate has continued to the present time. Weber felt that he had been misunderstood. Many felt that he was trying to replace Marxian economic determinism with a kind of Hegelian mysticism. Weber instead preferred to interpret his own work as a balanced view which treated economic, religious and social factors as interdependent.

Weber had originally intended to make studies of other religious systems to round out his analysis of Protestantism. The debate over his Protestant Ethic made this project even more necessary in his eyes. But it was not begun until at least 1913, nearly nine years after the initial publication of the first part of the Protestant Ethic. He completed studies of Confucianism, Taoism, Hinduism, Buddhism and Judaism.[27] He intended but was never able to analyze Mohammedanism, early Christianity and Catholicism.

In each of his religious studies, the interdependence of religion and economics, but especially the influence of religion on economics, was the central focus. In each case, he was able to conclude that religion and economics are to a certain extent independent of each other, but that each exerts a significant influence over the other. Because of the presence of the Protestant Ethic, capitalism developed in Western Europe. Because of the absence of the Protestant Ethic or some similar ethic in China, India and the Middle East, capitalism did not develop in these ares.

THE PROTESTANT ETHIC AND THE SPIRIT OF CAPITALISM

Weber's book The Protestant Ethic and the Spirit of Capitalism is one of the truly great classics of sociological literature. It is widely read in economics, history and sociology, and has become established in intellectual and cultural circles as one of those few books with which all educated persons are expected to be familiar. The term "Protestant Ethic" is widely used in everyday discourse. While the book has provoked a great deal of academic debate which continues to the present day, Weber's main thesis that there is a causal relationship between the ideas contained in the Protestant Reformation and the rise of capitalism largely has been accepted.

Weber clearly stated that his purpose in writing the book was to understand "the manner in which ideas become effective forces in history."[28] It is not possible, he argued, to explain the Reformation or the development of capitalism by reference to economic laws or forces alone. Protestantism and capitalism, as unique "historical individuals," are attributable to "countless historical circumstances." Among the most important of these was the peculiar constellation of ideas which came together to produce first Protestantism, then Capitalism.

DEFINING CHARACTERISTICS OF CAPITALISM

In the Introduction (written several years after the rest of the book), Weber began by comparing the East and the West. The essential difference between these two areas is in the greater development of rationality in the West. Historically, scholarship, art, music, and architecture are all well developed in other societies, but are not as rationally developed.

Next, Weber sought to develop an ideal-typical conception of the nature of "rational capitalism." This type of capitalism, found only in the West, is radically different from other types of capitalism, such as "adventure booty capitalism" found in many parts of the world at many different time periods. Capitalism does not come at one historical stage, as Marx argued. Rather it is widely distributed over both time and space. What is different in the West in the modern period, however, is the rationalistic development of a particular brand of capitalism. Let us quote at length Weber's definition of rational capitalism.

We will define a Capitalistic economic action as one which rests on the expectation of profit by the utilization of opportunities for exchange, that is on (formally) peaceful chances of profit. . . .

100

Where capitalistic acquisition is rationally pursued, the corresponding action is adjusted to calculations in terms of capital. This means that the action is adapted to a systematic utilization of goods or personal services as means of acquisition in such a way that, at the close of the business period, the balance of the enterprise in money assets (or, in the case of a continuous enterprise, the periodically estimated money value of assets) exceeds the capital, i.e., the estimated value of the material means of production used for acquisition in exchange. . . . The important fact is always that a calculation of capital in terms of money is made, whether by modern bookkeeping methods or in any other way, however primitive and crude. Everything is done in terms of balances: at the beginning of the enterprise an initial balance, before every individual decision a calculation to ascertain its probable profitableness, and at the end a final balance to ascertain how much profit has been made.[29]

In short, "capitalism is identical with the pursuit of profit, and forever <u>renewed</u> profit by means of continuous, rational capitalistic enterprise."[30] The essential defining characteristics of capitalism, then, are as follows:

1. The <u>sytematic</u> use of capital (goods or personal services).
2. <u>Calculation of profit</u> in terms of <u>money</u> or economic rewards rather than prestige, power, or other emoluments.
3. <u>Rational</u> calculation of profit through a comparison of expense to income.
4. Orientation to <u>continuous</u> economic activity. Restraint on behavior is used to enable the businessman to remain in business and to make a continuous profit over a relatively long period of time. This is in contrast to the capitalistic adventurer, whose behavior is speculative or who desires to make a large "killing" at a single point in time.
5. <u>Peaceful</u> rather than violent political action. Competition rather than

101

naked conflict is encouraged. Profit is not obtained by conquest, robbery, or extortion.

     6. <u>The principle of exchange</u>. Something valuable is given and something valuable is received. Both parties profit from the exchange.

These defining characteristics of capitalism are all couched in subjective terminology. They all have to do with the attitudes and values which motivate actors to act in the economic system. This definition, then, is very different from Marx's definition of capitalism couched in structural terms.

PRECONDITIONS FOR CAPITALISM

One of the most important aspects of Weber's argument in the <u>Protestant Ethic</u> is a discussion of the differences between economic organization in the West (Capitalism) and that found in the East. From his discussion, one can extract certain factors which Weber thought were <u>conditions necessary for the development of capitalism</u>. Weber's argument is that rationalization of the economy is dependent upon the following conditions:[31]

(1)   Free labor

(2)   A money economy

(3)   Separation of business from the home

(4)   Rational bookkeeping

(5)   Rationalization of law and administration

(6)   Modern science and technology

(7)   A religious ethic conducive to economic rationality

The first six preconditions of capitalism were viewed by Weber as subjective. Free labor, for example, is thought of by Weber as dependent upon the normative system of a particular society which defines the legal and social role of the laborer.

The seventh characteristic necessary for capitalism is a pervading attitude of rationality. This attitude is assumed in the previous six conditions, but also needs to be stated separately. This ethic of rationality, if it is to give rise to capitalism, must be found in all aspects of society. A religious system which is conducive to the rise of rationality and to rational economic action is necessary before capitalism can develop. A religious ethic which is traditionalistic or which involves a withdrawal from rational economic activity would be detrimental to the rise of capitalism. Only those religious orientations which favor or support rational economic attitudes are conducive to the rise of capitalism.

HOW PROTESTANTISM LEADS TO CAPITALISM

Weber observed an empirical correlation between the social class position of an individual and his religious affiliation. In each European nation, Protestants occupied higher status positions than Catholics. Equally important, those nations or regions within nations with the highest levels of economic development were dominated by Protestantism. This is true because the economic ethic associated with Catholicism is traditional, whereas the Protestants hold a more progressive economic ethic. Catholics prefer security and stability, even at the cost of lower pay; Protestants prefer risk and opportunity, which usually leads to better economic rewards.

The spirit of capitalism is a constellation of subjective values which taken together distinguish capitalism from other forms of economic organization. It is not a hedonistic one oriented solely to wordly pleasure. Under capitalism, monetary success is sought because of the existence of a cultural norm prescribing that it should be sought. Success is not an end in itself. It is viewed by members of the society as a duty for which each individual should strive. This cultural value placed on success, and the normative prescription that each individual should seek success, is precisely what needs to be explained, according to Weber. The presence of this spirit, rather than any structural feature of economic organization, is the most important social feature of capitalism. It is this that has enabled capitalism to develop so rapidly and so significantly in Western Europe.

The spirit of capitalism stands opposed to the spirit of traditionalism found during the Middle Ages. In the latter the worker was motivated to work as

103

little as possible. He was socialized to accept his traditional standard of living. "The opportunity of earning more was less attractive than that of working less."[32] People do not naturally wish to make more money by working harder. Such an orientation has to be inculcated over many years' time.

Weber argued that the spirit of capitalism is not directly correlated with economic conditions. In Florence in the 14th and 15th centuries, trade and commerce flourished without the spirit of capitalism. However, in the rural backwoods conditions in the United States in the 18th century, the spirit of capitalism predominated. "To speak here of a reflection of material conditions in the ideal superstructure would be patent nonsense."[33]

What was the influence of Protestantism on the development of the spirit of capitalism? Weber identified several influences. First, Luther succeeded in reorienting his followers from an "other-worldly" to a "this-worldly" orientation. This was accomplished by rejecting the Catholic teaching that righteousness could best be sought by withdrawing from the carnal world and seeking spiritual union with God. Luther taught that each man depended upon other men for sustenance. Labor in a "calling" was an act of brotherly love. To live a righteous life, each individual must fulfill his own occupation or "calling" adequately. Hard work was righteous, not something to be avoided.

Second, Calvin and other reformers carried the doctrines of (1) predestination, (2) the Fall, and (3) salvation by Grace to their logical extremes. Because of the Fall, no man on his own merits (or works) could be saved. Salvation came as a gift from God to show His mercy. To demonstrate His mercy, God grants salvation through Grace to some individuals. To demonstrate His justice, He damns some others. Salvation is not given simply to the most righteous, nor damnation to the less righteous. This would demonstrate neither mercy nor justice. Salvation cannot be earned, and is not correlated with works. Each man is predestined to either salvation or damnation as a result of an independent decision by God.

The result of these teachings was to create within the individual a "feeling of unprecedented inner loneliness."[34] Since the individual was not able to determine his salvation or damnation, he felt a sense of frustration or alienation--a sense of powerlessness. No one could help him, including his family, his priest, his church.

People cannot live long under such a powerful anxiety-producing situation. Therefore, eventually they adjust to this situation and create signs for determining whether a person is saved or damned. The Calvinists turned back to some of the other doctrines of Protestantism, notably the doctrines taught by Luther, to find a sign of salvation or damnation. God requires man to work for the benefit of others and to achieve success in the world as a means of bringing glory to God. It was an easy step from this belief to a belief that success in one's calling is a sign of personal salvation. Thus, although Calvin taught that there is no "sign" by which a person may know he is saved, the followers of Calvin took the financial success of a person as a sign that he had received Grace from God.

The result was to force most Calvinists into this-worldly economic activity. This-worldly activity was already seen as a positive virtue, and "intense worldly activity . . . dispurses religious doubts and gives a certainty of grace."[35] An individual who works hard for the benefit of others and who is able to achieve significant success in the world can feel much more secure that he has been predestined by God to salvation. Whereas the Catholics taught that a gradual accumulation of good works is rewarded in heaven, the Calvinists taught that only systematic self-control throughout one's whole lifetime--consistency in this-worldly activity--is a sign of salvation. Moral conduct cannot be planless. It has to be consistent, rational and systematic. Weber considered the systematic rational ordering of the moral life as the most important result of ascetic Protestantism.

This is essentially a psychological argument. The development of a rational systematic this-worldly orientation toward the economic system is seen as an adjustment to psychological frustration and anxiety. While other possible accommodations might have been made, the present one was chosen because it fit in well with the teachings of Calvin and Luther.

105

ASCETISISM AND THE SPIRIT OF CAPITALISM

Weber's analysis of the Protestant contribution to the rise of capitalism is rounded out by his discussion of asceticism, or self-denial. The Catholics practiced "other wordly" asceticism. They sought to escape from worldly things through a rejection of worldly pleasures. This reached its fullest expression in monasticism accompanied by vows of poverty, chastity and obedience.

The Protestant sects after the Reformation also practiced asceticism, but it took a different form--"this-worldly asceticism." Their religion taught them that they must deny themselves the pleasures of the world which were abundantly available to them because of their worldly success. Wealth was dangerous.

Protestant asceticsm affected the rise of capitalism in two ways. First, it produced a limitation on consumption. This limitation on consumption in turn resulted in the accumulation of large capital sums. Second, capital was invested in business enterprises. Therefore, the effect of asceticism was to decrease consumption and increase capital available for production. Both of these factors are necessary in any underdeveloped country before it can develop economically.

The result of the new teachings of Protestantism was thus a new economic ethic which pervaded Protestant areas and which was widely held by members of Protestant churches.

> A specifically bourgeois economic ethic had grown up. With the consciousness of standing in the fullness of God's grace and being visibly blessed by him, the bourgeois businessman, as long as he remained within the bounds of formal correctness, as long as his moral conduct was spotless and the use to which he put his wealth was not objectionable, could follow his pecuniary interests as he would and feel that he was fulfilling a duty in doing so. The power of religious asceticism provided him in addition with sober, conscientious, and unusually industrious

workmen, who clung to their work as to a life purpose willed by God.[36]

One need only compare the attitudinal characteristics produced by the Protestant Ethic to the defining characteristics of Capitalism to note their significant similarity.

CHARACTERISTICS OF THE PROTESTANT ETHIC	CHARACTERISTICS OF RATIONAL CAPITALISM
Rationality	Rational
Hard work	Continuous
Self-discipline, honesty	Peaceful
	Systematic use of capital
Accumulation, thrift, asceticism	Economic profit
	Principle of exchange
Acquisition, competition	
Individualism	

The correlation between the two sets of characteristics is notable. The development of an ethical set of ideas, i.e., the Protestant Ethic, had a causal influence on the development of a new form of economic organization, i.e., rational capitalism. The conjunction of these two in Western Europe during the 18th and 19th centuries was not accidental. The attitudes produced by the Protestant Reformation were necessary (but not sufficient) to bring about the rise of capitalism. Other factors, such as free labor, rational bookkeeping, etc., were also necessary. But given the presence of these factors, the development of a new religious ethic was sufficient to produce a capitalistic form of economic activity.

Weber's purpose was not to "substitute for a one-sided materialistic an equally one-sided spiritualistic causal interpretation of culture and history."[37] He sought only to demonstrate the important role of religious ideas, in conjunction with economic, political and other factors, in producing a particular kind of social organization. Ideas are not always causal. And they are not monistic causes. However, no analyst of historical or social events, as Weber demonstrated, can ignore the effect of ideas in any concrete situation.

WEBER'S OTHER RELIGIOUS STUDIES

As we have noted, Weber's book provoked much critical debate. This stimulated Weber to extend his studies of the relationship between religious ideas and economic organization to other geographical areas and other time periods. In these studies, he sought to demonstrate that economic factors alone were not sufficient to produce a new form of economic activity, since traditionalistic religious ideas often served as "fetters" to hinder the "pure" workings of economic forces. Specifically, he sought to show that in China, India and the Middle East, economic conditions were conducive to the rise of capitalism. However, because of the particular nature of the religious ethics in those nations, the economy remained traditionalistic far into the modern era.

> The Chinese in all probability would be quite capable . . . of assimilating capitalism . . . . But compared to the Occident, the varied conditions which externally favored the origin of capitalism in China did not originate in occidental or oriental Antiquity, or in India, or where Islamism held sway. Yet in each of these areas different and favorable circumstances seemed to facilitate its rise. Many of the circumstances which could or had to hinder capitalism in China similarly existed in the Occident and assumed definite shape in the period of modern capitalism.[38]

CHINA AND CAPITALISM

Why didn't capitalism develop in China? Weber discussed both the conditions favoring such development as well as those opposed to it. The acquisitive spirit, Weber notes, always has been an aspect of Chinese personality. Throughout the world the Chinese have been known for business acumen. Until the 19th century, China was as advanced technologically as any nation. Further, the growth of population provided the labor with which an industrial order might have been built. China was politically united to a much greater extent than was Europe, and except for certain periods, had relative internal peace.[39]

All these favorable conditions, however, were more than balanced by factors which served to limit capitalistic development. The most important of these were the strong patriarchal sib organization and the strong religious emphasis on traditional adherence to social proprieties. In addition, the economic interests of the literati and the highest strata of Chinese society were opposed to capitalistic development. The Chinese ideal of the gentleman came in conflict with the specialization of occupational activities necessary for economic development. The Chinese viewed the world as a harmonious physical social system with which the individual must adjust, rather than as a place which must be overcome by human initiative. These conditions, some economic and some ideational, together produced a religious and cultural system which "fettered" the economy and kept it on its traditional course.

To put the argument simply, China was more advanced economically than Western Europe right up to the time of the Industrial Revolution. If Marxism were correct and if only economic causes accounted for the development of capitalism, then China should have been the first nation to experience the industrial revolution and become capitalistic.

Western Europe, initially more backward than China in many ways, developed the Protestant Ethic at a time when its economy was feudalistic. But when people began to put the Protestant Ethic into action--began to strive for economic success, work hard, and use individual initiative--then economic progress was rapid, the Industrial Revolution occurred, and Western Europe quickly surpassed China in its economic productivity.

It was the new set of religious ideas which produced the motivating force by which capitalism and industrialization were accomplished. This argument stands as the most substantial refutation of Marxism found in the sociological literature.

THE RECIPROCAL INFLUENCE OF SOCIAL ORGANIZATION ON RELIGION

Weber often cautioned that one should not interpret his religious studies as an attempt to develop a one-sided ideational theory of society. He took care to note the many times historically that economic forces influenced the course of religious development. While his treatment of the economic conditions influencing the rise of Protestantism was almost wholly lacking,[40] he did include in his later works an extensive discussion of the social and economic conditions which were present in the society under consideration. His studies of China, India and Judaism begin with analyses of the social conditions in these societies which have an influence on the religious development of the society.

In his last work on religion, the section entitled "The Sociology of Religion" in Economy and Society, Weber clearly called attention to the great influence of economic factors in religious development. One might even make a strong case that Weber increasingly placed greater emphasis on structural factors at the expense of ideational factors in his later works.[41]

This should not be taken out of context. Intellectual reaction to his Protestant Ethic forced Weber to make more explicit the influence of structural factors upon ideational factors. He had never denied the importance of these former factors. His approach was always more balanced and less monistic than those of Marx and many of his contemporaries. There is a change of emphasis in his later works. Structural factors are discussed in more detail. But there is not significant change in Weber's general position that ideational factors have some autonomy from structural factors. No comprehensive analysis of social phenomena can ignore either of these two.

RATIONALITY

One of Weber's most distinguishing characteristics was his ability to place his society and time in perspective. Because of his breadth of scholarship, he was able as few men have been, to compare Germany with other societies with different characteristics and from different time periods.

One of Weber's most important insights had to do with the increasing rationality found in modern industrial societies. While many rational elements are to be found in most societies, even primitive societies, Weber concluded that rationality in a well-developed form is only found in industrial societies, particularly those with a developed capitalistic economy.

Nowhere was Weber's interest in rationality more clear than in his discussion of bureaucracy.[42]

Bureaucracy is an extreme form of rationality developed in Western society and particularly associated with capitalistic enterprises. Bureaucracy for Weber was an ideal type of rational administration. It represents the purest form of administration oriented toward efficiency and practicality. While the concept today carries with it some negative connotations of red tape and impersonality, Weber treated it as the most efficient form for dealing with the complex problems of administration found in large-scale organizations which has ever been devised.

A bureaucracy is controlled by legally established rules which govern the actions of bureaucratic officials. Adherence to these rules allows the greatest efficiency possible. Further, since supposedly the rules have been rationally determined as those which allow the greatest efficiency. Further, since each official is chosen solely on the basis of technical proficiency, the bureaucratic organization is further enabled to operate with a minimum of inefficiency.

The impersonality found in a bureaucratic organization is an integral part of the orientation of such an organization. Officials cannot be allowed to make independent and emotional decisions granting favoritism to some at the expense of others. Further, they cannot be allowed to use the organization for their own aggrandizement. Each client of the organization must be treated according to a specified system of rules such that each enjoys an equal position under those rules. While the impersonality of such a system may be frustrating to some, it is equally beneficial to both the system itself and to the customers it serves.

WEBER'S REJECTION OF MARXIAN THEORY

Much if not all of Weber's work has usually been interpreted as a revision or a rebuttal of the Marxian theories of social organization and social change. Weber recognized very early in his career some of the weaknesses of Marxism. He also had the ability to recognize important truths in some of the Marxian formulations. At many points Weber accepted Marx's analysis as correct, but sought to broaden and extend it to make it more comprehensive and accurate. In his studies of religion and in some of his essays, however, Weber directly rejected Marx's monism and materialism.

Weber made an important distinction--one which Marx never made--which is extremely fruitful in understanding the workings of the economic system. He formulated three categories, as follows:

(1) Economic events, "the economic aspect of which constitutes their primary cultural significance for use. These are _deliberately_ created or used for economic ends."[43]

(2) Economically relevant phenomena, which are noneconomic causes of effects--"they have consequences which are of interest from the economic point of view."[44]

(3) Economically conditioned phenomena, that is, phenomena which are noneconomic effects of economic causes. They are "more or less strongly influenced in certain important aspects by economic factors."[45]

These categories are not intended to be mutually exclusive. Depending upon the point of view, one phenomenon may be considered as being in any of the three categories. Weber recognized that almost any social phenomena may be placed in the third category, since the economy directly or indirectly affects "all spheres of culture without exception."[46] Just as accurately, all social phenomena may be placed in the second category, since

> all the activities and situations constituting an historically given culture affect the formation of the material wants, the mode of their satisfaction, the integration of interest-groups and the types of power which they exercise. They thereby affect the course of 'economic development' and are accordingly 'economically relevant'.[47]

Like Marx, Weber recognized the interdependence of all social phenomena. Marx had attributed this interdependence to the causal working of the economic substructure of society. For Weber, social phenomena are more truly _inter_dependent, since there is a genuine reciprocity among economic and noneconomic factors.

> The explanation of everything by economic causes alone is never exhaustive in any sense whatsoever in any sphere of

cultural phenomena, not even in the 'economic' sphere itself.[48]

Weber was careful to point out, however, that economic factors are powerful causal agents. The emphasis on "material" interests and the explanation of history in terms of these interests has proved most fruitful.

> Liberated as we are from the antiquated notion that all cultural phenomena can be deduced as a product or function of the constellation of 'material' interests, we believe nevertheless that the analysis of social and cultural phenomena with special reference to their economic conditioning and ramifications was a scientific principle of creative fruitfulness and with careful application and freedom from dogmatic restrictions, will remain such for a very long time to come. The so-called "Materialistic conception of history" as a Weltanschauung or as a formula for the causal explanation of historical reality is to be rejected most emphatically. The advancement of the economic interpretation of history is one of (our) most important aims. . . .[49]

Weber rejected the political dogmatism which is associated with Marxian theory, but nevertheless recognizes that it contains important elements which must be utilized in any future sociological theory of merit. Marx had overemphasized the role of economic factors in history. Weber cautioned against a reaction leading to an underestimation of these factors. In his own work, he consistently treated economic factors as important, while recognizing the equal importance of religious, legal and cultural phenomena.

Weber's recognition of the complexity of social phenomena has often been ignored, and has rarely been duplicated. It was to the examination of this complexity that he devoted his life. One cannot understand Weber's full genius unless one understands how he wrestled to conceptualize and clarify the relations among these complex and interrelated phenomena.

113

Weber, Marx and Durkheim

Durkheim and Weber were contemporaries; yet, each seemed to be unaware of the other. In conclusion, we should not the differences between Weber's sociological approach and that of Durkheim. First, Weber treated ideas as causes, and looked for their effects in such social organizations as capitalism. Second, his approach was a multiple causal one. Religious ideas combine with other causes, some of them subjective and some of them structural, to produce a given effect. Third, Weber himself did not examine the social causes of these ideas to the same extent as did Durkheim.

Weber provided the most notable example of a well-developed subjective theory of social phenomena which is available in the "classical" period in sociology. He gave much more emphasis to the independence of subjective phenomena than did either Durkheim or Marx. But he was also cognizant of the fact that structural and economic factors are significant in determining the course of social development. Rather than view Weber as occupying one extreme end of a structural-subjective continuum, with Durkheim and Marx at the other, we should view each theorist as occupying an intermediate position on this continuum, roughly as follows:

Structural			Subjective
Marx	Durkheim	Weber	

FOOTNOTES

[1]Robert Alun Jones and Sidney Kronus, "Professional Sociologists and the History of Sociology," unpublished paper, American Sociological Association, August, 1975.

[2]Many of Weber's works were published after his death. His most important work, Economy and Society, was not fully translated into English until 1968.

[3]Talcott Parsons, The Structure of Social Action (Glencoe: The Free Press, 1949), pp. 579-693; Talcott Parsons, "Max Weber's Sociological Analysis of Capitalism and Modern Institutions," in Harry E. Bernes, editor, An Introduction to the History of

114

Sociology (Chicago: University of Chicago Press), 1948, pp. 247-248; Don Martindale, The Nature and Types of Sociological Theory (Boston: Houghton-Mifflin), 1960, pp. 376-380.

[4]Max Weber, Economy and Society: An Outline of Interpretive Sociology (New York: Bedminster Press), 1968.

[5]Weber's method of verstehen is discussed in the following works: Max Weber, The Methodology of the Social Sciences (Glencoe: The Free Press, 1949), especially pp. 40-47 and 68-90; Economy and Society, vol. I pp. 4-23. See also Max Weber, The Theory of Social and Economic Organization (Glencoe: The Free Press, 1947), pp. 88-115. This latter work is an English translation of some parts of Economy and Society. See also Marcello Truzzi (ed.), Verstehen: Subjective Understanding in the Social Sciences. (Reading, Massachusetts: Addison-Wesley), 1974.

[6]The Methodology of the Social Sciences, p. 40 (herinafter abbreviated as Methodology).

[7]The Theory of Social and Economic Organization, p. 91 (herinafter abbreviated as Theory).

[8]Ibid., p. 92.

[9]Ibid., p. 95.

[10]Ibid., p. 96.

[11]Ibid., p. 97.

[12]Loc. cit.

[13]Loc. cit.

[14]Ibid., p. 99.

[15]Loc. cit.

[16]Ibid., p. 90.

[17]Ibid., p. 94.

[18]Loc. cit.

[19]Ibid., p. 113.

[20]Ibid., p. 118.

[21]"Purpose-rational" action is the English translation of zweckrationalitat, and "value-rational" action is the English translation of wertrationalitat. See Max Rheinstein, editor, Max Weber on Law in Economy and Society (Cambridge, Mass.: Harvard University Press, 1954), pp. 1-10.

[22]Theory, p. 115.

[23]Methodology, pp. 42, 90-91.

[24]Ibid., p. 90.

[25]Emile Durkheim, The Elementary Forms of the Religious Life (Glencoe: The Free Press, 1915).

[26]Max Weber, The Protestant Ethic and the Spirit of Capitalism (New York: Scribners, 1958).

[27]Max Weber, The Religion of China: Confucianism and Taoism (Glencoe: The Free Press, 1951); Max Weber, The Religion of India: The Sociology of Hinduism and Buddhism (Glencoe: The Free Press, 1958); Max Weber, Ancient Judaism (Glencoe: The Free Press, 1952); Max Weber, The Sociology of Religion (Boston: Beacon Press, 1963).

[28]Protestant Ethic, p. 90.

[29]Ibid., pp. 17-18.

[30]Ibid., p. 17.

[31]Ibid., pp. 21-26. See also Max Weber General Economic History (Glencoe: The Free Press, 1950), p. 277. In the latter work, Weber lists as the "presuppositions for the existence of capitalism:" (1) rational capital accounting as the norm for all large economic organizations, (2) freedom of the market, (3) rational technology, (4) calculable law, (5) free labor, and (6) commercialization of economic life (p. 277).

[32]Protestant Ethic, p. 60.

[33]Ibid., p. 75.

[34]Ibid., p. 104.

[35]Ibid., p. 112.

[36]Ibid., pp. 176-177.

[37] Ibid., p. 183.

[38]The Religion of China, p. 249.

[39] Ibid., especially pp. 54-55.

[40]See "The Reformation and Its Impact on Economic Life," in Economy and Society, vol. 3, pp. 1196-1200.

[41]Hans Gerth and C. Wright Mills, editors, From Max Weber: Essays in Sociology (New York: Oxford, 1958), pp. 63-64.

[42]Theory, pp. 329-341.

[43]Methodology, p. 64.

[44]Loc. cit.

[45]Loc. cit.

[46]Ibid., p. 65.

[47]Ibid., p. 66.

[48]Ibid., p. 71.

[49]Ibid., p. 68.

CHAPTER SEVEN

CLASSICAL SUBJECTIVISM: PARETO AND SUMNER

Weber's work stands as the epitome of subjectivism. In his methodology even more than his substantive writings, subjectivism was his dominant orientation. Two other "old masters" of sociological theory also made important contributions to subjectivism. Vilfredo Pareto, the preeminent Italian sociologist, and William Graham Sumner, the most important figure in the early development of sociology in the United States, developed different but complementary insights into the nature of social life. This chapter is devoted to a discussion of their theories.

PARETO ON SUBJECTIVISM

Pareto treated the subjective-structural issue as one of the most significant issues in sociological theory. He distinguished the subjective from the objective (structural) more clearly than the theorists who preceded him. His relatively balanced view of the relationship between these two aspects of social life preceded Thomas' better developed theory uniting the two. [1]

In Mind and Society, as in his earlier Les Systems Socialistes, Pareto made the distinction between objective and subjective aspects of social life. [2] The objective aspect is concerned with social phenomena as they are "in reality," and the subjective aspect with phenomena as they "appear to the mind." Pareto did not see this distinction as a metaphysical judgment of the nature of "reality." His purposes were scientific, not philosophic.

Pareto asserted that both aspects are "in reality" subjective, since all human knowledge is subjective. The objective is distinguished from the subjective chiefly by the "greater or lesser amount of factual knowledge" we possess about the event in question. If a great many observers agree on a given event as "fact," it becomes objective. It is the human mind which perceives, thinks, and chooses. Ultimate causation must be ascribed to the human mind, rather than to objective conditions. External causes may operate, but can only operate through the mind. The

119

mind is thus the intervening variable between structural conditions and human behavior.

A sociologist must study both objective and subjective aspects of social life. The purpose of studying objective aspects is to discover the relationships which exist among objective or "real" facts. For example, one studies the objective social conditions which lead to the "circulation of the elite." Subjectively, men substitute ideas for real events. The purpose of studying subjective aspects is to discover how people think of reality, how they manipulate ideas, and how ideas lead people to act in certain ways to create social systems or justify them.[3]

An individual's subjective perception of an objective condition is rarely a "faithful copy" of it. Pareto used the analogy of looking at a stick which is partly immersed in water. The stick is straight, but is perceived as being bent. The lack of correspondence between the subjective and the objective accounts for "non-logical" behavior.

NON-LOGICAL BEHAVIOR

Central to Pareto's theory of social life was his distinction between logical and non-logical behavior. Pareto used two criteria for distinguishing between the two. First, does the behavior in question involve the rational choice of a means to obtain a consciously held goal? That is, is the means related to a goal in a logical manner? Second, does the action appear to be logical both from the point of view of the actor and of objective observers? The latter criterion is necessary because of the strong tendency for people to think of their behavior as logical when it does not appear to be so to an external observer.[5]

The goal must be an immediate one which is directly "situated in the field of observation and experience." The goal must be consciously held and be real, not imaginary. That is, it must be objectively possible to obtain. And the means employed to reach the goal must be appropriate and logically tied to the goal.

Logical behavior necessitates a process of reasoning. One cannot act emotionally nor traditionally nor ritually. He must consider possible alternative means and choose that one which is most

120

appropriate to the goal being sought. Rationality attaches to both the goal being sought--since it must be real and attainable--and to the choice of means to reach the goal.[6]

Non-logical behavior is not necessarily "illogical." The means may be well adapted to the obtaining of the goal. However, if the individual acts emotionally, or fails to engage in a reasoning process, his behavior must be categorized as non-logical. Persons frequently act in traditional and conformist ways without considering or "reasoning" about their behavior. Much behavior is also emotionally caused rather than reasoned.

Pareto devoted a large portion of Mind and Society to an analysis of non-logical behavior. People frequently act non-logically in a trial and error attempt to adapt to their environment. When they are successful, they seek to discover the reasons for their success in order to be able to live more comfortably. This leads them eventually to develop logical explanations or motivations for behavior which originally was non-logical.

Very frequently, people attempt to rationalize behavior which remains irrational. The logical reasoning which justifies the behavior serves as a "mask" to cover the real and non-logical cause of the behavior. One of Pareto's major purposes was to strip off these logical masks to "reveal the things which are hidden beneath them."[7] Most human behavior is non-logical. Any attempt to explain human behavior must therefore explain it in non-logical terms. Further, social investigation must discover the reasons why people act as they do as well as the reasons they give for their behavior.

Most theorists have been aware of the non-logical nature of human behavior but have avoided dealing with these non-logical aspects. It is much easier, Pareto argued, to formulate explanations of human behavior in rational terms. Reason is a powerful tool in the hands of the analyst to explain behavior. The attempt to explain behavior in non-logical terms is infinitely more difficult. This kind of theory does not possess the simplicity and precision which a rational theory possesses. More importantly, we must "discover outside outselves, outside our own reasoning and personal experience, the material of inquiry."[8] In short, we

121

must use the inductive rather than the deductive method.[9] It is simpler to use deductive reasoning to arrive at general and comprehensive explanations of human behavior. Inductive studies, however, are more accurate.

RESIDUES AND DERIVATIONS

Pareto's specific explanation of non-logical social behavior made heavy use of the concepts of "residues" and "derivations." Residues are comparable to psychological instincts.[10] They involve more or less innate tendencies on the part of individuals to act in specific ways. The residues are expressed by "sentiments" which are held or present in the minds of individuals. In turn, these sentiments are manifested by actual patterns of behavior. Certain kinds of behavior may be used as indicators of sentiments, which in turn may be indicators of more deep-seated residues.

Pareto classified the residues into six classes: (1) instinct of combinations (with 11 sub-classes), (2) instinct of persistence of aggregates (9 sub-classes), (3) manifestation of sentiments by activity, (4) residues of sociality, (5) residues of integrity of the individual, and (6) sex residue.[11] The specific content of each of these residues need not concern us here. Pareto's brand of instinct psychology, and his particular classification of residues, has little interest or merit. We need add only that persons with the instinct of combinations correspond to what Pareto (and Machiavelli) call "Foxes," and those with the residues of the persistence of aggregates correspond to "Lions." It is these two groups which tend to replace each other in a cyclical manner in what Pareto called "the circulation of the elite."[12]

The "derivations" are also sentiments which derive directly from the residues. As the term implies, the derivations are based upon the more central and deep-seated residues. Pareto's definition of derivations was incomplete and fuzzy. He seemed to think of derivations as justifications, explanations, or assertions based upon the residues. The derivations were classified into four classes: (1) assertion, (2) authority, (3) accord with sentiments or principles, and (4) verbal proofs. From this classification, and his discussion based upon it, derivations seem to be those sentiments which

122

legitimize or explain actions and sentiments which derive from the residues. Again, this part of Pareto's work has little value or interest to contemporary sociology.

SUBJECTIVE VARIABLES AND SOCIAL STRUCTURE

Two further comments need to be made about Pareto's approach to the explanation of social behavior. First, he specifically rejected introspection as a means of obtaining knowledge. He consistently asserted the need for inductive and objective methods in the study of society. Following Durkheim rather than Weber, he argued that one must treat one's own experiences and thoughts as "things" rather than as ideas subject to manipulation.[13] He was critical of those who allow ideational labels or values to govern scientific work.[14] He even criticized his own past work as deriving from sentiment rather than fact.

Second, Pareto clearly recognized that subjective explanations do not exhaust the entire range of possible explanations. What we have called structural variables are also important in the determination and explanation of human behavior.

Given the conditions in which an individual lives, certain opinions can be expected of him; nevertheless he may not be aware of this relationship between his opinions and his circumstances, and will seek to justify the former on quite different grounds.[15]

External social conditions cause a large but still indefinite area of human behavior. In their explanation of their own behavior, people fail to comprehend these forces and causes. External and structural (or emotional) causes of this kind contribute heavily to non-logical behavior.

WILLIAM GRAHAM SUMNER: FOLKWAYS

William G. Sumner, the most important American sociologist up to the turn of the century, took a different point of view from Pareto. Sumner was influenced by Spencer's evolutionism, and became a strong advocate of this theoretical perspective in the United States. In his later life, he became increasingly interested in normative customs, which he

123

identified as folkways. His interest culminated in the book <u>Folkways</u>,[16] which has long been regarded as one of the most important classics of American sociology. Its influence upon sociology is difficult to overestimate. It provides a substantial basis for a subjective theory of social life as well as a foundation upon which to erect a bridge between the subjective and structural orientations.

FOLKWAYS

Folkways are the customary ways of thinking and acting common to the ordinary people (folk) within a society. They are the norms, customs, traditions, and usages of a society. People have in their minds certain expectations for behavior which derive from habit and custom. Especially in primitive societies, these norms (the more common term today) are fixed and unchanging, and the behavior which follows directly from the norms is likewise patterned, traditional, and unchanging.

Folkways develop directly out of the needs of individuals and groups to adapt to their environment. Historically, people have gradually developed customs or regularized methods for dealing with their physical needs. These usages or folkways have gradually become habitual and customary. Eventually they are adopted by more and more people until they become "mass phenomena." Folkways become "uniform, universal in the group, imperative, and invariable."[17] Consistent ways of acting are transformed into expectations for future behavior.

Folkways develop unconsciously. People usually do not set out consciously to formulate customs or rules for behavior. Folkways develop gradually and irrationally. "They are not noticed until they have long existed, and it is still longer before they are appreciated."[18] The origins of the first folkways can never be discovered, but through the study of simple societies we can gain the assurance that reason or human purposes were not contributory factors to the initial development of folkways. Folkways are rather "unconscious, spontaneous, uncoordinated."[19]

In a group of people who are engaged in task-oriented activities (adapting to the environment), there is a continual process of give and take, of suggestion and testing. The result of this process of selection is the development of a more efficient system of adaptation to the environment than could have been arrived at by the solitary individual. The group, according to Sumner, possesses a kind of natural wisdom which is not possessed by the individual.[20]

The processes of variation, selection and transmission are central to the development of the folkways. People vary their behavior in order to find what is best adapted to the environment. They select out those that are best fitted. Likewise, nature selects out those persons who adjust or adapt most effectively to the environment and eliminates the rest. The ways of acting which are most effective in adapting to the environment are transmitted to others and eventually become customary and habitual.

The folkways concerned with self-maintenance, which Sumner later called the "maintenance-mores," are most closely related to the conditions of existence and are the most easily tested for effectiveness. These norms are part of the "substructure" upon which is built a "superstructure" of norms governing other aspects of social life. Subsistence is basic, and other social customs and practices are derivable from the folkways governing subsistence.[21]

This argument is Marxian in orientation, especially in its use of terminology. However, Sumner's views of the nature of substructure and superstructure differed significantly from those of Marx. Customs or ideas, not structural or economic relations, are the essence of substructure according to Sumner. Marx distinguished structure from ideas. Sumner, in a brilliant synthesis, argued that the essential elements of social structure are normative ideas which define relations among individuals and groups, and which orient them to behave in a patterned or organized manner.

The folkways of a society are the social structure of the society, rather than being "reflections" of some more basic social processes. This idea was sometimes alluded to by Durkheim. But Durkheim maintained the distinction between structure and customs. Sumner's major contribution to sociological theory was in showing how normative ideas organize or structure man's behavior and give form and order to social life.

125

Norms are ideational or subjective in character. They exist as ideas in the minds of men. Rather than varying for each individual, however, there is widespread agreement on norms so that each individual adheres to the same norms that others do. These ideas derive directly from the experience of adaptation to the environment, and in turn determine all of the other social phenomena of a society. Folkways represent the most important single aspect of social life. The study of the folkways and their influences on human behavior is the central task of sociology.

MORES

Some important folkways become associated in men's minds with the general welfare of the total society. They are so central to the welfare of the group that the violation of these norms would threaten the existence of the group. Such folkways are called "mores." (The singular is mos. Both terms are derived from the Latin term for "customs.") Folkways are elevated to the status of mores when they become infused with moral notions as to their importance to the total society. Mores are distinguished from folkways in being (1) more important to the welfare of the society, (2) infused with a higher moral tone, and (3) more severely sanctioned. Folkways are considered expedient methods of acting but are not sufficiently important to carry moral overtones. He who disobeys the folkways is unintelligent and impractical. He who disobeys the mores is immoral.[22]

Laws are folkways or mores which have been formally legislated. They tend to have a more rational and practical character than the mores. People act toward them in a more conscious and voluntary manner than to the mores. To be effective, laws must derive from and be supported directly by the mores.[23] Mores are a type of folkway. When speaking of all norms of whatever kind, Sumner often used the terms interchangeably, referring sometimes to folkways and sometimes to mores.

The folkways have a strongly coercive power over the individual. A child is socialized to accept the folkways of his group and to conform to them completely. Sumner consistently used the term "coercion" in speaking about the influence of the folkways upon the individual. "All are forced to conform, and the folkways dominate the societal life."[24]

The result of this regulation of individual behavior is order and social organization. Individuals are able to live together in peace because they share a common normative system. Chaos would result from unregulated behavior. Because individuals know what to expect from others, and know how to act in any given situation, they are able to adjust their behavior to that of others and thereby deal effectively with others.

ETHNOCENTRISM

The folkways define what is right and wrong. The moral code of a society is contained in the folkways, and never has a separate existence. It is seldom subject to question or to independent verification. By definition, all folkways are "right." Social groups, especially primitive ones, never question the rightness or morality of their folkways. "The 'right' way is the way which the ancestors used and which has been handed down."[25]

This is why ethnocentrism is a characteristic of every social group. Each group uses its own folkways as a standard of behavior by which it judges the folkways and practices of other groups. Since folkways are accepted as "right," each group thinks of itself as morally superior to other groups. The group takes special notice of those of its folkways which are different from those of other groups. It tends to exaggerate and intensify these to magnify the differences between itself and other groups.[26] Patriotic identification with one's own group is accompanied by distrust or contempt for members of other groups. The "ethos" of a group--that which sets the group apart from others--is defined by the folkways of the group.[27]

PERSISTENCE AND CHANGE

According to Sumner, folkways have several important characteristics. First, within a given social group, there is a tendency toward consistency of all social norms. Norms are "subject to a strain of consistency with each other, because they all answer their several purposes with less friction and antagonism when they cooperate and support each

127

other."[28]   Integration of the normative system is one of the most important characteristics of any social group.

Second, folkways are characterized by persistence. There is a rigidity and stability built into the system of folkways. They serve as their own justification by defining the traditional as good and right.

> They never contain any provision for their own amendment. They are not questions, but answers, to the problems ot life. They present themselves as final and unchangeable, because they present answers which are offered as 'the truth.'[29]

Once they are established, folkways are extremely resistent to change. Individuals feel secure in situations which are ill-defined. They prefer to maintain their customary ways of acting and thinking because these allow them to deal with their environment and other people without the expenditure of needless energy.

This does not mean that folkways never change. The third characteristic of folkways is their variability. Each social group within a society has its own folkways (what we now call "subculture").[30] They are elastic as well as rigid. No child ever exactly imitates the behavior of his parents. Perhaps more importantly, the physical and social environment changes, necessitating a change in the normative means of adapting to the environment.

> It is necessary to prosperity that the mores should have a due degree of firmness, but also that they should be sufficiently elastic and flexible to conform to changes in interests and life conditions.[31]

Sumner was pessimistic about the possibility of bringing about changes in the folkways through planning or initiative. Attempts to effect changes in the folkways only result in agitation rather than change. Legislation and preaching are ineffective, especially if they seek marked changes over a short period of time. Only if other conditions allow change can change be effected through individual initiative. Sumner was a strong advocate of laissez-faire individualism, and did not believe that people could significantly improve social life through government intervention.[32]

The folkways are the property of the masses rather than the elite. Those who are better educated and superior in training and intellect (Sumner had a well-developed belief in the superiority of an elite) can use their creative energy to produce numerous ideas which would have the greatest positive effect upon the society. However, these changes cannot be put into effect until they are accepted by the masses. Only if the "masses" can be induced to imitate the behavior of the "classes" will society evolve and progress. Sumner recognized the cultural gap between the educated classes and the masses, and seemed perturbed by the difficulty of exerting leadership over the masses to accept the ideas of their "betters." Folkways are the ways of the "folk," not of the elite. The folkways of the society determine the course of evolution of the society and the course of events therein. While Sumner was an elitist in his own attitudes, his conclusions are opposed to elitist theory. The history of a society is not determined by the elite but by the masses.

CONCLUSION

In conclusion, Sumner's important contribution to sociological theory was to show the pervading importance of social norms in determining social behavior. Norms are the central feature of social organization. Once norms are developed, they are followed traditionally and irrationally by the members of the society. Children are socialized to accept the normative standards as given and to conform their behavior to normative expectations. If one seeks to explain human behavior, he must first seek to understand the normative system of a particular society. He must discover the processes by which individuals are socialized and motivated to conform to social norms. Any explanation of social behavior which fails to account for the subjective element of society as contained in social norms will be both invalid and ineffective. Social norms, as they are expressed in the ideas and behavior of individuals, are the essence of social life.

FOOTNOTES

[1] See Chapter 8 for a discussion of Thomas' theory.

[2] Vilfredo Pareto, The Mind and Society: A Treatise on General Sociology, New York: Dover, 1963; Vilfredo Pareto, Sociological Writings, New York: Praeger, 1966. See the quotations accompanying this chapter.

[3] Sociological Writings, pp. 125-126.

[4] Ibid., pp. 143-144.

[5] Sociological Writings, pp. 151, 185.

[6] See the excellent discussion in James Burnham, The Machiavellians, Chicago: Regnery, 1943, pp. 192-205.

[7] Sociological Writings, p. 194.

[8] Ibid., p. 196.

[9] Ibid., pp. 215-216.

[10] Ibid., p. 217.

[11] Ibid., pp. 222-223.

[12] Pareto's discussion of the circulation of the elite has provoked a good deal of interest, and has many important insights into the nature of power and government. We shall not deal with it in this book. For further information, see Sociological Writings, especially pp. 256-259, 267-275, 311-325. See also Burnham, op. cit., pp. 230-248.

[13] Sociological Writings, p. 173.

[14] Ibid., pp. 173-182.

[15] Ibid., p. 124.

[16] William Graham Sumner, Folkways, New York: Mentor, 1960.

[17] Ibid., p. 18.

[18]Ibid., p. 19.

[19]Ibid., pp. 23, 33.

[20]Ibid., p. 33.

[21]William Graham Sumner and Albert G. Keller, The Science of Society, New Haven: Yale University Press, 1927, Volume I, pp. 35-37.

[22]Ibid., p. 33 and Folkways, pp. 42, 48, 66-67.

[23]Folkways, pp. 63-64.

[24]Ibid., pp. 49, 70-72.

[25]Ibid., p. 41.

[26]Ibid., p. 28.

[27]Ibid., p. 76.

[28]Ibid., p. 21.

[29]Ibid., p. 83.

[30]Ibid., p. 50.

[31]Ibid., p. 87.

[32]Sumner and Lester F. Ward were intellectual enemies on this point, with Ward advocating the use of government programs for the improvement of social life. For Sumner's position, see Folkways, pp. 56, 89, 95, 101, 110.

CHAPTER EIGHT

CLASSIC SUBJECTIVISM: SYMBOLIC INTERACTION

Symbolic Interactionism is one of the most distinctive points of view in the early development of sociological theory. The leading exponents of this theoretical perspective, Charles H. Cooley, George H. Mead and William I. Thomas, advocated a subjective point of view as strongly as did Weber. Cooley's early writings provided the foundation for symbolic interactionism. Mead's lectures influenced a generation of sociologists, although his important writings date from a much later period than Cooley's. Thomas's published works span a great many years. More than the other two founders of symbolic interactionism, Thomas developed and changed his theoretical orientation during the course of his career. The writings of these three theorists lead to an appreciation of the strengths of the subjectivist position and the stages through which symbolic interaction passed.

COOLEY: THE LOOKING-GLASS SELF

Charles Horton Cooley's (1864-1929) contributions to the development of a subjectively oriented theory of human behavior are among the most important in sociology. Cooley was a shy, almost reclusive man who felt more comfortable when dealing with ideas than with people. Throughout his life he exhibited a timidity and reserve in his social relations.

Yet Cooley possessed a penetrating mind, and was capable of insightful analysis of personal relations which few sociologists have possessed. His methodology consisted of observation and introspection, yet he achieved a sophistication of description and an acuteness of analysis which surpassed that of most of his contemporaries. His writings, especially his first book, Human Nature and the Social Order,[1] provide one of the primary sources for the exposition of the subjective theory of society.

The level of analysis at which Cooley worked was far different from that of Weber. While Weber focused on broad cultural values at the national or cross-national level, Cooley and the other symbolic interactionists trained their attention on the small-group level. Cooley was primarily interested in

133

the effect of ideas on the development of the "self" or personality and on the patterns of interactions which take place among small groups of individuals.

SYMBOLIC INTERACTION

The basis of social life, according to Cooley, is social interaction. No individual is capable of living without interacting with others. People are forced to associate with others, and their social and biological needs can only be met through interaction with others.

Interaction is accomplished through symbols. Physical gestures carry certain meanings which are interpreted in the minds of others. Likewise, words have a symbolic meaning. Language is created through social interaction, and enables people to interact with each other on a more highly developed level. Communication through symbolic means is essential to social life.

The theoretical assertion that social interaction is the basis of social life led Cooley to a corollary. He argued that both "the individual" and "society" are "simply collective and distributive aspects of the same thing."[2] The individual personality develops only through interaction with other persons. Likewise, society represents the general aspects of the interactions among the members of a large social group.

When individuals interact, their interaction is essentially symbolic. That is, the words and gestures they use as they interact are impressed upon each actor's mind as ideas. The mind interprets the symbolic meaning of the words and gestures, and in turn makes some determination as to how to respond. Social reality, Cooley argued, is found in ideas.

Cooley noted that people generally think of the "individual" as a physical entity. As far as the social sciences are concerned, however, the physical aspects of the human being are secondary to the "mental and moral" aspects. The essence of the social individual is found in ideas, both those he possesses in his own mind about himself and those contained in the minds of others.

Society likewise consists basically in ideas. When large numbers of persons interact, their interaction is carried on in the mind. Further, each individual possesses ideas about other persons in his immediate social group, and about such larger groups as a nation or a church.[3] Both the individual and society exist as symbols in the minds of human beings. Ideas are the ultimate social reality. Sociology, therefore, must devote itself to the study of ideas.

THE LOOKING-GLASS SELF

Perhaps Cooley's single most important contribution to the development of sociological theory is found in his discussion of the development of the individual "self" through social interaction. This is an extremely seminal idea. Mead later built much of his own sociological theories upon this essential insight. It is the basis for the theoretical school of "symbolic interactionism." In addition to its theoretical importance, it is valuable as a practical guide to social relations and child rearing.

According to Cooley, each individual has an "instinct" to feel or regard himself as an individual entity. This derives from certain emotions which are physically present in each individual. But Cooley's emphasis was not on the physical or biological aspects of the individual. His discussion centered upon the ideational nature of the self. He noted that every individual tends to conceptualize himself as an individual. Such a fact is important to recognize, and needs to be explained by those who seek to study social life.

The distinctive idea of the self, according to Cooley, is "a characteristic kind of feeling which may be called the my-feeling."[4] Each individual has a sense of self-consciousness and of self-assertiveness. There is both an emotional and a cognitive aspect to this "self-feeling." While there are instinctual aspects to the sense of self, the self develops largely through social interaction. The resultant is an extremely complex entity. Certain general characteristics are found in each individual. But because of the complexity of the self, each self is also distinctly individualistic in its development and its ultimate form.

When people talk about themselves in the first person, their reference is almost always to their ideas, opinions, motivations, desires, etc.[5] Seldom do they include in their references to themselves their

135

physical body, "clothes, treasures, ambition, honors, and the like."[6] The ideas and self-feeling of the individual, rather than the physical being, are generally the phenomena which are represented by references to the self.

Cooley's analysis of how the individual gains this conception of himself is especially important. He observed the development of his own children, and noted that by age two his daughter, Margaret, had learned correctly the use of personal pronouns. This was significant to Cooley because he observed that these pronouns are used in many different ways, and that the use of one to apply to oneself, e.g., "my," is different in meaning than when the same word is used by another person. One therefore cannot learn the meanings of these terms purely through imitation. A great deal of reflective understanding is represented by correct use of personal pronouns.

Cooley reasoned that Margaret, his second child, had learned to use such words in her interactions with her older brother, Rutger. Her desire for certain things was essentially instinctual, and she felt a certain amount of opposition from her older brother. He often possessed things which she desired. He also pulled things away from her early in her life. Such behavior was often accompanied by statements by her brother that the object he was taking from her was "mine." Margaret, then, reflected upon this behavior and learned to use the same word when she appropriated objects from her brother or from others. The word is a sign, a symbol, of the aggressive behavior of appropriation.[7] The word stands for the behavior. Eventually, through reflection the child generalized this behavior and learned the abstract meaning of the concepts "I" and "you." The older brother, Rutger, learned these concepts more slowly than Margaret because of the absence of this kind of appropriative behavior in his relations with his parents.

The significant point to be derived from this discussion is that the concept of self develops in interaction with other persons. This was given a distinctive label by Cooley: "the looking-glass self." When one looks in a mirror, one sees a reflected image of oneself. He gains an impression of his physical appearance. In the same manner, each individual looks into the faces of others to see a reflected image of himself. Other people reflect back to us an image of ourselves. We get a definite impression of ourselves through the reactions of others. The emotions which we feel about ourselves are derived directly from these reactions by others. We see ourselves as others see us.

According to Cooley, there are three principal elements in the development of the looking-glass self. In the first phase of the looking-glass self, we imagine how we appear to a second person. It is important to note that this occurs in the mind of the first person. This imagination may be derived from his own knowledge of his clothing, appearance, and behavior. The individual, however, is "other-directed" in that he looks for signs as to how the other person views his appearance. No individual is so completely self-assured that he can divorce himself from how others view him.

This is closely related to the second phase, which involves the imagination by the first person of the judgment of his appearance by a second person. The individual looks for behavioral signs which will give him a clue as to how the other person is judging his appearance. He interprets these acts or reactions on the part of the other person. Again, this occurs in the mind of the first person. The second person may indeed present many clues, either through gestures or language, as to how he judges the appearance of the first person. But these clues must be interpreted to the first person. He alone gives meaning to these clues. For example, if the second person smiles at the first, the first person must interpret the meaning of that smile. Does it mean that his appearance is funny, and that the other person is laughing at him? Or does it show approval and pleasure on the part of the other person at his appearance? Irrespective of the content of the thought of the second person, the first person imagines in his own mind what judgments are being made in the mind of the other. He gets clues from the other person's behavior, but can never put himself in the other's mind and gain a direct knowledge of what the other is thinking.

Third, after imagining the judgment of the second person, the first person then feels some self-emotion or self-judgment. If he imagines that the other person's judgment of his appearance is favorable, then he feels pride or other favorable emotions. Conversely, if he imagines that the judgment of the

137

other is unfavorable, he himself judges his appearance as unfavorable, and feels an emotion appropriate to the judgment.

This total process occurs within the mind of the first person. His own behavior is the direct result of his thought processes. He acts in accordance with his conception of self, which in turn is derived from interaction with others. One's self-concept, then, is gained directly through interaction with other individuals. If one is treated with love, or imagines that others love him, then he comes to love himself. If he is rejected by others, he rejects himself.

The practical principle which is derived from Cooley's analysis is expressed in the following saying: If you wish a person to possess a certain characteristic, treat him as if he already possesses that characteristic. Robert Merton's later discussion of this subject drew its essential insights from Cooley.[8] Merton noted that people often make a prediction regarding some future state, particularly some future characteristic or behavior, of an individual. This prediction becomes a "self-fulfilling prophecy" because the act or acts of making the prophecy have an important influence in determining the final outcome. By defining a young man as "good" or "helpful" we create a condition which facilitates his becoming good or helpful.

This does not mean that the individual is totally passive in the process of the development of the self. Cooley took pains to note that the most essential characteristic of interaction is precisely that one person changes his behavior to adjust to another's appearance or behavior. The young child, he argued, learns very early in life that he can bring about a change in behavior of other persons through his own behavior. One gains a certain degree of control over others through one's ability to behave in certain ways. A child of six months, he observed, will consistently attempt to attract attention to itself. In addition, it learns that different kinds of actions provoke different kinds of responses in others.

The young performer soon learns to be different things to different people, showing that he begins to apprehend personality and to foresee its operation.[9]

Parents naturally seek to influence their children. They therefore react favorably to certain kinds of behavior of which they approve, and negatively to other kinds of behavior of which they disapprove. In other words, the behavior of the parent is conditional, at least to some extent, upon the behavior of the child. One might say with Cooley that the child has influenced the behavior of the parent, just as the parent has influenced the behavior of the child.

At an early age, children learn to carry on interaction without the actual presence of the other person. That is, they learn to symbolize in their minds the presence of the other person. They frequently carry on conversations with themselves, now playing the role of the other, now playing the role of self. They are able to do this because they have learned the typical reactions of other persons in given situations.

Since one can interact with others in one's own imagination, interaction can be carried on at the symbolic level as well as the physical level. In fact, Cooley argued that there is no essential difference between these two kinds of interactions. It is perhaps possible to distinguish interaction from thought analytically. But both are aspects of the same phenomena, according to Cooley. The significant factor present in the interaction which takes place when two individuals are physically present is also found in the ability of each to symbolize the behavior of the other. Interaction, then, is no different from that which takes place in the mind of one individual who imagines the presence or the behavior of the other. Each is interaction on the symbolic level. In each case, the essential reality is in the ideas in the mind.

It follows from this point that individuals are able to imagine "ideal" selves and "ideal" others. The ideal is built upon through imagination. Each individual is able to create in his mind certain ideal kinds of behavior, certain ideal social conditions, which may never be achieved in actuality but which may serve as important influences in his life. He is not limited by those conditions which he has actually observed. Instead, because of the ability of the mind to abstract out certain elements of a situation and generalize them to other situations, the individual can think about what he might do in certain future or imaginary situations. He can choose various

139

alternative behaviors and imagine the effect of each upon other persons. This kind of imaginary construction of situations often enables the individual to interact more effectively when the situation is finally presented. Further, such "ideal" kinds of actions can serve as a guide for behavior in situations which do not fully approximate the conditions which are imagined. Ideals, including religious ideals, are created in the mind through this process of selection and generalization.

PRIMARY GROUPS AND SOCIAL ORGANIZATION

The assertion that ideas are the essential facts of social life is the most important single theoretical proposition in Cooley's works. In Social Organization,[10] Cooley built an explanation of social organization upon this assertion.

When people interact, they tend gradually to develop consistent patterns of behavior and thought. They develop a kind of sympathy or a sharing of common mental states.[11] These similar patterns of behavior and thought become crystallized into the customs and norms of the social group. Since individuals have acted in certain ways in the past, they are expected to act in the same way in the future. Ideational expectations for behavior become the foundation of social organization. A group of people may be said to be organized when they have developed a consistent way of thinking and acting, and when these customary forms of thought and action influence the individual member of society to conform to them.

> Social organization . . . should not be conceived as the product merely of definite and utilitarian purpose, but as the total expression of conscious and subconscious tendency, the slow crystallization in many forms and colors of the human spirit.[12]

Aside from Cooley's concept of the "looking-glass self," no other concept developed by Cooley has such wide acceptance as that of the "primary group." Cooley's definition and discussion of the primary group has had a significant influence upon the development of terminology to describe social organization. Families, peer groups, and neighborhoods most closely illustrate this kind of social organization. Individuals are tied to other individuals through a common feeling that they

140

belong together. They share a sense of intimacy and cooperation, of sympathy and mutual identification, which they don't feel toward others. These ideas and mutual feelings bring the individuals together. They influence the individual to act in certain ways in order to maintain these "spiritual" ties to others. Ideas are the essence of a primary relation. Close association, face-to-face interaction, durable relations, similarities of personal characteristics, in and of themselves, do not create primary relationships. Only if people think and feel a certain way toward each other can they be said to form a primary group. These ideas, then, tie people together. They are the necessary and sufficient conditions for social organization.

OBJECTIVE INTROSPECTION

In his early works, especially Human Nature and the Social Order, Cooley unabashedly advocated a combination of observation and introspection as the method of collecting data about social life. While this position was strongly attacked by the behavioristic school of social psychology, Cooley never seriously wavered from this position. [13]

Ideas should be the major objects of scientific investigation. [14] Whenever possible, one should observe the behavior of an individual in order to gain some clues as to his thought processes or emotions. However, we cannot know the thoughts of a person directly through his behavior. [15] Instead, we are forced to interpret the process by which the individual's thought is linked to his behavior.

> Facial expression, tone of voice, and the like, the sensible nucleus of personal and social ideas, serve as the handle, so to speak, of such ideas, the principal substance of which is drawn from the region of inner imagination and sentiment. [16]

Behavior, including language, can serve as an indirect indicator of ideas. No direct indicators of another's ideas are available. It is impossible to observe the mind of a person directly.

In his later book, Social Organization, Cooley gave a more complete account of his view of introspection. Here, he argued that introspection

141

cannot be achieved by withdrawing from society and giving oneself up to one's inner thoughts. Instead, introspection must be carried out in close conjunction with personal experience and observation. Only by broadening one's own experience and interactions can one also broaden one's introspective abilities.

Cooley did not reject such methods as the collection of statistics, laboratory experiments, physical measurements, etc. He thought of these methods as valuable tools by which to gain knowledge of social reality. But their real purpose is to aid the mind in gaining insight into the nature of social reality. Introspection is the major method of gaining truth. Other methodological techniques are useful in providing the introspective mind with matter upon which to reflect.[17]

One needs only to read Cooley's works to feel the confidence and power with which Cooley himself used introspection. He prided himself on being an insightful observer, and in being able to draw from his observations of ordinary situations and ordinary people the fruitful generalizations which he felt were the results of introspection. His analysis of child development, of the nature of the primary group and social organization, of conflict and social classes, to mention only a few, have endured through many years. One test of an empirical generalization or of a theoretical proposition must be its continuing fruitfulness in aiding in the explanation, prediction and control of social phenomena for which social scientists ultimately strive.

MEAD: ROLE PLAYING

George Herbert Mead (1863-1931), a philosopher and social psychologist who taught at the University of Chicago from 1893 to 1931, is often regarded as the leading figure of "symbolic interactionism." Our own evaluation, however, is that Cooley contributed more to the establishment of symbolic interaction than did Mead. While Mead wrote many articles, he never systematized his theoretical approach in book form. After his death, some of his students, notably Charles W. Morris, published many of his important ideas, taken from stenographic notes of his lectures.[18] Mind, Self and Society[19] is derived from his course in social psychology, which he taught for many years and which influenced a generation of students and

142

colleagues. It is Mead's best expression of his theory of symbolic interaction, and has become a classic in sociological literature.

John B. Watson's theory of behaviorism had had a dominant influence on the psychology of Mead's day. Mead accepted Watson's major point that human behavior is the essential phenomena of psychology. He therefore called himself a social behaviorist. But Mead was not true to either Watson's methodological principles or his basic explanation of social reality. His criticisms of Watson's brand of behaviorism were incisive. They led to a reorientation of social psychology, with greater emphasis placed on "subjective" factors than Watson would have liked.

In <u>Mind, Self and Society</u>, Mead criticized Watson for his rejection of "subjective" and "ideational" factors such as ideas, mind, consciousness, thought, etc. Mead asserted (with very little supporting data other than his own introspection) that there is a realm of phenomena--of thought, experience and feeling--that "belongs (experientially) to the individual qua individual, and is accessible to him alone."[20] This "inner experience" is part of the data which social psychology must explain. When individuals behave in a certain manner, their behavior is influenced by the subjective ideas which they possess.

Mead discussed what he called the "act" as the unit of analysis of social psychology. Each separate act is composed of the external behavior which is openly exhibited and available for observation, and the internal subjective states which precede the external behavior and largely determine it.

> But part of the act lies within the organism and only comes to expression later; it is that side of behavior which I think Watson has passed over. There is a field within the act which is not external, but which belongs to the act, and there are characteristics of that inner organic conduct which do reveal themselves in our own attitudes, especially those connected with speech. Now, if our behavioristic point of view takes these attitudes into account we find that it can very well cover the field of psychology.[21]

143

Mead exhibited some ambivalence but seemed to accept the belief that introspection is the major method of gaining information about these inner subjective factors. He recognized that external behavior may serve as an indicator of the presence of these subjective factors. However, subjective factors cannot be observed directly, but only through the external behavior which more or less truly represent them. Mead's own methods of description and analysis made use of both observation and introspection.

SYMBOLIC GESTURES

Two biological organisms which meet may communicate with each other through what Mead spoke of as gestures. He gave the example of two dogs who growl and bark at each other, and by their posture and movements communicate their aggression toward each other. The action of one dog provokes a response in the second, which in turn provokes a different behavior or response in the first dog. The two, then, are interacting. They are acting in awareness of each other. The behavior of each provokes a response in the other, so that the specific behavior that emerges from their interaction is a resultant of their mutual adjustive responses to each other. The dynamic aspects of their interaction take on great importance.[22]

The interaction which human beings engage in is of the same type, although more complex. The gestures which each individual mades toward the other are meaningful, both to the actor and to the other person. They express the feelings and emotions of the actor. The other person observes the gestures, interprets their meaning, and adjusts his behavior in accordance with his interpretation. Each gesture has symbolic meaning to the other actor. It becomes what Mead calls a "significant symbol."[23] Meaning precedes the behavior and in large part determines it. It is important, according to Mead, to explain the process by which gestures take on meaning.

MIND

"Mind" can be said to be in existence when individuals are able to internally manipulate the meanings of symbolic gestures and words. Individuals "think" when they interact with themselves by using the symbols which have been given a fixed meaning by the social group.

Only in terms of gestures as significant symbols is the existence of mind or intelligence possible; for only in terms of gestures which are significant symbols can thinking--which is simply an internalized or implicit conversation of the individual with himself by means of such gestures--take place.[24]

Individuals interpret the gestures of other individuals--that is, they give meaning to them--through role taking. Each individual places himself in the position of the other person. If he feels anger and makes a gesture to demonstrate that anger to the other person, he implicitly takes the point of view of that other person and imagines the meaning which his gesture has to that other person. He projects his own subjective state and assumes that the other person feels the same way about his gesture as he does. Likewise, when the other person gestures to him in some manner, he places himself in the role of the other and interprets the meaning of the behavior in terms of how he would feel if he had behaved in the same way. Social learning, then, involves a process of socialization by which each individual learns to take the role of the other person in interpreting his own behavior.

The meaning of gestures which are repeatedly used becomes fixed. This facilitates the socialization process as well as enabling the individual to respond more accurately to the gestures made by others. The meaning of these gestures, therefore, becomes a part of the culture of the group.

Language, which is so important to interaction between human beings, is simply a series of vocal sounds which, like gestures, are given meaning by interacting individuals. Words are symbols. They communicate the feelings and attitudes of individuals in the same manner as do gestures. They "stand for" or are representative of the behavior or object to which, by agreement of the group members, they refer. Through interaction all members of a social group come to interpret the meaning of a vocal sound in the same way. This agreement on meaning allows communication through language to take place.

Language differs from gestures, however, in a crucial way. When animals or people communicate by means of gestures, according to Mead, the action of one provokes a different response in the other. If one attacks, for example, the other assumes a defensive position, or he flees. The two acts are complementary, but are not identical. In language, however, the word (as a significant symbol or gesture) has the same meaning for both the speaker and the listener. Both individuals are able to react to the same stimulus, because the words used have similar meanings to each actor.

This point is all the more important because of the relationship of language to role taking. Because words have similar (if not always identical) meanings to two interacting individuals, one individual is enabled more effectively to take the role of the other and see his own behavior in this perspective. Language facilitates role-taking behavior.

According to Mead, a gesture or word has meaning in behavioral terms. A gesture indicates to the other individual a response which he should take.

> If that gesture does so indicate to another organism the subsequent (or resultant) behavior of the given organism, then it has meaning . . . . The gesture stands for a certain resultant of the social act, a resultant to which there is a definite response on the part of the individuals involved therein; so that meaning is given or stated in terms of response.[25]

The response of the second individual to the gesture of the first, however, is not automatic or instinctual. Lower animals act towards each other on the basis of instinct. What separates man from lower animals is precisely the ability to interpret the gestures of the other in terms of some common set of meanings. Mind, then, is an intervening variable between the stimulus and the response. The response of the second party is adjustive in that it is oriented to the behavior of the first party. It enables the second party to behave in such a way that his behavior is brought into line with that of the first, either by being similar or complementary to it.

A crucial point made by Mead is that language enables the individual to "pick out responses and hold them in the organism."[26] That is, the thinking individual is able to delay his response to the stimulus, rather than act automatically to it. The individual is able to think about various alternative responses to the stimulus and choose which of these responses he will make.

The essence of mind, then, is the ability to reflect on possible alternative responses, make predictions about the possible consequences of each alternative (by predicting the responses of other individuals to his action), and choose both the behavior he will engage in and the timing of his behavior.

The reflection upon future possibilities is an important element in the thinking process. Mead assumed that lower animals (which many behavioral psychologists have used as the bases of their studies) cannot take the future into consideration, since their responses to stimuli are instinctual and non-reflective. Mind, then, sets man apart from other biological organisms, a conclusion as old as Greek philosophy, yet crucial to the modern development of the social sciences.

Mead's discussion of mind, then, centered on the interactive process by which people adjust their behavior to each other. This process of interaction results in the development of significant symbols, both verbal and nonverbal. People manipulate these symbols in their minds, and choose a single course of action from among many which are possible and which are also present in the mind. Delayed action and choice of alternative courses of action are behavioral indicators of the existence of the mind. Since the mind develops out of social interaction, it is essentially social in nature.

SELF

Mead's concept of the "self" is a seminal one in the development of social psychology. The self, according to Mead, refers to the subjective aspect rather than the biological aspect of man. The self is not present at birth. It develops gradually through the process of social interaction. Mead's definition of the self stressed the subjective or attitudinal aspects of the mind of an individual.

147

The young child interacts with his environment and with the individuals who are part of this environment. He initially regards these individuals as objects which are similar to other physical objects present in his environment. However, he quickly learns that people respond to his behavior in a totally different way than do objects. Physical objects are passive; people are active. By manipulating his own behavior, he can influence the behavior of other persons.

Mead asserted that the young child initially experiences himself subjectively, through his psychological and biological mechanisms. Mead sought to examine those behavioral experiences which enable the individual to "get outside himself . . . in such a way as to become an object to himself."[27] One can become conscious of himself only to the extent to which he is able to view himself objectively--from the point of view of other persons. Through the process of social interaction, the individual gradually learns to take the role of the other and to treat himself as an object. He learns to carry on a conversation with himself in the same way he converses with others. He anticipates the behavior of others toward himself, and tends to develop a self-image of himself in comformity with the reactions of others toward him. However, Mead did not develop this point with the same cogency as did Cooley.

According to Mead, there are two stages to the development of the self. In the first stage, the individual responds to specific other persons, and incorporates into himself the specific attitudes and behavioral patterns which are directed toward him by others. This process of incorporation or internalization is one of organization, since the individual tends to organize his attitudes toward himself by selecting out those features of the behavior of others toward him which are common or consistent.

This organization of attitudes is more complete in the second stage of the development of the self. Here, the individual tends to generalize the behavior of other persons in an organized way. By generalizing the behavior of others, he is enabled to respond to persons in terms of social categories rather than to specific individuals. He responds to the "generalized other" rather than to specific others. Such behavior represents a significant social development for both the group and the individual. The individual attains

148

the full development of his self only by learning to take the role of the generalized other.

The social group cannot be organized or function properly unless the individual members of the society develop this generalized other. Mead argued that the "complex cooperative processes and activities and institutional functionings of organized human society" cannot proceed without the development of the generalized other on the part of group members. Social interaction enables people to live together, but the complex problems of living together could not be solved unless people were able to generalize their experiences with other individuals.

This does not mean that the individual self precedes the development of the social group. Mead argued forcefully that the development of the self presupposes the existence of the social process of interaction. Without association with other individuals, the self could never develop. Mind and self, as well as society, are essentially social phenomena. Both (a) the process of interaction and (b) society as an entity precede the development of mind and self.[28]

The development of the generalized other is illustrated by Mead in his often-quoted discussion of role taking in play and the game. Here he makes excellent use of two of his most important concepts--role-taking and the generalized other. Often when a child is playing by himself, he will imagine himself as occupying another role. He plays at being a policeman, or a father, or a doctor. He attempts to act and think in the way in which he has observed the other person acting and thinking.[29] Play helps the child learn to take the role of others. This in turn facilitates his own ability to respond to such persons when called upon to interact with them. He is better able to predict their behavior because he has "been in their shoes" so to speak.

Organized games represent a more complex and sophisticated form of role taking. In such a game, there are a specified set of roles. Each role has a set of behavioral expectations which govern how the role is played. To play the game successfully, the child must know what is expected of each role, and must be able to place himself subjectively into each role. Mead gave the example of the baseball game, in which

149

each player must be able to take the role of each other player in order to anticipate the kinds of behavior in which each will engage. Any organized activity can be carried on only if each participant is able to role-play effectively. Social life is a game in which people play specified roles.

THE SELF AND THE SOCIAL PROCESS

Mead recognized that every individual interacts with a multitude of other individuals. He learns to generalize these interactions and to conceive of a generalized other. However, it is also important to recognize that because these other individuals differ markedly from each other in many ways, the actor must learn to take into account the peculiar as well as the general aspects of his interaction with others.

One way we learn to adjust to the individual differences of those with whom we interact is to recognize the different roles which they hold. One of the most important factors contributing to the consistency and predictability of behavior is that persons who hold the same role tend to act in the same way. However, persons who hold the same role may act differently. Since interaction is a complex process of adjusting one's behavior and attitudes to others, the content of a given process of interaction may be quite different from that of another among individuals with similar roles.[30]

In any interaction between two individuals, neither actor expresses himself completely. Only part of one's personality and attitudes is invoked in any given interaction.

> We carry on a whole series of different relationships to different people. We are one thing to one man and another thing to another. There are parts of the self which exist only for the self in relationship to itself. We divide ourselves up in all sorts of different selves with reference to our acquaintances . . . . There are all sorts of different selves answering to all sorts of different social reactions.[31]

The social self tends to be integrated in normal people so that there is a consistency of behavior from role to role and interaction to interaction. However, the self also has multiple manifestations. Mead recognized the normality of a "multiple personality" in that each individual expresses himself in a multitude of different ways corresponding to the multitude of interactions in which he engages.

Mead spoke of the self as both a structure and a process. The self is a <u>structure</u> to the extent to which the attitudes and behavioral responses are organized.[32] Since society tends to prescribe certain kinds of attitudes and behaviors for certain situations, the self takes on a consistency and organization. A partial rigidity of personality develops. The self is not completely plastic, able to act in any way at any time. Rather, there is a consistency to one's behavior and attitudes. The individual suffers psychically if he tries to incorporate too many conflicting elements into his self. Likewise, society tends to eliminate the extreme forms of conflict in norms, roles and cultural values in order to bring harmony and balance to the society.

The self is also a <u>process</u>, according to Mead. While Mead did not define what he meant by a process, the implied meaning is that a process refers to an ongoing series of changes which enable the organism to adjust adequately to its environment. Interaction itself is a process in this sense, since it is an ongoing activity of mutual adjustment between two or more individuals. This process of interaction, of relating oneself and adjusting one's behavior to others, was spoken of by Mead as both the precondition for the development of the self and the essence of the self as an entity.

It is probably not important to argue with Mead about his use of these terms. The important point he wished to make is that there is a definite consistency in the individual's tendencies to respond to others; likewise, the individual is constantly incorporating into his self new attitudes because of the diversity of his experience. The self is constantly adjusting as it comes in contact with new persons and new situations.[33] However, it also maintains a consistency because these new elements are combined and organized with the previous elements which compose the self. The self, then, attempts to achieve a balance of flexibility and stability, of change and of organization.

SOCIETY

Like Cooley, Mead was at his best when he was analyzing social relations at the small-group level. His discussion of the development of the self and of the intimate interplay of influences between two interacting individuals is rightly regarded as brilliant. However, when he moved to the societal level and applied his analysis to larger groups, the weaknesses of his approach became evident. In his discussion of "society," Mead argued that larger social groups like families and governments grow out of symbolic interaction at the small-group level. He extrapolates the principles he had developed to explain intimate interaction to a higher level, and assumed that the same orientation which aided him so successfully to explain micro-social phenomena could also be used to explain macro-social phenomena.

Mead accepted a relatively simplistic theory of evolutionary progress as the basis for his explanation of the development of society. He took for granted the physical and physiological conditions which influence social life. Social evolution proceeds from instinctual interaction to gestures at the level of the lower animals, through the development of language, mind and self, to the development of society as such. Society is viewed as the product of the growth of population with its accompanying increasing complexity of social interaction, together with the development of a generalized other of increasing scope and inclusiveness.

The family is the basic unit of social organization. Social institutions, such as the state and the economy, are simply composed of a large number of families tied together by interaction and the resulting generalized set of attitudes and behavior patterns to which all individuals are socialized and to which they conform.

I have tried to bring out the position that the society in which we belong represents an organized set of responses to certain situations in which the individual is involved, and that in so far as the individual can take those organized responses over into his own nature, and call them out by means of the symbol in the social response, he has a mind in which mental processes can go on, a mind whose inner structure he has taken from the community to which he belongs. [35]

Large organizations, such as a society, have needs which are similar in most respects to smaller groups such as the family. Each needs a division of labor, replacement of population, regulation of behavior, etc. Because of the larger size of a society, however, the organization which it develops must be more complex, and the integration which it achieves must be extensive.

Ultimately and fundamentally societies develop in complexity of organization only by means of the progressive achievement of greater and greater degrees of functional, behavioristic differentiation among the individuals who constitute them. [36]

What is needed to support Mead's argument is a detailed analysis of the manner in which interactions among individuals become translated into social institutions or social norms. Mead's discussion of society unfortunately did not build the bridge between small interaction and large-scale social organization. When Mead explained the development of the individual self, his interactional orientation worked beautifully. When he attempted to explain society, his orientation lacked precision and explanatory power. Symbolic interaction is a powerful tool to explain micro-social phenomena, but seems to lack power at the macro-social level.

THOMAS: THE SITUATIONAL APPROACH

William Isaac Thomas (1863-1947) is the third of the major figures in the development of the symbolic interactionist approach. His writings were much more extensive than either Cooley or Mead, yet his theoretical statements are less extensive. Thomas was primarily engaged in presenting and interpreting data. His theoretical statements are therefore made in intimate relationship to data. They are scattered throughout his works, rather than being drawn together in a single work.

Like many researchers, Thomas was theoretically flexible, and went where his studies took him intellectually. One can see in his works a marked development of theoretical conceptions. He discarded concepts that did not aid him in his most recent studies, and developed new ones which were more utilitarian. Likewise, he discarded older philosophical notions of the nature of social laws and causation[37] and took a more moderate approach to these problems.

Thomas did maintain a consistent orientation throughout his works, however. This was his subjective approach to the study of social phenomena. This orientation is found in his earliest writings, and was maintained throughout his long professional career. He built upon the insights of both Cooley and Mead, of John Dewey and James M. Baldwin. He accepted the assertion that people have minds. They think, perceive, select, choose and act. They are not simply acted upon by external forces, as is a chemical element for example. People act and react to their environment. They possess an _internal_ environment, so to speak, in their own minds.

Thomas was less concerned than Cooley or Mead with the specific phenomena of mind, language and consciousness. These had been well analyzed previously, and he felt no obligation to proceed further in this direction. His approach was to use these essential insights to explain particular kinds of behavior.

Thomas's studies ranges over an extremely broad spectrum of phenomena. His first interests were in primitive societies, especially sexual and racial differences between primitive and modern societies. Later he turned to an analysis of social organization and disorganization. This interest culminated in his classic work The Polish Peasant in Europe and America,[38] published between 1918 and 1920 in five volumes, which he coauthored with Florian Znaniecki. This was a monumental study of Polish immigrants to the United States. In order to analyze this phenomenon effectively, Thomas and Znaniecki studied patterns of peasant life in Poland as well as the adjustment of individuals to immigration and the establishment of a new pattern of social organization in the New World.

Thomas continued his interests in adjustment in two important works, The Unadjusted Girl (1923) and The Child in America (1928).[39] These continued his interests in social disorganization and deviant

154

behavior. Finally, he returned to his initial interest in primitive cultures in his final book <u>Primitive Behavior</u> (1937).[40]

Thomas's major theoretical contribution of interest to us here has been labeled "the situational approach." His discussion of the objective and subjective conditions present in any situation and his influential notion of the "definition of the situation, are especially important. Thomas's discussion provides a valuable vehicle for the analysis of the relationship of subjective to structural factors.[41]

The Situation

The "situation" is a general term which encompasses all those conditions which are available for observation by a scientific investigator. These include all physical conditions (i.e., the temperature of the room) as well as the biological state of the interacting organisms. However, to Thomas, the important elements in the situation are the social ones. All aspects which can be observed, including patterns of behavior and such ideational factors as attitudes and values (as they are indicated in actual behavior) are included in the situation. The social relations between individuals or groups are especially important.[42] Thomas spoke of the situation as primarily composed of those social and ideational factors which influence the individual to act as he does. Physical factors are included only if they exert some influence upon the individual's thought processes, either consciously or unconsciously.

The Definition of the Situation

Watson and the behaviorists had argued that any explanation of social life must include only "situational" factors. That is, only those factors subject to direct empirical observation could be utilized in a scientific investigation. Thomas rejected this behavioral view. He asserted that the individual is not simply a passive entity through which objective social causes operate to produce social effects. Instead, the individual possesses the ability to reflect upon his external environment, select out those elements most important to him, ponder alternative courses of action, and finally choose a particular way of acting. He reacts to his

155

environment, not in any mechanical manner, but as a subjective, thinking, feeling actor.

> (Behaviorists) ignore largely questions of the organic causation of behavior, the "why" of behavior reactions, and limit themselves to the observation, measurement and comparison of behavior manifestations--how the individual behaves in specific situations.[43]

In his earlier works, Thomas emphasized the concepts of "values" and "attitudes" as most useful in dealing with the subjective elements of society. These two concepts were central to his discussion of the process of adjustment of Polish peasants to American life.[44] Later, in The Unadjusted Girl, he developed the concept of the "Four Wishes" to explain the psychological processes by which individuals come to differ from others in their same social group.[45] In his last works, Thomas refers increasingly to his important concept, "the definition of the situation."[46]

Thomas believed that the individual "defines" or looks at a situation in a given way. His interpretation of the situation is "real" for him, and he acts on the basis of this interpretation. The individual's behavior is, therefore, influenced by the situation, but is determined by the individual's definition of the situation. Every individual is forced to make an adjustment to the situations in which he finds himself. The process of adjustment is neither automatic nor determined mechanically either by the biological state of his body or through some automatic process of imitation. The individual must make his own adjustment. He must choose how he will respond to his environment. If his response is incorrect, he will suffer the consequences. If his response is correct, he will derive benefit from the situation and achieve a higher level of coordination with his environment. All social life involves adjustment. Adjustment is a constant process by which all individuals accommodate to other individuals, groups and the external environment. Adjustment is one of the most important concepts in Thomas's explanation of social life.[47]

In a primitive society, in which the rate of change is extremely slow, there is almost (but not quite) universal agreement on how to define each situation which confronts the group. Because of this, the individual who is properly socialized is able to define the situation in the same way all others define it. (See the chapter on Sumner for a discussion of how definitions at the macro-social level are developed). In such cases, the individual is able to act in traditional and habitual ways, seldom "coming to attention" or consciously planning his behavior. Adjustment is nearly automatic in such cases.

However, no individual is ever able to gain full knowledge of all aspects of the situations in which he lives. He is always being confronted by new situations, new individuals whose roles or patterns of behavior he does not know, and new external environments. Even in the most stable society, the individual is faced with new situations which force him to determine his own definition of the situation, or at least consciously determine which of many former situations the present situation is most like.

In more complex societies with more specialized roles, a larger number of social norms, and a much broader range of social situations, the process of defining the situation becomes much more difficult. A wide range of possible definitions and resultant patterns of behavior is available. Because there is a plurality of possible definitions and actions, the individual must find some way to make a choice.

The most frequently used method of defining the situation is to find in one's consciousness or imagination some other situation which seems to be most like the one in question. One then simply generalizes from a familiar situation to a new one. He uses the behavior appropriate in one situation to apply to the new situation. If the situation is not similar to any other situations, or if the individual cannot find these similarities, he is forced to develop a new definition of the situation and a new way to act in it.

Thomas argued that "the definition of the situation is equivalent to the determination of the vague."[48] In the modern world, many situations are ill-defined, and fewer clear-cut definitions are available to the individual.

> . . . not only particular situations but the most general situations have become vague. Some situations were once defined and have become vague again; some have arisen and

157

have never been defined. . . . There are
rival definitions of the situation, and none
of them is binding.[49]

Because of the complexity of modern life, the
individual is faced with a multitude of possible ways
to define a given situation. He is forced to reflect
upon the situation and choose his own definition.
Thomas assumed that this definition is a personal one,
and is largely unpredictable to an outside observer
with no other information than his own observations of
the external situation.

Symbolic Interaction and Social Change

In almost every social situation, the definition
of the situation must be attained by the individual
through the reflective process. Some alternatives of
choice are available to him. A certain vagueness
pervades the situation. Because of this, the
individual has an expanded latitude of response. He
puts his own unique and personal stamp upon his
response to the situation. As individuals act, they
adjust their behavior to each other. The resulting
behavior is a product of these individual choices and
adjustments. Even in traditional societies or
situations, new forms of behavior constantly emerge
because of the nature of the interactive relationship.

This explains how social change takes place. For
Thomas, social change occurs at the small-group level.
New patterns of behavior and new definitions of the
situation emerge from the interactive process. In
turn, these relatively minor changes affecting only a
few people are multiplied by the thousands of similar
events which occur each day. New definitions at the
small-group level eventuate in changing moral codes,
normative prescriptions, and cultural values.

Although Thomas did not attempt to explain
technological change, the same argument may be applied
to this question. As people interact and new
definitions of situations emerge, the possibilities for
invention increase. The minds of people are gradually
freed from traditional ways. As new social conditions
emerge, the need for new technological inventions
increases, and intelligent people are more highly
motivated to pursue them.

Interaction and Macrosociology

The symbolic interactionist approach was developed primarily by persons who thought of themselves as social psychologists. They were interested in the influence of the group upon the behavior of the individual. General group tendencies were of only secondary importance to them (although both Cooley and Thomas made important contributions to analysis at this level). One does not find in Thomas' works an extensive discussion of the relationship between interaction at the small group level and larger organizations. However, one does find an implicit theory of social organization at the macrosocial level.

In his initial statement on the definition of the situation, Thomas noted that the individual is socialized to a definition of the situation by his parents and other agencies.

> This defining of the situation is begun by the parents in the form of ordering and forbidding and information, is continued in the community by means of gossip, with its praise and blame, and is formally represented by the school, the law, the church. [50]

In other words, the individual is taught the culture of the group, which includes standard definitions of situations commonly found in the group. The code of behavior of the group is formalized in the major societal institutions. Formal and informal sanctions are brought to bear upon the individual to conform. He is taught how to define certain situations and is motivated to act in accordance with the group's norms.

This kind of explanation is widely accepted by sociologists, and does not differ from the assertions of Durkheim, Sumner and a host of previous sociologists. However, it should be noted that it is an explanation of the perpetuation of a code of conduct and its associated definitions of situations. It does not, however, explain the creation of such codes. The question becomes, therefore, how does a general code of conduct grow out of the initial interactions among men in small groups?

Thomas gave a relatively simplistic answer to this question in his methodological chapter in The Child in America. He noted that greater progress has been made in explaining behavior at the small group level than at the "mass behavior" level.

> With the progress of our studies of the various behavior-forming situations we may hope to approach the still more obscure problem of mass behavior--the participation of whole populations in common sentiments and actions. . . . We are able to define this total situation satisfactorily, but it involves the interaction of language and gesture and gossip and print and symbols and slogans and propaganda and imitation, and seems, more than anything else, the process eventuating in the formation of the distinctive character of communities, nationalities and races. <u>The process itself may be described as a series of definitions of situations whereby behavior norms are established.</u>[51]

Individuals first interact in small groups. In such groups, agreement on definitions of situations is achieved. The normative standards of behavior found in large groups are simply the result of countless interactions at the small group level with their resulting agreement on definitions. If there are no barriers to interaction, such agreement eventually spreads to the entire group. A normative code, then, has no separate existence apart from the subjective orientations of individual actors.[52] A general norm (such as "Thou shalt not kill") is found only in the minds of individuals in the form of definitions of how one should act in a given situation. The individual definitions, which are often transmitted from person to person, are the essential elements from which the general code is derived. There seems here to be a clear if implicit assumption that the whole is a sum of all the parts, with no separate existence of characteristics than those found in each of the parts. This position, of course, is directly contrary to Durkheim's position.

The definitions of situations developed through social interaction become embodied in a "code" of conduct. This code defines the rules of behavior to which individuals are then expected to conform. The code defines abstract ideals (such as honesty or chastity) by defining how individuals should act in specific situations.[53] These rules of conduct give

160

organization to social life. Social organization, for Thomas, consists of social rules of conduct developed through symbolic interaction.

> The rules of behavior, and the actions viewed as conforming or not conforming with these rules, constitute with regard to their objective significance a certain number of more or less connected and harmonious systems which can be generally called <u>social institutions</u>, and the totality of institutions found in a concrete social group constitutes the <u>social organization</u> of this group.[54]

This view of social organization differs from those emphasizing patterns of behavior (Simmel) or particular structural arrangements (Marx and Durkheim). It may be argued, however, that these other views of the nature of social organization may be adequately incorporated into the subjectivists' conception that the essence of social organization is rules of conduct. Subjectivists argue, for example, that there is nothing to social structure but norms and definitions of situations. A status is simply a collection of rights and duties--that is, normative definitions as to proper behavior in particular situations. Theories of social structure which emphasize such concepts as social class, kinship organization, status or position, etc., often fail to see that a social class, a kinship organization, or a social status has no reality other than in the minds of individual actors. The definitions which these actors have in their minds of the nature of such structures, and how the occupants of such statuses should act in particular situations, are the essence of social organization.

The power of the social group over an individual is therefore not some abstract entity deriving from any powerful, independent forces. Rather, it derives from the influences of particular other persons who share with the actor certain common definitions of situations and who are likely to sanction his behavior if he does not conform to their expectations. The power which is exerted upon the individual rests with other individuals, not in some external and metaphysical entity called "society."

> . . . (T)he values which (sociology) studies draw all their reality, all their

power to influence human life, from the social attitudes which are expressed or supposedly expressed in them; if the individual in his behavior is so largely determined by the rules prevailing in his social group, it is certainly due neither to the rationality of these rules not to the physical consequences which their following or breaking may have, but to his consciousness that these rules represent attitudes of his group and to his realization of the social consequences which will ensue for him if he follows or breaks the rules.[55]

Any "deterministic" influence which the group might be said to have over the individual is exercised through other individuals. The actor may choose to regard or disregard such individuals. In his choice, he considers the consequences of each alternative. The group "determines" the behavior of the individual only to the extent to which it forces him to consider the consequences of his choice and makes him suffer these consequences.

The Relationship of the Situation and the Definition of the Situation

Let us now present a diagram of Thomas's basic situational approach and discuss some of its ramifications.

Figure 8:1   Thomas's Situational Theory

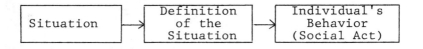

Thomas treated the individual's definition of the situation as the mediating factor between the situation and the individual's behavior. It is the individual who perceives the situation, defines it, and chooses how to act within the situation.

We wish to consider two possibilities. First, what are the implications for sociological theory and research if the individual's definition of the situation coincides with the situation? Second, what are the implications if the definition of the situation does not coincide with the situation?

Consistency of Situation and Definition

In the first case, the individual's definition of the situation coincides with the situation as it is defined by the total social group. Such a condition is more likely to be found in small primary groups, in primitive societies, or in other situations of stability and slow social change. Even here, we may not find complete agreement among all the individuals as to the definition of the situation. However, where a general consensus is achieved, the individual actor may feel that there is strong support for a given definition of the situation.

In such a situation, the social researcher may be able to establish through research that there is a stable relationship either (1) between the situation and the behavior, or (2) between the definition of the situation and the behavior. Since the situation and the definition of the situation coincide, either may serve equally as a predictor of the other. Knowledge of either the situation or the definition of the situation would enable the observer to make an accurate prediction about the resultant behavior.

Since the situation is generally more easily observed and objectively described than the definition of the situation, the researcher can make an accurate prediction of behavior through a study of the characteristics of the situation itself. It is in precisely such situations that the structural approach to the explanation of social life is most effective. In those situations where (1) the social group has substantial agreement on how given situations should be defined, and (2) where these group definitions are both well known and consistent with structural conditions, the researcher can make accurate predictions about behavior from an analysis of the structural conditions present in the situation. For example, in a given society lower-class persons may tend to vote for liberal political parties. The cultural definitions found among lower class people are internally consistent, and coincide with the structural conditions present in the group. In such a situation, the researcher may accurately predict the voting behavior of an individual by ascertaining his social class membership, without reference to "subjective" variables

163

or the individual's definition of the situation. This is possible, however, only because subjective variables are taken for granted, and because the researcher has some previous knowledge of the integration of cultural definitions with structural cultural definition of a given situation, then knowledge of social class membership can lead to accurate prediction of resulting behavior.

Sociologists often assume that these group definitions of the situation are "consistent with" the structural conditions. Thus, most American sociologists assume that liberal attitudes are consistent with low status. They have an implicit (and sometimes explicit) theory which links low status to liberal attitudes. But the subjectivists would argue that there is nothing "necessary" or predetermined about the linkage of these two. In many societies, i.e., India, low status is "consistent with" conservative attitudes. Rather than there being any necessary linkage between a structural condition and cultural norm (or a group definition of the situation in Thomas's terms), the only necessity is given by the consistency with which the cultural norm is held. All individuals in the society may think of this as a necessity because there is agreement on the norm in their society. An opposite condition may be just as natural and considered to be just as necessary by persons in another society.

The structural condition, then, should not be considered to be the cause of the resultant behavior. This is true even if the researcher can make accurate predictions of the behavior simply by studying the social structure (the situation). The situation is consistent with the behavior only because there is substantial agreement in the group as to the cultural definition of the situation. This group definition of the situation, rather than the situation itself, must be considered as the cause of any behavior which may result in the situation.

There is nothing automatic about people's responses to given situations. Only if a response were automatic could the situation be said to be the cause of the behavior. Any time that the individual thinks, interprets or defines the situation, this process of definition becomes the immediate cause of the resultant behavior.

Further, there is nothing automatic or "natural" about the relationship between the situation and the definition of the situation. Situations may be defined in a variety of ways by a particular group or individual. Any situation, no matter how simple, is subject to many different interpretations. One need only note the variety of interpretations of such standard human evens as birth, death or sexual union among the cultures of the world.[56] The situation cannot be said to be the cause of the definition of the situation. It may greatly influence it. But many components besides the situation enter into the individual's definition of the situation. In Figure 8:1, then, the line connecting the situation and its definition should not be regarded as causal.

Discrepancy of Situation and Definition

This brings us to the second case, in which there is a discrepancy between the situation and the definition of the situation. This discrepancy may be the result either of (1) the vagueness, internal inconsistency of instability or the situation, or (2) the inability of the individual to perceive, integrate, understand or otherwise internalize all of the elements of the situation. According to Thomas, in modern societies, few if any situations are found in which the situation is so simple and pure that it affords no alternative definitions. Some definitions may be more likely, or follow more logically from the conditions present in the situation. However, in almost every case (one is tempted to use an absolute here) other alternative definitions are possible.[57]

Where the situation and its definition do not coincide, or coincide only in part, accurate prediction of behavior in the situation is possible only by knowing the definition of the situation. In such cases, knowledge of the situation itself would be at best only partially useful. The researcher must direct himself to the definition of the situation, the individual and subjective element, in order to understand and make accurate predictions about behavior. No matter how discrepant the definition from the actual situation, the individual will still act "as if" his definition of the situation were accurate. Thus Thomas's famous dictum: "If men define situations as real, they are real in their consequences."[58]

165

No matter how sound and stable the financial
position of a bank, if the depositors of the bank
believe that it is going to fail, they will act upon
the definition. Their actions derive from the
(objectively false) definition rather than the
(objectively true) situation itself. The behavior
which individual's engage in as a result of an
initially false definition of the situation can often
(but not always) change the objective situation to
coincide with their definitions of it.[59] Thus, the
bank may eventually fail, no matter how stable its
original condition before the false definition of the
situation led to a run upon its assets.

Thomas rejected the assumption that changing the
structure (or situation) of a society will
automatically result in a change of its culture (or
definition of the situation). He labeled as fallacies
the assumptions:

(1) that men react in the same way to
the same influences regardless of their
individual or social past, and that therefore
it is possible to provoke identical behavior
in various individuals by identical means;
(2) that men develop spontaneously,
without external influence, tendencies which
enable them to profit in a full and uniform
way from given conditions, and that therefore
it is sufficient to create favorable or
remove unfavorable conditions in order to
give birth to or suppress given tendencies.[60]

Both of these assumptions are central to
structural theory. Thomas supported his rejection of
them with data from The Polish Peasant. Polish
immigrants often retained almost intact their original
peasant culture despite the marked structural
(situational) changes which occurred in immigrating to
the United States. When cultural norms and definitions
of situations changed, the process was not automatic
nor governed directly by the new structural conditions
or situations. The reflection of the individual upon
his changed situation mediated the relationship between
changed conditions and changed behavior. It was always
a significant factor, and could be said to be the cause
of the change of behavior if such in fact occurred.

Whether the definition of the situation fits the
situation or not, the "true" cause of the observed

behavior is found in the subjective element of the definition of the situation, not in the objective situation. While some understanding can be gained, and predictions can sometimes be made with accuracy by studying only the situation (or the structural factors), complete understanding and accuracy of prediction can only be achieved by studying the subjective definition of the situation.

The Methodology of Symbolic Interaction

The most telling criticisms of symbolic interaction have been directed to the methodology by which the researcher studies the subjective phenomena of mind and interaction. Behaviorists have been especially critical of symbolic interactionism. They argue that only human behavior can be scientifically observed. Subjective states of mind, definitions of situations, attitudes, values, etc., can be observed only as they are expressed in behavior. Behaviorists, therefore, argue that in order to be scientific one must attempt to establish relationships, causal if possible, between certain situational conditions and the behavior patterns found under these conditions. Since the subjective element cannot be observed, it must be eliminated from any analysis of social life which seeks to be scientific.

Thomas tried to meet this criticism in The Child in America. He argued that observation in a variety of situations together with insightful introspection and analysis of the subjective factors in the situation will yield more fruitful results than simple observation without the use of the researcher's own subjective experience.

It has been strongly objected, especially by the adherents of the school of "behaviorism," that this introspective method has no objectivity or validity. What they mean is that these records will not reveal the mechanisms of behavior, the process of consciousness, what is going on inside of us when we think and act, and with this we are in agreement. But the unique value of the document (life history) is its revelation of the situations which have conditioned the behavior, and concerning this there can be no doubt.[61]

167

In The Polish Peasant, Thomas and Znaniecki had made extensive use of the case study or "life history" techniques of gathering data. Using diaries and other documents written by the actor himself about his life and his subjective reactions to his experiences, the authors had made an analysis of the adjustment of individuals to new conditions.

Thomas acknowledged that such documents might be extremely subjective. To him, that was their value. They enabled the researcher to gain insight into the actor's interpretation of the situations in which he was placed. These data could not be gained in any other way.

> . . . (T)he behavior document (case study, life record, psychoanalytic confession) representing a continuity of experience in life situation is the most illuminating procedure available. In a good record of this kind we are able to view the behavior reactions in the various situations, the emergence of personality traits, the determination of concrete acts, and the formation of life policies and their evolution.[62]

Since the reaction of the individual in an interactive situation is the essence of social life, no method which deals only with external conditions or behavior can eve reach this subjective essence. The life history or other personal document allows the researcher to gain some introspective understanding of the feelings of the individual as he himself expresses them. The value of a life history is proportional to the ability and creativity of the researcher who uses it.

Thomas did not argue that the case study approach should be the only one used by sociologists. He advocated the use of statistics and experimental method whenever possible. He believed that case studies are more valuable at the descriptive and exploratory levels of research, where the researcher has little previous data on his subject, is still groping for the correct concepts by which to conceptualize his subject, and has not developed exact measuring instruments for his important variables.

Statistics and experimental methods are more useful as the research progresses, especially in hypothesis testing. However, case studies are still needed to provide general background information.[63] The strengths of the case study method include (1) use of a time dimension which facilitates attribution of causation, (2) wealth of data provided on a wide number of variables, and on the subjective state of the individual. Its important weaknesses are (1) lack of objectivity of the record, (2) the expense in time and money to obtain each life history, and (3) the tendency to use only a few life histories with resultant problems stemming from a small sample.

Thomas did not directly meet the objection of the behaviorists. He was forced to admit that his data were themselves behavior. That is, the act of telling or writing one's personal history is itself a behavioral act. It gives indirect but not direct evidence as to the subjective state of the individual. No direct method is ever available to enable the research to "know" what is going on in the mind of the subject.

Equally important, the researcher must use his own introspection to interpret the document and gain insight into the workings of the subjects mind. The process of interpretation weakens but does not destroy the scientific value the data might have.

Although Thomas did not directly answer this charge, symbolic interactionists have replied that all data, no matter by what techniques they have been gathered, are subject to the interpretation of the researcher. No fact is meaningful of itself. The meaning and interpretation is given to it by the researcher. This subjective process of interpretation is therefore no different when one is dealing with case histories than when one is dealing with replies to questionnaires or demographic statistics. No scientist can avoid the interpretation of his data. What is necessary, therefore, is to be as open as possible about one's own preconceptions, strive for as much objectivity as possible, and check one's interpretations with other qualified observers.

Thomas's theoretical contributions are less heralded than those of Cooley and Mead. However, his concept of the definition of the situation and his discussion of the relationship of the situation and the definition of the situation have proved most fruitful. Together with Cooley and Mead, Thomas had provided a significant theoretical foundation for a subjectivist orientation to social psychology. Its influence, however, has primarily been confined to microsociology rather than macrosociology--to small group interaction rather than societal or institutional phenomena.

FOOTNOTES

[1]Charles H. Cooley, Human Nature and the Social Order, (New York: Scribner's, 1902).

[2]Ibid., p. 2.

[3]Ibid., pp. 84-85.

[4]Ibid., p. 137.

[5]Ibid., p. 144.

[6]Ibid., p. 140.

[7]Ibid., p. 160.

[8]Robert K. Merton, "The Self-Fulfilling Prophecy," in Robert K. Merton, Social Theory and Social Structure, revised edition, (New York: Free Press of Glencoe, 1957), pp. 421-436.

[9]Cooley, Human Nature and the Social Order, pp. 165-166.

[10]Charles H. Cooley, Social Organization, (New York: Scribner's, 1909; reprint ed., New York: Schoken Books, 1962).

[11]Cooley, Human Nature and the Social Order, pp. 102-103.

[12]Cooley, Social Organizations, p. 22.

[13]See Charles H. Cooley, "The Roots of Social Knowledge," in Sociological Theory and Social Research, (New York: Holt, 1930).

[14]Cooley, Human Nature and the Social Order, p. 87.

[15]Ibid., p. 86.

[16]Ibid., p. 81.

[17]Charles H. Cooley, Social Process, (New York: Scribner's 1918), p. 167.

[18]George H. Mead, The Philosophy of the Present, (LaSalle, Illinois: Open Court, 1932); George H. Mead, Movements of Thought in the Nineteenth Century, (Chicago: University of Chicago Press, 1936); George H. Mead, The Philosophy of the Act, (Chicago: University of Chicago Press, 1938).

[19]George H. Mead, Mind, Self and Society From the Standpoint of a Social Behaviorist, (Chicago: University of Chicago Press, 1934).

[20]Ibid., p. 5.

[21]Ibid., p. 6.

[22]Ibid., p. 63.

[23]Ibid., p. 45.

[24]Ibid., p. 47.

[25]Ibid., p. 76.

[26]Ibid., p. 97.

[27]Ibid., p. 138.

[28]This point will be discussed more extensively in Chapter   .

[29]Mead, Mind, Self and Society, p. 150.

[30]Ibid., p. 191.

[31]Ibid., p. 142.

[32]Ibid., p. 140.

[33]See Chapter   .

[34]Mead, Mind, Self and Society, p. 229.

[35]Ibid., p. 270.

171

[36]Ibid., p. 310.

[37]See Chapter   .

[38]William I. Thomas and Florian Znaniecki, The Polish Peasant in Europe and America, Chicago: University of Chicago Press,   ; reprinted, New York: Knopf, 1918-1920).   and Richard G. Badger).

[39]William I. Thomas, The Unadjusted Girl: With Cases and Standpoint for Behavior Analysis, (Boston: Little, Brown & Company, 1923); William I. Thomas and Dorothy Swaine Thomas, The Child in America: Behavior Problems and Programs, (New York: Knopf, 1928).

[40]William I. Thomas, Primitive Behavior: An Introduction to the Social Sciences, (New York: McGraw-Hill, 1937).

[41]See the excellent summary in Edmund H. Volkart, editor, Social Behavior and Personality: Contributions of W. I. Thomas to Theory and Social Research, (New York: Social Science Research Council, 1951), p. 2.

[42]Thomas, The Child in America, p. 572.

[43]Ibid., p. 558.

[44]"Methodological Note to The Polish Peasant," in Volkart, Social Behavior and Personality, pp. 49-50.

[45]Thomas, The Unadjusted Girl, pp. 1-40.

[46]Thomas first introduced this concept in "The Persistence of Primary-Group Norms in Present-day Society," in Herbert S. Jennings et al., Suggestions of Modern Science Concerning Education, (New York: Macmillan, 1917), pp. 167-187; see also Volkart, Social Behavior and Personality, p. 226.

[47]Thomas, Primitive Behavior, pp. 1-2.

[48]W. I. Thomas, On Social Organization and Social Personality ed. Morris Janowitz, (Chicago: University of Chicago Press, 1966), p. 240.

[49]Ibid.

[50]"The Persistence of Primary-group Norms in Present-day Society," in Volkart, Social Behavior and Personality, p. 227.

[51]Thomas, The Child in America, p. 575.

[52]Thomas, Primitive Behavior, p. 7.

[53]"The Persistence of Primary-group Norms in Present-day Society," in Volkart, Social Behavior and Personality, p. 227.

[54]"Methodological Note," Ibid., p. 52.

[55]Ibid., pp. 52-53.

[56]Thomas, Primitive Behavior, p. 8.

[57]Thomas, The Child in America, p. 572.

[58]Ibid.

[59]Robert K. Merton, "The Self-Fulfilling Prophecy," in Robert K. Merton, Social Theory and Social Structure, revised edition, (New York: Free Press of Glencoe, 1957), pp. 421-436.

[60]"Methodological Note," in Volkart, Social Behavior and Personality, pp. 44-45.

[61]Thomas, The Child in America, p. 571.

[62]"The Relation of Research to the Social Process," quoted in Volkart, Social Behavior and Personality, p. 20.

[63]Ibid., p. 93.

CHAPTER NINE

THE STRUCTURALISM-SUBJECTIVISM ISSUE
IN CONTEMPORARY SOCIOLOGY

The most fundamental cleavage in sociological theory is that which separates subjectivists from structuralists. As we have observed previously, this issue is a longstanding one in philosophy and has been continually debated throughout the history of sociology. Altogether it is the most enduring and fundamental issue in sociological theory.

This observation holds true for contemporary sociology every bit as much as for previous eras. The division between symbolic interactionists and behaviorists, or between ethnomethodologists and neo-positivists, is probably as great today as that which separated Marx and Weber. This is true in spite of continual efforts to synthesize the two approaches and arrive at a workable solution to the issue.

Our intention in this work is to explicate the positions taken by the classical theorists in the history of sociology on the most important issues of sociological theory. It is not possible for us in this book to address the many ways in which these issues are being worked out in contemporary sociology. But in a brief compass here, we wish to indicate some of the ways in which the issue is being addressed and the theorists whose writings have been most significant.

As an overview, we have compiled a list of important sociological theorists past and present who have taken a relatively consistent stand on the structuralism-subjectivism issue. This classification scheme is presented below:

STRUCTURALISTS	SUBJECTIVISTS

Classical Structuralism
    Marx and Engels
    Durkheim
    Simmel
    Comte
    Spencer
	Classical Subjectivism
	    Weber
	    Sumner
	    Ward
	    Pareto

Neo-Marxism and Critical Sociology
    Habermas
    Frankfurt School
    Mills
	Neo-Subjectivism
	    MacIver
	    Znaniecki
	    Sorokin

Modern Conflict Theory
    Dahrendorf
    Coser
    Collins
	Social Action Theory
	    Parsons

Structural-Functionalism
    Radcliffe-Brown
	Pure Functionalism
	    Malinowski

Structural Symbolic Interactionism
    Stryker
	Symbolic Interactionism
	    Cooley
	    Mead
	    Thomas

Behaviorism
    Watson
    Skinner
	Blumer
	    Goffman
	    Turner

Positivism
    Lundberg
    Blalock
	Ethnomethodology and Phenomenology
	    Garfinkel
	    Schutz

Exchange Theory
    Homans
    Blau
	Tiryakian
	    Berger
	    Luckmann

Macro Structuralism Blau	

French Structuralism
    Levy-Strauss
    Piaget	

Linguistic Structuralism
    Chomsky
    Saussure	

Mathematical Structuralism White	

Such a categorization as this is, in many cases, very difficult to make, especially for some theorists. The primary reason for this difficulty is that many theorists begin their academic careers by taking a rather extreme position on the issue; then, in later years or later publications, they tend to modify this extreme position and move to more moderate ground somewhere between the two extremes. John Finley Scott has noted the shift in Talcott Parsons's career from extreme subjectivism toward a more structural position.[1] Both Marx and Engels, but especially Engels, moderated their extreme structural position in later writings. The same is true of Durkheim.

Closely related is the tendency for later theorists to modify or redirect a theory away from an extreme position taken by earlier theorists. Sheldon Stryker has recently published a structural version of symbolic interaction.[2] Aaron Cicourel is a less extreme ethnomethodologist than Harold Garfinkel and has been talking more about structure.[3] George Ritzer interprets Goffman's writing on frame analysis as a move away from his earlier extreme subjectivist position.[4]

Some notable theorists do not appear on our list because they are difficult to classify. Robert Merton has published work which is both subjectivist (especially "The Self Fulfilling Prophecy" essay[5]) and structuralist ("Social Structure and Anomie" and his later essay on structuralism[6]). And Anthony Giddens, an important young theorist, has tried to synthesize a subjectivist viewpoint with Marxian analysis.[7]

We conclude, therefore, that it is difficult to maintain an extreme position on this issue and that the tendency is to take a more moderate position as time goes by. While both structuralism and subjectivism have obvious merits and can be supported by strong arguments, both have significant weaknesses which can be exploited by persons of an opposite persuasion. Thus, in the long run, the merits of both cases seem to lead sociological theorists to position themselves somewhere in the middle of the structuralism-subjectivism continuum.

A second generalization can also be derived from the classification of theorists. In contemporary sociology, subjectivism is represented almost exclusively in two theoretical schools: symbolic interaction and ethnomethodology. There are obviously variations within each school, but subjectivism tends to be encompassed by these two. Conversely, the diversity of structural approaches is much greater in contemporary sociology. Structuralism is represented in the theoretical viewpoints as diverse as conflict and critical theory, French structuralism, behaviorism and neo-positivism, exchange theory, and structural-functionalism.[8]

Structuralism is also exposed to diverse influences. The linguistic structuralism of Noam Chomsky has influenced both the mathematical structuralism of Harrison White, the developments of French structuralism, and the cognitive sociology of Aaron Cicourel.[9] White has also been influenced by Levy-Strauss.[10] Blau's influence on the development of exchange theory was very significant,[11] but recently his work has been centered on macro-structural issues.[12] Critical theory and other neo-Marxist approaches have received much recent attention,[13] d structural approaches are still strong within the functionalist tradition.

We do not mean to imply by this that structuralism is more viable presently than subjectivism (although this may indeed be the case), but it certainly appears to be more diverse.

Can the structuralism-subjectivism issue be resolved? Is there a possible synthesis which will bring the two positions closer together? Such a synthesis is not now present, but the beginnings and outlines of one are available. Let us begin with a reformulation of several of Anthony Giddens's propositions:

1. Human beings have minds and agency; they create their own subjective world and choose their own behavior and attitudes.

2. Human agency and thought are powerfully influenced by social conditions, both subjective (values, norms, group-shared attitudes) and structural (level of economic development, degree of democracy of the political system, size of the middle class, etc.).

3. People "produce society, but they do so as historically located actors, and (seldom) under conditions of their own choosing."[15]

4. Unseen forces (economic, political, spiritual, historical) exert a powerful but not determinative influence on the social lives of human beings.

5. Despite these forces, human beings have sufficient freedom and agency to influence and direct the course of their own lives; human individual differences are variegated and significant.

6. Once established through largely subjective processes, ideational aspects of social life (values, norms, etc.) tend to become institutionalized and structuralized over time. Thus ideas are transformed into structures which maintain their subjective properties and yet still act in structural ways to influence social events.

7. The result is enough consistency and structure in society and history to allow structuralists to find patterns and predict rates of behavior, and yet enough variation and individual initiative to enable subjectivists to locate ideas and treat them as causes in history. Social life is both predictable (in part) and unpredictable (in part). Both ideas and structures serve as causes (and as effects) in the events of social life.

In conclusion, we believe the best way to view this issue is through the perspective of "dual tendencies."[16] This theoretical point of view recognizes that in social life there are frequently forces or tendencies which work at cross-purposes, which exert their influence in opposite directions. Two (or more) tendencies can be identified, and both are legitimate subjects for sociological investigation. To utilize one at the expense of the other is to miss a significant portion of social life. But social life is not simply a sum of the two tendencies. Since both operate, society occasionally shifts its position between the two tendencies as one or the other exerts a more powerful influence. Both tendencies, however, are important and both must be recognized as fundamental to an understanding of social life.

FOOTNOTES

[1]John Finley Scott, "The Changing Foundations of the Parsonian Action Scheme," American Sociological Review 28 (October 1963), 716-735.

[2]Sheldon Stryker, Symbolic Interactionism: A Social Structural Version. (Menlo Park: Benjamin/-Cummings), 1980.

[3]Aaron Cicourel, Cognitive Sociology. (New York: Free Press, 1974), pp. 74-98.

[4]George Ritzer, Contemporary Sociological Theory. (New York: Knopf), 1983, p. 285. Erving Goffman, Frame Analysis. (New York: Harper), 1974.

[5]Robert K. Merton, "The Self Fulfilling Prophecy," in Social Theory and Social Structure, Revised Edition. (Glencoe: Free Press), 1957, pp. 421-436.

[6]Robert K. Merton, "Social Structure and Anomie," Ibid., pp. 131-160; "Structural Analysis in Sociology," in Peter Blau (ed.), Approaches to the Study of Social Structure. (New York: Free Press), pp. 21-52.

[7]Anthony Giddens, New Rules of Sociological Method. (London: Hutchinson), 1976, especially pp. 160-161.

[8]Richard T. DeGeorge and Fernande M. DeGeorge (eds.), The Structuralists: From Marx to Levi-Strauss. (Garden City: Doubleday), 1972.

[9]Nicholas C. Mullins, Theories and Theory Groups in Contemporary American Sociology. (New York: Harper), 1973, pp. 250-269; and Cicourel, op. cit., chapters 2 and 3.

[10]Harrison C. White, An Anatomy of Kinship. (Englewood Cliffs: Prentice-Hall), 1963.

[11]Peter M. Blau, Exchange and Power in Social Life. (New York: Wiley), 1964.

[12]Peter M. Blau, Inequality and Heterogeneity: A Primitive Theory of Social Structure. (New York: Free Press), 1977.

[13]For a brief introduction to this literature, see Julius Sensat, Jr., Habermas and Marxism: An Appraisal. (Beverly Hills, Sage), 1979.

[14]George Ritzer, Sociology: A Multiple Paradigm Science. (Boston: Allyn and Bacon), 1975.

[15]Giddens, op, cit., p. 160.

[16]Reinhard Bendix and Bennett Berger, "Images of Society and Problems of Concept Formation in Sociology," in Llewellyn Gross (ed.), Symposium on Sociological Theory. (Evanston: Row, Peterson), 1959, pp. 92-118; James T. Duke, "Toward a Theory of Dual Tendencies: A Propositional Inventory of Sociological Theory," Pacific Sociological Association, San Francisco, April 1980.

CHAPTER TEN

DURKHEIM AND THE CLASSICAL GROUP APPROACH

Sociology is the scientific study of the human group, or social (i.e., group) life. Sociology identifies itself as a scientific discipline and emphasizes the use of the scientific method to describe and explain social life. As a science, it is distinguished from other endeavors associated with social life: religion, social philosophy, mysticism, law, etc. While there is substantial agreement on this point, it should be noted that there is also substantial disagreement among sociologists on the implications of science for the study of sociology.

One would imagine that there would be agreement among sociologists on one other important point--the nature and influence of the social group. Alas, this has never been true. One of the major issues which has divided sociological theorists is concerned with the "groupness" of social life and the related influence of the individual human being upon social life. Some sociologists like Emile Durkheim and George Lundberg have argued that the group has a reality <u>sui generis</u>. It is different from the sum of its individual parts (the individuals who compose it). In social life, the group has a profound effect upon the individual members who compose it. The individuals, in turn, have very little influence upon the group.

Further, these theorists believed that the events of social life are susceptible to scientific study and to reduction to a set of scientific laws which describe and explain them. Group life is not random or planless. It is subject to uniformities in the same sense as are physical phenomena. Through the use of the scientific method, the uniformities of social life can be identified and formulated into sociological generalities or laws. We may label this approach the "group" approach for our purposes. It tends to be relatively deterministic in its orientation, and to play down the influence of individuals and individual choices in social life.

The alternative orientation found among sociologists may be labelled the "individualistic" approach. It emphasizes the importance of taking the individual into account in the study of social life. Such theorists tend to argue that individual human

183

beings possess volition and mind. They are able to think, choose and act upon their choices. Since a group is composed of individuals, it seems logical to these theorists that the individual should become the startingpoint in the study of the group. The influence of the individual upon the group is emphasized in this orientation, and the purely "group" characteristics of social life are viewed as less important. Those who fall within this group tend to be more varied in their outlook and to differ among themselves on some essential implications of this orientation. For example, Weber argued that the possession of volition and choice by individuals resulted in the emergence of constantly new "historical individuals" or events which could not be formulated into scientific laws. He made a strong argument against the search for rigidly defined scientific laws for the social sciences. Others, like George Homans have argued that laws can be formulated which describe and explain social life, but that these laws can ultimately be derived deductively from the laws of individual behavioristic psychology.

From these two general orientations, then, it is possible to observe several sub-issues, as follows: What is the basic unit of analysis of sociology, the group or the individual? Is the group simply a result of the characteristics of its individual parts, or does it possess social characteristics which are different from those of its individual parts? Is it possible to describe and explain social life by reference to a set of scientifically formulated laws, or is social life so variable as to necessitate the rejection of the search for laws in social life? To what extent does man possess free will, or are his actions determined by social laws? What are the political policies which are most directly implied by this issue? What is the influence of the "great man" upon the society in which he lives?

We shall begin our discussion of this issue by turning to the classical "group" orientation in sociology formulated by Emile Durkheim.

THE POWER OF SOCIAL FACTS

Perhaps Durkheim's major accomplishment was the establishment of sociology as a separate academic discipline in France. He instituted the first course in sociology ever taught at a university in France. He held the first chair of social science established in

184

France, as well as the first professorship which carried sociology in its title. He established the first journal devoted to sociology to be published in France.

Durkheim approached his task with a pioneer's spirit. His enthusiasm was boundless. He inspired others to follow him and to work with him to build up the discipline. His works were criticized, often brutally, by those in other disciplines who failed to see the necessity of developing a new discipline called sociology. Many had vested interests; philosophers, psychologists and biologists all laid claim to the study of social groups.

Durkheim reasoned that in order for sociology to be recognized as a separate discipline, it must deal with phenomena which are qualitatively different from those of any other discipline. He felt that only if he could demonstrate that sociology was devoted to the study of facts which were purely social, and which were not encompassed in the other scientific disciplines, could he justify its existence. Such facts would be preeminently social, in that they would refer to characteristics of the group itself rather than to the biological and psychological characteristics of the individuals who were members of the group.

THE DEFINITION OF A SOCIAL FACT

In his classic little book, The Rules of Sociological Method,[1] Durkheim addressed himself to this task. He sought to demonstrate that what he called "social facts" are of a different order than facts of any other discipline, such as psychology or biology. Social facts point to a different thing--a unique entity. In studying facts, one makes observations of the phenomena which are not within the province of any other subject matter. Durkheim's famous definition of a social fact is as follows:

> A social fact is every way of acting (thinking or feeling), fixed or not, capable of exercising on the individual an external constraint. . . .[2]

This definition was filled with meaning for Durkheim. The two most important words in the definition are "external" and "constraint." Social facts are "external" in the sense that they exist in

185

the collective conscience rather than the individual consciousness. Social facts exist prior in time to the individual. The individual is born into an ongoing social group in which the social facts are fully developed. Social facts are also prior to the individual in the sense that because they come from the group, they exert influence upon the individual's conscience. In almost every case, the individual is not able to change the social fact through an exercise of his own willpower or reason.

This leads us to Durkheim's second characteristic of a social fact: constraint. The social group uses sanctions to make sure that the individual's behavior is in conformity to the social facts. Durkheim placed more emphasis on negative than positive sanctions in this early work, although in his later <u>Moral Education</u>[3] he gave equal weight to the two. The individual is coerced by social pressures to act in a manner different from that which he would have chosen without coercion.

The best proof that social facts are external and constraining is found in child-rearing practices. Durkheim recognized that through the imposition of sanctions, children are taught patterns of behavior which are not "natural."[4] Let us use socialization to toilet training as our example of this. It is not "natural" for a child to eliminate his wastes into a round porcelain bowl called a toilet. In many societies, elimination is relatively public, with little modesty or shyness attached to it. In American society (and many others), however, the child is taught that the only proper place to eliminate his wastes is in the bathroom, and in private. Such a practice is not "natural" but social. It is a cultural pattern which is held by the social group and which is taught to the individual with appropriate (and sometimes inappropriate) sanctions.

However, once the individual has internalized (an extremely meaningful word) this pattern, he no longer feels constraint. Only if he suddenly begins to deviate from the pattern does he feel the weight of society against him. Conformity is usually perfect, at least for the great majority of adults. The pattern is taken for granted to the point that individuals are often unaware of the coercive nature of the social group in imposing the pattern upon them. In fact, most individuals feel totally free to choose the time and

place for such elimination. They feel that their
behavior is individualistically chosen, rather than
determined by the social group. Thus, rather than
recognizing this normative pattern as social, they
regard it as a matter of personal choice.

We have used as an example of a social fact what
is today called a social norm. Durkheim characterized
these as "established beliefs and practices." He gave
as examples of social facts such things as "legal and
moral regulations, religious faith, financial systems."
Individuals cannot easily or effectively change the
legal or financial systems of their society. If you
think so, try using French francs (if you can find
them) in the local supermarket the next time you go
shopping. Individual behavior is constrained by
group-held patterns of behavior and expectations.

Durkheim also noted that there is a second
category of social facts "without such crystalized
form" which he called "social currents."[5] These are
the facts of collective behavior which are less
normative but which still exert a strong influence on
the individual. The behavior of mobs, crowds and other
temporary groups are of this character. Individuals
often act differently in groups than they otherwise
would act as isolated individuals. Mobs may engage in
riotous behavior, whereas isolated individuals
infrequently act in such aggressive ways. The
spectator at a baseball game acts in a jubilant and
boisterous manner because the social situation
encourages such behavior. The same individual may find
it very difficult to express himself in this manner
while alone.

THE SOCIAL CAUSES OF SUICIDE

Durkheim's most forceful proof of the importance
of studying social facts is contained in his study of
suicide. Suicide,[6] published in 1897, was by far the
best statistical study of social phenomena to appear up
to that time. Durkheim gathered data on suicides from
a number of different nations and provinces within
nations. More importantly, he personally studied
approximately 25,000 cases of suicide from the years
1889-1891 in France and classified these suicides for
his own purposes. While statistical analysis was
little developed at that time, he was able to make an
amazing number of crucial tests with his data.

Durkheim's choice of suicide as an object of sociological investigation was a shrewd one. Suicide seems at first glance to be an individualistic phenomena. Suicides are rarely committed in the presence of other people. Several persons almost never commit suicide together, the Jim Jones group in Guyana being a very notable exception. Suicide is a highly personal act, and until Durkheim's time was universally attributed to individualistic causes.

Durkheim chose as his subject a phenomenon which had always been regarded as individualistic. He reasoned that if he could show that such an act can be fruitfully analyzed sociologically, and especially if he could show that it is subject to social rather than individual causes, he could assuredly win his case that sociology should be a separate discipline.

But Durkheim did not study individual suicides. Instead, he focused on the suicide rate of a given group at a given time period. He demonstrated that the suicide rate of a nation tends to be constant over time, rather than varying widely. For example, between 1849 and 1855 the suicide rate in France varied between 9.4 and 10.5 per 100,000 inhabitants, with an average of 10.1. During the same time period, the death rate in France varied between 21.4 and 27.4, averaging 24.1.[7] He concluded from this and other evidence that the suicide rate is less variable than the death rate. This is an extremely momentous conclusion, for death seems to be due to natural causes whereas suicide is thought to be due to individual choices. If the suicide rate is more stable and uniform than the death rate, this fact gives substantial support to the conclusion that it is subject to law-like social influences.

Durkheim further demonstrated that different nations have widely different suicide rates. For the period 1866-1870, for example, the suicide rate in France was 135 (per million inhabitants). Other nations were as follows: Italy, 30; England, 67; Sweden, 85; Prussia, 142; and Denmark, 277.[8] In each of these nations, such rates were consistent with those of previous years. Suicide rates for a given nation do change, but only when the nation is facing a social crisis. If a marked change takes place and becomes permanent, this is a sign that "structural characteristics of society have simultaneously suffered profound changes."[9] Durkheim concluded that a suicide rate is "not simply a sum of independent units . . . but is itself a new fact sui generis, with its own unity, individuality and consequently its own nature--a nature, furthermore, dominantly social."[10] This conclusion is expressed time and again throughout the book, and is the point to which the whole book is addressed.

Durkheim rejected insanity, alcoholism, race and other hereditary factors, climate and seasonal factors, and imitation as causes of suicide. Let us briefly summarize his arguments against insanity as a cause of suicide in order to illustrate his method.[11]

Durkheim first noted that many "alienists" (psychiatrists) have observed a pathological state of insanity in many persons who commit suicide. He argued, however, that such alienists study only persons who were already mentally ill before the suicide took place. These people study only one of the four cells in a correlation matrix--only one of four types of persons who need to be studied.

		Suicide	
		Yes	No
Insane	Yes	x	
	No		

Without data on the other three types, no definitive conclusion can be reached.

Further, since a common practice is to label as suicides only those acts which seemed to have no motive, there is a definitional correlation established between suicide and insanity. Heroic and other acts with a definite and apparent motive are not called suicides, although the individual often clearly had prior knowledge that he would die as the result of his act.

Durkheim's argument became even stronger when he turned to data for support. He noted that the link between insanity and suicide can be established only if the variations of the suicide rate coincide with those of the insanity rate. This led Durkheim to examine certain social variables and their correlation with suicide. With regard to sex, Durkheim noted that women are slightly more likely to be found in insane asylums than men, yet men are much more likely to commit suicide than women. Further, more insanity is found among Jews than other religious groups, with Protestants and Catholics relatively equal in their rates of insanity. Yet Protestants have a higher rate of suicide than Catholics, with Jews having the lowest rate. In the case of religious groups, "suicide varies in inverse proportion to psychopathic states."[12]

With respect to age, suicide rates regularly increase from childhood to old age. Durkheim argued fallaciously that insanity is rare before maturity, reaches a peak at about age 30, then decreases at old age. Again, no correlation is found between insanity rates and suicide rates. Further, in comparing one nation to another, "the countries with the fewest insane have the most suicides."[13] Suicide as an individual psychological phenomenon determined by abnormal or aberrant psychological conditions (insanity) is therefore rejected by Durkheim. One cannot attribute the observed variations in the suicide rate to individualistic causes. Social causes, rather than individual causes, must be sought.

On turning to the social causes of suicide, Durkheim argued that there may be several types of suicide, each with its own distinctive cause. This led him to develop his famous typology of suicides: egoistic, altruistic and anomic suicide.

EGOISTIC SUICIDE

Durkheim first examined statistics regarding suicide rates among religious groups. In every country at every time period that Durkheim studied, Protestants had a higher suicide rate than Catholics, with Jews lower than Catholics. This difference is not attributable to the different teachings of the churches regarding suicide, since Durkheim argued that Protestants and Catholics "prohibit suicide with equal emphasis."[14] Further, Jews are less likely to place a religious sanction on suicide than the other two groups, yet have a lower suicide rate.

Protestantism is associated with a "spirit of free inquiry" not found in Catholicism.[15] This spirit results from the greater freedom of the individual within Protestantism, which is in turn a result of the separatism which characterizes the social organization of Protestant churches. The Catholic church, on the other hand, has a high degree of central authority, a well-organized social structure, and a strong, unified and extensive <u>credo</u> covering all aspects of individual life. In short, the Catholic church is more strongly <u>integrated</u> than the various denominations of Protestantism.[16] The suicide rate varies inversely with the rate of social integration. Thus, malintegration is the major cause of one type of suicide, which he labels "egoistic" suicide.

Before examining the mechanism by which lack of integration leads to suicide, however, Durkheim sought for further evidence of an inverse relationship between integration and suicide. He reasoned that marriage and family life is one of the most significant features of social life contributing to social integration. He therefore examined data regarding the relationship of marital status to suicide. He showed statistically that married persons are less likely to commit suicide than unmarried people when age is controlled. Further, widowed persons <u>who have children</u> are less likely to commit suicide than widowed persons with no children or unmarried persons of the same age. This is of course due to their greater degree of integration into a family unit. Finally, unmarried women have a lower suicide rate than unmarried men. Durkheim reasoned that unmarried women are more likely to remain in an ongoing family unit than unmarried men. Their greater integration provides a social protection against suicide.[17]

In addition, Durkheim provided data to show that the suicide rate goes down whenever a society faces a political crisis.[18] This is because the integration of the society always increases in the face of a threat from the outside. Great wars and even election campaigns reduce the suicide rate, but "purely dynastic wars" where the people are little affected and which do not result in a greater integration of the society have no such preservative effect from suicide.

In each case--religion, family, political crises--it is not the "sentiments" or ideas of such groups which give them their preservative effect against suicide. It is instead their social organization--their integration. "When a society is strongly integrated, it holds individuals under its control . . . and thus forbids them to dispose wilfully

191

of themselves."[19] If society loses some of this integration, however, the individual becomes detached from society and "his personality (tends) to surmount the collective personality."[20]

This led Durkheim to a description of the mechanism by which lack of integration causes a high suicide rate.[21] Individuals who belong to poorly integrated social groups do not receive group support for their activities. Having no social group on which to depend, such individuals must rely upon their own abilities and judgment. This in turn leads to "excessive individualism," in which the individual has no restraints and no close ties to other people. He may have a strongly formulated moral code to which he adheres; the Protestant does not differ from the Catholic in this regard. However, without the support and restraint exercised by other members of a well-integrated social group, he is able to develop private sentiments and principles which he uses to govern his life. When adversity strikes, he is less likely to receive emotional support from a group, and more likely to feel unwanted and unfulfilled. Suicide is more likely to occur under such circumstances.

Durkheim's argument here is closely akin to that made in the Division of Labor[22]: primitive societies characterized by mechanical solidarity are well integrated, and the individual is closely restricted by the collective conscience. As society develops, however, tradition tends to break down and the individual is emancipated from the ties of the social group. Thus, any force which contributes to individualism or to a weakening of the integration of the group will result in an increase in the suicide rate. As corollaries, educated people, especially those in the liberal professions, are more likely to commit suicide than less well-educated persons. Persons in rural areas are less likely to commit suicide than those living in cities.

Excessive individualism, then, is a pathological state which results from a breakdown of societal integration through rapid social change. Individualism itself then becomes the cause of the high suicide rate found in groups with excessive individualism. Durkheim's major thesis may be diagrammed as follows:

192

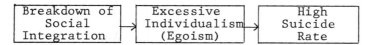

Breakdown of Social Integration	→	Excessive Individualism (Egoism)	→	High Suicide Rate

Durkheim noted that this explanation also fits the commonly accepted belief (for which he had no data) that the suicide rate is higher in nations with less traditionalistic ways--nations, in other words, with greater economic development and industrial technology. Unlike most experts of his time, however, he recognized that suicide, and even a high rate of suicide, may be found in what he calls "lower" societies. Such suicides are due to far different causes than those attributed to egoism in highly developed societies.

ALTRUISTIC SUICIDE

Durkheim sought to show that suicides in lower societies are especially prevalent among three classes of people: (1) "men on the threshold of old age or stricken with sickness," (2) women whose husbands have just died, and (3) "followers or servants on the death of their chiefs."[23] Such people commit suicide because they feel it is their duty to do so. Altruism and conformity are the main motives which activate such behavior. Society places an obligation on the individual. "The weight of society is . . . brought to bear on him to lead him to destroy himself."[24]

Such suicides occur because the individual is "almost completely absorbed in the group." That is, the group is integrated to such an extent that each individual has very little value in and of himself. Since the society has no social need for such people, and since they often are a heavy burden on the meager resources of the group, the society requires that the individual kill himself, and the individual altruistically complies. The individual makes a sacrifice of his own life as a gift to his society.

Durkheim noted other forms of altruistic suicides: that performed by individuals in societies where suicide is a praiseworthy act which confers social prestige (e.g., Japanese Hara Kiri), and that performed by individuals dominated by mystical ideas of Nirvana, of renunciation of the physical body and physical world, and of aspirations for communion or reunification with a mystical or spiritual essence.

Altruistic suicide also may be practiced in advanced societies. Durkheim had more "hard" data to rely on here. He chose the suicide rate in the army to illustrate this point. In the army, the suicide rate is higher among officers and non-commissioned officers than among privates, higher among volunteers than among conscripts, and higher among elite troops than among regular troops. Thus, suicide occurs among "those who are most inclined to (an army) career, who are best suited to its needs and are best sheltered from its disadvantages and inconveniences."[25] But these are precisely the soldiers who are best integrated into the army, who feel the greatest sense of duty to it and their country. Such suicides, then, result from very strong ties to the social group with a concurrent weakening of individualistic tendencies. Altruism rather than egoism characterizes the behavior of such individuals.

Durkheim's argument here seems to be the opposite of his previous argument about egoistic suicide. Altruistic suicide varies directly with the degree of integration of the individual in a social group. He recognized that in some groups, the group becomes overintegrated to the point where an individual feels his own life is secondary to the needs or desires of the group. Altruistic suicide occurs among persons who are highly integrated into a group if the group requires their suicide. That is, altruistic suicide occurs in conformity to group pressures to achieve specific goals which are highly valued. Altruistic suicide does not occur in all groups with an extremely high degree of integration, only those whose organization, cultural values and specific goals make it necessary or desirable that some should take their own lives. In such cases, it is precisely those who are most closely integrated (or most expendable) who commit suicide.

This conclusion is much less satisfactory than Durkheim's argument regarding egoistic suicide, and is based on much weaker data. However, Durkheim made an honest effort to explain facts (however poorly supported by adequate research) which seemed to be at variance with his initial theoretical formulation. Altruistic suicide was to him a distinctly different kind of suicide than egoistic suicide, and he did his best, with inadequate data, to explain it.

Some facts still remain to be explained. Durkheim's statistics on the rate of suicide in given nations over a period of years show that the suicide rate increases whenever there is a significant change in economic conditions. This is true of both economic crises and abrupt prosperity. Poverty in itself does not produce this rise in suicide. Generally, the suicide rate is low in countries with high levels of poverty, such as Ireland or Spain. Such increases in the suicide rate occur because any significant change in economic conditions brings about "disturbances of the collective order."[26]

Every society has need for a "moral force" to regulate passions and aspirations. An equilibrium between resources and aspirations must be attained. Regulative norms are institutionalized to perform this function. They generally are accepted without question by members of the society. Such norms are considered "just" by the people involved, and are maintained by custom rather than external force. However, when crises or abrupt changes occur, the stability of the normative system of the society is disturbed. If a financial crisis is involved, many people are not able to meet their traditional expectations. They are prevented from enjoying the level of living to which they are accustomed. If prosperity occurs, those who benefit from the prosperity no longer accept their traditional place in society. Their aspirations arise, yet their demands cannot be met.[27] Even though their lot has improved, their expectations can no longer be fulfilled, and frustration results.

Such a condition was described by Durkheim as a state of normlessness. The individual's activity lacks regulation. "In anomic suicide, society's influence is lacking in the basically individual passions, thus leaving them without a check-rein."[28] Anomie is a state of normlessness, not in the sense that there are no relevant norms to govern behavior, but in the sense that the norms which formerly applied to certain individuals no longer fit their changed position in society. Since the social organization has changed, and since the individual's place in society has changed, the normative system must change too (again a structural argument). But since social organization can change more rapidly than the normative system (another indication of its causal nature), a disequilibrium results until the normative system can be brought back into balance. In the meantime, people's aspirations are unregulated, or poorly regulated, and anomic suicide results.

Durkheim noted the similarity between this type of suicide and egoistic suicide.[29] Both result from social disorganization, and both come about through excessive individualism. Egoistic suicide occurs as a result of loss of social ties, while anomic suicide results from loss of social norms. A Protestant commits suicide (egoistic) not because of a lack of normative teaching but because of a lack of social ties to his religious group. A businessman commits suicide (anomic) when he loses his fortune, not because of fewer ties to wife or family, but because it is too painful to remain in a situation where he cannot meet his social obligations to those with whom he has social relations. The normative expectations applied to him no longer fit his objective situation. Thus while these two types of suicide may be difficult to distinguish in any individual case because they often result from similar social conditions, they still need to be distinguished theoretically.

THE SOCIAL NATURE OF SUICIDE

Up to this point in _Suicide_, Durkheim had presented his classification of the three types of suicide, analyzed a great deal of data, and demonstrated forcefully the effect of social conditions upon the suicide rate. But he felt it necessary to spend a further 110 pages discussing the implications of this analysis. His intention was to make it very clear that suicide is a social rather than a purely individual phenomenon. After all, he was fighting for the establishment of an entire discipline--a discipline to which he was personally committed and of which he was the acknowledged leader in France. His battle was very real and very earnest, for there were many who opposed him. He had to demonstrate, beyond question, the efficacy of his sociological approach to this phenomenon which appeared to be so individualistic.

Durkheim left open to his opponents an area for compromise. He acknowledged that not all aspects of suicide can be explained sociologically.

Each victim gives his act a personal stamp which expresses his temperament, the special conditions in which he is involved, and which, consequently, cannot be explained by the social and general causes of the phenomenon.[36]

Thus suicide might fruitfully be studied psychologically, medically, legally, economically, etc. But this should not deter the sociologist from making his studies of the social nature of suicide.

Durkheim then returned to his major premise: each social group possesses its own tendency toward suicide. This tendency is determined by the conditions of egoism, altruism and anomie currently present in the group. This group tendency toward suicide should be thought of as the cause of the suicide <u>rate</u>. Individuals who commit suicide are strongly influenced by this group tendency, although they seldom recognize it. Since the group rate of suicide is more stable than its membership, which changes constantly, the suicide rate cannot be caused by individualistic causes.

Individuals may blame their suicides on poverty, financial crises, problems with relatives, rejection of lovers, failure to achieve in a chosen vocation, etc. But many who have similar problems do not commit suicide. If the individual is not well integrated into a social group, if his behavior is no longer regulated by relevant norms, then any problem may lead to suicide. If, however, the individual is tied closely to his group, such problems may cause suffering but rarely lead to suicide. It is easy to place the blame on individualistic circumstances. Social causes have such control over individuals that these individuals frequently are totally unaware of their existence, so completely do such causes pervade their lives. It has been well said, the last thing a fish is likely to discover is water. Perhaps the last thing an individual discovers are the social forces impinging upon him. That is why it is important to recognize these social causes and not let individualistic biases hinder our understanding of our behavior.

According to Durkheim, the stability of suicide statistics cannot be accounted for by reference to individuals. Individuals are changeable and malleable; societies are less so. Individuals' lives can be measured in tens of years; the lives of societies must be measured in hundreds of years.

Is it not possible, however, as Durkheim's critics have suggested, that the stability of social phenomena is due to the combined actions of individuals rather than social causes? Durkheim faced this question squarely. Such an argument assumes that the "whole is qualitatively identical with the sum of its parts, that an effect is qualitatively reducible to the sum of its productive causes."[31] Durkheim had rejected this once before in his _Rules_. His argument in _Suicide_ took much the same form.

First, he asserted that social facts are qualitatively different from individual facts. Society is made up of individuals, but it is also made up of material things. Methods of transportation and communication, types of architecture, and technology, are all embodied in material things. Legal and moral precepts and religious dogmas "become fixed externally in a consecrated form."[32] But even more important, the intensity of individual and social phenomena differ. While a social group may have an extremely restrictive set of moral standards, "the morality of the average man is of only moderate intensity."[33] In many ways, the orientation of the group differs markedly from the orientation of the average man or from the great majority of men. Moral facts cannot be attributed to individuals acting individually. Instead, their combination, their association, brings into existence social facts which have an existence _sui generis_.

Second, social facts are external to and constraining on the individual. They are prior in time to the individual--they existed before he was born. They are also prior in authority, constraining the individual to conform to their requirements.

Third, individual characteristics cannot be the cause of social facts because they do not vary together. Individual characteristics, at least those which are suitable to explain social phenomena, are general and immutable. Society changes much more rapidly than human nature, at least that part of human nature which is not formed socially. For individualistic variables to explain social variables, the former would need to vary with the latter, which has not been demonstrated. In fact, Durkheim assumed that individualistic characteristics are constants rather than variables, and could not then be the cause of social facts.[34]

198

In summary, Durkheim forcefully demonstrated that (1) suicide rates are consistent over time, (2) suicide rates differ widely from one group to another, (3) suicide rates vary with social conditions, and (4) no individualistic characteristics can be found which vary with suicide rates. He concluded that the suicide rate depends upon social causes. Sociology may validly study the suicide rate and its social causes without infringing upon the province of any other discipline, since the suicide rate is a social fact with a reality sui generis. The social group has a character which is different from that of the individuals which make up the group. Therefore, the social phenomena which are generated within the group are different from individual phenomena. Durkheim, at least in his own mind, had established sociology as a separate discipline.

THE GROUP POINT OF VIEW

This led Durkheim to the consideration of a further question which has been a point of contention between the advocates of the "group" and "individual" approaches: from whose point of view should social life be studied? Most sociologists previous to Durkheim had taken the point of view of the individual--the actor. Spencer and most of the evolutionists, Toennies, Simmel, Ward and Giddings, among others, took this point of view.

Durkheim believed that the only way to establish sociology as a separate discipline was to look at the behavior of man from a point of view different from that of other sciences, especially psychology. Since he believed that social phenomena are qualitatively different from those of psychology, they can only be studied with a different methodology. In the Rules of Sociological Method, he enunciated one of his cardinal methodological rules.

> When . . . the sociologist undertakes the investigation of some order of social facts, he must endeavor to consider them from an aspect that is independent of their individual manifestations.[35]

Social principles cannot be discovered, according to Durkheim, by studying "individual manifestations." Since the group is different from the individuals who compose it, a study of individuals will not yield reliable information about the nature of the social group. A study of motives for committing suicide, for example, gives the sociologist no information about the different rates of suicide among different groups, or about the stability of the suicide rate. Durkheim therefore criticized those who take the individual as the starting point of an investigation of social phenomena. He argued that "every time that a social phenomenon is directly explained by a psychological phenomenon, we may be sure that the explanation is false."[36]

What data are available for sociological investigation? Durkheim's answer to this question can best be seen by a look at his own studies. In Suicide, as we have shown, Durkheim took as his major dependent variable the suicide rate of a particular group at a particular time period. Social integration, as the major independent variable, was a most significant choice. As we have pointed out earlier, integration is clearly a "social" variable, since integration is achieved only through the coordination of the many individual units which make up the group. One cannot speak of the integration of a single unit, only of a multiplicity of units.

In the Division of Labor, Durkheim focused on another purely group phenomenon--the division of labor. Such a variable, like integration, is a property of a group, not an individual. While an individual may be specialized, only a group can possess a differentiated and coordinated division of labor. Durkheim further explained that different types of societies have different degrees of labor. These differences are due to the influence of group variables, such as physical and dynamic density.

In his study of religion Durkheim analyzed group beliefs and rituals. He viewed the development of both beliefs and rituals as a purely sociological phenomenon, since religion serves the functional needs of the society for integration, manipulation of the social environment, etc. One cannot understand religion as being due to individualistic attitudes or to any "natural" inclination of individuals to believe in the supernatural. Society creates religion because society needs religion. Religion serves social ends, and can best be studied through an analysis of group phenomena rather than individual attitudes.

200

In his studies of morality, education and economics[37] he consistently looked to institutionalized practices, normative rules, and the social organization of the group as the major indicators of social phenomena. Legal rules embodied in a written code, economic practices embodied in institutionalized role definitions and normative practices--all are examples of the social facts which are the objects of sociological analysis. Durkheim followed his own rule. He consistently rejected the point of view of the individual manifestation, choosing instead to focus his studies on group, i.e., social phenomena.

THE ROLE OF INDIVIDUALS IN SOCIAL LIFE

One might conclude from the foregoing discussion that Durkheim was a strict sociological determinist, and that he did not leave a place in his sociological orientation for individual choice and initiative. Many sociologists have interpreted Durkheim in essentially this way. During his lifetime, Durkheim was frequently criticized for his alleged sociological determinism and his rejection of individual influences upon social life. He found it necessary on several occasions to explain his stand. At such times he consistently took a nondeterministic point of view with regard to the individual. In many of his less-well-read works, he developed cogent arguments concerning the relationship of the individual to the social group.

In his book, Education and Sociology,[38] Durkheim recognized that all individuals have "innate predispositions." But he questioned whether people have any instincts which are deterministic of behavior. He argued that what innate predispositions people have are general and flexible. They do not predispose humans to any one kind of behavior. Unlike animals dominated by instinct, human beings are relatively free to choose many kinds of behavior within the broad limits set by their physical constitution.

> To say that innate characteristics are for the most part very general, is to say they are very malleable, very flexible, since they can assume very different forms.[39]

The child enters the world with few predetermined behaviors and with a great capability to adapt to a variety of socially prescribed conditions. The purpose of socialization and formal education is to make the child into a social being, to teach him the culture of his group and fit him into his proper place in social life. Customs, patterns of behavior, attitudes and values must be taught the child to enable him to live happily with others.

This theme was further developed in Durkheim's Moral Education.[40] Here he recognized that the individual is not totally passive in his behavior. He does not automatically conform to the pressures of social norms or other deterministic feathers of the social world. Instead, he individualizes the social facts. He interprets them, and in so doing, gives them his own individualistic form and interpretation. Rather than simply being acted upon, he reacts back on society. In short, he acts like a conscious, willing, choosing being in his relations to other people and to social conditions.

No society, however well integrated, has a perfectly consistent set of normative rules which can be perfectly followed by all individuals. Further, according to Durkheim, there are no general rules of morality which apply to all situations. For Durkheim, morality "consists in an infinity of special rules, fixed and specific, which order man's conduct in those different situations in which he finds himself most frequently."[41] The individual must be aware of the "infinity" of rules which society promulgates to govern behavior. Further, the individual is usually confronted with conflicting or ill-defined expectations of behavior. Conflicting alternatives are presented to him from which he must choose the most appropriate (and moral) behavior. Every society allows the individual some choice in bringing his behavior into conformity with the normative expectations of the group.

One of Durkheim's strongest statements on individualism was developed in his discussion of "autonomy" in Moral Education. His argument here is intriguing. He posed the hypothetical situation: suppose that we are omniscient in regard to the physical world. We have an idea about everything in the physical world.[42] Once we understand the world in this manner, we understand the laws which govern it. We understand the reasons for everything. "Hence . . . we can conform, not simply because we are physically restrained and unable to do otherwise without danger, but because we deem it good and have no better alternative."[43] While Durkheim admitted that such total knowledge is not possible for us, the principle still remains the same: as we increase in knowledge, we become more autonomous. Our greater autonomy leads us to great conformity to the laws of nature--to greater harmony with "the nature of things."[44]

Likewise with the social world, as we increase in our knowledge of the social world through social science, we gain greater mastery and control over social phenomena. We have more power to act, rather than to remain passively to be acted upon--we become more autonomous. But our mastery over the social world should also lead us to recognize that we must bring our individual choices in line with the workings of social causes. We must use social forces rather than oppose them. Things are as they are because of the influence of sociological laws, and changing things can only bring disharmony with nature. Thus our greater knowledge leads us to greater submission to the laws of nature. Our freedom and autonomy lead us to conformity.

If, perhaps, pathological or abnormal conditions occur, we certainly can act, using our knowledge of the laws of nature, to bring conditions back to normal. We can act upon our world as well as submitting ourselves to it. But such actions are in reality in conformity with the natural laws of society. Autonomy, rather than being antithetical to conformity to moral precepts, leads us to greater conformity.

This discussion led Durkheim to a conclusion about what society must do to educate its members to act morally.

> To act morally . . . we must have knowledge, as clear and complete an awareness as possible of the reasons for our conduct. . . . (T)he rule prescribing (our) behavior must be freely desired, that is to say, freely accepted. . . . This explains the place we accord the teaching of morality in our schools. For to teach morality is neither to preach nor to indoctrinate; it is to explain.[45]

In <u>Moral Education</u>, Durkheim pleaded forcefully for the necessity of greater individualism. An individual should have greater freedom of thought and action. Human dignity must be recognized and extended. A greater part of social behavior (especially education) must be based on rationally developed principles. This must be done by changing social relations to bring them into adjustment with individualism. Individualism is not achieved by freeing the individual from social relations, but by freeing him from unjust discipline and other harmful restraints. According to Durkheim, individualism is achieved by inculcating a secular morality, based on reason rather than revelation. Such a moral system maintains rules and sanctions, but such are used to direct the individual toward greater use of reason--to give greater dignity and social justice to the individual.[46]

> Individuals, while conforming, must take account of what they are doing; and their conformity must not be pushed to the point where it completely captures intelligence. Thus, it does not follow from a belief in the need for discipline that discipline must involve blind and slavish submission.[47]

One can make a strong case that Durkheim was a champion of individual initiative. He recognized the strong influences of the social group, and felt that their influences were generally for the well-being of society. But the individual must also be accorded an important place in society. He must have some freedom to develop autonomy and independence. He must exercise self-control through intelligence and reason, rather than having his behavior constantly and thoroughly controlled by the group.

The group must have a certain amount of stability in order to survive, but it also must maintain flexibility to adjust to new conditions. Only through individual differences can change be introduced which allows the society to react flexibly to new conditions. In both his writings and his life, Durkheim exhibited a moral regard for both the freedom of the individual and the beneficial influence of the social group.

INDIVIDUALISM AS A RESULT OF THE DIVISION OF LABOR

The preceding discussion allows us to gain new perspective on Durkheim's first great work, The Division of Labor in Society. This work was originally conceived as an analysis of the relationship of the individual to society. Durkheim posed this question: "Why does the individual, while becoming more autonomous, depend more upon society? How can he be at once more individual and more solidary?"[48] Durkheim found the answer to this question in the increasing division of labor. Only a social factor which varies directly with the increase of individualism in society can be the cause of such an increase. Both individualism and an increasing division of labor gradually increase throughout the course of history.

Durkheim distinguished two different types of societies, based on their degree of division of labor. The first type, found in primitive societies, is characterized as having mechanical solidarity. The second type is prevalent in advanced societies, and is characterized by organic solidarity.

Durkheim tied this definition of types of societies to a discussion of individualism. And in his characteristic fashion, he could not discuss a subject without first defining it. The definition of individualism was, for Durkheim, quite simple. Individualism involves "how much of our own individual qualities we have, what distinguishes us from others."[49] That is, we are individuals to the extent to which we are different. If we are easily distinguishable from others, then individualism exits.

In a mechanical society, individualism is severely limited. Such a society is a homogenous one, in which individuals closely resemble each other, not only in physical type but in occupation, standard of living, daily tasks, behavior and personality. However, as society progresses and the division of labor proceeds, individualism also develops. Each individual must become occupationally specialized in order to compete successfully in a highly developed society. Occupational specialization, of course, brings with it other individual differences in both behavior and outlook. Durkheim recognized that it was socially imperative that the individual be granted some freedom and initiative in order that specialization could be accomplished.[50] Individuality results from the social need for occupational specialization. The society leaves it to the individual, in fact makes it incumbent upon him, to develop his own individuality <u>in the sphere of specialization of function</u>. The greater complexity of society which comes from a highly

205

developed division of labor makes individual differences both desirable and inevitable.

In many ways, this argument is similar to Durkheim's discussion of the influence of social conditions upon suicide rates. Here, Durkheim treated individualism as a sociological variable. Individualism is a characteristic found in every social group. It is a variable. Groups differ widely in the extent to which they grant individualism to their members. Most importantly, individualism varies with other social conditions, such as economic development and the division of labor. One can treat individualism as a sociological variable and calculate the rate of individualism in each group. The rate of individualism will in turn be correlated with the degree of division of labor and other sociological characteristics found in the group.

This does not mean that individual behavior can be predicted. Sociologically, Durkheim was able to predict the rate of suicide of a given group, but not which individuals would commit suicide. Here, Durkheim seemed to be saying that it is possible to predict sociologically the rate of individualism without a concurrent prediction of each individual act. Just as a "suicidogenetic current" does not determine which individual will commit suicide, an "individualistic" tendency in a particular group does not determine precisely how each individual will act. It is left to the individual to choose how he will specialize in order to compete occupationally. Likewise, he is able to choose within limits a great many other individualistic behaviors which cannot be predicted from a knowledge of sociological principles. The sociological investigator is able to predict the rate of individualism in a group but not specific acts of individual behavior. Individual behavior may be explainable through psychological or biological principles, but may not be predicted from sociological generalizations.

SOCIOLOGICAL LAWS AND DETERMINISM

Durkheim believed strongly in the presence of natural laws governing social life. He was a "realist" in the sense that he believed sociological laws were not mere theoretical constructs but existed "in reality." Much of his work was devoted to identifying and describing the uniformities in social life and the

206

sociological laws which produced these uniformities. His study of <u>Suicide</u> is one of the most successful of such enterprises in all sociological literature.

However, Durkheim did not believe that the existence of such sociological laws strictly determined individual behavior. Just because statistics show a consistency in social behavior, one should not conclude that people are not free or that they do not have free will. While social facts do have an influence on the individual, he is able to act for himself and exert a personal force in opposition to the social tendencies which impinge upon him.[51]

In fact, according to Durkheim, the assertion that social facts influence the behavior of individuals is less deterministic than the more common assertion that individuals produce social phenomena. If one tried to explain social uniformities from an individualistic point of view, he would be forced to revert to factors inherent in the individual's constitution, which would lead to the "strictest determinism." Social uniformities which result from external social facts do not:

> determine one individual rather than another. (A social fact) exacts a definite number of certain kinds of actions, but not that they should be performed by this or that person. It may be granted that some people resist the force and that it has its way with others. Actually, our conception merely adds to physical, chemical, biological and psychological forces, social forces which like these act upon men from without. If the former do not preclude human freedom, the latter need not. . . . When an epidemic center appears, its intensity predetermines the rate of mortality it will cause, but those who will be infected are not designated by this fact. Such is the situation of victims of suicide with reference to suicidogenetic currents.[52]

Durkheim's determinism was a determinism of a limited nature. Social facts determine other social facts. Social facts have variable but usually great influence on individuals. But such social facts do not strictly determine the behavior of each individual. Social facts determine that one group will have a higher suicide rate than another, but do not determine which individuals in the group will turn to suicide. Thus Durkheim opted for a limited conception of both determinism and individualism. Determinism operates within the sphere of social facts. But where individuals are concerned, individualistic and deterministic tendencies are both operative, and tend to limit each other.

FOOTNOTES

[1]Emile Durkheim, The Rules of Sociological Method (Glencoe: Free Press), 1950.

[2]Ibid., p. 13.

[3]Emile Durkheim, Moral Education (New York: Free Press), 1961.

[4]Rules, pp. 5-6.

[5]Ibid., p. 4.

[6]Emile Durkheim, Suicide (Glencoe: Free Press), 1951.

[7]Ibid., pp. 47-49.

[8]Ibid., p. 50.

[9]Ibid., p. 46.

[10]Loc. cit.

[11]Ibid., pp. 57-81.

[12]Ibid., p. 72.

[13]Ibid., p. 73.

[14]Ibid., p. 157.

[15]Ibid., p. 158.

[16]Ibid., p. 159.

[17]Ibid., pp. 197-202.

[18]Ibid., pp. 202-208.

[19]Ibid., p. 209.

[20]Loc. cit.

[21]Ibid., pp. 209-216.

[22]Emile Durkheim, The Division of Labor in Society (New York: Free Press), 1933. It should be noted here that this is a structural argument, as discussed more fully in Chapter Three.

[23]Suicide, p. 219.

[24]Loc. cit.

[25]Ibid., p. 233.

[26]Ibid., p. 246.

[27]Ibid., p. 253.

[28]Ibid., p. 258.

[29]Loc. cit.

[30]Ibid., pp. 277-278. See also p. 294.

[31]Ibid., p. 311.

[32]Ibid., p. 314.

[33]Ibid., p. 317.

[34]See Harry Alpert, Emile Durkheim and His Sociology (New York: Columbia University Press), 1939, and Harry Alpert, "Explaining the Social Socially," Social Forces, 17 (March 1939), pp. 361-365; and "Emile Durkheim: Enemy of Fixed Psychological Elements," American Journal of Sociology, 62 (May 1958), pp. 662-664.

[35]Rules, p. 45.

[36]Ibid., p. 104.

[37]Emile Durkheim, Education and Sociology (Glencoe: Free Press), 1956; Moral Education (New York: Free Press), 1961; Professional Ethics and Civic Morals (Glencoe: Free Press), 1958; Socialism and Saint-Simon (New York: Antioch Press), 1958; and Journal Sociologique (Paris: Presses Universitaires de France), 1969.

[38]Op. Cit.

[39]Ibid., p. 84.

[40]Op. Cit.

[41]Ibid., p. 25.

[42]Ibid., p. 114.

[43]Ibid., p. 115.

[44]Loc. cit.

[45]Ibid., p. 120.

[46]Ibid., especially p. 12.

[47]Ibid., p. 52.

[48]Division of Labor, p. 37.

[49]Ibid., p. 129.

[50]Ibid., pp. 129-131, 403-404.

[51]Suicide, p. 325.

[52]Ibid., p. 325.

CHAPTER ELEVEN

THE GROUP AND THE INDIVIDUAL IN CLASSICAL SOCIOLOGY
COMTE, MARX, and SPENCER

In this chapter we examine the works of three classical sociological theorists--Comte, Marx and Spencer--to see how they approached the issue of the group vs. the individual. Comte's orientation was positivistic. He achieved a statement of the necessity for the scientific study of social life which is amazingly relevant to contemporary sociological concerns. Marx's orientation is essentially deterministic, with a strong emphasis on the influence of the group upon individual behavior. However, one also finds a growing awareness in later Marxian writings of the importance of individual initiative in the process of history. Finally, Spencer was the champion of individualism during the latter part of the 19th century. He provided many of the important political and philosophical foundations which even today underlie American thinking. Yet his sociological writings--as opposed to his political writings--provide strong support for a "group" or "collectivist" orientation in sociological theory. We turn now to an examination of each of these separate threads in the fabric of sociological theory.

AUGUSTE COMTE AND THE DEVELOPMENT OF POSITIVISM

Auguste Comte, more than any other man, was responsible for establishing sociology as a scientific discipline. He enunciated the important principles of scientific method which he believed must be applied to the study of social phenomena. Further, it was he who by his brilliance and perseverence forced the intellectual world to consider and come to terms with the claims for scientific independence of this new field of study.

In Comte's works, especially in the first two chapters of his <u>Philosophie Positive</u>,[1] can be found the fundamental principles of scientific method and their applicability to social phenomena. Most of these principles have since been incorporated into the body of philosophical, theoretical and methodological assumptions by which sociologists order their professional lives. Many of these principles of positivism are so basic to the contemporary scientific orientation of sociology that we believe it would be profitable to list them first before discussing them.

Fundamental Principles of Positivism

The fundamental principles of positivism which Comte enunciated may be summarized as follows:

1. Each scientific discipline and each individual develops intellectually through three stages: (1) theological, (2) metaphysical, and (3) positive.[2]

2. The positive or scientific orientation is the culmination of a development process, and supplants speculative and "spiritualistic" interpretations of the nature of the world.[3]

3. Sociology, or the study of social phenomena, must become and is now (1830) becoming positivistically oriented.[4]

4. Only through the application of positive methods can accurate information and explanation be obtained regarding social phenomena.

5. The fundamental object of sociology is to discover the laws of social phenomena.[5]

6. The laws of social phenomena do not refer to "ultimate causes," but to "invariable relations of succession and likeness."[6]

7. Laws may be discovered and established only through empirical observation.[7]

8. Introspection or "inner observation" is not an objective nor effective method of arriving at empirical laws.[8]

9. A body of scientific laws is arrived at through the process of induction rather than deduction.[9]

10. Through induction and synthesis, the number of laws is reduced to the "least possible number"--parsimony is the goal of scientific explanation.[10]

212

11. The gathering of facts through observation, and their explanation through the use of theory, are mutually dependent. There is a reciprocal relationship between theory and fact.[11]

12. As a scientific discipline develops, it should and does pursue "pure" rather than practical research. "Abstract" principles are more fundamental than "concrete" principles.[12]

13. The simplest phenomena are also the most general, and should be studied first.[13]

14. Each scientific discipline is moving towards greater and greater specialization.[14]

15. Despite this increasing differentiation, there is a fundamental unity of the sciences.[15]

16. One special science is needed to study the similarities among the sciences. This special science is sociology. Sociology, therefore, has two separate but reciprocal provinces: (a) to study social phenomena scientifically, and (b) to develop generalizations tying together all sciences.[16]

17. No single principle or law which attempts to explain all phenomena is possible. Monism must be rejected in favor of a parsimonious but multiple-causal theoretical system.[17]

18. Social phenomena cannot be ultimately reduced to physiological phenomena; they are essentially different and more complex in character.[18]

19. The study of all living beings may be classified under two main headings: statics and dynamics.[19]

20. As a discipline becomes more scientific, it achieves greater precision and coordination through the use of quantification and mathematical analysis.[20]

21. Once knowledge of the world has been gained through the scientific method this knowledge should be used to improve the world. Knowledge of social laws should be used to reorganize society and education.[21]

The above principles of positivism are so

important (and so well stated) that Comte's introductory chapters to Philosophie Positive deserve to be much more frequently read than is currently the case among sociologists. Books have been written about each of these principles. In the space which we have available to us here, it is possible to discuss only the most pertinent and important of these principles.

Sociology as a Scientific Discipline

Comte began his discussion of positive philosophy by asserting that he had discovered the "law of three stages." Every discipline develops through three stages--the theological, the metaphysical, and the positive. In the theological stage, events are explained through the workings of supernatural agents. Here, one seeks for "the inner nature" of things, for "first and final causes."[22] The metaphysical stage is a transitional one. Supernatural agents "are replaced by abstract forces," that is by "Nature." One still seeks ultimate causes and the "essence" of things.

The positive or scientific stage is achieved only after the other two stages have been passed. Here, people give up the search for ultimate truths and final causes. They seek instead to explain occurrences in terms of "laws." Causation is of a more limited sort. If a regularized event (cause) is always followed by another regularized event (effect) a law is said to exist. There must be a similarity in all of the events which are classified as causes, and in those which are classified as effects. Further, the effect must follow successively from the cause. Comte treated a law as invariable: the effect always follows the occurrence of the cause.

Sociology, like every other scientific discipline, must pass through each of these stages. In the past, people explained the workings of social phenomena and the behavior of individuals as being due to, first, supernatural influences, and second, "natural" or metaphysical forces. Now, such explanations must be seen to be false. Instead, investigators must seek to explain social phenomena through observation--that is, through the use of the scientific method. Facts regarding the actions of people must be collected and analyzed. Scientific laws must be developed which incorporate these facts and explain them.

Observation vs. Introspection

The ultimate goal of any science, including sociology, is the discovery of a parsimonious system of laws by which all phenomena (in any given discipline) may be explained. Such a system of laws can only be discovered inductively. People have tried for centuries to discover such laws through reason. Comte argued that this has only led to confusion and multiplication of possible explanations. He challenged those who advocate either reason or introspection as the methods of discovering laws to point to any one law which has been discovered and verified using these methods.

Comte referred to the method of "illusory psychology" which "claims that it can discover the fundamental laws of the human mind by contemplating it in itself, without paying any attention either to the causes or the effects of its activity."[23] Introspection, according to Comte, must be rejected. It is impossible through introspection to rid one's mind of subjective elements and to observe objectively these "internal" elements in one's mind. Introspection "gives rise to almost as many divergent opinions as there are so-called observers"[24] because no individual's introspective experience is subject to corroboration through similar observations by a second observer. Observers cannot agree because they cannot observe the same (internal) phenomena.[25]

Sociology as a Generalizing Science

Comte observed that there is an increasing tendency for each science and each scientist to become more specialized and differentiated. This is necessary because of the rapid growth of knowledge and the difficulty of anyone gaining proficiency in more than one specialized area. This specialization, however, has a serious drawback. Scientists who are narrowly specialized fail to see the relationship of the facts they are studying to other facts observed by other scientists.

In order to overcome this difficulty, Comte argued that there needs to be one specialized discipline whose task it is to synthesize and generalize facts derived from all the other specialized sciences. This discipline is sociology.

215

It would be (sociology's) function to
determine exactly the character of each
science, to discover the relations and
concatenations of the sciences and to reduce,
if possible, all their chief principles to
the smallest number of common principles,
while always conforming to the fundamental
maxims of the Positive Method.[26]

All scientists would receive training in these general
principles discovered by sociologists, as well as in
the specific principles of the science of their
choosing. Comte was not completely consistent in his
discussion of this point. He implied that sociology
(generally encompassing all the social sciences) must
be specialized toward the study of social phenomena.
At the same time, a special branch of scientific
endeavor, also labelled sociology, must study the
relations among all the sciences.

Comte did not make it clear why this specialized
and generalizing science is not also distinct from
sociology. By extrapolation, one may argue that social
phenomena are more complex than other kinds of
phenomena, and that other kinds of phenomena
(astronomical, physical, chemical, and biological) are
included in the social. Since social phenomena include
all other phenomena, it follows that sociologists are
the most natural persons to study the general laws
which tie together all phenomena.

The Unity of Science

Comte believed that there is an essential unity of
all phenomena, resulting in a unity of all sciences.

The divisions which we establish between the
sciences, although not arbitrary, as some
people suppose, are yet essentially
artificial. In reality, the subject of all
our researches is one; we only divide it so
that we may, by separating the difficulties,
resolve them more easily.[27]

This does not mean, however, that the phenomena of each
discipline are identical to those of other disciplines,
or reducible to these other disciplines. Comte clearly
argued that sociological phenomena are qualitatively
different from those of physiology or other sciences.
One cannot explain the behavior of humans by reference

to physiological processes. While each scientist should seek for bridges between the various sciences (and Comte clearly believed that such bridges are present), he must not seek to reduce all phenomena to a single principle.

Comte rejected monism. "It is my deep personal conviction that these attempts at the universal explanation of all phenomena by a single law are highly chimerical. . . ."[28] The world is too complicated to be reduced to a single law. Even if a single law could be developed, Comte believed that few advantages would be achieved by possessing such a law.[29]

The unity found in science is a unity of <u>method</u>. The approach and attitude of mind which each discipline takes to its data must be the same.

> The only indispensable unity . . . is that of Method, which can and evidently must exist, and is already largely established. As to the Doctrine, it is not necessary that it should be <u>unified</u>; it is sufficient if it be <u>homogeneous</u>.[30]

Comte did not explain what he meant by homogeneous, but the implication is that the <u>relative</u> similarity of phenomena leads to a relative similarity in theoretical or "doctrinal" propositions. A homogeneous body of propositions could then be tied together by a parsimonious set of general propositions which would bind all the sciences together into a unified whole.

Quantification

Finally, Comte saw clearly that quantification is an important accompaniment of the development of science. He noted that those sciences which have achieved the greatest development are the same sciences which most fully use mathematics. Mathematics can be utilized both as a means of expressing abstract relationships in formula form and as a methodological means of description and hypothesis testing.

In order for the social sciences to gain the same scientific development, Comte believed it is necessary for them to gain increasing proficiency in the application of mathematics to social phenomena. Quantification in the social sciences should be pursued with vigor. While Comte recognized some differences

217

between social and physical phenomena, these differences were not such as to limit the use of quantitative methods in the study of social phenomena.

Mathematics is not a separate scientific discipline, but rather the basis of all of the sciences. Every well-educated scientist, no matter in which discipline he chooses to specialize, must receive a grounding in mathematics. A major portion of Comte's Cours en Philosophie Positive was devoted to the application of mathematics to the study of natural phenomena, including social phenomena.

A great many of Comte's most important ideas have been incorporated into contemporary sociology. His influence is clearly seen in the works of positivist George Lundberg and in many of the methodological practices of contemporary researchers. There are certainly sociological theorists--most notable Max Weber--who have developed theoretical orientations opposed to that presented here. However, contemporary sociology has developed along the lines Comte suggested, and many of his fundamental principles have become basic tenets of contemporary sociology, as we shall see presently.

Comte did not come to grips as well as many later theorists with the relationship between the group and the individual. The importance of Comte's positivism here is that it sets the stage for the major intellectual battles in more recent times over the related questions of deterministic social laws and the freedom of the individual to influence social life.

MARX AND ENGELS:
DOES THE INDIVIDUAL MAKE HISTORY?

The question of the relation of the individual to the group is much more clearly raised in the works of Marx and Engels. Perhaps one of the most widely debated points in interpretation of Marxian theory is the relationship of the individual to the events of history. Some argue that Marx was a strict determinist: history follows certain laws which are deterministic; the course of history is inevitable, and man cannot change this course. Others see in Marxian theory an emphasis on the individual. They argue that Marxism is essentially a humanistic theory which is highly critical of capitalism for seeking to destroy human individuality. People can revolt against their

218

social conditions. In a revolution, the actions of individual people are often the deciding factor in the success or failure of the revolution.

There is ample evidence in Marxist literature to support either interpretation. Both interpretations have strong supporters, and each position can be justified by quotations from Marx's writings. Let us examine each of these interpretations.

Marxism as Determinism

Marxism has usually been interpreted in a deterministic way, especially in the United States. From this perspective, Marx's main goal was to discover the essential social laws of human behavior.[31] Within a given historical epoch, a set of social laws operates to govern social life.[32] History is a process conformable to equally certain social laws--it follows the dialectic. There is a natural contradiction between the forces of production and the relations of production which produces change and revolution. Such changes are inevitable, and take place irrespective of the will of individual people.

Human beings cannot change the course of history, because social laws operate independently of individual will. Much of Marx's writing was devoted to an analysis of these social laws, especially those governing capitalism. In such writings, little place is given to individual initiative.

In his book, <u>Ludwig Feuerbach</u>, written after Marx's death, Engels detailed this point of view more specifically.

> . . . each person follows his own consciously desired end, and it is precisely the resultant of these many wills operating in different directions and of their manifold effects upon the outer world that constitute history . . . the many individual wills active in history for the most part produce results quite other than those they intended--often quite the opposite: their motives therefore in relation to the total result are likewise only of secondary significance. On the other hand, the further question arises: what driving forces in turn stand behind these motives? What are the

historical causes which translate themselves into these motives in the brains of these actors? Answer: production.[33]

In this passage, Engels took a point of view much like Durkheim's. He assumed the existence of the individual as an acting, willing entity. But the results of the individual acts and wills do not add up to history, and history does not follow the rational or emotional desires of human beings. It is conformable to its own laws, specifically, those governing the economic conditions of the time and the conflict between the forces and relations of production in that era.

Marx rejected the "great man" theory of history. Rather than seeing the French Revolution as the history of the actions of Napoleon and other great men, he believed it was necessary to grasp the broad principles operating in history. Groups with different economic interests are in a struggle with each other. Such group interests, together with the state of the society's institutions (economy, government, religion, etc.) are the real forces of history. Engels even went so far as to argue that any "great man" could and would have been replaced in history. History would have developed in the same way irrespective of the people who acted upon the stage of history.

> That a certain particular man, and no other emerges at a definite time in a given country is naturally pure chance. But even if we eliminate him, there is always a need for a substitute, and the substitute is found tant bien que mal; in the long run he is sure to be found. That Napoleon--this particular Corsican--should have been the military dictator made necessary by the exhausting wars of the French Republic--that was a matter of chance. But in default of a Napoleon, another would have filled his place; that is established by the fact that whenever a man was necessary he has always been found: Caesar, Augustus, Cromwell.[34]

It is easy to point to instances in science where a monumental discovery was made by a brilliant scientist. But just as often, one can find other people who made the same discovery independently, or who were on the verge of making it. Engels seems to be

220

arguing that, given the social conditions in France in the early 19th century, many people as well as Napoleon could have accomplished the same thing. The revolution in England would have been accomplished with someone else as leader if Cromwell had not been on the scene.

Determinism and Alienation

In some of their earlier writings, most notably the Economic and Philosophical Manuscripts of 1844 and The German Ideology,[35] Marx and Engels built upon Hegel's notion of alienation and developed their own theory on this subject. Marx's later writings, especially Capital,[36] detailed the manner in which capitalistic production produces alienation. The German word entfremdung (Marx also used the words entausserung and verausserung) has been translated variously as "alienation," "estrangement" and "self-estrangement." The German word fremd means stranger. "Entfremdung is the activity or process by which someone becomes a stranger to himself." Alienation involves a separation of the person from his real self.[37]

In The German Ideology, Marx argued that originally the laborer was paid with the fruits of his labor. However, as a money economy developed, the laborer increasingly received money for his labor rather than goods. He was thus cut off from the fruits of his own labor. This separation of the individual from what he produces is the essence of alienation. Marx spoke of alienation in several other ways. First, man becomes alienated when he seeks for his own personal interest in a competitive struggle against other laborers, rather than seeking the common good of all laborers. Such a person is alienated or separated from his "real" self and his "real" interests. Man is estranged from other men. Second, the development of classes brings about an estrangement between classes. This is the main and fundamental separation under capitalism. Third, the power of the bourgeoisie over the proletariat brings an estrangement. Marx wrote of this as an "alien force existing outside them" which is viewed by the worker as exploitative.[38] The worker by being forced to do things he would not have chosen voluntarily is alienated from his true nature.

Alienation, then, is a variable found in a number of specific social situations. Marx did not speak of alienation as a psychological variable as is frequently

221

done today. For Marx, alienation was a structural variable which in turn is reflected in the minds of human beings. The essence of alienation is social, not psychological--man becomes alienated in the psychological sense precisely because he is first alienated in a social (or structural) sense.[39]

One may interpret this argument in several ways. It certainly shows Marx's keen interest in the individual and the way in which society has done harm to the individual nature. But the cause of alienation lies outside the individual. The individual cannot escape his alienation simply by taking thought. He is acted upon but has little room to act himself.

Marxism as Individualistic

There is an equally valid interpretation of Marxism which stresses Marx's emphasis on individualism rather than his determinism. While this interpretation is not as frequently advocated as its opposite, it has equally persuasive supporters.[40]

In The German Ideology, Marx began by recognizing that the first premise of all social life is the existence of the individual.[41] Throughout this work, Marx was concerned about the individual and his place in society. He rejected the notions of social contract and of the "pure" individual alluded to by many writers of his time. However, he did recognize that the individual personality is not totally shaped by the social conditions of his existence.

In Marx's discussion of alienation, he observed that there is "a division within the life of each individual, in so far as it is personal and in so far as it is determined by some branch of labour and the conditions pertaining to it."[42] The "personal" individual seems to refer to the characteristics and behavior of the individual which are not socially determined. Marx spoke of this part of the individual as relatively free--able to act "individualistically." The other part of the individual--and he never discussed how large a part this is--is "determined" by his social and economic conditions.

Marx took care to note that man's individuality is becoming more and more restricted, that the worker under capitalism has less individuality than he had under feudalism.[43] Thus, the influence of social

222

(especially economic) conditions on human behavior is variable, but increasing. Once the communist revolution took place, however, the assertion was clearly made that the individual would be much more free to determine his own behavior without social constraints.

Marx felt it is not possible to detail completely the social conditions to be expected under pure communism--these are subject to observation, not prophecy. But he did argue that under pure communism people will be able to decide their own fate. Rather than being alienated, they will be whole persons. Social conditions will be subject to their decisions, and men and women will act rather than merely be acted upon. This assertion was most clearly stated by Engels.

> The laws of (man's) social activity, which have hitherto confronted him as external, dominating laws of nature, will then be applied by man with complete understanding, and hence will be dominated by man. Men's own social organization, which has hitherto stood in opposition to them as if arbitrarily decreed by nature and history, will then become the voluntary act of men themselves. The objective, external forces which have hitherto dominated history, will then pass under the control of men themselves. It is only from this point that men, with full consciousness, will fashion their own history. . . .[44]

The relationship between the group and the individual is a variable, not a constant. In certain historical periods, social conditions deprive people of control over their own fate. Their decisions and actions have little if any effect on social conditions or even the course of their own lives. But people can revolt (if the conditions are right) and change the nature of their social world. New social conditions can be created which will allow humans to act individualistically to govern their own lives. In other words, some social conditions are conducive to individual behavior and development, others are not. The relationship of the individual to the group is complex and changeable, and one cannot make any generalization about this subject that applies to all cases and all historical stages.

223

Marx's view of social laws as deterministic is also informative. Especially in his later works, Marx came to recognize that the alleged inevitability of the proletarian revolution would not allow him to predict exactly when the revolution would take place. He felt certain it would take place, but many factors, including individual behavior, would influence when and how the revolution would occur.

> World history would indeed be a very easy thing to make were the struggle to be carried on only under conditions of unfailingly favorable chances. Its nature would have to be of a very mystical kind if "accidents" played no role. These accidents naturally fall within the general path of development and are compensated by other accidents. But the acceleration and retardation of events are very largely dependent upon such "accidents" among which must be reckoned the character of the people who stand at the head of the movement.[45]

"Accidents," or the working of chance, are operative in history. This does not preclude the existence of social laws, but it does mean that social laws are not totally deterministic. Chance events may influence the course of events, and in particular, may speed up or slow down the natural changes in society.

In his more journalistic writings, especially those which sought to analyze a given event--The Class Struggle in France, The 18th Brumaire, The Civil War in France--Marx frequently concerned himself with the actions of particular individuals. Such writings show clearly that Marx did concede to the individual a great ability to affect the course of history. It is unquestionable that Marx saw himself in this light--as a genius who by his own actions could change the course of history.

In summary, one can interpret Marxian theory either as being strictly deterministic or as allowing an important place for individual action in influencing the course of history. While the deterministic interpretation is the most frequently used, either interpretation can be amply supported from a resort to Marxian literature. Like all people whose writings span a period of 40 years, Marx was not completely consistent. His major desire was to show the effect of economic conditions on the life of human beings. There is no question that he made this point strongly and effectively, and that since his time it has been impossible to ignore economic influences. Still, Marx seems to have left in his theory an important place for individual initiative and action.

HERBERT SPENCER ON INDIVIDUALISM VS. DETERMINISM

Herbert Spencer has often been identified as the leading exponent of individualism in the 19th century. His evolutionary theories and the political doctrines which were derived from them have consistently been used to support a rather extreme form of laissez-faire individualism. Spencer placed great emphasis upon the individual and advocated political doctrines designed to strengthen the individual against the encroachments of government and other social groups.

However, the relationship between the individual and the group was much more complex in Spencer's mind than the usual simplistic interpretations of his theories would lead us to believe. What has become fixed in the popular mind is a notion of Spencer as a political exponent of laissez-faire capitalism and unrestrained individualism. What has generally been forgotten is that Spencer developed some of the most important early arguments in support of sociological analysis, in which considerations of individual behavior were subordinated to considerations of the effects of collective action.

One needs to separate Spencer's writings and consider the various purposes which he had in mind in writing them. In this section, we will consider separately Spencer's thought under the following topics: (1) the group bases of social life; (2) social laws and determinism; and (3) the principle of non-interference, or politically oriented individualism.

The Group Bases of Social Life

Like Durkheim and indeed all social theorists, Spencer began his discussion of the nature of the group by recognizing the existence of the individual. Unlike Durkheim, however, Spencer attributed to the individual the determination of the nature of the group. For Spencer, the nature of the individual is the most important single factor in determining the nature of the group.

To illustrate his point, Spencer told a story of a man piling up bricks. Through the use of bricks made with good materials and with square corners and flat sides, a brick mason can build a square wall of considerable height without mortar. With inferior brick with irregular shape, the wall cannot be built as high with the same stability. In contrast, if the same brick mason attempted to build a square wall with cannon-shot, he would not be able to do it. Cannon-shot can be piled symmetrically, but the pile will not have square sides, and must have a much thicker base than a wall made of bricks. The principle illustrated by this comparison is simple: the nature of the units determines the nature of the aggregate. Given certain kinds of units, only certain kinds of aggregates can be formed.[47]

The sociologist therefore must begin with an analysis of the essential features of the individual person. People have need for food, water and other physiological needs. They are subject to injury and pain. They have emotional needs. They like those who supply their needs and dislike those who don't. The first task of sociology is to utilize the comparative approach to determine what characteristics all people have in common, no matter what kind of society they live in. These common traits will then be used to provide the basis of a scientific sociology.

This does not mean that the nature of the individual is the sole determinant of social phenomena. The environment, including both the physical and social environment, is an important determinant of social life. The nature of the individual sets broad limits within which other factors operate to determine the peculiar nature of each social group. Contemporary sociologists have tended to view these limits as extremely broad, so that almost any type of society is possible because of the flexibility of the human personality and its physical needs. Spencer saw the limits placed on social life by the nature of the individual to be restrictive but still broad enough to enable a multitude of variations of social conditions and group organization.

Spencer was not a reductionist, however. He did not believe that all social phenomena can be explained

226

by reference to the characteristics or behavior of individuals. Spencer argued that a social group has a life and characteristics apart from the individuals who compose it. When individuals interact, they form a group whose characteristics are different in nature from those of the individual members. Society is an entity because of its permanence and its structure. It is to the characteristics of the total aggregate, particularly the "growth, development, structure, and functions of the social aggregate,"[48] that the sociologist must devote his attention.

Spencer illustrated his argument by reference to the principles of mechanics exhibited in an explosion of a bomb. A scientist studying such an explosion could predict many occurrences. He could predict that fragments from the device would rise to certain specified heights depending upon the explosive charge in the device, and that these fragments would then fall to the earth. They would be distributed in some predictable pattern, with more pieces falling near the explosion than far away. Further, the path of each fragment can be represented by a curve, and each curve will be alike in most respects.

However, before the explosion, the scientist cannot make a prediction as to the specific height, direction, or eventual resting place of some specific piece of the device, say the section on the left side three inches from the front and four inches from the top. Prediction can be made about the aggregate effects of all fragments, but not of each individual fragment. Predictions are general in nature, rather than specifically applying to each individual unit.[49] The predictions made in the physical sciences are of this nature. The botanist does not try to predict which individual seeds of wheat will grow; he contents himself with predicting that a certain volume of seed will produce a certain volume of wheat under given conditions of soil, climate, etc. The chemist does not predict which individual molecule of oxygen will combine with which molecules of hydrogen to produce water. He predicts only that under certain conditions, some unspecified molecules of oxygen and hydrogen will combine to produce water.

Likewise, a sociologist can predict that a certain percentage of persons will unite themselves in marriage without predicting which individuals will marry which others. Predictions about aggregates do not

227

necessitate predictions about the units of which the aggregates are composed. Sociology devotes itself to analyses and explanations of social groups, but it does not encompass in its domain the necessity to explain or predict individual behavior.

The group as the focus of sociological explanation was especially stressed in the second chapter of The Study of Sociology, in which Spencer entertained other possible explanations of social behavior, including the so-called "great man" theory of history. Spencer noted that many people see "in the course of civilization little else than a record of remarkable persons and their doings."[50] Much of history and popular culture (including the contemporary press, who use it as standard procedure) is written as the exploits of particular individuals. The story of a hunt, a battle, or an athletic competition is presented as the story of one or a few individuals, neglecting the contributions and effects of countless others.

Spencer asserted that the great man theory is readily accepted because (1) there is a "universal love of personalities,"[51] (2) it is used as instruction to gain knowledge upon which one's own life can be modeled, and (3) it is easily understood because it simplifies reality. However, when we ask the question "Whence comes the great man?" we are immediately led to an analysis of social conditions. The great man is produced by the social group of which he is a member: he is a product of social causes. (Today, the "great man" is often a woman.)

Specific social conditions produce given kinds of personalities. This assertion does not detract from the greatness of the accomplishments of these great men, but it does recognize that if they were born in a different time and place, their accomplishments would be of a far different order. Da Vinci failed to invent an airplane, not because of his lack of talent or industry, but because his society had not yet produced a base of technological inventions upon which he could build.

A great man may have some influence upon his society. One person may alter the course of history to some small degree, but he is still a product of his times. While the individual may be regarded as the proximate cause of a particular event, the ultimate cause must be sought in the stage of evolution of a particular society and the social conditions present in that stage.

Social Laws

Spencer believed strongly in the existence of a set of natural laws which govern social life. Given causes always produce specific effects. There are uniformities in social life which can be measured and studied. One of the characteristics of the society in which Spencer lived was the increased recognition of the presence of such laws governing the lives of human beings.[52] According to Spencer, a law is a statement of uniformity existing between a cause and an effect, of the kind "If A, then B." Such a generalization can only be established after observation of a great many empirical instances.

Because of the very nature of uniformities and laws, a law does not change. Therefore, once it has been discovered it can be used from that time forth by all who are acquainted with it. This assumption led Spencer to an inevitable conclusion: the total realm of phenomena in the world are constantly being reduced to laws. This means that the total number of phenomena not explained by laws is constantly being reduced. Eventually, all phenomena, whether of the physical or social worlds, will be included in some set of laws. Not only is a single law universal, but all phenomena are explainable through laws. The world is a world of law, and the province of science is to discover these laws so that they may be used by people to control the social world. This perspective, of course, has the major defect of reifying social laws--of treating them as real entities.

The Stages of Evolution as Determined

Spencer and most of the later evolutionists treated the process of evolution as a deterministic process. Spencer believed that society moves inexorably from simple to complex, from homogeneous to heterogeneous. Evolution is an "ultimate principle" in that it is the direct result of the working of a particular and specific cause in human affairs, which Spencer identified as the "Persistence of Force."[53] In the First Principles, Spencer set for himself the task of tracing and analyzing the nature of social evolution, the major causal agents of evolution, and the principle effects to be expected. Spencer believed that evolutionary principles operate on both the macrosocial and the microsocial levels. Each individual event or interaction provides evidence of the workings of evolutionary principles. All are eventually reducible to one ultimate cause. Spencer did not believe it would ever be possible for humans to understand completely this ultimate cause. However, he believed scientists could develop, first, a set of empirical generalizations, and second, a set of "rational generalizations" which would give a close approximation to the ultimate cause.[54]

Free Will

The existence of laws does not necessitate a rejection of free will or individual initiative. In The Study of Sociology, Spencer attempted to answer the arguments of those who contend that a science of social life is not possible because of the volition of human beings. Spencer noted that the arguments in support of free will usually imply two assertions. First, it is asserted that human volition is incalculable--that is, that because individuals think and choose and act that no calculations or generalizations can be developed which apply to such actions.[55] Second, it is asserted that because human beings possess volition, "there are not causal relations among his states of mind."[56]

Spencer did not deny the ability of the individual to think, choose and act--to exercise volition. But he did reject the above two assertions which are supposedly based on the assumption of volition. He pointed to the countless situations in which individuals base their own behavior upon calculations, often very accurate, as to what other people will do or say. In given situations, human behavior is predictable to a remarkable extent.

If, in crossing a street, a man sees a carriage coming upon him, you may safely assert that, in nine hundred and ninety-nine cases out of a thousand, he will try to get out of the way.[57]

The "predominant activities" of people have this same degree of regularity. In many fundamental social areas, human behavior is extremely regular and predictable. It is only because the behavior of others is predictable that we are able to deal effectively with other people and have the organized kind of social life which we all have come to expect.

Regarding the second assertion, Spencer argued that causal relations, expressed in the form of social laws, do indeed operate in social life. Social life is not planless or disorganized. Rather it tends to be highly organized, and subject to the operation of laws which are universal. However, Spencer did accept the assertion that social laws are never perfectly exact or invariable, and that they "have various degrees of definiteness."[58] While generally it is warmer in the summer than in the winter, it may turn cold or even snow during the summertime. Likewise, while most people may regularly perform a certain act in given circumstances, some exceptions may always be found. In both the physical and social sciences, one must speak in terms of probability rather than universality.

Spencer noted that the "law of gravity" may be "overcome" if one catches a falling stone and inhibits it from falling. However, the law is still operating, and the forces of attraction existing between the earth and the stone are still present. Likewise, certain social forces or tendencies may remain in operation even though people take actions which seem to thwart or overcome them. While a great many people may conform to a given expectation, others may deviate in their behavior in unpredictable ways. The social laws are still operable, and the deviants may feel the power of the forces operating toward conformity. However, prediction is reduced through such actions. While every action of every person cannot be predicted, it is possible to predict with a great degree of accuracy the average behavior of all people, or most behavior of most people. While the possibilities for understanding and predicting human behavior are not limitless, they are great enough to encourage and even necessitate the development of the social sciences.

Noninterference

Although Spencer accepted the basic principles of social determinism and rejected the reductionist point of view, he reached different conclusions about the respective roles of government and the individual than other sociologists did. Spencer was a strong advocate for individual liberties and the limitation of government.[59] This position was politically very controversial during Spencer's life. He received a great deal of praise for this position, especially from prominent conservatives in the United States during a triumphant tour there in 1882. However, Spencer was also consistently attacked by liberals and radicals who advocated the extension of state powers to include provisions for personal and group welfare.

Spencer argued that no society is possible without protection of individual life and property.[60] Government, therefore, can never be dispensed with. The proper function of government is to assure the continuance of social life by protecting each individual against the encroachments of others. However, the assertion that some government is necessary should not be used as a basis for unlimited extension of governmental powers to other areas of life. Government should be strictly limited in its powers to influence or regulate individual initiative and freedom.

Spencer viewed with alarm any attempt to extend the role of government into other fields. He strongly believed that society is progressing from the authoritarian and military organizations of primitive society toward a more democratic and less restrictive organization found in modern society. Any attempt to increase the authority of government over the individual contradicts the overall and long-range process of evolution. Individual freedom and restriction of the role of government are the ends toward which society is evolving. Only those who fail to understand the course of evolution can advocate extensive government legislation in the fields of education, commerce, etc.

During the last twenty years of his long life, Spencer devoted much of his time to writing essays (for both learned journals and popular newspapers) denouncing the extension of government and advocating greater individual freedom. He consistently predicted that the trend toward welfare legislation and governmental regulation would have a deleterious effect upon the course of evolution. However, Spencer did not oppose individual meliorative actions or philanthropic endeavors. These should be carried on in moderation, however, since the chief danger of such activities is in thwarting the natural tendency of society to eliminate the unfit. By keeping unfit people alive and allowing them to reproduce, one can countermand the evolutionary tendencies of his own society. Individual

232

actions should be directed toward creating the proper conditions for evolutionary development.[61]

Spencer did not think of himself as primarily a conservative. He accepted the implication of organicism that past governments, even very violent and authoritarian ones, had been adapted to the stage of evolution in which they were found. While such behavior would not be acceptable in a more advanced society, it was natural and necessary in a previous stage. Present conditions have been achieved through the process of adaptation. Nonadaptive conditions tend to be eliminated, so that which is presently found is by definition natural and good. Spencer readily admitted that this is an extremely conservative position.

However, Spencer did not believe that one must seek at all costs to maintain the status quo. Since society is continually evolving, one must recognize that change is essential. Spencer recognized the inevitability of change. Over the long run, such changes would be extremely radical, bringing a totally different society than that presently in existence. Spencer looked forward to these changes and to the ideal state toward which society is evolving.[62]

Spencer's position on the group vs. individual issue is often misrepresented and misunderstood. He was a forceful advocate of individual freedom and restricted government. He recognized the importance of individual characteristics, and believed that these have an important effect on social life. Yet he also was a strong advocate of the existence of natural social laws and of a positivistic approach to the study of social life. He opposed the great man theory, and took an essentially Durkheimian position that the social group exists as an entity with characteristics different from those of its individual components. He saw some conflict between the interests of the group and the individual, but believed that the process of evolution would finally usher in a period of peace, prosperity, and great individual freedom and initiative. Social change, according to Spencer, is leading to greater individualism--a conclusion directly the opposite from Marx's more pessimistic judgment.

FOOTNOTES

[1]Auguste Comte, <u>The Fundamental Principles of the Positive Philosophy</u>, tr. by Paul Descours and H. Gordon Jones (London: Watts and Company), 1905. See also Auguste Comte, <u>The Positive Philosophy of Auguste Comte</u>, tr. by Harriet Martineau, 3 volumes (London: George Bell & Sons), 1896.

[2]<u>Fundamental Principles</u>, pp. 22-23.

[3]<u>Ibid</u>., p. 23.

[4]<u>Ibid</u>., pp. 28-29.

[5]<u>Ibid</u>., pp. 22-24, 26, 36.

[6]<u>Ibid</u>., pp. 22, 26.

[7]<u>Ibid</u>., p. 23.

[8]<u>Ibid</u>., pp. 33-34.

[9]<u>Ibid</u>., p. 40.

[10]<u>Ibid</u>., p. 26.

[11]<u>Ibid</u>., p. 24.

[12]<u>Ibid</u>., pp. 25, 46-47.

[13]<u>Ibid</u>., p. 53.

[14]<u>Ibid</u>., p. 31.

[15]<u>Ibid</u>., pp. 37-38, 41.

[16]<u>Ibid</u>., p. 32.

[17]<u>Ibid</u>., p. 40.

[18]<u>Ibid</u>., p. 55.

[19]<u>Ibid</u>., p. 33.

[20]<u>Ibid</u>., pp. 58, 62.

[21]<u>Ibid</u>., pp. 36, 44.

[22]<u>Ibid</u>., p. 22.

[23]Ibid., p. 33.

[24]Ibid., p. 34.

[25]Ibid., pp. 33-34.

[26]Ibid., p. 32.

[27]Ibid., p. 37.

[28]Ibid., p. 40.

[29]Ibid., p. 40.

[30]Ibid., p. 41.

[31]C. Wright Mills, The Marxists (New York: Dell), 1962, pp. 90-92. See also the following: John Lachs, Marxist Philosophy: A Bibliographical Guide (Chapel Hill: University of North Carolina Press), 1967; Sidney Hook, The Hero in History (Boston: Beacon), 1955; M. D. Kammari, Der Marxismus-Leninismus über die Rolle der Persönlichkeit in der Geschichte (Berlin: Dietz), 1955;

[32]Karl Marx, "Preface to the 2nd Edition," Capital (New York: Modern Library), 1906, pp. 22-23.

[33]Friedrich Engels, Ludwig Feuerbach (New York: International Publishers), 1935, pp. 58-59.

[34]Friedrich Engels, "Letter to Bloch," quoted by Sidney Hook, Towards an Understanding of Karl Marx (New York: John Day), 1933, p. 170.

[35]Karl Marx, Economic and Philosophical Manuscripts of 1844, (New York: International Publishers), 1964, and Karl Marx and Friedrich Engels, The German Ideology (New York: International Publishers), 1947.

[36]Marx, Capital, op. cit.

[37]Raymond Aron, Main Currents in Sociological Thought, tr. by Richard Howard and Helen Weaver (Garden City, New York: Doubleday), 1968, Volume 1, p. 185.

[38]Marx, The German Ideology, p. 24.

[39]See the excellent footnote #23 in Ibid., p. 202.

235

[40]Hook, op. cit.; Plekhanov, The Role of the Individual; and Delfgaauw, p. 66.

[41]Marx and Engels, German Ideology, p. 7.

[42]Ibid., p. 76.

[43]Ibid., p. 77.

[44]Friedrich Engels, "Socialism: Utopian and Scientific," Selected Works (New York: International Publishers), no date; quoted by Mills, op. cit., p. 78.

[45]Karl Marx, "Letter to Kugelman, April 12, 1871," quoted in Hook, Toward an Understanding of Karl Marx, pp. 174-175.

[46]See MESW (Marx and Engels, Selected Works).

[47]Herbert Spencer, The Study of Sociology (New York: Appleton), 1896 (1873), pp. 44-45.

[48]Ibid., p. 47.

[49]Ibid., pp. 49, 101-102.

[50]Ibid., p. 26.

[51]Ibid., p. 28.

[52]Herbert Spencer, "Laws, and the Order of Their Discovery," in "Three Essays," Humboldt Library of Science, 68 (June, 1885):441.

[53]Herbert Spencer, First Principles (New York: DeWitt Revolving Fund, Inc.), 1958, p. 395.

[54]Herbert Spencer, "Progress: Its Law and Cause," in Illustrations of Universal Progress: A Series of Discussions (New York: Appleton), 1883, pp. 30-31.

[55]The Study of Sociology, p. 33.

[56]Ibid., p. 34.

[57]Loc. cit.

[58]Loc. cit.

[59]See especially: "Postscripts," The Study of Sociology, pp. 369-386; "The Coming Slavery" and "The Sins of Legislators," Humboldt Library of Science, 103 (May 1888):1-41; "Over-Legislation," Essays: Moral, Political and Aesthetic (New York: Appleton), 1889 (1857); The Principles of Ethics (New York: Appleton), 1898, Volume Two; and The Man Versus The State (Caldwell, Idaho: Caxton Printers), 1946, especially "The New Toryism," pp. 1-21.

[60]Herbert Spencer, Social Statics, Abridged and Revised Edition (London: Appleton), 1910 (originally published in 1850, abridged in 1890), pp. 126-127.

[61]The Study of Sociology, p. 366.

[62]Ibid., pp. 364-367.

CHAPTER TWELVE

THE DEVELOPMENT OF POSITIVISM: GEORGE LUNDBERG

Auguste Comte provided the foundation of positivistic principles upon which sociology initially developed. Although his principles have been imperfectly practiced by every generation of sociologists since his time, his basic approach has gradually gained acceptance. Durkheim gave these principles a significant impetus in France at the turn of the century. American sociologists, especially in the 1920s, increasingly turned to these principles for guidance. Yet the resistance to positivism was still substantial. This was especially true in Germany, where idealistic philosophy, supported by Weber's subjectivist orientation, led to a less positivistic emphasis.

The man most closely identified with the recent development of positivism in American sociology is George A. Lundberg. Lundberg's influence was most fully felt in the late 1920s and early 1930s. His influence has continued up to the present day, but his significant impact came in this earlier period.

The essential principles of positivism were enunciated by Comte, but Lundberg developed certain of these principles to a higher level than that of Comte. Since this approach today is widely accepted in contemporary sociology, a statement of Lundberg's major points is almost like a restatement of current methodological principles in sociology. There are, however, significant points upon which debate has centered.

The Natural Science Method

Lundberg believed that sociology is a natural science, and can be studied with the same methods and logic as that used by other sciences. In fact, he preferred the label of "natural scientist" to that of "positivist." He accepted the postulate of the inherent unity of all the sciences; the same general laws, according to Lundberg, may be applicable to both natural and social phenomena.[1] The essence of the scientific method is the objective observation of facts. The state of mind of the scientist, the way he approaches his data, distinguishes him from moralists or theologians. This objective method can be used

239

equally by all scientists of every discipline. Lundberg believed that sociology would be able to make consistent and significant gains if it were to model itself more fully after the natural sciences.

Scientific Language

Many non-scientists assume that language fully denotes "the nature of things."[2] For Lundberg, a word is a verbal symbol which we agree to apply to a particular object or class of events. As long as people agree on the referent of the word, communication is possible. What is necessary in science is the development of a body of concepts which are rigidly defined. This will enable scientists to be more precise in their designations of phenomena, and therefore more precise and accurate in the propositions they develop using these terms.

According to Lundberg, the best type of scientific definition is the "operational definition." An operational definition specifies the operations or acts which an observer must perform in order to measure or otherwise observe a certain phenomena. Rather than defining a concept "in terms of" other words, an operational definition is defined by the operations performed.

The operationist merely tries to make his language denote actual operations as specifically as possible. . . . If he cannot make the operations clear verbally, he should perform them, as one does in teaching language to children, after which language may be used to denote operations.[3]

Intelligence is best defined in terms of an IQ test, that is, the specific operations necessary to measure intelligence, just as temperature is best defined in terms of the operation of reading a thermometer. What is crucially important is that people learn to think in terms of operational definitions. In the physical sciences, this has been achieved. In the social sciences, the mode of reasoning and conceptualization still has not fully encompassed quantitative and operational orientations.

Postulates of Science

In his book Foundations of Sociology, Lundberg discussed five postulates of science. These postulates are quite different from other widely accepted postulates, and Lundberg did not imply that his list of postulates was comprehensive or supplanted other statements of postulates. His list of postulates was developed primarily to show the similarity in methodological operations in both the physical and social sciences.

1. All data or experience with which man can become concerned consist of the responses of the organisms-in-environment. This includes the postulate of an external world and variations both in it and in the responders to it.

2. Symbols, usually verbal, are invented to represent these responses.

3. These symbols are the immediate data of all communicable knowledge and therefore of all science.

4. All propositions or postulates regarding the more ultimate "realities" must always consist of inference, generalizations, or abstractions from these symbols and the responses which they represent.

5. These extrapolations are in turn represented symbolically, and we respond to them as we respond to other phenomena which evoke behavior.[4]

Lundberg ignored the philosophical issue of the relative "reality" of physical and social phenomena. Instead, he argued that every scientist responds to symbols or conceptualizations of his data. The symbols, rather than the "real" substance which is observed, become the data. These symbols are then manipulated and scientific generalizations are constructed. The important point is that the process or method by which the physical scientist approaches his data is identical to that used by the social scientist. This unity of method of all disciplines must be recognized by social scientists.

241

Propositions

The aim of every science is to develop a set of propositions which have been verified through scientific operations and which allow prediction and control of a specified set of phenomena, according to Lundberg.

> In its maturest form the content of science consists of a body of verified propositions so related that under given rules (logic) the system is self-consistent and compatible with empirical observation. The more universally applicable these propositions are, i.e., the greater the variety of phenomena covered by the propositions, the more adequate is our knowledge of the field which they cover.[5]

This statement implies several criteria by which a set of propositions may be judged. First, have they been verified? Do they fit the facts of experience and observation? What is the level of probability for each of the propositions included? Second, can the propositions be interrelated through some system of logic? Third, what is the range of phenomena covered by the propositions? What degree of universality do the propositions have? The greater the correspondence between the facts and the propositional (theoretical) statements, the greater the logical consistency of the propositions, and the greater the universality of application of the propositions, the better is the theory. The close association of theory and fact is clearly recognized by this statement.

Quantification

Lundberg asserted that any quality or characteristic of social life has certain quantitative implications or uses. Any quality may be put into a contingency table as being either present and/or absent. Further, the number of cases in which it is present and/or absent may be counted and used as a quantified variable. Lundberg argued that there is no essential difference between qualitative and quantitative aspects. Both may be treated as quantitative. Statistical manipulation of both qualitative and quantitative aspects of social life is both possible and desirable.

Measurement and quantification of sociological variables is often a difficult task. For this reason, many sociologists have preferred to treat sociological variables as qualitative, according to Lundberg. This has not prevented them from making generalizations. Such generalizations almost always take the form of "more than" or "less than," implying some inherent quantifiability of the variables. Sociologists who deal with qualities, then, prefer "informal, impressionistic and imaginary statistics" rather than the more difficult task of developing accurate measurement of the variables they use. According to Lundberg, every variable is ultimately quantifiable if it is properly defined. Even such a variable as sex is quantifiable if the particular qualities of "maleness" or "femaleness" are properly identified. The qualitative noun "male" usually is used to denote a variety of qualities. If these qualities are identified and conceptualized, a quantifiable measure of each quality can be developed.

Explanation vs. Description

Lundberg noted that many persons have criticized the positivists for failure to achieve explanation. By this they mean that scientific propositions or generalizations are adequate as descriptions of the phenomena or relations among phenomena, but do not "explain" why such conditions are present. A statement such as "males have a higher rate of crimes committed than do females" describes a situation but does not tell "why" males commit more crimes.

Lundberg rejected this mode of thinking. To him, explanation is contained in the generalization. Explanation consists of relating an antecedent condition (sex distribution) to a succedent condition (crime rate).

All that science does is to describe concisely and objectively certain sequences in the behavior of the phenomena it studies. The only "explanation" known to science is conceptualized description.[6]

Any other meaning of the term explanation has metaphysical connotations which were rejected by Lundberg. The answer to "why" is contained in the statement itself, or may be spelled out by further propositions having the same general form: "the higher the personal aggressiveness (a variable directly related to socialization to the male role), the higher the rate of crimes committed." All scientific explanation consists of relating an antecedent and a succedent condition. Both empirical generalizations and higher-level theoretical propositions take this same form. An empirical generalization is explained when it can be deduced from a set of higher-order propositions. Descriptive and explanatory propositions are identical in form, and may be distinguished only on the basis of the intent of the investigator. A descriptive proposition has explanatory content, however, when it is placed in a more comprehensive set of propositions arranged in deductive order.

THE SCIENTIFIC METHOD

According to Lundberg, one of the most essential assumptions of positivism is that the world is experienced through the senses. One does not seek to gain knowledge of the world through pure reason, communication with the supernatural, or through self-analysis. Instead knowledge is gained through observation. Only that which is subject to observation can furnish the data for science. Any realm of the world, whether real or imaginary, which is not subject to experience through the senses cannot be studied scientifically. Accurate and reliable information cannot be gained about such realms.

Observation, however, is subject to the same biases as any perception. Science seeks to eliminate these biases in several ways. First, the scientist is trained to be objective. He attempts as much as possible to eliminate his preconceptions and to gain knowledge of his own biases in order to control them. Second, the testimony or evidence of one scientist is never taken as final. Agreement among a number of observers gives added weight to the observations of each. Each observation must be performed in such a way that it can be replicated by other trained observers. Third, scientists attempt to develop instruments to aid them in observation.[7] The thermometer is used to observe temperature. The ruler is used to observe length. The Guttman scale is used to observe social attitudes. These instruments facilitate the making of accurate and consistent observations. Quantification aids observation. If the scientist is able to define his subject matter in such a way that it becomes subject to quantification, validity is improved. The

244

scientist is also able to manipulate or utilize a greater number of cases or observations. This in turn increases the reliability of his observations.

Positivism developed in opposition to rationalism. It specifically rejected the rationalistic assertion that one can gain truth a priori through the use of reason. The rational faculties of the scientist are an important tool which he can use, but they must always be used in conjunction with observation. One cannot use reason to determine the number of teeth in a horse's mouth or the number of suicides in New York City in a given year. These facts can better be determined through observation.

Positivism likewise rejects introspection as a method of gathering data or testing hypotheses. Lundberg argued that the best way to gain information about behavior is to watch people behave, rather than think introspectively about one's own behavior. Introspection was advocated by some (e.g., Weber) as a means of gaining information about the subjective experience of the individual. Lundberg argued that through the use of observation and scientific experiments, more reliable information can be gained about the determinants of individual behavior. By showing that certain conditions lead to certain patterns of behavior, the behavior can be explained more accurately and more objectively than through the use of introspection.

Introspection is difficult to communicate. One person's introspective interpretation of a situation may differ markedly from another's. Further, there is no way to place a probability value upon a conclusion which is arrived at introspectively. Any number of interpretations may be plausible, but without observation and quantification, probability values cannot be determined. [8]

These questions were discussed more extensively in the section on the structuralism-subjectivism issue. In review we may say that Lundberg and other positivists rejected a subjective theory of social life. They replaced it with a structural theory which emphasized the causal links between given social conditions or stimuli and given patterns of behavior or responses. These causal links must be established through scientific observation. Any subjective intervening variables were rejected because they are

245

not available for scientific observation. Introspection was rejected as a scientific method because it is not subject to empirical validation.

Through much of his professional career, Lundberg carried on a running battle with those who advocated introspective and subjective methodologies. Herbert Blumer, an eminent champion of symbolic interactionism, was his most important protagonist. Lundberg's influence has been decisive in contemporary sociology. The major thrust of sociological methodology for many years has been positivistic. It has emphasized observation, experimentation and quantification. The development of increasingly sophisticated statistical and measurement techniques in recent years is one of the significant developments in contemporary sociology. Lundberg has clearly won the battle. He has not as clearly won the war. Subjectivists remain active and influential. Goffman and Garfinkel are perhaps the best of a number of recent sociologists who have found great worth in the subjectivist orientation and who still seek to utilize introspectionist techniques to gain greater knowledge of the social world.

Social Laws

As positivism defines it, the ultimate goal of science is the development of a system of laws which explain a particular realm of phenomena and from which predictions can accurately be made. Lundberg argued that this is the supreme goal of sociology. Through the use of objective scientific methods in the study of behavior, a set of social laws which explain behavior can be formulated. In turn, these laws can be used to predict and control events in the social world.[9]

Lundberg's definition of law was rather complicated.

. . . (A) scientific law is a generalized and varifiable statement, within measurable degrees of accuracy, of how certain events occur under stated conditions. More specifically then, a scientific law is (1) a group of verbal or mathematical symbols (2) designating an unlimited number of defined events in terms of a limited number of reactions (3) so that the performance of specified operations always yields predictable results (4) within measurable limits.[10]

It is important to note that a law need not be invariable in Lundberg's definition. Modern practice in both the physical and social sciences is to state laws in terms of probability, rather than assuming they are invariable.

Lundberg distinguished two types of laws. One is a scientific tautology. Here, the "conclusion stated is inherent in the definition of the words employed." These may be useful as statements of abstract principles, because theorems may be deduced from them which help to explain concrete phenomena.[11]

The second type of law "states the statistical probability of the occurrence of an event under stated conditions." In essence, this type of law specifies a correlation between two events. "The ultimate end is the correlation of two disparate sets of behavior phenomena so that the statement of their relationship will be consistent with sense experience."[12] One event always precedes in point of time the second event. The time interval between these two events, however, may be so small that it is difficult to measure. The first event is variously called the cause, the determinant, the independent variable, or the antecedent condition. The second event may be called the effect, the result, the dependent variable, or the succeeding variable. While no definite limits can be set upon the degree of correlation, it is generally agreed that the term "law" cannot be applied to the relationship unless the correlation is relatively high. Since the time sequence is important in determining causation, the relationship between the two variables must be sequential and irreversible.[13]

In almost every case, a number of conditions can be identified which influence the production of a given effect. This is what is meant by "multiple causation." In practice, one of these conditions, usually the most important one (judged either statistically or theoretically), is singled out as the cause. The other conditions are retained in the causal explanation, usually under the label "conditions."

247

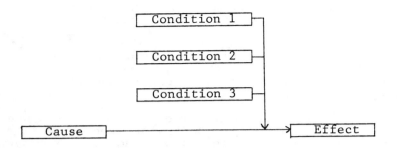

The decision to label one event as a cause and another event as a condition is usually arbitrary, and depends upon the purposes of the investigator. In one situation, one event may be defined as the cause of a given effect. In another situation, a second event may be labeled the cause, and the first event may be labeled a condition.

Lundberg noted that one of the most significant drawbacks in the establishment of relationships between social variables as laws is that "we do not know under what specific conditions they are true and to what degree they are verifiably true under these conditions."[14] Further research on establishing the conditions under which causal relationships exist will aid in the establishment of laws of social relations.

In order to establish a law, each variable must be measurable. One of the chief tasks of any researcher is to develop objective and operational definitions of his subject matter. As we have said before, the development of quantitative indices and instruments of measurement greatly facilitate accurate measurement.

Arguments Against Establishment of Social Laws

In The Foundations of Sociology, Lundberg discussed a number of arguments by persons who contended that it is not possible to establish laws in the social sciences. These may be discussed under two headings: (1) the variability of the social world, and (2) the nature of human volition.

Arguments regarding the variability of the social world take several forms. Some argue that the social world is infinitely complex, much more so than the physical world. Others contend that the great

248

varieties of different cultures, with their different patterns of behavior and personality, make any cross-cultural generalizations impossible. Still others believe that the high rate of social change, unlike the stability of the physical world, leads to variability and indeterminism.

Lundberg's answer to these arguments was to point to the abstract nature of laws. Any law, whether it applies to the physical or social world, is an abstraction. Only certain aspects of reality, usually conceptualized in highly artificial terms, are abstracted out for use in the development of laws. The law applies only to these abstract and artificial aspects of any particular case, not to all aspects. For example, statements about the boiling point of water refer to "pure" water, that is, H_2O, under constant pressure at sea-level. Impure water, or water under different pressures, does not fit the law perfectly, but these variances from the law can be calculated.[15] Likewise in the social sciences, certain abstract and artificial conditions must be selected in establishing laws. Variances from these conditions should be studied and incorporated into our explanations if possible. For example, we may be interested in those aspects of all revolutions which are similar. Through research, we can abstract out these consistent and ever-present features of all revolutions and formulate a law which states the relationships among these conditions. This does not mean that the French Revolution is not dissimilar in many respects from the Russian Revolution. It does mean, however, that all revolutions have common features which may serve as the bases for the establishment of social laws.

Lundberg noted that the physical sciences do not attempt to explain all occurrences in the phenomena they study. They do not attempt to explain or describe the path of each molecule in a pan of water over a fire. Instead, they predict the total volume of molecules striking the sides of the pan at any given time period, and thereby explain the phenomena of "boiling." Rather than seeking explanations at the microscopic level, they are content with explanations at the macroscopic level. In the same manner, sociology will be able to make more accurate and meaningful statements of relationships at the macroscopic level of social life, rather than at the level of explanation of each specific behavior of each

249

specific person. Lundberg recognized that many events, such as the number of automobile thefts in a given city, can be predicted with great accuracy. The rate of auto thefts, rather than which car will be stolen or which person will steal it, is the proper level of study for sociological purposes.[16]

A misconception of the nature of scientific laws leads some people to assume that no scientific laws can be developed which will explain social phenomena. They assume that laws are invariable. Since some sociologists believe in the extensive variability of social phenomena, they have made the mistaken assumption that invariable laws are not possible in sociology. Lundberg asserted that this assumption depends upon the mistaken belief that "real" invariable relations exist among physical phenomena, and that physical laws reflect this "reality." In fact, according to Lundberg, laws in the natural sciences are based on probability, and apply to "highly standardized and artificial conditions."[17] These conditions may include such abstractions as a frictionless plane, a perfect vacuum, or pure water. In the same way, social laws may be developed which apply to artificial conditions in social life. While these conditions may never be fully achieved in real life (as a frictionless plane is not), the laws based on such abstractions may still enable us to predict and control social life. Rather than seeking for "ultimate" truths, we should seek instead for abstract yet usable statements of relationship.[18]

The second argument against the possibility of establishing social laws has to do with the alleged volitional character of individual human beings. Some theorists attribute "all kinds of metaphysical characteristics, such as will, choice, whims, notions, mind, consciousness, etc.," to social phenomena.[19] To Lundberg, these notions are antiquated. Through behavioristic psychology and sociology, adequate statements of human behavior can be made without reference to these terms. Lundberg argued that sociological investigation has shown that accurate predictions of events which appear to be almost totally subject to personal choice can be made. For example, Lundberg noted that accurate predictions of death rates, which are supposedly not subject to choice, may be made. Equally well, the rates of marriage for a given group during a given time period can accurately be predicted, even though marriage is volitional in character. By studying the social conditions which lead to marriage--that is, by relating certain features of the social structure to this pattern of behavior--accurate predictions can be accomplished. Despite the alleged volitional character of most social events, proper research can lead to accurate predictions of such events at the macro level. The ultimate test of the positivistic orientation is its ability to develop social laws from which predictions can be made. Lundberg contended that many such laws have already been formulated, and that positivism offers the best hope for the future development of scientific explanations of social phenomena.

A corollary to the above argument is one which asserts the impossibility of developing social laws because of the ability of the human being to react to the process of observation. This argument is similar to Heisenberg's famous Principle of Uncertainty as applied to subatomic particles. The observation of these particles by an electron microscope is itself an act which influences their nature and movements. Likewise, the presentation of a questionnaire to an individual is a social act which an affects his life. Lundberg argued that the social scientist must seek to overcome this difficulty in three ways:

> (1) (D)evise methods of observing under which the observed is not aware of it . . . (2) develop indifferences to observation on the part of the observed . . . (3) discover and measure exactly what difference in behavior results from being observed, and allow for this difference in our correlations and conclusions . . .[20]

Lundberg took the position that the sensitivity of human beings to sociological observation need not vitiate the scientific development of sociology. While he conceded that the very process of observing people may change them, he believed that sociological methodology can take account of such changes as may occur. The use of "unobtrusive" measures[21] to study social phenomena seems to be an important implication of Lundberg's argument here. The volitional or reactional character of human beings need not detract from the possibility of developing adequate explanations for social behavior.

In conclusion, social laws are possible in the social sciences according to Lundberg. Through the use of natural science methods, social phenomena can be studied in the same way, and ultimately with the same degree of accuracy, as physical phenomena.

. . . (T)he apparent difficulty of applying the methods of natural science to societal phenomena flow not from any intrinsic characteristics of these phenomena but from the retention in the latter field of postulates long since repudiated in the other sciences.[22]

Resort to the methods of positivism rather than to introspection or reason eventually will enable the social scientist to explain social behavior with a high degree of precision and accuracy. Social laws can then be used as the basis for the establishment of the kind of social order which is popularly desired. Social relations will then be subject to social control, a goal very attractive to Lundberg.

INDIVIDUALISM AND DETERMINISM IN CONTEMPORARY SOCIAL RESEARCH

Contemporary sociological research almost universally follows in the long tradition of Comte, Durkheim and Lundberg. Every effort is made to "eradicate preconceptions," to reduce measurement error, and to increase the validity of questionnaires, the representativeness of samples, and the size of correlation coefficients. Strong emphasis is placed by contemporary sociologists upon training in objectivity. The methodological procedures used in a sociological study become the prime criteria by which the fruitfulness and the validity of the study are judged. In short, sociological researchers have made great efforts to attain the scientific ideals of the natural sciences and their own positivistic forefathers. This is true even though there have been some attempts to broaden the scope of methodological procedures used by sociologists to include such "soft" research as observation and the study of documents. Very few sociologists can be found, at least in the United States, who openly advocate an introspective point of view. Even such subjectivists as Blumer, Garfinkel and their respective schools of symbolic interaction and ethnomethodology are committed to positivistic research.

252

The point we wish to make in this discussion is that the current emphasis upon positivistic methodology also has important implications for the theoretical issue we are discussing. Determinism clearly seems to be implied by current sociological research methodologies. Little place is given to the individual as an entity, or to individual initiative, choice or behavior. The intent of sociological research is usually to establish empirical generalizations between given antecedent conditions (usually social conditions or characteristics) and succedent conditions (usually opinions, attitudes or specific patterns of behavior). The individual and his volitional capabilities are treated as constants, not variables entering into the system. Individual choice and variability are treated as residual categories which are useful only to explain why observed correlations were not as high as the researcher hoped they would be. Seldom in sociological research reports does the researcher address himself to the influence of the individual on the subject he is studying.

It is no wonder, then, that sociological research (and the sociologists who do it) are sometimes rejected by non-sociologists. The common American finds little sense in a discipline which attempts to explain why a man voted as he did or committed a crime without coming to grips with motives, emotions, thoughts, etc. The average person seeks explanations in terms of individuals, not social conditions. He wants to know the mechanisms by which poverty or discrimination or wealth produce people who refuse to work, or people who vote Democratic. He wants to know individual effects, not just collective effects or average tendencies. Much of sociological research is meaningless to him because of the level of analysis to which it is geared.

We should also note the vociferous and growing minority of professional sociologists, most of them relatively young, who approach the study of society from a humanistic rather than a scientific perspective. They also object to treating individual human beings as robots, as objects rather than subjects of sociological forces and pressures. They argue instead for a subjective and humanistic approach based on a different set of values--values stressing individual dignity and ability rather than scientific objectivity. The positivistic orientation in sociology is entrenched solidly. The humanistic orientation is just emerging from infancy. It will certainly have some influence upon the future of sociology, but it is still early to make a judgment as to the direction or success of that influence. There is little likelihood, however, that the positivistic approach will be rejected and replaced by a less-positivistic and more humanistic approach.

FOOTNOTES

[1]George Lundberg, "The Natural Science Trend in Sociology," American Journal of Sociology, 61 (November, 1955), pp. 191-193.

[2]George Lundberg, "Operational Definitions in the Social Sciences," American Journal of Sociology, 47 (, 1941-42), p. 739.

[3]Ibid., p. 2, 731. See also Bridgeman.

[4]George Lundberg, Foundations of Sociology, (New York: David McKay), 1964 (1939: Macmillan), p. 5.

[5]Ibid., p. 2.

[6]George A. Lundberg, "The Logic of Sociology and Social Research," in George A. Lundberg, Read Bain and Nels Anderson, editors, Trends in American Sociology (New York: Harper), 1929, p. 401.

[7]George A. Lundberg, Can Science Save Us? (New York: Longmans, Green), 1947, p. 24.

[8]Theodore Abel, "The Operation Called Verstehen," American Journal of Sociology, 54 (November, 1948), pp. 211-218.

[9]Foundations of Sociology, pp. 137-160, and George A. Lundberg, "The Concept of Law in the Social Sciences," Philosophy of Science, 5 (April, 1938), pp. 189-203.

[10]Foundations of Sociology, p. 137.

[11]Ibid., pp. 138-139.

[12]Ibid., p. 140.

[13]See Hans Zetterberg, On Theory and Verification in Sociology (Totowa, New Jersey: Bedminster), 1965, pp. 69-74.

254

[14]Foundations of Sociology, p. 143.

[15]Ibid., p. 142.

[16]Ibid., p. 152.

[17]"The Logic of Sociology and Social Research," p. 403.

[18]Foundations of Sociology, p. 107.

[19]"The Logic of Sociology and Social Research," p. 403.

[20]Foundations of Sociology, pp. 145-146.

[21]Eugene J. Webb, Donald T. Campbell, Richard D. Schwartz, and Lee Sechrest, Unobtrusive Measures: Nonreactive Research in the Social Sciences (Chicago: Rand McNally), 1966.

[22]Foundations of Sociology, p. 155.

CHAPTER THIRTEEN

THE CLASSICAL INDIVIDUALISTIC APPROACH:
MAX WEBER AND LESTER WARD

We now turn to the classical sociological theorists who most strongly emphasized the "individual" approach in the study of social life. Their approach contrasts strongly with that of Durkheim, who believed that any reference to "individual manifestations" took the investigator out of the realm of sociology. The theorists whose work we shall discuss in the next two chapters took an opposite point of view--they stressed the importance of the individual to sociological analysis. In their written works, they exhibited a theoretical interest in the individual as the unit of analysis of social life, and developed theories which attempted to account for social life as the actions of individual actors.

THE INDIVIDUAL ACTOR AS THE UNIT OF
SOCIOLOGICAL ANALYSIS: WEBER

Max Weber is certainly the most important sociologist to develop a sociological orientation based upon the individual actor. Weber's reasoning has provided a foundation for those few contemporary sociologists who have broken from the Durkheimian tradition and accepted the individualistic orientation. Weber's subjective orientation, which we discussed in Chapter 6, goes hand in hand with his emphasis upon the individual as the unit of sociological analysis.

In his section on "basic concepts" in Economy and Society, Weber defined sociology as the scientific discipline which studies the "social action" of individual actors through "interpretive understanding." Action is social to the extent to which individual actors attach subjective meaning to the behavior of themselves and others. Individuals "take account of the behavior of others" and "orient" their own behavior to the behavior of others."[1] Weber treated the individual as a thinking, choosing, acting person. Because of the nature of the individual, it is necessary for sociological theory to take into account the subjective orientation of the individual. Any study of social life would be incomplete and inaccurate if it did not begin with the point of view of the actor.

Weber argued that one of the major errors made by sociological theorists is the "reification" of sociological concepts such as "society," "state," etc. That is, many sociologists treat these collective entities as if they were real entities, capable of acting and thinking. According to Weber, such collective entities are merely abstract concepts which enable us to speak meaningfully about a multitude of individual actions. It is the individual who acts, not "the state" or "the group." The government does not levy a tax; tax laws are passed by legislators who are specific and individual human beings, and taxes are collected by other individuals who are equally specific and real.

In this connection, Weber referred to what he called the "organic school of sociology,"[2] whose orientation was to the "whole" within which the individual acts. From this perspective, the individual units of a functional system are of interest only to the extent to which they are integrated with other units and contribute to the entire system. Such an approach may be instructive and lead to important insights. But Weber cautioned that "if its cognitive value is overestimated and its concepts illegitimately 'reified,' it can be highly dangerous."[3] Such was Weber's treatment of the budding field of functional analysis. Since functional analysis is nonsubjective in character, and since it tends to ignore the individual and his most fundamental social characteristics, Weber had little use for it. He much preferred a sociological orientation which placed emphasis upon individual behavior and values, and upon the specific historical and cultural conditions which resulted from the social action of individual actors.

The real significance of collectivities is that as collectivities they have a subjective meaning to individual actors. People act "as if" collectivities have a real existence. They "pattern" their behavior after that of other actors in such a way as to conform to group norms. In this way, the collectivities "have a powerful, often a decisive, causal influence on the course of action of real individuals."[4] For ease of expression, we continually refer to groups rather than individuals. But if it suited our purposes, we could completely change our terminology and refer only to the actions of individual persons.

Weber cautioned that he did not mean to imply that the sociological investigator must always focus only upon the individual as his unit of analysis. He distinguished three possibilities: (1) "concrete individual action," (2) the "average" subjective meaning or behavior for a group of individuals, and (3) "a scientifically formulated pure type . . . of a common phenomenon."[5] In his own empirical studies, most of which were written before his more general statement in Economy and Society, Weber usually utilized numbers two and three above. He usually referred to social collectivities as entities and spoke of the values and actions of such entities. He frequently used ideal types for comparative analyses, enabling him to discuss such topics as capitalism and Judaism without constantly referring to individual people. What distinguished Weber's approach, however, was that he consistently referred back to subjective orientations of individual actors both in the formation of his important concepts and in his empirical generalizations of concrete historical events. He sought to make the subjective orientation of individual actors explicit in a way totally different from Durkheim's use of collective data. In much of his work, Durkheim treated groups as acting entities with a powerful influence upon individual actors. In contrast, Weber treated individual actors as acting entities with an equally powerful influence upon specific groups and events. The difference of emphasis of the two theorists is crucial to the manner in which their theories were developed. Because they differred so drastically in the orientations with which they approached the study of societal phenomena, it is not surprising that the kinds of studies they pursued and the kinds of conclusions they drew from their investigations differed significantly from each other.

THE NATURE OF SCIENTIFIC LAWS
IN THE SOCIAL SCIENCES

Weber's individualistic and subjective orientations had a profound influence upon his views about the proper role of the social scientist. His discussion of the proper methodology for the study of social life represented a major departure from both his precursors (i.e., Comte and Marx) and his contemporaries (i.e., Durkheim). We should note at this point that the great bulk of sociologists since the time of Weber and Durkheim have followed Durkheim's orientation. Weber's approach had a significant impact

259

in Germany for many years. Even there, however, the growth of positivism and the impact of American sociology have eroded Weber's influence in his native land. His approach has much to recommend it, however. Weber provided perhaps the most pervasive critique of the positivist orientation yet found in sociological literature. He used his emphasis on the subjective orientation of individual actors to develop a profound argument against the kind of methodology utilized most frequently by contemporary sociologists.

Weber believed that most sociologists were attempting to use the natural sciences as a model for their own discipline. He thought this was a fundamental mistake which has led sociology into serious theoretical errors. His argument against the natural science model is best developed in an essay entitled "'Objectivity' in Social Science and Social Policy" published in The Methodology of the Social Sciences.[6] In order to make an effective criticism of it, Weber set out to define and describe the natural science model of theoretical development as follows:

> In the natural sciences (there is) the hope . . . of attaining a purely "objective" (i.e., independent of all individual contingencies) monistic knowledge of the totality of reality in a conceptual system of metaphysical validity and mathematical form.[7]

Such a model assumes the existence of scientific "laws" which govern the causal relationships among physical phenomena and which lead to both "regularity" and "universality" in the physical world. Some events are assumed to be universal in that they are unfailingly produced by the workings of physical causes. Scientists who follow such an approach seek to develop a deductive system of propositions which will explain all sociological and historical events. Such laws are assumed to be both general and comprehensive.[8] Universal and recurring conditions and events become the focus of analysis, and unique or emergent conditions and events are assumed to be unimportant for scientific analysis.

Weber rejected this model of social reality most explicitly. He did not believe that it will ever be possible to develop a system of concepts and propositions which will apply generally to all cultures at all time periods. He himself never attempted to develop such a propositional theory. Weber believed in the "emergent" nature of social reality. New "historical individuals" such as rational capitalism are constantly arising, due to unique combinations of historical forces.

Social phenomena are qualitatively different from those of the natural sciences. No one can claim to be a sociologist who has not recognized this point. According to Weber, the methods and assumptions of science per se are indispensable to sociology. But the particular methods and assumptions, the definitions, propositions and theories of the natural sciences cannot be utilized in sociology because of the qualitative differences in the phenomena under investigation in the two scientific areas. Rather than borrowing methods and assumptions from the natural sciences, sociology should develop its own, and these should be in conformity with the special subjective nature of social phenomena.

In the above-mentioned essay, one can find at least seven[9] reasons why Weber rejected the natural science approach. These arguments center upon Weber's assertion that deterministic and universal laws are not present in social life. He believed it is therefore not appropriate that sociologists should seek to build their science upon the assumption that the end product of every science is a set of laws which can be ordered deductively. Let us first summarize these seven reasons for Weber's rejection of the natural science model before discussing them more fully:

1. The social sciences deal with "ideas" while the natural sciences deal with objects.

2. Individual free will and choice make deterministic laws impossible.

3. The processes of abstraction and selection utilized by the social sciences make the notions of invariability and universality untenable.

4. The multiple causation found in social phenomena also makes the assumption of invariability utenable.

5. The social sciences are interested in the "individuality of a phenomena" rather than in its universality.

6. Particularistic statements rather than general statements or systems of statements (theories) are most fruitful and contain the most information.

7. Society is characterized by change rather than stability.

Some of these arguments have been more fully discussed in Chapter Six. Some comments, however, should be made on each of these points here. In the pages which follow, we will discuss more fully Weber's arguments and his insistence that sociology must follow new paths never explored by the other sciences.

1.) IDEAS VS. OBJECTS

In the chapter on Weber's subjective theory, we discussed more fully his assertion that "ideas" are the subject matter of sociology. The following comments, however, seem necessary here. Men and women differ from physical phenomena in that they can think. No similar behavior has ever been observed in the phenomena dealt with by the physical sciences. Other organisms, even the so-called "higher mammals," appear to react to instinct rather than to reflection. A person's ideas represent an intervening step between the stimuli found in a given situation and the individual's reaction to the situation. Ideas never perfectly reflect the situation. Perception is a variable, not a constant. Thought processes lead to choices (discussed in #7) which are "free" rather than determined. Because ideas differ from objects, and because they are much more variable than objects, the approach taken by the social sciences must be far different from that taken by the natural sciences.

Scientific laws can never give information about the cultural significance of cultural phenomena. Weber argued that even if it were possible for sociologists or psychologists to separate subjective ideas into "elementary factors" and then to classify them and formulate them by empirical observation into laws, one would still not "understand" the significance of such ideas. This is the ultimate goal of sociology. Any statement of laws which might govern the ideas of men would still only be preliminary to the real work of sociology: understanding and explaining the cultural significance of ideas. Sociology's distinctive approach must be to study those aspects of social life which are significant from a subjective point of view.

It would be a waste of time for the sociologist to study social facts which have no significance to a society.

2.) FREE WILL VS. DETERMINISM

Weber's subjectivism led him logically to a second important assertion: because people exercise volition and act upon their social world, no purely deterministic forces operate in social life to produce predetermined effects. The behavior of individuals is influenced but not determined by the social conditions in which they live. People have some (admittedly variable) degree of freedom to choose the kinds of behavior in which they engage. They <u>will</u> act in what they <u>think</u> are their own best interests. Weber used this as an argument against the development of deterministic social laws to explain social behavior. He assumed that the social action of individuals would consistently result in emergent conditions not fully explainable by scientific laws.

Weber never fully came to grips with the philosophical issue of free will versus determinism. At many points he seemed to assume a position in favor of free will and opposed to determinism. However, this position is implicit rather than explicit in his writings. For Weber, social action in terms of specifiable personal goals is always problematic. One can ascertain patterns of values and choice, but these do not always produce a predictable pattern of behavior. Weber argued that only by knowing the totality of all previous conditions and choices can one make a reasonably certain prediction about a future state.[10] But such complete knowledge is never available to the human mind, according to Weber, and if it were, there would be no need for the development of deterministic scientific laws.

The social investigator should instead concentrate on identifying <u>specific</u> goals, values, choices and other subjective orientations of <u>specific</u> actors in order to arrive at an adequate causal explanation of a <u>specific</u> event. Such an approach has less general applicability, but gains in precision and meaningfulness over attempts to develop <u>general</u> scientific laws.

3.) ABSTRACTION VS. UNIVERSALITY

We have also previously discussed Weber's contention that all ideas, including scientific concepts, represent abstractions from reality.[11] Reality is extremely complex. In order to deal with this complexity, the mind selects or abstracts out only certain parts of reality for conceptualization and study. Further, a sociologist is interested in only certain aspects of the real world. He uses his own interests as criteria for determining which aspects of social reality will be conceptualized and examined. Countless other aspects of social life are left unrecognized and unconceptualized. Evidently, the process of abstraction is subject to variability and individual choice. These abstractions may be manipulated and reformulated at will. For example, one may develop any number of ideal-typical concepts about capitalism, each of which might be useful for a given purpose. Capitalism does not exist in the same sense that a planet exists, for it exists only in the mind of the individual. The process of abstraction thus is contradictory to the assertion that "real" objects exist with certain invariable and predictable relations among them.

What determines the specific content abstracted out from the complexity of reality? Weber's answer again stressed the importance of human values. Only those aspects of reality which have a cultural significance to the scientist and his society are chosen for study. Cultural values bring order to the otherwise chaotic plethora of possible individual goals. By making these cultural values the major object of study, and by studying only those aspects of social life which have cultural significance, the sociologist is able to achieve order in both his scientific explanations and in the methodology by which he pursues these explanations. The social and cultural (i.e., subjectively meaningful) causes of culturally significant social phenomena must become the object of causal explanation if sociology is to have a practical value, according to Weber.

4.) MULTIPLE CAUSATION

Weber's view of the nature of causation flows directly from this. Causal relations must be established, if possible, among those aspects of reality which have been abstracted out and conceptualized. Any causal statement is itself an abstraction from reality, and must be carefully considered as such. Weber consistently warned that all aspects of our scientific work, including attributions of causation, must be recognized for what they are: conceptions in the mind of the scientist. We should not attempt to attribute to them any objective reality. If we recognize that causal statements simply represent our current state of thinking about the world, we will not treat them as fixed and immutable laws which cannot be revised to suit our changing needs.

Weber assumed that in this subjective process of attributing causation, one would be able to find many relationships among variables which might be labeled as causal. For example, in one situation, A might be labeled the cause of B, with C, D, and E being considered as necessary conditions. In another situation with another point of reference, C might be considered the cause of B, with A, D, and E considered as conditions. A, C, D, and E are all necessary to produce B, but different purposes or different points of view may lead the observer to emphasize one at one time, and another at another time.

> The number and type of causes which have influenced any given event are always infinite and there is nothing in the things themselves to set some of them apart as alone meriting attention . . . an <u>exhaustive</u> causal investigation of any concrete phenomena in its full reality is not only practically impossible--it is simple nonsense. We select only those causes to which are to be imputed in the individual case, the "essential" feature of an event.[12]

Any event can be conceptualized as "caused" by a number of antecedent conditions. Here Weber assumed that the complexity of social causation in concrete reality is so extensive that a great many "causes" may be identified for any given effect. It therefore becomes necessary to abstract out those causes which have the most significance <u>from the point of view of the cultural values which the scientist holds</u>. It is the scientist who draws upon his own culturally-conditioned values to make an attribution of causation in any given case. From this premise, Weber concluded that the notion of the existence of scientifically

265

valid laws which are universal and deterministic is simply untenable.

5.) INDIVIDUAL VS. UNIVERSAL PHENOMENA
    GENERAL VS. PARTICULAR STATEMENTS
    CHANGE VS. STABILITY

The other three arguments Weber used against the natural science model can only be briefly summarized here.

Weber argued that it is precisely the unique and different events of social life which should be the objects of explanation by sociologists. His own work clearly demonstrated his values here. Rational capitalism, for example, is a unique historical event (or "historical individual") which came into existence under the influence of a multitude of specific causes. One should not attempt to derive such events from general causal laws. Rather, the investigator should seek to identify the specific constellation of causes which together produced this unique event. It will never occur again in precisely the same way.

General propositions, according to Weber, have very little explanatory value because of their abstract nature. Specific causal statements used to explain specific events were preferable to general causal statements which were directed to the explanation of broad and often undefined social conditions. Weber himself did not seek to establish universal generalizations applicable to all societies, although some of his definitions are of this type. Rather, he contented himself with the analysis of specific events which could be explained by particular causal statements subject to direct verification.

Finally, Weber recognized the changeability of social life. Being trained as an historian, he was oriented to observe those aspects of social life which emerged anew. Rather than seeking to explain stability, he sought to explain change. Rather than utilizing general explanations of universals, he sought specific explanations of emergent events. This aspect of his thinking was decidedly different from that of Durkheim and the positivistic school. Both were looking at different aspects of social life. Through their choice of a given orientation--universals or emergent events--they arrived at different conclusions about the proper methodology and the proper theoretical orientation of sociology.

THE ROLE OF LAWS IN THE SOCIAL SCIENCES

We have summarized above Weber's argument that the goal of the cultural sciences is to develop causally adequate explanations of specific events rather than universalistic social laws. We should make it abundantly clear, however, that Weber did not assert that social laws are nonexistent. Much of his work assumed rather that social laws of some sort do exist. But he did not view these laws as "natural." There are no self-existing laws present in the universe which operate on people irrespective of their conscious awareness of such laws. Weber argued against such "realism." Social laws are constructed in the minds of social scientists to enable them to understand social phenomena.

> It is customary to designate various sociological generalizations . . . as scientific "laws." These are in fact typical probabilities confirmed by observation to the effect that under certain given conditions an expected course of action will occur, which is understandable in terms of the typical motives and typical subjective intentions of the actors. These generalizations are both understandable and definite in the highest degree. . . .[13]

Causal imputations can certainly be made because understanding and, to a certain extent, prediction and control, are possible. But social laws are still essentially subjective, and no purpose would be served by considering them as anything else but fruitful ideas--as brilliant insights perhaps, but still ideas.

The practical uses of social laws, rather than any philosophical assertions concerning the nature of laws, was the focus of Weber's thinking on this point.[14] If a universal proposition serves to give us understanding of a particular historical case, it should be used. But we should expect from it no more than an "adequate" explanation of causation. The word "adequate" here is contrasted with "perfect" or "universal." It implies a lesser degree of probability than is ordinarily expected from causal statements. The relationship need not be invariant--the correlation between the cause and

267

the effect need not be perfect. A causal assertion is adequate if it can be communicated in a meaningful way to the scientist (and presumably to his readers) and if it seems to explain to their satisfaction the relationship involved.

In conclusion, Weber's main contributions to the "group vs. individual" issue were (1) his development of the rationale for studying social phenomena from the point of view of the individual actor, and (2) his rejection of deterministic and universal social laws for a more limited conception of laws applicable to specific historical events. In both cases, Weber took a position opposed to Durkheim and the positivist school. His position has not been accepted as popularly as has Durkheim's. It frequently tends to be misunderstood and misinterpreted. But Weber should receive great credit for the potency of his argument and for perhaps the highest development of the "individualistic" orientation.

THE INDIVIDUAL AS A CAUSE OF SOCIAL EVOLUTION: WARD

Lester Frank Ward (1841-1913) was one of the strongest advocates among American sociologists in the classical period of a sociological theory based upon individual action. Ward's influence upon his times was exceedingly great. Today, however, his major works are all out of print and few sociologists feel any need to review his theories.

Ward adopted evolutionary theory but took a far different view of the political implications of this theory than did Spencer or Sumner. The latter theorists believed that evolution followed the course of deterministic natural laws, and that people should not interfere in the course of evolutionary development. They accepted the laissez-faire doctrine advocating limited government and personal rather than social meliorism.

Ward took an opposite position. He believed strongly in the ability of the individual to influence the course of history. The social group is composed of individuals, and one should not think of it as a "real" entity. It should not be personified. "The only real thing is the individual."[15] One seeks to improve society only in order to improve the lives of its individual members. Throughout his career, Ward carried on a polemic with Sumner regarding the role of the individual in history. Ward advocated individual initiative to influence society and improve the social life of all people. He opposed the "individualism" of Spencer and Sumner which supposedly favored the individual and restricted governmental and other social action. He argued that this type of individualism gives little support to the possibility of individuals creating social organizations which will advance the level of civilization of their society. The laissez-faire evolutionists advocated individual initiative in economic spheres but foresaw little influence of the individual in directing the course of evolution and improving society. Ward believed that individuals can change the course of history and evolution with properly designed social programs.

In his first major work, Dynamic Sociology (1883), and even more in his Pure Sociology (1903),[16] Ward recognized two major spheres of social causation. The first he labelled "genesis," by which he referred to those "blind" natural forces which exert an influence on the course of history. All of the biological forces influencing the behavior of human beings are included here, as well as those forces operating in the evolutionary process which are not subject to the control of individuals.

The second category of forces are labelled "telesis." These encompass those forces set in motion by purposive actions--that is, through the individual's mind. In his concept of "mind," Ward included the intellect, the desires and the will of human beings. He devoted the whole of the volume The Psychic Factors of Civilization[17] to an analysis of the influence of the mind on social life.

The individual himself can be a cause in the social world. In fact, Ward refers to human purposive action as the "final" cause (a la Aristotle). It is the ultimate repository of causation: a cause from which the scientist cannot retreat to a further level of abstraction. Human purposive action is "ultimate." It is itself largely uncaused, and gives final direction to the course of history.[18]

Human purposive action includes a number of elements. First, the actor anticipates or knows in advance the end or result of his actions. Second, in order to attain his goal, the actor must understand other forces (genesis) which are operating in nature and foresee the consequences of his own action. Third, the actor acts to make use of these genetic forces to achieve his desired end. [19]

> The final cause is the mind's knowledge of the relations that subsist between the means and the end. But the chief of these relations, and the only practical one, is the action of other natural forces outside of the agent's will-power or muscular strength. What the mind sees is that such forces exist and are operating in certain directions. What the intelligent agent does is to place the thing he desires but lacks the power to move into the current of such a force which moves it for him. This is the type of teleological action. It is illustrated in its simplest form by the lumberman who puts his logs into the river and lets the current float them to their destination. [20]

The human agent makes use of natural forces, which may be called "efficient causes." [21] But the actor with a proper understanding of these forces can produce results which would not have occurred if he had not acted. The purposive act of the individual is thus the "final" cause. By taking action the person can utilize the forces of nature to produce the results he desires and can mold the type of society he chooses.

Much of Ward's theoretical work rested upon certain assumptions derived from the psychology of his day. Chief among these was the assertion that people always seek pleasure and avoid pain and that they are ultimately oriented to increase their own happiness. According to Ward, sociology can only be developed properly when psychology has been sufficiently developed to enable the explanation of individual behavior. Sociology "rests directly upon psychology." [22] Sociology applies psychological principles to the relations among individuals and their larger social groupings. Ward, however, believed that it is necessary to place greater emphasis upon society rather than the single individual and to engage more strongly in collective action. [23]

In summary, Ward's position was that society is a creation of human beings ultimately reducible to individual actions. The individual actor is the final cause of social phenomena, and can direct the course of social evolution and history. Ward's emphasis upon individual action and the important place of the individual in social life stands in contrast to more deterministic writers who tend to emphasize the causal role of social forces or social facts while neglecting or denying the role of individual action in social life.

FOOTNOTES

[1]Max Weber, Economy and Society: An Outline of Interpretive Sociology (New York: Bedminster Press), 1968, Three Volumes. Our references to this work will be taken from Max Weber, The Theory of Social and Economic Organization, tr. by A. M. Henderson and Talcott Parsons (Glencoe: Free Press, 1947). See especially p. 88.

[2]Theory, p. 102.

[3]Ibid., p. 103.

[4]Ibid., p. 102.

[5]Ibid., p. 96.

[6]Max Weber, The Methodology of the Social Sciences, tr. by Edward A. Shils and Henry A. Finch (Glencoe: Free Press, 1949).

[7]Ibid., p. 85. Italics Weber's. See also p. 106.

[8]Ibid., pp. 72-73.

[9]We don't wish to quibble about the specific number of objections. One might wish to group them or subdivide them into a greater or lesser number. These seven appear to us, however, as distinct.

[10]Ibid., p. 88.

[11]Ibid., p. 78. See Chapter Six.

[12]Ibid., p. 78.

[13]Theory, pp. 107-108.

[14]Methodology, pp. 79-80.

[15]Lester F. Ward, The Psychic Factors of Civilizations (Boston: Ginn), 1893, p. 99.

[16]Lester F. Ward, Dynamic Sociology (New York: Appleton), 1883 (Two volumes), and Pure Sociology (New York: Macmillan), 1903.

[17]Op. cit.

[18]Pure Sociology, pp. 466-468.

[19]Ibid., p. 467.

[20]Lester F. Ward, Outlines of Sociology (New York: Macmillian), 1904 (1897), p. 245.

[21]Pure Sociology, p. 466.

[22]Psychic Factors, p. 97.

[23]Ibid., pp. 313-333.

CHAPTER FOURTEEN

SYMBOLIC INTERACTIONIST APPROACHES TO THE RELATIONSHIP
BETWEEN THE INDIVIDUAL AND THE GROUP

In this chapter we shall continue to examine the
theoretical issue of the relationship of the individual
to the group by examining the work of three classical
symbolic interactionists: Cooley, Mead, and Thomas.
Since symbolic interaction is such an important theory
in contemporary sociology, it is instructive for us to
examine the approach which the founders of this
theoretical orientation took to what they considered to
be one of the most important issues in sociological
theory.

THE INSEPARABILITY OF THE SOCIAL
AND THE INDIVIDUAL: COOLEY

Charles Horton Cooley's contributions to the group
vs. individual issue are some of the most significant
in all sociological literature. He viewed the issue in
quite different terms than previous sociologists, and
his orientation to the nature of the individual is also
different from that of most theorists. Cooley's
argument about the inseparability of the social and the
individual has served to redirect thinking on the
subject ever since his time.

Cooley argued that most theorists make a false
distinction between the individual and society. They
think of these two concepts as denoting two distinctly
different forms of reality. In opposition to this
view, Cooley asserted that the individual and the group
are aspects of the same social reality: social
interaction. Every group is composed of individuals,
and any discussion of the larger group presupposes the
existence of these smaller units. This point of view
is widely held and generally well accepted. The
corollary of this view, however, is rarely discussed
and understood: the individual has no separate
existence apart from the group. What we call the
individual (or in Cooley's terms the "social self") is
in fact composed largely of representations and images
which the person receives through interaction with
other individuals. The individual personality develops
through social interaction. Without social
interaction, the personality could not develop. What
we think of as our own personality--our own
individuality--is directly derived from the images and

273

reactions which we receive from other persons about the nature of our own self.[1]

In Chapter Eight, we discussed Cooley's concept of the "looking-glass self." Cooley believed we gain a concept of the nature of our self as an individual not by looking in a mirror but by looking in the faces of others with whom we interact. The reactions of others to us gives us the essential information we must have about the nature of our own characteristics. Therefore, the way we think about ourselves--that is, the content of the "self" and the view that we have of ourselves as differentiated from others--is derived from others through social (i.e., symbolic) interaction.

Cooley noted that those who argue for the distinctiveness of the individual and society often refer back to some supposed prehistoric condition when individuals existed separately before they were joined together in a social group. While Cooley recognized that any discussion of the first origins of social relations is subject only to speculation because of the unavailability of data, he argued that individuals could never have existed without interaction with other individuals. The existence of one individual presupposes the existence of others as well.

Any idea which the individual has about himself also contains some social aspects, according to Cooley. The very reference to oneself has no meaning without the implied existence of other individuals as significant other persons. The existence of language and of communication precedes, then, the development of the self. (Cooley did not make this point as clearly as did Mead many years later in Mind, Self, and Society.)[2] Consciousness and other subjective processes, even emotion, are largely derived from the process of interaction. With the possible exception of instinctive emotional reactions, all thought presupposes the existence of other people.

The human organism, according to Cooley, coordinates and integrates certain basic capabilities or tendencies, including emotion, thought, and intelligence. Through social learning, the individual also internalizes the traditions and roles of his society. All these elements, then, tend to be integrated within the individual. They are in a state of readiness to act. Cooley spoke of these tendencies

as the "explosive material stored up" in the
individual. These tendencies "to live, to feel, to
act" are released through social interaction.[3] In one
sense, these basic human tendencies are created through
social interaction. In another sense, they are
released only through interaction. Without other
individuals with whom to interact, and without actual
interaction taking place, the individual remains a
bundle of capabilities and nothing more. Only the
social process of interaction turns loose these
capabilities and allows the person to develop the
individuality and potential which he or she possesses.

THE NATURE OF THE SOCIAL AND THE INDIVIDUAL

Cooley asserted that there are three usual
meanings of the term "social."[4] First, it "denotes
that which pertains to the collective aspect of
humanity, to society in its widest and vaguest
meaning." Second, it refers to social interaction
among individuals--"to the life of conversation and
face-to-face sympathy." Third, social is contrasted
with anti-social, and tends to mean that which is
"conducive to the collective welfare." In each of
these meanings, the existence of the individual is
assumed. But more important, according to Cooley, in
none of these senses is the social opposed to or in
conflict with the individual or with individuality.
Those who seek to contrast the social with the
individual, or who argue that they are mutually
exclusive, do not have a correct view of social life.
Social life is a "vital whole," not simply an
"aggregate of physical bodies."[5]

To strengthen his argument on this point, Cooley
then discussed four ways in which people think about
the individual person. In the first, which Cooley
called "mere individualism" the individual traits of
each person are emphasized. "Each person is held to be
a separate agent, and all social phenomena are thought
of as originating in the action of such agents."[6] The
second way of looking at the individual in his relation
to society was labeled by Cooley as "double
causation."[7] Here, both the individual and society are
conceived as separate, and each may have a causal
influence on the other. Cooley argued that this is the
most widely held notion. Partly because of this, both
the individual and the society tend to be conceived in
vague and ill-defined terms.

The third view is called "primitive individualism."[8] This view results from a "crude evolutionary philosophy," and conceives of the individual as being prior in time to the social. Through evolutionary development, the group "emerges" at a later time on a different level than the individual. The fourth and final view is the "social faculty view." Here, the social aspect of life is conceived of as including "only a part, often a rather definite part, of the individual."[9] Human nature is divided into social and non-social aspects. The individual is partly social, partly non-social.

The inherent weakness of each of these definitions of the individual is that it assumes that the individual can be separated empirically from the social process. Cooley argued that the separate individual is only an abstraction which has gained currency in contemporary thought. The essential insight which he had to offer in its place is the empirical generalization that the individual self develops only in social interaction and is totally a social product. What the sociological investigator observes is social interaction. If he chooses, he may divide this empirical reality into the social and the individual for purposes of abstraction. In reality, however, they are one. Cooley's wish was that future conceptualizations of the group and the individual will be brought more closely in touch with empirical reality.

THE SOCIAL NATURE OF INDIVIDUAL CHOICE

Cooley noted that those who argue for the separability of the individual from the social often base their arguments on the "innate" ability of the individual to exercise volition. They assert that because the individual is able to make choices, he is thereby "free" to act in a manner of his own choosing, independent of social influences. To Cooley, choice is a complex process of thought. In choosing, the individual takes account of all aspects of the situation, or as many as he can. He creates in his mind, through the thought process, a synthesis of the social aspects of the situation. His choice, then, reflects the influence of the situation upon the thought processes of the individual. Since both the elements of the situation and the thought processes of the individual are social in nature, the choice which results must also be social in nature. "Any choice that I can make is a synthesis of suggestions derived in one way or another from the general (social) life."[10]

As the individual grows and develops, he learns to take account of the social influences of other individuals upon his life, and to adjust to these influences. The whole process of symbolic interaction involves an adjustment of behavior to that of other individuals. Their expectations of us, and their reactions to our behavior, enter into our consciousness and become integral aspects of our own choices and behavior.

> Our particular minds or wills are members of a slowly growing whole, and at any given moment are limited in scope by the state of the whole, and especially of those parts of the whole with which they are in most active contact. Our thought is never isolated, but always some sort of a response to the influences around us, so that we can hardly have thoughts that are not in some way aroused by communication.[11]

Cooley believed that if the surrounding social environment is simple and homogeneous, so that few if any alternatives are presented to us, then our choices are almost automatic and unreflective. However, if the environment is complex and presents us with a variety of alternatives, choice becomes more difficult. Choice is still made among those alternatives provided by the social environment. But because the number of possible alternatives is much greater, the province of "free" choice is increased markedly. Cooley argued that the nature of social organization and the complexity of the social environment determine the alternatives from which individual choice is made, but there is no strict determination of which particular alternative will be chosen. The individual chooses his action through the process of cognitive synthesis of the social elements with which he is presented.

> It is the variety of social intercourse . . . the character of social organization, that determines the field of choice; and accordingly there is a tendency for the scope of the will to increase with that widening and intensification of life that is so conspicuous a feature of recent

277

history. . . . We are still dependent upon
environment . . . but environment is becoming
very wide, and in the case of imaginative
persons may extend itself to almost any ideas
that the past or present life of the race has
brought into being. This brings opportunity
for congenial choice and characteristic
personal growth, and at the same time a good
deal of distraction and strain. . . . Choice
is like a river; it broadens as it comes down
through history--though there are always
banks, and the wider it becomes the more
persons drown in it. Stronger and stronger
swimming is required, and types of character
that lack vigor and self-reliance are more
and more likely to go under.[12]

This conclusion coincides with that made by Durkheim in
his The Division of Labor in Society.[13] As society
develops and becomes more complex, the range of
alternatives from which behavior may be chosen
increases markedly. This in turn increases both the
individual's freedom to choose and the difficulty of
making choices. The alternatives from which the
individual can choose are still provided by his
society, but because the range of alternatives is
increased, the freedom of choice of the individual is
also increased.

INDIVIDUAL CHOICE AND DETERMINISM

This led Cooley to a digressive footnote on the
question of free will versus determinism.[14] He noted
that some persons conceive of each person's mind as
being a fortress besieged by an army (i.e., the social
group). The individual is attempting to repel the
external influences, while society is attempting to
breach the walls of his mind and force him to act as it
dictates. According to Cooley, this view does not
coincide with what actually takes place in society. He
argued that human life is a whole, and that each
individual is a member of his society. By stressing
this unity of individual and society, he attempted to
reorient the question of free will versus determinism.
Each individual is constantly willing and choosing, and
the general will of the society as a whole is simply
the general manifestation of these individual wills.
Since the individual and the group are both
manifestations of the same reality, they are not
opposed to each other, but inseparably connected.

278

Cooley believed, therefore, that the issue of free will versus determinism has not been decided, but rather has been rendered obsolete.[15] Philosophical discussions about this issue can be replaced with empirical studies of the nature of individual choice and the influence of each situation upon such choices. The sociologist need not debate the philosophical merits of each side. His work is to study social behavior and describe it as meticulously and accurately as possible. Cooley was confident that his own position as to the inseparability of the social and the individual would be justified by such research.

INDIVIDUAL CHOICE, NONCONFORMITY AND LEADERSHIP

Cooley used this theoretical position to explain both nonconformity and leadership. In every case, according to him, nonconformity is a matter of degree. From one point of view, the individual is acting in a deviant manner, but from the perspective of some other group, his behavior is totally conformist. Since many alternatives are possible, almost any choice and action will bring the individual to be identified as a nonconformist by some segment of his society. Much that is identified as nonconformity involves conformity to a different value, a higher principle. Here Cooley used Thoreau's analogy of marching to a different drummer. One still marches in conformity to the beat of a drum, but the beat that he marches to is different from that of others in his immediate group. One must then ask himself what influences the individual is obeying, rather than supposing that he is totally out of touch with his environment.

> All non-conformity that is affirmative or constructive must act by this selection of remoter relations. . . . There is, therefore, no definite line between conformity and non-conformity; there is simply a more or less characteristic and unusual way of selecting and combining accessible influences.[16]

No act is purely mechanical or imitative. One always puts his own stamp on his behavior. In Cooley's terms, he puts "something of his idiosyncrasy into it."[17] Just as truly, no act is purely individualistic. Everything that an individual does is derived in some part from his social environment.

Cooley noted, however, that psychologically some individuals have an "impulse" to nonconformity. They gain a greater sense of "self" or individuality by acting differently from others. They possess a "spirit of opposition," and gain a sense of courage, joy and self-fulfillment from nonconformity. Such nonconformist tendencies are found in every individual, but vary widely from one to another. Cooley treated these "impulses" as relatively innate predispositions. However, they are not purely instinctual, since they are reinforced or punished by persons with whom the individual interacts. They therefore take on a social aspect.

Leadership is much like nonconformity. Some individuals have greater needs for self-assertion than others. These needs are often spoken of as if they are innate traits, but Cooley argued that they are developed largely through social interaction. Leaders have a sense of self-reliance, of personal assertion, of confidence which others possess in lesser degrees. They also tend to represent in their behavior and personalities the most positive features of their social environment. They embody more fully than others the values and aspirations which the society seeks to inculcate in all its members. The majority of people are impressionable individuals who react positively to leaders and who tend to follow them emotionally.

Many characteristics contribute to leadership. Cooley mentioned personal judgment, reputation, past record, aggressiveness, definiteness of plan, and self-confidence among others. The important point to note, however, is that leadership is exerted through social interaction between leader and follower. Each communicates to the other, and their mutual reinforcement of each other's aspirations and values bonds them together into a leader-follower relationship. One cannot understand the phenomenon of leadership, then, unless one also understands the symbolic nature of social interaction and the close integration of individual and social aspects of human life.

In summary, Cooley's discussion of the relationship between the group and the individual is one of the most extensive in all sociological literature. Its emphasis upon the inseparability of the social and individual aspects of social interaction has contributed to a reorientation of thought on the subject. Cooley's argument, however, is frequently neglected in contemporary sociology.

THE INDIVIDUAL AND THE SITUATION: THOMAS

W. I. Thomas's view of the nature of the individual was similar in most respects to Cooley's. His emphasis on the situational approach, however, made him express his ideas in a different manner. Further, his discussion of the influence of "great men" departed from the approaches taken by Mead and Cooley.

According to Thomas, an individual acts in an individualistic manner if his behavior is not strictly determined by the traditions, norms and sanctions of his social groups, but rather is subject to the individual's free choice. Individualism is a matter of degree. The greater the influence of the social group in the form of definitions of the situation, traditional normative codes and severe sanctions for nonconformity, the less the individualism. On the other hand, the weaker the sanctions, the wider the limitations placed by social norms, the greater the leeway allowed without sanction, and the greater the number of alternative definitions of situations and forms of acceptable behavior, the greater the individualism.

> Individualism . . . means the personal schematization of life--making one's own definitions of the situation and determining one's own behavior norms.[18]

The behavior of the individual, even in primitive societies, is never completely determined. Numerous situations present themselves. For each situation, alternative modes of defining the situation are possible. For each alternative definition of the situation, alternative courses of action are available. People differ in their biological makeup, previous experience, and rigidity of personality. All these conditions facilitate individualistic behavior, and might be said to be causes of individualism. Thomas noted that a wide variety of behaviors result from seemingly similar conditions.[19]

> Examining this standpoint among primitive groups we find that they notice and magnify situations which we fail to notice, or disregard; that different tribes define the

281

same situation and pattern of behavior in precisely opposite ways; that the same tribe may define the situation for one set of objects in one way and for another set in another . . . that the same pattern may include a variety of meanings and applications . . . that a pattern may change to its opposite and back again, and even back and forth, with changing circumstances . . . that there is a tendency (which may be termed "perseverative") to step up patterns to unanticipated extremities.[20]

Because different groups behave differently in the same situations, Thomas argued that the social situation cannot be the determinant of patterns of behavior. The group's definition of the situation is the primary force in influencing the behavior of members of the group in each situation. Such group definitions may and do change relatively rapidly.

Every individual tends to conform to the prescriptions of his social group. No individual may be said to be completely individualistic. On the other hand, no social group completely prescribes or determines the actions of the individual. Some flexibility and alternatives are provided by every group, and in almost every situation. Individualism, therefore, is a matter of degree. It is subject to the influence of social variables such as type of social organization, consistency of cultural norms, types of sanctions used, rapidity of social change, etc. Thomas obviously believed that individual initiative accounts for a greater part of social behavior than do most sociologists, who tend to follow Durkheim's orientation.

THE GREAT MAN[21]

Given that every person acts individualistically at least part of the time, it seems apparent that some individuals might be considered extreme in their degree of individualism. In some cases, this individualism is quickly punished or squelched. In others, the person who acts in this manner may become a great leader who exerts a significant influence upon his society.

In his early work, Source Book for Social Origins,[22] Thomas discussed the presence of "extraordinary individuals" in a group. These individuals help their societies adjust to "crises," and by so doing exert a particularly significant influence on the society as a whole. Thomas mentioned Moses, Mohammed, Confucius, and Christ as examples of these "great men." He was quick to note, in addition, that primitive societies have been heavily influenced by great individuals. He mentioned the influence of Dingiswayn and Chaka on their Oulu tribesmen as an example of the influence of great individuals on a primitive society.

These great people exert their influence primarily on the subjective side of social life. They are "special definers of situations" who can direct a whole society toward a certain course of development or action because of their influence. Often they are occupationally specialized. They are the medicine men, the lawgivers, the scientists or the prophets. They have the ability to create and direct social movements through their power to influence the definitions of situations of the members of their society.

> . . . (C)ulture epochs and mass conversions (Christianity, Mohammedanism, the German Reformation, the French Revolution, popular government, fascism, communism, prohibition, etc.) are inaugurated by the propaganda of definitions of situations.[23]

Most sociologists have attempted to explain such broad social changes as Thomas mentioned here by reference to other social processes. They generally attempt to explain history without reference to individual people . Thomas's emphasis on the influence of "great men" therefore is distinctly different from that of most sociological theorists. Thomas's analysis of the influence of individuals is superficial since he did not attempt to show how a particular person changed the course of history for any given society. He did not mention the influence of other factors which might contribute to social change in addition to the acts of great individuals. But he clearly argued that certain people, through the new definitions of situations which they promulgate, can radically change the way of life of an entire society.

Thomas's contributions on this issue were not as extensive or significant as those of the other sociologists we have so far discussed. However, his relatively extreme position (among sociologists) on the

283

influence of the individual on the social group needs to be recorded. His significant theoretical contribution--the discussion of the definition of the situation--was closely related to his view that individuals make their own interpretations of social conditions and choose their behavior accordingly.

THE SELF AS A SOCIAL PRODUCT: MEAD

Like Thomas, George Herbert Mead's contributions to the understanding of the relationship between the group and the individual were not as seminal as his predecessor Cooley. Mead's discussion of the process of role playing and of the development of language represented significant advances over Cooley's symbolic interactionism. However, Cooley's discussion of the development of the self and of the interactive relationship between the self and the group are both better though-out and better expressed than Mead's.

Mead's orientation toward the individual was directly related to the fact that his disciplinary affiliation was as a social psychologist.[24] As such, he was interested primarily in the analysis and explanation of the influence of the social group on the individual. The dependent variable he dealt with was the individual--his personality, his attitudes, and his behavior. Only secondarily was he concerned with the reciprocal influence of the individual on the society.

His approach, then, differed markedly both from those of Cooley and Durkheim. Durkheim opted for a "pure" sociology in which the existence of the individual was assumed but in which individual characteristics were treated as constants for purposes of analysis. Durkheim was interested in social rates of behavior; Mead was interested in the behavior of the individual. The difference between them is a matter of choice. Each chose to explain a different aspect of social phenomena.

In many of his statements about the relationship of the group to the individual, Mead took a position which was as deterministic as Durkheim's. However, in his analysis of what he called the "I" and the "Me" he took a much more individualistic and less deterministic stance. We shall discuss both of these facets of his writings below.

284

THE "I" AND THE "ME"

According to Mead, the individual self has two phases or parts, which were labeled respectively the "I" and the "Me." The "Me" represents those aspects of the self which are derived from the generalized other. This is the "conventional individual."[25] The "Me" encompasses those attitudes and behavior patterns which are consistent with other individuals in the group. It represents the conformist side of the self.[26]

The "I" on the other hand represents those aspects of the self which are unique to the individual. It encompasses the spontaneous, impulsive and essentially irrational behavior of the individual. It is variable, unpredictable and free. Mead argued that the individual sometimes acts without reflection. Conscious awareness of such behavior is an indicator of the presence of the "I" as an essential part of the self.

Both the "I" and the "Me" are combined in each individual. For some, the "Me" or conventional self is almost totally in control. For others, the "I" is less restricted and accounts for a much greater percentage of the individual's behavior.

> We speak of a person as a conventional individual; his ideas are exactly the same as those of his neighbors. . . . Over against that there is the person who has a definite personality, who replies to the organized attitude in a way which makes a significant difference.[27]

Perhaps the reason that one does not find more empirical generalizations at the macro-social level in Mead's writings is because of his belief in this individualism, this unpredictability of the actor. Since every individual possesses an "I" as well as a "Me," the behavior determined by the "I" always introduces a new emergent element into social reality which is unpredictable from past knowledge of the individual or of the society.

Mead argued that "great men" can have an extremely important influence on the societies in which they live because of the force of their personalities as expressed through their individuality. Major social changes result largely from the actions of such people.

The individual, then, is an essential element in the explanation of the broad evolutionary changes which are occurring in society, as well as the particular changes found in any single society or social group.

However, one should not overemphasize this point. Mead recognized that such changes as are introduced by these "great men" are usually in keeping with the major values of the society. He argued that Socrates embodied in an almost perfect form the rationality which was an increasingly important aspect of Greek society. Likewise, Jesus carried to the extreme the emphasis on moral purity which was an essential element of Hebrew culture. By expressing a cultural principle in a pure form such individuals were carrying to the logical extreme the tendencies which were already present in their societies. Rather than being divorced from social conditions, therefore, their individualistic behavior was directly related to the ongoing trends in the societies in which they lived.

THE SELF AS A SOCIAL PRODUCT

The individual self, then, is composed of both individualistic and conformist tendencies. Even those aspects of the self which are most particularistic are often influenced by or oriented to the social conditions present in the society. Mead recognized the intimate connection between individual behavior and social structure.[28] While much of his analysis was devoted to an explanation of individual behavior, he clearly recognized that the self is a social product.

The self and the generalized other were generally treated by Mead as separate and distinct phenomena. However, they are differential aspects of the same social reality--interaction. The self cannot develop or have an existence apart from the others with whom it interacts. Likewise, the generalized other has no existence apart from the social selves which give it life. The "individual," then, is an abstraction from reality. The reality is social interaction among human beings. Certain aspects of this reality are abstracted out and labeled the self. Other aspects are abstracted out and labeled the "group" or the "generalized other."

The self is developed by internalizing the attitudes and patterns of behavior of the social group to which the individual belongs. The individual takes the role of the other and views himself from the point

286

of view of the generalized other. Mind, thought and language are results of the social process of interaction, as are the self and the generalized other.[29]

Mead's basic approach, therefore, was to explain the development of the self and the behavior of the individual from the point of view of the society in which the individual lives. The group is logically and temporally prior to the individual.[30] The process of social interaction is prior in time to the development of language, mind and the self. The society exerts a significant influence upon the individual, whose very self is dependent upon the perception of itself as an object. Such perception grows only through social interaction. The self and the generalized other are both distributive aspects of the process of social interaction.

At the same time, the self is composed of two aspects, the "Me" which is the conventional or conformist part and the "I" which represents the unique and individualistic part. The assertion of the "I" in social behavior leads to the emergence of new social phenomena and to social change. Some "great men" have an important influence on the course of history because of (1) their unique characteristics and behavior, and (2) their extension and embodiment of social tendencies present in their societies.

CONCLUSION

In the last two chapters we have discussed the works of those theorists who have most fully taken an individualistic approach to the study of social phenomena. Few were extreme in their individualism, and all recognized the important influence of the group on the individual. Yet all of these theorists suggested that the individual be taken as the point of reference in the study of social life. Their various positions contrast distinctly with those of Durkheim and the theorists who have taken a more "social" and deterministic orientation to the study of social phenomena. We turn now to a discussion of the manner in which this issue has been addressed by more contemporary sociologists.

FOOTNOTES

[1]Charles H. Cooley, Human Nature and the Social Order (New York: Scribner's), 1902, pp. 1-2, 11-12, 91-92.

[2]George H. Mead, Mind, Self and Society From the Standpoint of a Social Behaviorist, edited by Charles W. Morris (Chicago: University of Chicago Press), 1934 (posthumous).

[3]Human Nature, p. 285.

[4]Ibid., p. 4.

[5]Ibid., p. 8.

[6]Ibid., pp. 8-9.

[7]Ibid., pp. 9-10.

[8]Ibid., pp. 10-11.

[9]Ibid., p. 12.

[10]Ibid., p. 17.

[11]Ibid., p. 32.

[12]Ibid., pp. 38-39.

[13]Emile Durkheim, The Division of Labor in Society (Glencoe: Free Press), 1960.

[14]Human Nature, pp. 18-19. See also Charles H. Cooley, Social Organization (New York: Schocken Books), 1962 (published in 1909 by Scribner's).

[15]Human Nature, p. 19.

[16]Ibid., p. 271.

[17]Loc. cit.

[18]W. I. Thomas, On Social Organization and Social Personality, edited by Morris Janowitz (Chicago: University of Chicago Press), 1966, p. 244.

[19]See Edmund H. Volkart, Social Behavior and Personality: Contributions of W. I. Thomas to Theory and Social Research (New York: Social Science Research Council), 1951, pp. 9-10 for an especially good discussion of the individualistic implications in Thomas's work.

[20]W. I. Thomas, Primitive Society, p. 8.

[21]From the current perspective, discussions of the great man theory seem very sexist. Seldom was there a recognition that the great man could be a woman. Even in traditional and patriarchal societies there have been notable examples of women who have had a major influence on the history of their society (e.g., Joan of Arc in France).

[22]W. I. Thomas, Source Book for Social Origins (Chicago: University of Chicago Press), 1909.

[23]Primitive Society, p. 7.

[24]Mind, Self and Society, p. 7.

[25]Ibid., p. 200.

[26]Ibid., pp. 173-177.

[27]Ibid., p. 200.

[28]Ibid., pp. 164, 201-202.

[29]Ibid., pp. 191-192.

[30]Ibid., p. 186.

CHAPTER FIFTEEN

THE DEVELOPMENT AND CONTEMPORARY RELEVANCE OF THE GROUP VS. INDIVIDUAL ISSUE

In the past five chapters, we have found that a great variety of positions have been taken by classical sociological theorists on the question of the relationship between the group and the individual. Some consistent tendencies, however, seem to be present. Those who stress the importance of the social group in determining individual behavior tend to follow Durkheim's lead in being relatively deterministic and positivistic. On the other side are found those who, like Weber, treat the individual as the unit of analysis of sociological investigation. They tend to be relatively subjectively oriented, to be much more flexible and less positivistic in their methodology, and to give much greater weight to individual initiative and lesser weight to deterministic social laws. We want to emphasize again that many different ideas have been advanced on this issue, and that the above tendencies are not perfectly or consistently followed by any of the theorists we have discussed.

In turning to the contemporary development and relevance of this issue, we find at least a partial breakdown in the before-mentioned tendencies. Those who place most stress upon the influence of the group still tends to be positivistic in their methodology and relatively deterministic in their conclusions. However, among those who can be classified as adhering to the individualistic position, two distinct trends are found. The first, centering around Talcott Parsons, tend to follow Weber's position very closely. They treat the individual actor as the unit of analysis of social action and take a subjectivist theoretical position. The second, represented best in sociological literature by George Homans, argues that sociological generalizations can be ultimately deduced from theoretical propositions of behavioristic psychology. The individual is treated as the ultimate source of all sociological action. Those who take this orientation, however, are strongly positivistic in orientation. They stress the importance of the use of experimental methods to develop empirical generalizations regarding individual behavior. They tend to be more deterministic than the Durkheimians in their conclusions, although they work from an entirely different set of assumptions about the nature of the

relationship between the individual and group than did
Durkheim. In this chapter, we shall attempt to sort
out these various tendencies in order to come to a
fuller picture of the present position of sociologists
on this issue.

Talcott Parsons and George C. Homans were long
associated together at Harvard University. Both have
many adherents. The Parsonian influence was far-
reaching but is now waning. Homans's intellectual
disciples have built upon his "exchange" theory a
significant new theoretical alternative to contemporary
sociologists.

The Point of View of the Actor: Parsons

Max Weber's chief disciple in contemporary
American sociology has been Talcott Parsons. Parsons
studied for his doctorate at Heidelberg only a few
years after Weber's death. He translated Weber's
Protestant Ethic and the Spirit of Capitalism and the
seminal first section of Economy and Society into
English,[1] and in many ways has helped to popularize
Weber's work in the United States. Parsons also was
influenced by Durkheim, Pareto, Malinowski and Freud,
and by his initial interest in economics and biology.[2]
Yet the major influence on his own thinking and style
of work has certainly been Weber. This is most evident
in Parsons's basic theoretical orientation, which he
initially called the voluntaristic theory of action.[3]
Weber's emphasis upon taking the point of view of the
actor in seeking to understand the subjective
orientation of the individual which leads to his social
action was taken over almost totally by Parsons.

Parsons argued in his great first book The
Structure of Social Action that the point of view of
the actor must be the starting point in the development
of any theory which seeks to explain social action.[4]
His theory not only assumed the existence of the
individual actor, but made the individual a key factor
in the study of social phenomena. Each actor is
oriented to the achievement of particular goals, many
of which are derived from the normative structure of
his social group. He must take into account the
"conditions" over which he has no control as well as
the available "means" which he can utilize to gain his
ends. Parsons asserted that no full understanding or
theoretical explanation of the social action of the
individual can be achieved without seeking to describe

292

both the normative and structural context of the action
and the actor's subjective orientation to goals, means
and conditions.

Once he had made this theoretical assertion,
however, Parsons followed Weber in devoting his
attention to broad cultural values and norms rather
than to individual choices in specific situations. His
subjectivism assumed a conscious, willing actor, but
his level of analysis was usually societal rather than
individual. Some of Parsons's work, especially with
Robert F. Bales, was on small social groups, including
the family.[5] However, the great majority of his work
was geared to the societal or institutional level. In
John Finley Scott's analysis,[6] Parsons quite
consistently moved from a subjectivist and
individualist theoretical orientation to a more
structural and determinist orientation. In this
regard, also, he was similar to Weber, who emphasized
structural features much more in his later than in his
earlier writings.

It is therefore difficult to make a final
conclusion about Parsons's orientation. Like all good
theorists, his theoretical orientation changed and
developed. His initial position asserting the priority
of taking the individual into account in the
development of sociological theory gave way to a more
structural and Durkheimian orientation.

The Individual and Sociological Generalizations: Homans

Certainly the most different and controversial
position taken by a sociologist on the group vs.
individual issue was that of George C. Homans.
Homans's book The Human Group,[7] was widely read and
extremely influential in support of a systems approach
in sociology. Homans's later work, however, has taken
a far different approach. In Social Behavior: Its
Elementary Forms and The Nature of Social Science,
Homans has developed an orientation which is both
individual-based and deterministic in orientation, now
commonly referred to as "Exchange Theory."[8]

Rejecting his earlier systems orientation, Homans
based his later work on behavioristic psychology. Put
simply, Homans's theoretical position was that all of
the social sciences are but aspects of a single and
unitary discipline he called social science,[9] and that

all social science is founded on the general propositions of behavioristic psychology.[10] What gives unity to all of the social sciences is that their generalizations are ultimately derivable from psychology. Psychology provides the theoretical foundation--the core principles--on which the other social sciences, which deal with aggregates rather than individuals, are built.

The individual is the basic foundation of all studies of social life, according to Homans. Not only are individuals the fundamental units upon which all social science must be based, but all situations, institutions and events are the results of individual characteristics and behavior.[11] No generalizations which refer to aggregates or rates of behavior, such as Durkheim's generalizations about suicide, are complete without relating them to the more general propositions regarding individuals.

Homans recognized that there is substantial disagreement among behavioral psychologists on the fundamental general propositions of individual behavior.[12] In his Social Behavior, however, he discussed seven propositions which he believed were both well-substantiated and theoretically fruitful.[13] Using these propositions, he was able to develop a broad "exchange theory" of social life. He asserted that people act in an essentially rational manner in pursuing goals which are valuable to them. Their behavior involves exchange--of material as well as social goods--with other persons. Each individual seeks to receive social approval, prestige and other valuable rewards through interaction with others. In order to receive, he must also give something valuable in return. Social interaction, then, involves a constant exchange of rewards and punishments with others. Each individual weighs the cost of his behavior against the rewards he will receive from his behavior. Generally, a balance is reached such that each person receives either goods or social rewards equal to those he gives.

Homans used his exchange theory to explain influence, authority, competition, status placement and conformity, among a host of other social phenomena. Perhaps his major weakness is found in his explanation of power phenomena. Here he spoke of forced compliance to authoritative commands as exchange, in that the individual chooses to obey rather than take a punishment for non-conformity. Such interaction is certainly asymmetrical, and bears little resemblance to the voluntary exchange of economic goods in the marketplace. It is on this point that other exchange theorists, notably Peter Blau, differ most significantly from Homans.

Homans's view of theory coincides with that generally accepted in science and logic. Theory represents a system of propositions ordered in a meaningful way, such that specific empirical facts and generalizations can be deduced from the more general propositions of the theory.[14] In Homans's scheme, the general propositions are psychological ones, and refer to the behavior of individuals. Other propositions, including sociological generalizations relating to rates of behavior and historical generalizations referring to specific events, can be deduced from the general propositions. Homans's gave the following example:

1) The greater the value of a reward to a person the more likely he is to take action to get that reward.

2) . . . William the Conqueror . . . did not find the conquest of Scotland at all valuable.

3) Therefore he was unlikely to take action that would win him Scotland.[15]

In this example, William the Conqueror's decision not to invade Scotland after conquering England was derived from the general psychological proposition that a person does only those things which are rewarding to him. Homans admitted that the above reasoning is simple and obvious. He argued that it is so obvious that it tends to be rejected by intellectuals who disdain the obvious for the obscure. Rather than having contempt for the familiar, Homans believed that it is precisely the familiar which must be the starting point in the explanation of social life.[16]

The main weakness in the above example, at least from an historical point of view, is that there is no independent way to measure the second proposition relating to William's values. It is therefore necessary to deduce his values from his observed behavior. That he did not invade Scotland is given as proof that he did not value Scotland. This turns the theory into a definitional tautology, and destroys its explanatory value.

Individualism and Determinism in Homans's Writings

Homans recognized that the theoretical propositions of behavioristic psychology are similar in many respects to the "rational-choice model" of human behavior.[17] They assume a conscious, thinking and willing human actor who can modify his behavior in order to adjust to the varying situations in which he finds himself. Homans also asserted that this approach is similar to historicism, which tends to treat each event as unique rather than as similar to other events.[18] The past conditioning and experience of the individual influence him in choosing his behavior. This results in the constant emergence of new behavior and new situations which were not observable previously.[19] In this regard, Homans's position is similar to Weber's and the classical individualistic approach.

However, Homans's drew a different conclusion which unfortunately he did not elaborate. He asserted that he believes that the actions of individuals, and therefore the course of social history, is "absolutely determined."[20] He acknowledged that he and other social scientists are very far from being able to predict in advance the behavior of an individual in even very general terms. Yet he held to a kind of mystical acceptance of determinism which seemed to derive more from personal values than from observed facts. He believed that individual choice is an "illusion" which enables people to accept the world in which they live and strive to change it.[21] Even those like the Marxists who believe strongly in the existence of natural law still act as if their own behavior will enable them to influence the course of history. Homans obviously thought that this was a beneficial illusion, although he seemed to have cured himself of it. (One might wonder whether he felt that his own act of writing his books was absolutely determined.)

Homans admitted that his position was reductionist.[22] He supported his argument by asserting that reductionism is found in all sciences. The classic example, of course, is Gibbs's reduction of the laws of thermodynamics to the simpler laws of statistical mechanics.[23] Much of biology is now being reduced to chemistry and physics. Homans believed that the social sciences must exercise faith that the aggregative laws of sociology and history can ultimately be reduced to the individualistic laws of psychology. One of his strongest arguments in this regard was that sociology has never been able to develop general propositions which can stand alone without some psychological underpinnings. He argued that those who disagree with him must take the responsibility for showing that the empirical findings of sociologists can be deduced from more general propositions which are purely sociological rather than psychological. Their present inability to do so accounts for the sterility of contemporary sociological theory and for the manic-depressive feelings of many sociologists.[24]

Homans believed that sociologists should give up the Durkheimian belief that sociological facts and theories can be strictly separated from those of other sciences. A retreat from their grandiose belief in the separability of their science may be difficult, but it will ultimately result in greater development and therefore greater respectability of sociology and sociologists. Treating sociology as a branch of psychology does not mean that sociologists need feel inferior, nor that they no longer will have work to do. Their function in the scientific division of labor will be to study collective aspects of social life and relate their findings to the general propositions of psychology. The strength that will come to sociology through this process will more than compensate for its loss of claim as an independent science. The unity of science and interdisciplinary work are much more fruitful bases for sociology than the fragmentation of science and single-minded attention to a narrowly defined subject matter.

Homans's position has not been popularly received by sociologists, which was to be expected. Some few social psychologists find it enticing, while many find it threatening. It does represent the most radical reorientation of sociological perspective since the time of Durkheim. As such, it has and will continue to receive considerable attention and discussion from sociological theorists. As a clearly formulated alternative to the more widely accepted Durkheimian position that the group and the individual are separable features of social life, Homans's orientation deserves extensive scrutiny.

297

INDIVIDUALISTIC VS. STRUCTURAL APPROACHES

Bruce Mayhew has recently argued forcefully that almost all contemporary sociology is "individualist" in that it takes as its starting point the individual and his basic nature.[25] Sociology tends to be interested in "human behavior," rather than social phenomena, and tends to define its domain in such a way that individuals become the focus of analysis. Mayhew blames Weber as the classical champion of this position, but is especially condemnatory of Parsons and Homans as the chief representatives of this position in contemporary sociology. Both symbolic interactionists and behaviorists are also in this camp according to Mayhew.

The opposite of individualism, according to Mayhew, is structuralism. This poses the issue in different terms than we have done here, but the differences are more apparent than real. We have noted before that almost all structuralists take the point of view of the group and explain social events from this perspective. Conversely, most (but not all) subjectivists take an individualistic point of view. We believe it is important to separate these two issues at the abstract level while recognizing that there is a substantial correlation between the issues at the practical level. We also believe that there is much more structuralism in contemporary sociology than Mayhew admits, but recognize that during the 1970s and 1980s there has been a swing back toward a more individualistic position by some sociologists.[26]

Mayhew attributes this preponderance of individualistic approaches in the United States to American values (a non-structuralist explanation). Because of the great emphasis on individualism in the U.S., American sociologists assume uncritically an individualistic theoretical position. His argument here is much like the one enunciated in our first chapter: that theoretical orientations are often assumed as postulates, without proof or attempts at securing evidence in support of these postulates. These theoretical orientations guide all intellectual work and influence all research, analysis and theoretical exposition. One of our purposes in discussing these issues is to expose these assumptions and bring them to the light for discussion and debate. Only then will the issues come to be resolved. We therefore believe Mayhew's position is a useful one, even if it is overtly polemic.

CONCLUSION

It would be premature and presumptuous to attempt to resolve all of the questions raised concerning the issue discussed here, but we shall make some conclusions which represent our current thinking on the issue. These are not made to curtail or conclude discussion but to encourage further examination of the questions raised here.

First, individuals are actors and not just reactors, and have the ability to act on nature and on other individuals. They possess free will, and are responsible agents.

Second, while part of the self is social, another part of the self is unique and individualistic. A person's behavior is thus partly conformist and determined, and partly individualistic and undetermined. Since there are many social influences which operate on individuals, and since individuals also have the ability to make choices among these influences, people are (at least partially) responsible for their choices and actions. And social conditions have some influence on the degree of individualism present among people in a given social group.

Third, social relationships are also "real." While a social relationship does not have the capacity to "act" in the same way an individual does, it does exert an influence on individuals through the quality and nature of the relationship, etc.

Fourth, the actions of people become embodied in social groups and their products: norms, rules, books, social roles, organizations, corporations, churches, etc. These social embodiments do not have the capacity to "act" in the same way an individual does, but they do exert an influence on individuals (partly by themselves and partly through other individuals).

Fifth, both practically and theoretically it makes sense to talk about groups and to study social phenomena apart from their individual manifestations. This is a fruitful approach which has yielded much benefit for sociology. Such an approach does not imply the denial of the existence or importance of individuals. A theorist or researcher should be free to choose to take either the point of view of the individual or of the group.

Sixth, history is not determined solely by the play of objective and inanimate social forces. Human choices and the actions of individuals, both great and small, also determine history.

Seventh, arguments in favor of social determinism are weakened by the inability of social scientists to establish invariant laws of social behavior (with high rates of probability) or to predict social events. Social predictions tend to be accurate in the short run and under very restricted conditions, but do not apply to very different cultures or social conditions. Whether social laws in fact exist is still a moot question.

FOOTNOTES

[1]Max Weber, The Protestant Ethic and the Spirit of Capitalism, trans. Talcott Parsons (New York: Scribner's), 1958 (1930); and Max Weber, The Theory of Social and Economic Organization, trans. A. M. Henderson and Talcott Parsons (Glencoe: Free Press), 1947.

[2]Talcott Parsons, The Structure of Social Action (New York: McGraw-Hill), 1937, and "A Short Account of My Intellectual Development," Alpha Kappa Deltan 29 (Winter 1959), pp. 3-12.

[3]The Structure of Social Action, p. 11.

[4]Ibid., pp. 44-47, 640-687. See also Talcott Parsons, The Social System (Glencoe: Free Press), 1951, pp. 4-9, 24-26; and Talcott Parsons and Edward A. Shils, editors, Toward a General Theory of Action (Cambridge: Harvard University Press), 1951, pp. 4-7, 31-38.

[5]Talcott Parsons and Robert F. Bales, _Family Socialization and Interaction Process_ (Glencoe: Free Press), 1954; see also Talcott Parsons, _Social Structure and Personality_ (New York: Free Press), 1964; "Age and Sex in the Social Structure of the United States," _American Sociological Review_ 7 (October 1942), pp. 604-616; and "The Kinship System of the Contemporary United States," _American Anthropologist_, 45 (January-March 1943), pp. 22-38.

[6]John Finley Scott, "The Changing Foundations of the Parsonian Action Scheme," _American Sociological Review_ 28 (October 1963), pp. 716-735.

[7]George C. Homans, _The Human Group_ (New York: Harcourt), 1950.

[8]George C. Homans, _Social Behavior: Its Elementary Forms_ (New York: Harcourt), Revised Edition, 1974, and _The Nature of Social Science_ (New York: Harcourt), 1967. See also Peter M. Blau, _Exchange and Power in Social Life_ (New York: Wiley), 1964; see also George C. Homans, "Social Behavior as Exchange," _American Journal of Sociology_ 63 (May 1958), pp. 597-606; Richard M. Emerson, "Power-Dependence Relations," _American Sociological Review_ 27 (February 1962), pp. 31-41; and John W. Thibaut and Harold H. Kelley, _The Social Psychology of Groups_ (New York: Wiley), 1959.

[9]Ibid., pp. 3-43, 106, and _Social Behavior_, p. 6.

[10]_Nature of Social Science_, pp. 35-36, 44-45, 56; and _Social Behavior_, p. 12. See also George C. Homans, "Bringing Men Back In," _American Sociological Review_ 29 (December 1964), pp. 809-818; and Morton Deutsch, "Homans in the Skinner Box," _Sociological Inquiry_ 34 (Spring 1964), pp. 156-165.

[11]_Nature of Social Science_, p. 61.

[12]Ibid., pp. 36-37.

[13]_Social Behavior_, pp. 53-75.

[14]_Nature of Social Science_, pp. 22-28.

[15]Ibid., p. 44.

[16]Ibid., p. 73.

301

[17]Ibid., p. 38.

[18]Ibid., pp. 90-96.

[19]Ibid., p. 59.

[20]Ibid., p. 103.

[21]Ibid., p. 104.

[22]Ibid., pp. 80-86.

[23]Ibid., p. 83.

[24]Ibid., pp. 5-6.

[25]Bruce H. Mayhew, "Structuralism Versus Individualism: Part I, Shadowboxing in the Dark," Social Forces 59 (December 1980), pp. 335-375; and "Structuralism Verses Individualism: Part II, Ideological and Other Obfuscations," Social Forces 59 (March 1981), pp. 627-648.

[26]Randall Collins, "On the Microfoundations of Macrosociology," American Journal of Sociology 86 (March 1981), pp. 984-1014.

CHAPTER SIXTEEN

CAUSATION IN CLASSICAL SOCIOLOGICAL THEORY:
EMILE DURKHEIM

The third issue addressed in this volume will be the causation vs. system issue. Both the concepts of "cause" and "system" have had a varied and thorny route in sociological theory. Sociological theorists have usually not been well versed in the philosophical debates surrounding the notion of causation, and have not been particularly concerned with it. We may conclude that their attitude is much like ours: scientific issues addressed to matters of data and data interpretation are both more important and more substantive than philosophical debates concerned primarily with ideas. Empirical conclusions are much more likely to change philosophy than vice versa. Still, the tendency of sociological theorists, including ourselves, to ignore philosophical issues should not lead us to misinterpret what we are doing in this volume. We are concerned here primarily with theoretical orientations, similar in practical respects to philosophical assumptions about the nature of social life.

Sociological theorists, of both the past and present eras, may be categorized according to their acceptance of either a causal or systemic orientation to the explanation of social life. Those who accept the causal orientation assume that certain conditions or events (causes) tend to produce other conditions or events (effects). A cause is an event or condition which produces or results in another event or condition. If the cause is present, then the effect naturally follows. The cause is the necessary condition for the occurrence of the effect. In the case of single causation, the cause also becomes a sufficient condition for producing the effect. The effect is <u>dependent</u> upon the occurrence of the cause. In statistical language, therefore, the cause is spoken of as the independent variable, and the effect is the dependent variable.

Systems theorists take an opposing orientation. Many do not reject the concept of causation outright, but their view of social life is not essentially causal. Systems theorists assert that social phenomena are essentially reciprocal. Rather than one event always producing another, they stress the mutual interdependence of two or more events or conditions upon each other. No variable or condition is independent of others. Instead, all variables are viewed as belonging in a system in which all are mutually influenced by each other. The systems orientation replaced causation with reciprocity.

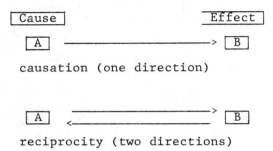

causation (one direction)

reciprocity (two directions)

THE CLASSICAL SOCIOLOGICAL STATEMENT OF CAUSATION: DURKHEIM

Emile Durkheim's statements regarding causation in sociology have become classics in sociological literature. More than any of the classical theorists, Durkheim came to grips with the sociological issues involved in attempts to discover social causes. His position on this issue has not been a particularly popular one in contemporary sociology, but almost all students of social life can benefit from a close inspection of Durkheim's arguments.

Durkheim assumed that sociology must be scientific, and that the basic scientific pursuit is to identify causal relationships. He believed that the assumptions that nature exhibits regularities and that these regularities are due to the operations of natural causes were essential to science. It seemed self-evident to Durkheim that social causes operated in social life. The basic task of sociology, he felt, is to discover and describe the causal relations among social phenomena.

THE MEANING OF "CAUSE"

The original meaning of the term cause came from ancient legal practice, and involved the attribution of

304

responsibility to an accountable actor.[1]   Thus, if a theft was discovered to have been committed, the question was raised: who is the person responsible for this event?   The notion of causation carried with it the meaning that a responsible actor had produced a given result through his own action.

As the term causation eventually came to be applied to scientific events, the notion of responsible actor was replaced with the conception that an event or condition served to produce an effect.   For example, a fire might be started either by an individual lighting a match or by sparks thrown from a turning mill stone. But while the idea of responsible agent was eliminated in such scientific meanings of causation, the idea of the production of an effect was retained.   The causal event in question operated in such a way as to produce or create the effect being investigated.[2]

The significance of this meaning becomes greater when we distinguish between a cause and "mere" conditions.   The term cause is applied to that person or event which acted to create or produce an effect, while conditions are necessary to the result but do not themselves produce the result.   To use an example from the recent philosophical literature on causation, lightning striking a barn caused the barn to burn. Necessary conditions to the burning of the barn were that it was made of combustible material (wood) and that oxygen was present in sufficient quantity to allow combustion to take place.   What distinguishes the cause from the conditions is that (a) the conditions were present both before and after the fire started, and (b) were equally present in other barns in the vicinity which were not burned.   Comparison of the barn which burned with other barns enables us to demonstrate that the single circumstance in which the burning barn differed from other barns was that it was hit by lightning.   Lightning, therefore, must be attributed as the cause of the fire, with the presence of combustible material and of oxygen being treated as "mere" conditions.   In like manner, poverty cannot be viewed as the cause of crime because (a) poverty exists both before and after the crimes are committed, and (b) it does not distinguish between criminals and noncriminals, since many person sin poverty do not commit crimes.   Poverty may be an antecedent condition of criminal behavior, but another cause for the criminal behavior should be sought.

305

In ordinary language, the notion of causation is expressed in many phrases and is implied in most active verbs. In the sciences, however, there is a tendency for causal language to disappear as the science advances. Causal formulations tend to be replaced by explanations of the hypothetico-deductive variety in which consequences (empirical generalizations) are deduced from a law or theoretical generalization which summarizes available knowledge.[3]

In sociology, the existence of such hypothetico-deductive theories unquestionably seems to be on the increase. It is therefore interesting that there also is an increase in the development of causal models in recent sociological literature, which follows a period of little interest in causation in sociology, especially during the 1950's.[4] A cursory look at the literature of the 1950's, and a comparison with the literature of the 1970's and 1980's leads one inescapably to the conclusion that there is more interest in causation and more written about causation today than in the previous two or three decades.

The rest of this chapter will be devoted to a discussion of Durkheim's principles of causation, which we regard as the classic statement on causality in sociology. The following chapter will look at other classical theorists who supported the causal side of the causation vs. system issue.

DURKHEIM AND SCIENTIFIC EXPLANATION

As Emile Durkheim viewed it, scientific explanation "exclusively" involves establishing causal relations among social phenomena. He believed the assumption that causal relations exist among phenomena is essential to science, and that the scientific endeavor should be devoted exclusively to the attempt to discover and establish such causal relations.[5] Durkheim set as his task the establishment of sociology as a scientific discipline in France, and embarked upon the search for sociological laws, e.g., the causal relations among social phenomena.

Durkheim attributed to Montesquieu the development of the idea that scientific causal laws operated in social phenomena as they did in physical phenomena. His interesting little book Montesquieu and Rousseau,[6] the first part of which is derived from his Latin doctoral thesis, was devoted to exploring this idea.

Following Montesquieu, Durkheim argued that science involves both description and interpretation. One must first observe social phenomena and seek to generalize the uniformities observed. Once these uniformities have been established, one needs to interpret them. Interpretation involves establishing relations of causation.

> To interpret things is simply to arrange our ideas about them in a determinate order, which must be the same as that of the things themselves. This presupposes that an order is present in the things themselves, that they form continuous series, the elements of which are so related that a given effect is always produced by the same cause and never by any other. If we assume, however, that there is no such causal relationship and that effects can be produced without a cause or by any cause whatsoever, everything becomes arbitrary and fortuitous. . . . Hence, a choice must be made: either social phenomena are incompatible with science or they are governed by the same laws as the rest of the universe. . . . [7]

Durkheim felt he was acting in a long tradition stretching back through Comte and Saint-Simon to Montesquieu in seeking to discover the definite and invariable social laws which exist in nature. While both Montesquieu and Durkheim allowed for a certain contingency in these social laws,[8] this contingency was of a limited sort and did not destroy the essential notion that what happens in society is due to causes which are determinate and can be studied scientifically.

THE DEFINITION OF CAUSE

Durkheim felt it necessary only once, late in his life, to give a definition of causation. His singular attempt at definition was not very sophisticated, but it is instructive of the way Durkheim thought of causation.

> The first thing which is implied in the notion of the causal relation is the idea of efficacy, of productive power, of active force. By cause we ordinarily mean something capable of producing a certain change. The

307

cause is the force before it has shown the power which is in it; the effect is this same power, only actualized. Men have always thought of causality in dynamic terms.[9]

Several points stand out in this definition. First, Durkheim believed that the notion of causation was always present in the thoughts of human beings. The causal order of nature is reflected or "represented" in the people's minds. Second, an important aspect of the definition of causation is the idea of "force." A cause is a force, a power, which produces an effect. Since social forces are impinging on individuals, these individuals are able to develop ideas of causation which embody the concept of force. The idea of force derives directly from social forces existing in society.

It is society which classifies beings into superiors and inferiors, into commanding masters and obeying servants; it is society which confers upon the former the singular property which makes the command efficacious and which makes power. So everything tends to prove that the first powers of which the human mind had any idea were those which societies have established in organizing themselves: it is in their image that the powers of the physical world have been conceived.[10]

Here Durkheim made the important point that people originally developed their conceptions of force through their experiences in social groups. Once they had developed this concept, they then applied it to the "powers of the physical world." Our conception of causation and of law and order in the physical world originated through experiences with social groups, and the order we observe in nature is but a reflection of the order we first observed within our social group.

Another important aspect contained in the idea of causation is that of association. If two events are always associated together, especially if one event always precedes another, the notion of causation arises. This may be true even if no concept of force is present to unite the two events into a causal connection. This may lead to erroneous attributions of causation, since the association of two events does not necessarily mean that one is the cause of the other. A gesture, an idea, a totally separate event may be thought of as the cause of an act or event. Because of this, Durkheim argued that it is necessary to search for the cause of a social fact in the social constitution of the group and in the social events which preceded the social fact. One must not attribute causation to individualistic ideas or behavior.[11]

BASIC PRINCIPLES OF CAUSATION

Durkheim's basic principles of causation are developed most fully in his methodological classic The Rules of Sociological Method.[12] His discussion contains at least five principles, which we shall first summarize briefly and then discuss in greater detail. First, any effect has only a single cause. Second, the only useful method of establishing causal relations in sociology is correlation. Third, the study of causes must be separated from the study of effects or "functions." Fourth, social facts are always caused by other social facts. Fifth, establishing causal relations is the essence of scientific explanation.

SINGLE CAUSATION

Durkheim's conception of causation was what today would be labeled single causation. His famous dictum concerning this point was short and to the point: "A given effect has always a single corresponding cause."[13]

According to this rule, no effect or dependent variable can have anything other than a single cause. Durkheim specifically rejected the notion that things occur by chance, and problablistic notions are not generally found in Durkheim's writings. But most importantly, Durkheim rejected any assertion that an effect could be caused by more than one causal agent.

Durkheim's rule encompasses several kinds of causal models, all of which might be thought of as single causation. Let us diagram and discuss three possibilities.

(1) One cause, one effect. This is the simplest type of causal model. The effect is attributed to one and only one cause, and no other variables are included in the model (see Figure 16:1). This involves concentration on only one effect, and study

309

Figure 16:1. One cause, one effect.

A ————————> B

(Note: Causal influence is denoted by an arrow →)

and analysis is pursued to the point which one and only one cause can be determined as operating. If additional causes seem to be present, further analysis and/or conceptual definitions are carried out to enable the investigator to eliminate possible causes until a single cause is isolated. The effect can be said to be explained once we have identified its cause.

(2) One cause, multiple effects (see Figure 16:2). In this model we have several effects, but each one of these effects is produced by the same

Figure 16:2 One cause, multiple effects.

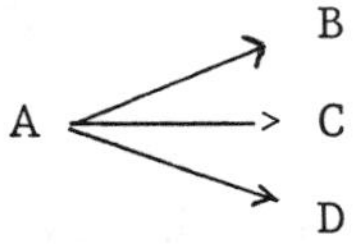

cause. In his example of egoistic suicide, for example, Durkheim argued that egoism (excessive individualism) produces both a higher suicide rate and a higher rate of attendance at universities. Both college education and suicide, then, are effects of egoïsm. Some may make the mistake of attributing college education as the cause of suicide, since both vary together; the real case, however, is that both are effects of the same cause.[14]

(3) Causal chain. In this causal model (see Figure 16:3), several variables are involved. A is the cause of B. B, in turn, is the cause of C. C, in turn, is the cause of D. The cause of A is not

Figure 16:3. Causal chain.

A ————————> B ————————> C ————————> D

specified by the model. Each of the other variables has only a single cause. While some theorists and philosophers introduce the language of "first cause," "proximate cause," etc., Durkheim had little use for

310

such language. A and B should not be viewed as the cause of D; only C is the cause of D. As we will show later, when an investigation seems to show that A, B, and C are all causally related to D, further analysis will often show that these variables are related in a causal chain, and what appears to be multiple causation can be reduced to single causation.

MODELS OF MULTIPLE CAUSATION

Multiple causation may be represented by the model shown in Figure 16:4. In such a model, A, B, and C are all considered to be causes of D. That is, A by itself can produce D; B by itself can produce D and C by itself can produce D. In short, any of the

Figure 16:4 Multiple causation.

causes independently can produce the effect without the operation of the other causes. The effect can be produced by any of a number of causes, and these causes must be clearly specified and observationally validated.

A more complex model of multiple causation is what we have called "conjoint multiple causation," and is diagrammed in Figure 16:5. In such a model, it is asserted that all of the causal variables, e.g., A, B, and C, must be present conjointly or simultaneously in

Figure 16:5. Conjoint multpile causation.

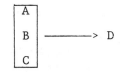

order for the effect to be produced. Each of the so-called causes is a necessary condition for the production of the effect, but all must be present before the effect occurs.

311

DURKHEIM'S REJECTION OF MULTIPLE CAUSATION

Durkheim felt that the concept of multiple causation allowed too many complexities to be introduced, which thereby changed the very meaning of causation. If we assume that a number of causes will produce a given effect, then it is not possible to state clearly that any one is the cause, since the causal variable, and it alone, does not produce the effect. Durkheim therefore argued that we should reserve the term "cause" to be applied only to those events or conditions which clearly and consistently produce known effects. "This supposed axiom of the plurality of causes is, in fact, a negation of the principle of causality."[15] According to Durkheim, the very meaning of the term causation is negated or destroyed when a multiple causal model is introduced.

Durkheim believed that multiple causation conceals sloppy or incomplete empirical investigation. It is relatively easy to establish that several phenomena vary together, and it is tempting to imply that this demonstrates that multiple causation is operating. If it can be demonstrated that several of these variables precede in time the dependent or effect variable, then it is tempting to call all of the antecedent variables causes. It is much more difficult to proceed beyond the establishment of correlations to demonstrate that one or several variables actually produce the effect which is being investigated. Therefore, many investigators use the language of causation and either implicitly or explicitly assume that a given effect has several causes.

REDUCTION OF MULTIPLE CAUSATION TO SINGLE CAUSATION

If it appears that several causes seem to produce one effect, Durkheim believed that further investigation or analysis should be made to discover the "true" cause of the effect in question. That which seems to exhibit multiple causation, Durkheim believed, would eventually be discovered to be reducible to single causation. His work provides us with ample demonstrations of three different ways in which this can be accomplished.

(1) Division of effects. If several causes seem to produce a single effect, we might ask ourselves first whether this effect is genuinely a singular effect, or whether in fact there are several effects

present (see Figure 16:6). Often it will be discovered that the effect produced by cause A is different from the effect produced by cause B, even though at first they appeared to be the same thing. A reconceptualization of the effect, often preceded by further observation and data analysis, results in a change of the causal model from a multiple causal model to a single causal model.

Figure 16:6.   Division of effects.

A			A ————> D_1
		is	
B ————> D		transformed	B ————> D_2
		into	
C			C ————> D_3

Durkheim did this in his classic work, Suicide (1951), when he discovered that suicide was not in fact a singular sociological phenomenon. Rather, there were three different types of suicide, which he labeled respectively egoistic suicide, altruistic suicide, and anomic suicide. Each of these types of suicide was elicited by a different cause, and each had only a single cause. Superficial analysis might have made it appear that suicide had several causes, when in fact more extensive analysis enabled him to separate the effect into three different effects rather than one. Likewise, contemporary analyses of crime rates, aspirations for a college education, or rates of social mobility might make it appear many variables contribute to these effects. Durkheim's point of view would lead us to ask whether the researchers studying these phenomena have yet gone far enough to assure us that these are not divisible effects which might yet be shown to be caused by single causes. For example, crime might be divided into crimes against persons and crimes against property a la the Uniform Crime Reports, or broken down further to effects like murder, child abuse, auto theft, etc.

(2)   Reduction of causes. A second way in which a multiple causal model may be reduced to a single causal model is through the reconceptualization of the causal variables. Using this technique, the investigator looks at all of the causal variables to see if he can discover whether they all contain some factor in common which may be producing the effect (see Figure 16:7).

Figure 16:7. Reduction of causes.

```
A                              A
            is                          are
B ———> D transformed   B indicators X ———> D
           into                         of
C                              C
```

Here A, B, and C are found to have in common a single
factor, which we call X, and which is the "real" cause
of D. Variables A, B, and C may serve as indicators
for this single factor X, but they are not themselves
causes of D.

In his analysis of the cause of egoistic suicide,
Durkheim found that Protestants had a higher suicide
rate than Catholics, single persons had a higher rate
of suicide than married persons, and that people living
in times of peace had a higher suicide rate than people
living in times of war.[16] Rather than treating
Protestantism, single marital status, and peacetime
conditions as causes of suicide, Durkheim looked for
the factor which these variables had in common. That
factor, according to Durkheim, was a condition of
malintegration resulting from excessive individualism
and a lack of social ties within the social group.
Such a condition of malintegration (egoism) was the
"true" or "real" cause of egoistic suicide.
Superficial analysis might have made it seem that
egoistic suicide was caused by three variables, when in
fact all of these variables had one condition in common
which served to cause egoistic suicide.

Here Durkheim went up the "ladder" of generality
to a higher level of abstraction to find his cause,
while in the former case (division of effects) he went
down the ladder of generality to a more specific level
of abstraction. Since the attribution of causation is
a matter of abstraction, one should change his level of
abstraction until he has reached the level which will
allow him to posit a single cause for any given effect.

(3) Reduction to a causal chain. We have already
discussed the model of causal chain. We need indicate
here only that when several variables seem to be
causally related to a given effect, it is often
possible to discover that these variables occur in a
time sequence and that they can validly be placed in a
causal chain rather than in a multiple causal model.
For example, if we discover that higher socioeconomic

314

status, membership in a country club, and exposure to friends with conservative economic attitudes are all correlated with voting for the Republican party, we may find upon further analysis that these variables can be placed in a causal chain according to the time order in which they occur, as represented in Figure 16:8.

Figure 16:8.   Reduction to a causal chain.

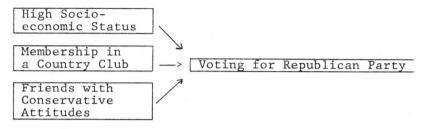

can be reduced to:

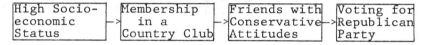

To summarize again, Durkheim argued that a multiple causal model represented a negation of the principle of causality, since it is not possible using a multiple causal model to clearly and unequivocally link a cause to an effect. In other words, given a specific effect, we are not able to predict its cause using a multiple causal model. Sloppy and incomplete investigation usually results in multiple causal models, whereas painstaking research and reconceptualization over a long enough period of time will enable us to develop a single causal model which will adequately explain a given effect.

SOCIAL CAUSATION

In Chapter Ten we discussed Durkheim's notions about the relationship of the individual to the group. Durkheim strongly believed that the group has a reality sui generis, a reality of its own apart from the individuals who compose it. Emergence occurs when individuals associate together. New phenomena are created which are peculiarly social. These social facts are the proper domain of sociology. Thus it

315

follows that one should not seek for the causes of
social facts in psychological facts, biological facts,
chemical facts, etc.[17]   Only social facts can be the
causes of other social facts.   Social facts are of a
different order of reality than other facts, and must
be studied in their own right.   Social laws govern
social facts.   To discover causal relations in social
phenomena, one must not move outside the range of
social facts.

Durkheim consistently followed this rule.   One
need not multiply examples, since they are found in all
his writings.   Suicide is caused by social integration.
The division of labor is caused by physical and dynamic
density.   Religious rites and beliefs are caused by the
social organization of the society.   Accepting the
structural orientation, Durkheim believed that the
internal constitution of the group was the key factor
in the causation of other sociological phenomena found
in the group.[18]   Durkheim's emphasis upon social
causation was closely allied with his structuralism.

Durkheim frequently implied, however, that social
facts may be used as explanations of psychological
facts.   The social group has great influence on the
socialization and behavior of the individual.   Facts of
a "higher order" thus may be deterministic of "lower
order" facts, but the reverse is not true.

SEPARATING CAUSE FROM FUNCTION

Durkheim was highly critical of the frequent
practice in his day of "intuiting" the causes of social
phenomena.   Once an investigator has "discovered" how a
phenomenon has contributed to society, he often
believes his analysis is complete.   Durkheim argued
that the sociological investigator must clearly
separate in his own mind the cause from the effect.
Some effects make important contributions to the
existence of the group in its environment.   Durkheim
used the term "functions" to apply to such effects, and
developed in a rather crude form an early functional
theory.

Durkheim felt that many investigators confused
function with cause.   They mistakenly believed that the
function was identical with the cause.   Durkheim argued
that "the need we have of things cannot give them
existence, nor can it confer their specific nature upon
them."[19]   The investigator should fist seek to identify

the cause which brings some social conditions into existence. Then he may study, if he is interested, the positive effects of this condition upon the survival of the society. The study of causation should precede that of function. Establishment of the cause of a phenomenon will aid in determining its function, whereas the opposite is not true, according to Durkheim.

This argument is clearly applicable to much of functional theory today. Contemporary functionalists have generally ignored this basic rule formulated by one of the founders of functionalism. The great majority of functional analyses contain no mention of causation and no investigation of the operation of causal relations in the specific situation. Their intent seems only to show the function of a given phenomena--in Durkheim's words, how it is useful. This is probably one of the most significant weaknesses of contemporary functional theory.

Method of Establishing Causation. Demonstrating causation has always been a difficult matter for sociologists. Durkheim faced the question directly, but many will doubt that his answer solves the problem.

Durkheim rejected the method of experimentation simply because social facts are "not within our control."[20] Without control over all variables in the analysis, no true experiment can be performed. This leaves sociologists with what Durkheim (following John Stuart Mill) called the "indirect experiment, or the comparative method."[21] One must wait until a certain event occurs in nature. Then one compares this event to other events in an attempt to discover its cause.

Durkheim rejected Mill's methods of agreement, difference, and residues (and by implication the joint method of agreement and difference) as not practical for use by sociologists.[22] He did accept Mill's fourth method, that of correlation or concomitant variation. He believed that through establishing a correlation between two variables, the investigator could most clearly prove their causal connection. If two variables are correlated, they must be causally related. But one still does not know which is the cause and which the effect. Further, both may be effects of a third cause. The correlation must be "interpreted."[23] This interpretation must be "methodically conducted." Through deduction, the

317

investigator hypothesizes a particular causal connection between the two variables. New data are gathered to test this hypothesis. Again, correlational analysis is used as the basis for making conclusions. This is repeated until the investigator feels that he has amassed enough data and made enough comparisons to enable him to feel confident that the proof has been made.

This method is not very exact, and depends a great deal on the interpretive skill of the scientist. Yet Durkheim believed it is the most fruitful method of establishing causation in sociology. And unlike the other methods suggested by Mill, correlational analysis can be made with a few observations, a few facts, rather than a great multiplicity of observations necessitated by the other methods. One must establish the correlation "in a sufficient number and variety of cases,"[24] but one need not have all the data before he makes a causal generalization.

This argument is not completely consistent with Durkheim's position on single causation. Single causation would necessitate a correlation of 1.00. Every time a cause occurs, the effect should be invariably produced, according to Durkheim. Durkheim recognized that perfect correlations had not yet been found. He himself worked primarily with percentage analysis rather than with statistical correlations (which of course had not been developed to any great extent in his day). Durkheim maintained the faith, however, that careful sociological investigation would be rewarded with perfect or near perfect correlations. With the possible exception of such correlations as split-half reliability tests, sociologists almost never work with correlations of the magnitude of .90. Many are happy with correlations of .50 or even .25, and many such correlations are statistically significant. Durkheim's fond hope for single causation, as exhibited by perfect correlations, is far from realization yet.

DURKHEIM AND THE SYSTEMS APPROACH

Durkheim's influence upon contemporary sociology, especially the functional school of sociological theory, has been notable. This has been due in large part to Durkheim's emphasis upon integration, which is a central concept of modern functionalism. It is interesting to note, however, that Durkheim did not couple his integrationist orientation with a systems

318

model of social life. In his mind, it was not necessary to assume a systems orientation in order to hold to a integrationist perspective. He consistently treated integration within a causal framework. In Suicide, integration was viewed as the cause of suicide. In the Elementary Forms, integration was treated as an effect of religious beliefs and practices. In both cases, however, causation rather than reciprocity was used as his theoretical model.

However, Durkheim did make use of the term "system," and in a relatively modern sense. Several quotations may be instructive.

Educational practices are not phenomena that are isolated from one another; rather, for a given society, they are bound up in the same system all the parts of which contributed toward the same end. . . .[25]

Thus the men of the clan and the things which are classified in it form by their union a solid system, all of whose parts are united and vibrate sympathetically.[26]

For Durkheim, a system contains a number of units which are united together and which vary together (vibrate sympathetically). The notion of reciprocity here cannot be ignored. Durkheim recognized the interdependence of some social facts. But he also consistently maintained that such interdependence was due to the natural operation of causal laws. Causation rather than reciprocity characterized Durkheim's writings.

In his Fourth Lecture on Pragmatism,[27] Durkheim specifically rejected the notion of system as a monistic explanation of social reality. He noted that what he called the "monistic point of view" assumes that "the universe is actually one in the sense that it forms a closely linked system, all the elements of which imply each other, a system where the whole commands the existence of the parts and where individuals are only appearances that in sum constitute one being."[28] Durkheim, following the pragmatist William James, opted for a more pluralistic point of view, which sees the world "made up of parts which are linked to each other by certain relationships, but which, nevertheless, remain distinct and retain a

319

certain independence, a certain autonomy, so that there is room for change, diversity, and contingency."[29]

The world is made up of an incalculable number of networks that unite things and beings with each other. These networks are formed of complicated and relatively independent links. The elements that they connect are not fixed, and the very form of the network is subject to change. Made up of a plurality of small systems, each of which is endowed with an autonomous life, it is ceaselessly formed, deformed, and transformed.[30]

Durkheim thus agreed with William James that the unity of the world is "partial, relative, and progressive." It does not have "the beautiful order" that many attribute to it.[31] Rather then viewing the social world as one large system, one should view it as a complex entity with a multiplicity of social laws and causal relations operating in it.

In conclusion, many of Durkheim's important principles of causal analysis are not followed in contemporary sociology. One of the special merits of studying Durkheim, even when one believes him to be wrong, is that he made forceful and cogent arguments for the theoretical positions he took. This is especially true of his discussion of causation. Contemporary sociologists still have not come to grips with many of the basic issues raised by Durkheim. Careful study of Durkheim's writings on causation and resolute debate with the ghost of Durkheim on his major points is strongly to be recommended.

FOOTNOTES

[1]Patrick H. Nowell-Smith, "Causality," Encyclopedia Britannica (1966) Vol. 5, pp. 104-107.

[2]Ibid., p. 105.

[3]Ibid., p. 105.

[4]Talcott Parsons, "Cause and Effect in Sociology," in Daniel Lerner (ed.), Cause and Effect. New York: Free Press, pp. 51-73.

320

[5]Emile Durkheim, The Rules of Sociological Method. Glencoe: The Free Press, 1938, p. 125.

[6]Emile Durkheim, Montequieu and Rousseau. Ann Arbor: University of Michigan Press, 1960.

[7]Ibid., p. 10.

[8]Ibid., pp. 44-47.

[9]Emile Durkheim, The Elementary Forms of the Religious Life. Glencoe: Free Press, 1915, p. 363.

[10]Ibid., p. 363.

[11]Ibid., p. 367.

[12]Durkheim, Rules, op. cit.

[13]Ibid., p. 128, italics Durkheim's.

[14]Emile Durkheim, Suicide. Glencoe: Free Press, 1951, pp. 168-169.

[15]Rules, p. 127.

[16]Suicide, pp. 152-208.

[17]Rules, especially pp. 110-111.

[18]Ibid., p. 113.

[19]Ibid., p. 90.

[20]Ibid., p. 125.

[21]Loc. cit.

[22]Ibid., p. 129.

[23]Ibid., P. 131.

[24]Ibid., p. 130.

[25]Emile Durkheim, Education and Sociology (Glencoe: Free Press), 1956, p. 95. See also p. 65.

[26]Emile Durkheim, The Elementary Forms of the Religious Life (Glencoe: Free Press), 1915, p. 150.

[27]Emile Durkheim, et al., Essays on Sociology and Philosophy, edited by Kurt H. Wolff (New York: Harper), 1964, pp. 412-420.

[28]Ibid., pp. 416-417.

[29]Ibid., p. 417.

[30]Ibid., p. 418.

[31]Ibid., p. 419.

CHAPTER SEVENTEEN

CLASSICAL CAUSATION: WEBER, SPENCER AND THOMAS

As we continue to explore the arguments in favor of a causal explanation of social life, we shall discuss in this chapter the writings of three important contributors to causal explanation in sociology: Max Weber, Herbert Spencer, and W.I. Thomas. All three approached the explanation of social facts from a causal standpoint, but each dissented from the extreme model of causation expounded by Durkheim. The three theorists to be discussed here represent three steps in a retreat from classical causation toward the abandonment of causation in sociology.

WEBER'S ORIENTATION TOWARD CAUSATION

Weber used a critique of a book by Eduard Meyer as a vehicle for developing his ideas regarding "interpretive" sociology. He started with the assumption that "an infinity of causal factors (had) conditioned the occurrence of the individual 'event' . . ."[1] It is therefore necessary to select from this infinity of factors those which are to be used in the analysis. This is done, first, by the criterion of interest. If we are interested in the sociological principles which led to a particular event (say a revolution), we will select out different factors than if we were interested in the medical or legal or technological factors involved.[2]

> . . . (H)istory is exclusively concerned with the causal explanation of those 'elements' and 'aspects' of the events in question which are of 'general significance' and hence of historical interest from general standpoints. . . .
> Hence, there is involved in the problem of the assignment of historical causes to historical effects . . . the exclusion of an infinity of components of a real action as 'causally irrelevant.' A given circumstance is, as we see, unimportant not only when it has no relationship at all with the event which is under discussion . . . it is indeed sufficient to establish the causal irrelevance of the given circumstance if the latter appears not to have been the co-cause of that which alone interests us, i.e., the concretely essential components of the action in question.[3]

ABSTRACTION

Any causal analysis, then, involves abstraction. Only certain phenomena are abstracted for causal analysis, while others are ignored. This is not an automatic process which can be engaged in purely objectively; rather, the process of assignment of causality takes place in the mind, as the term "abstraction" suggests. Scientific work, then, is subjective in its very nature.

Our real problem is, however: by which logical operations do we acquire the insight and how can we demonstratively establish <u>that</u> such a causal relationship exists between those 'essential' components of the effects and certain components among the infinity of determining factors. Obviously not by the simple 'observation' of the course of events in any case, certainly not if one understands by that a 'presuppositionless' mental 'photograph' of all the physical and psychic events occurring in the space-time region in question--even if such were possible. Rather, does the attribution of effects to causes take place through a process of thought which includes a series of <u>abstractions</u>. The first and decisive one occurs when we <u>conceive</u> of one or a few of the actual causal components as modified in a certain direction and then ask ourselves whether under the conditions which have been thus changed, the same effect (the same, i.e., in 'essential' points) or some other effect 'would be expected'.[4]

SUBJECTIVITY

We want to emphasize two important points contained in this argument. First, all scientific work is essentially "subjective" in the sense that (a) it occurs in the mind, (b) it deals with concepts, and (c) all such concepts represent abstractions which do not fully reflect the real world. A scientist may manipulate objects or people, but he also manipulates ideas in his mind. And these ideas are not mere "reflections" of the objects observed in the mind through the process of abstraction. Historical and scientific work

324

involves first the production of--let us say
it calmly--'imaginative constructs' by the
disregarding of one or more of those elements
or 'reality' which are actually present, and
by the mental construction of a course of
events which is altered through modification
in one of more 'conditions'.[5]

THE PROCESS OF RECONSTRUCTION

The second point is that the scientist arrives at
an attribution of causation through reconstructing in
his mind the essential social conditions which led to a
given effect. Then he imagines what might have
happened if one of these conditions had been otherwise.
He may proceed through the analysis by taking each of
the "essential" conditions (or causes) and imagining
what might have happened were this factor to have been
nonexistent or changed in some way. If any condition
can be changed without a corresponding change in the
effect, then the condition is not a cause of the
effect--it is not essential. If, however, a change in
one of the conditions preceding the effect would have
produced a different effect, then the condition is
essential, i.e., causal.

If now one examines . . . the
propositions regarding what 'would' happen in
the event of the exclusion or modification of
certain conditions . . . there can be no
doubt that it is a matter of isolations and
generalizations. This means that we so
decompose the 'given' into 'components' that
every one of them is fitted into an
'empirical rule'; hence, that it can be
determined what effect each of them, with
others present as 'conditions,' 'could be
expected' to have, in accordance with an
empirical rule.[6]

Such a method is usually called a Gedanken-
experiment, or a "thought-experiment." While the
development of the experimental method has enabled
researchers to vary these essential conditions in a
laboratory rather than just in the mind, the Gedanken-
experiment is often useful.

In order to do this, one must have some previous
knowledge about the results of a given factor. One
must be able to generalize in some fashion about the

relationship between a cause and an effect. Let us give an example used by Weber. Two shots were fired in a mob of people in Berlin. This incident led to serious street fighting. The question then became: were the two shots causally significant in producing the street fighting, or, would any incident have produced the same results. In this case, Weber argued that the two shots were not causally significant, since the street fighting could be causally explained by reference to other social conditions present in the situation. The results would have been the same whether the shots were fired or not. In this case, the "unique" event of the decision of an individual to fire two shots cannot be said to be the cause of the resulting fighting which followed. One has reached the point of what Weber called "adequate causation" when one has shown

> that in the given historical constellation certain 'conditions' are conceptually isolatable which would have led to that effect in a preponderantly great majority of instances given even the co-presence in that constellation of other possible conditions. . . .[7]

A number of social conditions are typically abstracted out from objective reality. These conditions are then synthesized into an historical unity. The observer imagines how these conditions came together in a particular historical instance to produce a given effect. No one single cause, in Weber's view, could by itself produce a given result: all explanations in the social sciences (and presumably in all sciences) are multiple-causal.

According to Weber, the scientist should not seek for a perfectly valid and universally applicable statement of a cause and effect relationship in the form of a scientific law. Rather he should seek for a statement of causality applicable to the specific problem to which he has addressed himself, and "adequate" for his own purposes. Causal adequacy is relevant to many factors, including the goals of the investigator, the quality of data available, the uses to which causal knowledge will be put, etc.

Further, while Weber admitted the possibility of "chance" occurrences, he believed that most historical events could be explained in terms of "adequate causation"--that is, in terms of the action of a number of social conditions. Chance causes were simply those which were due to factors which were outside the purview of the theory or which had not been sufficiently conceptualized nor analyzed. The language of causation could be used to explain individual decisions as well as to explain the occurrence of categories of behavior or historical events.

SOCIOLOGICAL METHODOLOGY

Weber rejected the then commonly held notion that the social sciences, because they deal with subjective abstractions, need a methodology different from the natural sciences. Instead, he argued that the process of scientific work is a unitary process. The phenomena under investigation, whether they be fields of wheat, chemical compounds, or historical events, must be studied and explained in the same manner: by abstraction, imaginative construction, and generalization.

All science initially involves observation of a given effect. Then the causes of this effect are observed and analyzed. Scientific explanation proceeds from effect to cause. Once this is accomplished, the explanation is used as a prediction, and an observation or an experiment is made in which the cause is seen to produce an effect. Only when a specific effect can be predicted from a given cause is the explanation accepted as fully satisfactory.

One result of this point of view is that all scientific explanations of causation are characterized by "possibility" rather than "certainty." The best explanation is thus said to be the one most likely to be correct. It cannot be an absolute explanation, for it depends upon abstraction. If one chooses to abstract out other characteristics, the causal explanation will be changed. This does not mean that all characteristics are equally useful as causal factors in a scientific explanation. But the usefulness of any factor is dependent upon the way in which it is conceptualized.

The degree of probability is variable. One explanation is more probably correct than another. But one can never assign a strict "numerical measure of chance" because "this presupposes the existence of absolute chance" or specific measurable or countable aspects of phenomena or results as the sole object of scientific interest."[8]

MULTIPLE CAUSATION

Weber believed that a number of factors, taken together, may be said to be the causes of a particular event or phenomenon, and he specifically rejected both monistic causal theories and the Hegelian (dialectical) notion of historical causality. Instead, he strongly supported a multiple-causation approach to causation.

> (T)he totality of all the conditions back to which the causal chain from the 'effect' leads had to 'act jointly' in a certain way and in no other for the concrete effect to be realized.[9]

In his historical analysis of the development of capitalism in Western Europe, Weber gave an excellent example of multiple causation. In The Protestant Ethic and the Spirit of Capitalism,[10] Weber analyzed the causes which produced the industrial revolution and the rise of rational capitalism in Western Europe. As we noted in Chapter Six, Weber's basic thesis was that Marx had confused the causal priority of historical variables and had treated religious ideas solely as effects of economic causes. Weber reversed the causal priority of these variables, and argued that the ideas and values which resulted from the Protestant Reformation were causally prior to and had the effect of producing the economic changes characterized as the industrial revolution and the development of capitalism. The Protestant Ethic had a significant causal influence on the development of the Spirit of Capitalism, which in turn had a significant causal influence on the development of rational capitalism.

Weber identified seven factors which occurred prior to the development of rational capitalism and which had a causal significance in producing it. Weber's causal model is diagrammed in Figure 17:1.

Figure 17:1. Weber's Causal Model of the Development of Rational Capitalism.

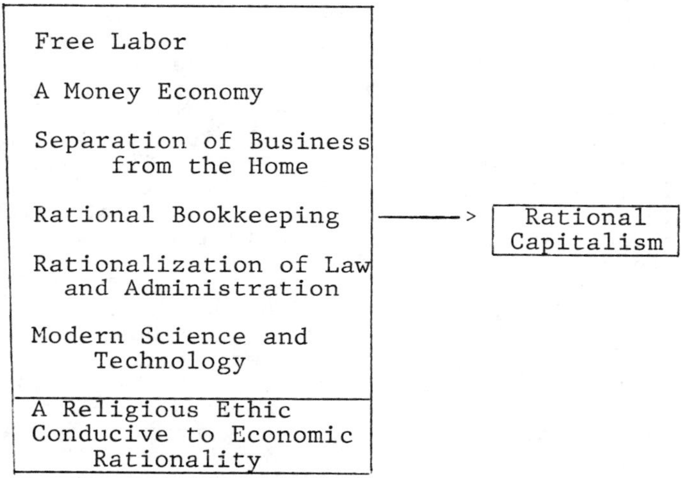

```
┌──────────────────────────────┐
│ Free Labor                   │
│                              │
│ A Money Economy              │
│                              │
│ Separation of Business       │
│    from the Home             │
│                              │                    ┌──────────────┐
│ Rational Bookkeeping         │────────>           │ Rational     │
│                              │                    │ Capitalism   │
│ Rationalization of Law       │                    └──────────────┘
│    and Administration        │
│                              │
│ Modern Science and           │
│    Technology                │
├──────────────────────────────┤
│ A Religious Ethic            │
│ Conducive to Economic        │
│    Rationality               │
└──────────────────────────────┘
```

This model is of the type which we called conjoint multiple causation in Chapter Sixteen. It was alleged by Weber that all of the seven causal factors must occur jointly in order to produce rational capitalism, and that rational capitalism would not have occurred if any one of the conditions had not been present jointly.

We feel it is important to note that, while Weber was not perfectly clear on this point, it appears that he believed that the single unifying element in all of the causal variables was rationality. In his introduction to the Protestant Ethic, Weber argued that one of the most significant long-term trends in history is toward an increase in rationality. It is this element of rationality which unites free labor, modern science, rational bookkeeping, a rational religious ethic, etc., into a single whole. This has the effect of subsuming all causes into one single cause which is very general and abstract, very similar to Durkheim's mode of explanation.

THE "UNIQUENESS" OF HISTORICAL EXPLANATION

One final point needs to be made concerning Weber's explanation of the development of rational capitalism. Weber argued most validly that this historical explanation applies only to one historical instance: the development of rational capitalism in Western Europe. There is no case of rational capitalism found in history previous to this one. In later cases where rational capitalism is found, it is due to entirely different causes. The most significant of these is the diffusion of capitalistic ideas from the West into other geographical areas, which are then forced to compete economically with capitalistic enterprises.

It is possible to make some generalizations which span many historical time periods, such as that subjective religious values will always have a significant effect upon the type of economic organization found in a society. Such general statements, however, are not very fruitful and give us relatively little information, or so Weber believed. The most fruitful historical and sociological investigations, according to Weber, are those which concern themselves with historically unique configurations of elements which possess cultural significance to the investigator and to his society.[11]

THE NATURAL SCIENCE MODEL

Weber believed that most sociologists were attempting to use the natural sciences as a model for their own discipline, which he believed to be a serious mistake. Such persons seek to discover "laws" which were invariant or probabilistic, in which specific conditions unfailingly produce a given effect. They look for general and comprehensive laws which encompass universal and recurring conditions and events, and which can be deduced from a system of propositions which explain all sociological and historical events. Weber rejected the natural science model for reasons which we discussed extensively in Chapter Thirteen. These include subjectivism, voluntarism, the process of abstraction, multiple causation, historical uniqueness, social change, and the relative importance of particularistic explanations in the social sciences. We have discussed most of these topics in this chapter.

In summary, Weber advocated specific historical and sociological investigations into culturally significant topics, such as the development of rational capitalism in Western Europe, even if and largely because these events represented unique or special conditions which could not be deduced from a covering law such as those found in the natural sciences. Multiple causes produce all significant historical and sociological effects, and such causes can be discovered through observation and the use of "imaginative constructs."

THE REGRESSIVE MULTIPLICATION OF CAUSES: SPENCER

Herbert Spencer's published writings on causation are not nearly as important as those of Durkheim or Weber. Yet in one brief essay published at the very end of his life (at the age of 82), Spencer developed a notion of multiple causation which deserves brief attention here. Its importance derives primarily from the observation of the author that it fits the common-sense lay view of causation better than any other model developed by sociological theorists.

Spencer had long maintained a clearly multiple-causal view of social life. But in an essay entitled "The Regressive Multiplication of Causes," Spencer claimed that only after a full career of scholarship did this principle become clear to him. According to Spencer, social causes are like a family tree. Two parents unite to form a single child. But these two parents are in turn the offspring of four grandparents, eight great-grandparents, sixteen great-great-grandparents, etc. Similarly for each given effect, a number of causes have combined to produce it. Each of these causes was in turn produced by a multiplicity of other composite causes. As one works backwards through history to trace the causes of a particular event, the investigator finds a regressive multiplication of causes.

REGRESSIVE MULTIPLICATION OF CAUSES

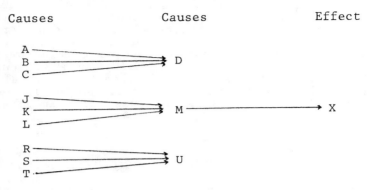

Further, each particular cause is a compound entity rather than a single entity. Each cause may be broken down into a number of components. It is treated as a single unit only for ease of analysis and purposes of exposition.

The reverse is of course also true. Each cause produces more than one effect, so that there is a "progressive multiplication of effects."

PROGRESSIVE MULTIPLICATION OF EFFECTS

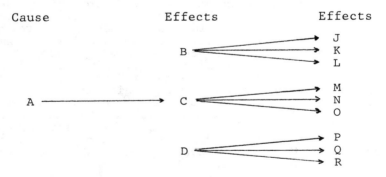

Spencer used this argument to support his assertion that evolution always progresses from simple to complex, from homogeneous to heterogeneous.

In his essay, "Progress: Its Law and Cause," Spencer stated as his basic law: "<u>Every active force</u>

produces more than one change--every cause produces more than one effect."[13] Society evolves because each force tends to produce multiple effects. Society is continually getting more complex and heterogeneous because every cause produces a variety of effects which act to produce a more complex society. This latter idea, of course, is fully consistent with the position of Durkheim on single causation.

It is interesting that there should be a gap between the general sociological view of causation and the common-sense view. I find my students readily accept Spencer's orientation to causation and frequently wonder why it should even be necessary to discuss it. Yet such an apparently self-evident point of view is difficult to find in sociological literature. I have found it expressed only in the obscure essay cited, which was written in Spencer's dotage. Perhaps this is because it is also so self-evident to sociologists that it is assumed as given rather than openly discussed. Yet classical writings on the subject, notably Durkheim's and Weber's seem to take a different point of view.

THOMAS ON CAUSATION

W. I. Thomas developed a point of view about the nature of causation that was radically different from that of Durkheim. This conception of causation is found only in Thomas's later writings. Its significance to contemporary sociology will be readily apparent. Our discussion of Thomas's writings will be divided into two sections, the first on social laws, the second on causation. The two are obviously related, but for clarity of discussion, we wish to distinguish them analytically.

SOCIAL LAWS

In the great classic The Polish Peasant in Europe and America,[14] Thomas and Znaniecki took the common orientation of the period regarding social causation. They assumed that social laws exist and that social research will enable sociologists to discover these laws. Once social laws have been discovered, they can be used for practical purposes to improve the social life of mankind.

If we want to reach scientific explanations, we must keep in mind that our facts must be

333

determined in such a way as to permit of their subordination to general laws. . . . And only if social theory succeeds in determining causal laws can it become the basis of social technique. . . .[15]

This view of the nature of social laws coincides with those of Durkheim, Spencer, Comte, Marx and the great majority of pioneer sociologists (but not with Weber).

THE REJECTION OF SOCIAL LAWS

As much as anyone in his day, W. I. Thomas was a researcher as well as a theorist. Thomas was consistently engaged in the process of fitting research findings to theory and vice versa. His views about causation may therefore be said to have grown out of more practical experiences than did those of many others who took a more philosophical approach (e.g., Mead). Perhaps for this reason, Thomas became frustrated with the attempt to establish social laws as invariant relationships among variables. Thomas found that he could sometimes establish relationships among variables, but that such relationships as he and other researchers were able to establish were far from meeting the criteria for acceptance as scientific laws. For this reason, in his later works, Thomas rejected the point of view that scientific laws could be established in the social sciences.

In The Child of America,[16] Thomas devoted the last chapter to a consideration of methodological issues raised by the book. Here, Thomas pointedly rejected the possibility of establishing social laws in sociology. He first noted that scientists in most disciplines are able to establish "a limited number" of scientific laws. His definition of a law is very simple: if under certain established conditions, a particular cause invariably is followed by a given effect, a law is said to exist. However, the establishment of a scientific law does not also imply that the scientist can give a "complete causal explanation" of a phenomenon.[17] A complete causal explanation would involve the explanation of the coming into existence of the cause and the conditions which influenced the causal relationship. This is a far different matter than stating that given certain conditions and the existence of a cause, a particular effect will follow. In order to make this more complete causal explanation, the scientist must "determine every force and measure every influence in the universe in order of their reciprocal action" from the creation of the world to the present instance. This, of course, is impossible.

Accepting the symbolic interactionist point of view, Thomas argued that social relations are based on interactions among individuals. Such interactions tend to achieve an aspect of consistency and stability. This leads to common definitions of situations and common behavior under similar conditions. Social institutions and all collective forms of behavior, then, are built up from these interactions among individuals. (This point is discussed more extensively in Chapter Ten.)

Any social act is influenced both by the conditions present in the situation (both social and nonsocial) and by the individual's definition of the situation.

> . . . (W)hile the effect of a physical phenomenon depends exclusively on the objective nature of this phenomenon and can be calculated on the ground of the latter's empirical content, the effect of a social phenomenon depends in addition on the subjective standpoint taken by the individual or the group toward this phenomenon and can be calculated only if we know, not only the objective content of the assumed cause, but also the meanings which it has at the given moment for the given conscious beings.[18]

The subjective element, the capability of the individual to think, makes the causal relationship among social phenomena more complex than that among physical phenomena. This complexity must be taken into account in the causal principles utilized by the social sciences.

It follows, then, that a sociologist will never be able to give a complete causal explanation of any particular social act. According to Thomas, each act grows out of interaction. It is an emergent entity subject to the influence of previous experiences by all the actors involved in the interaction. Therefore, no complete explanation of an act can be given without tracing back through history every interaction which has contributed to the determination of the act under

investigation. By implication, this means _every_
interaction.

This was an extremely important point for Thomas,
since he viewed social phenomena as possessing
characteristics radically different from physical
phenomena. Human beings think, choose, reflect, and
exercise will. This is not true of physical entities
studied by the physical sciences. For this reason, the
social scientist must take into account the experience
and reflection of the individual actor in his attempt
to establish social laws. The unit of analysis (the
individual) has a volitional character which sets him
apart from the units of analysis (e.g., molecules of
water, fields of wheat) studied by other sciences.

The volitional character of the individual,
together with the changing nature of society which
results from this volitional character, makes social
laws impossible. Thomas strongly implied in this
particular work that such invariant laws do not exist
in the realm of social phenomena. If they do not
exist, there is no possibility of discovering them or
otherwise establishing them.

> The individual is changing, under influences
> which cannot be measured. His response in
> situations changes with periods of physical,
> mental and emotional maturation and as the
> result of experiences in an endless variety
> of preceding situations. The student of
> behavior can therefore not hope to establish
> even the limited number of laws possible in
> the case of the exact scientist. He may hope
> to be able to determine that in certain
> situations certain reactions will usually
> follow. He will be able to make inferences
> but probably unable to establish laws. This
> would imply, then, not a complete but an
> adequate causal explanation of behavior.[19]

In his later publications, Thomas consistently
advocated objective scientific research to establish
"adequate" relationships. This is a more practical and
attainable goal than establishing causal laws. This
point of view was strongly stressed in his article "The
Relation of Research to the Social Process." While
advocating experimentation as the major method of
establishing causation, he recognized that no control
of all relevant variables is possible when dealing with

336

social phenomena. Because of this, he argued that no inferences derived from social experiments or statistical studies will gain the status of scientific laws.[20] The social scientist should seek for higher and higher probabilities, but his efforts will never culminate in the establishment of social laws.

INTERACTIVE CAUSATION

Durkheim had argued that every social effect must be caused by a social fact. No individual facts or "manifestations" can be brought in and assumed to be causally related to a social effect. Likewise, most psychologists had used psychological or individual facts as causes of other psychological facts. Sociological facts were considered to be on a different level than psychological facts. Any mixing of the levels produced spurious research findings or theories.

In the famous "Methodological Note" in the Polish Peasant, Thomas and Znaniecki developed a point of view of causation opposed to Durkheim's formulation. The "fundamental methodological principle" which must be utilized by both sociology and social psychology was stated by Thomas and Znaniecki as follows:

> The cause of a social or individual phenomenon is never another social or individual phenomenon alone, but always a combination of a social and an individual phenomenon.[21]

As stated, the view of causation here presented may be diagrammed as in Figure 17:2.

337

Figure 17:2

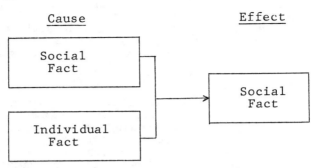

This is the typical sociological causal explanation. The form of explanation in psychology is similar (Figure 17:3).

Figure 17:3

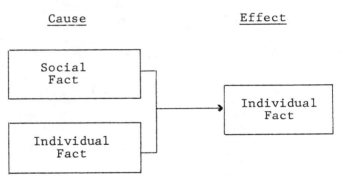

However, Thomas and Znaniecki paid greater attention to the cause rather than to the effect. Most statements of causation take this form. They assume the effect as given, and establish rules for determining a cause. However, if we consider the position of symbolic interaction in general and Thomas in particular, there is no reason why the effect is not viewed in the same way as the cause. If the effect, like the cause, is treated as a combination of social and individual phenomena, then the following diagram of causation is most accurate (Figure 17:4).

338

Figure 17:4

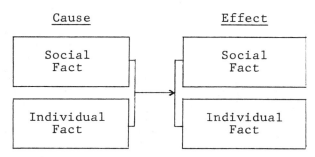

    In this view, the cause is always a combination of a social and an individual fact. Likewise, the effect is a combination of both a social and individual fact. In attributing causation, one cannot ignore either the social condition present in the situation or the individual or "meaningful" conditions present in the individual's definition of the situation. Both are always present.

    This does not mean necessarily that each factor has equal weight as a cause. One may be more important in one situation, the other may have greater causal weight in another. Causation is always <u>multiple</u> in that both social and individual factors are always present. One can distinguish the social from the individual only analytically. Following Cooley's insight about the "real" intermixture of these two, one would have to say that the process of interaction, involving both social and individual aspects, must always be treated as causal. The nature of the effect is not equally as clear. For analytical reasons, we may wish to distinguish the social from the individual. In reality, however, they are inextricably intermixed.

ABANDONMENT OF CAUSATION

    With Thomas's changing views on the nature of social laws, he also changed his views on causation. In his later work, he advocated the abandonment of the idea of causation and its replacement with the idea of relationship. Thomas implied that social relations might better be characterized as reciprocal rather than causal, although he never explicitly stated this point of view. However, it is clear that he felt it most important to pursue social research as practically as possible. Any philosophical notions of causation must not be allowed to get in the way of concrete research. If one found causal relations, and could establish their invariability, that would be fine with Thomas. In the meantime, however, one should not worry about attaining this degree of certitude. At the level at which researchers were working in his day (and perhaps in ours, too) the best one could hope for was establishing a correlation. One should seek to refine one's measurements and theory in order to include other relevant factors and thereby increase the statistical probabilities present in the relationship. But the search for invariant causation seemed very remote to Thomas in his later works.

SUMMARY

We have found that there are many facets to the causal point of view. Some of the classical theorists, notably Durkheim, asserted the efficacy of the causal viewpoint. They believed that the assumption that causes operate in social life was basic to the development of sociology. And they believed that the major task of sociology was the discovery of cause and effect relations. Others like Weber took a more moderate view of causation. Weber retreated from the realist position and argued that any causal statement involved abstractions from reality. Causal statements were subjective constructs to aid sociologists in making "adequate" explanations of events. All events were produced by a multiplicity of causes rather than any one single cause, to which Spencer readily agreed. Thomas's orientation was close to that of Weber. Accepting a subjectivist orientation, he argued that individual choice as well as social conditions contribute to any specific social event. He developed a multiple-causal orientation based upon the workings of both psychological and sociological forces to produce any given effect.

Later, Thomas retreated even from this mild point of view to a belief that causal terminology was relatively fruitless in sociological investigation, and that sociologists should cease the attempt to discover invariant social laws and seek more limited generalizations based on probable relationships.

FOOTNOTES

[1]Max Weber, "Critical Studies in the Logic of the Cultural Sciences," in Methodology of the Social Sciences, tr. by Edward A. Shils and Henry A. Finch (Glencoe: Free Press), 1949, p. 169; italics Weber's.

[2]This is what Merton called "orientation." Robert K. Merton, Social Theory and Social Structure, revised edition (Glencoe: Free Press), 1957, pp. 87-89.

[3]The Methodology of the Social Sciences, pp. 169-171, italics Weber's.

[4]Ibid., p. 171, italics Weber's.

[5]Ibid., p. 173.

[6]Loc. cit.

[7]Ibid., p. 184.

[8]Ibid., p. 138.

[9]Ibid., p. 187.

[10]Max Weber, The Protestant Ethic and the Spirit of Capitalism (New York: Scribners), 1958.

[11]Methodology, pp. 72-76.

[12]Herbert Spencer, "The Regressive Multiplication of Causes," Facts and Comments (New York & London: Appleton), 1902, pp. 210-215.

[13]Herbert Spencer, "Progress: Its Law and Cause," The Humboldt Library of Science, 17 (March 1881), p. 243, italics Spencer's.

[14]William I. Thomas and Florian Znaniecki, The Polish Peasant in Europe and America (New York: Knopf), 1918-1920 (five volumes).

[15]"Methodological Note," in Ibid. See also Edmund H. Volkart (ed.), Social Behavior and Personality: Contributions of W. I. Thomas to Theory and Social Research (New York: Social Science Research Council), 1951, p. 54.

341

[16]William I. Thomas and Dorothy Swaine Thomas, _The Child in America: Behavior Problems and Programs_ (New York: Knopf), 1928.

[17]_Ibid_., p. 553.

[18]"Methodological   Note"   in   Volkart,   _op_.   _cit_., pp. 54-55.

[19]_The Child in America_, p. 554.

[20]Volkart, _op_. _cit_., p. 89, footnote #3.

[21]_Ibid_., p. 55.   Italics Thomas's and Znaniecki's.

CHAPTER EIGHTEEN

CLASSICAL SYSTEMS THEORY:
SPENCER, PARETO, AND RADCLIFFE-BROWN

The systems orientation in sociological theory stands in marked contrast to the causal orientation. While the two should not be thought of as complete opposites, those who take one orientation tend to make different kinds of analyses than those who take the other orientation. It is our intent in this chapter to discuss the perspectives of the classical sociological theorists who have utilized the systems orientation and to contrast this approach with the causal orientation.

THE ROOTS OF THE SYSTEMS ORIENTATION:
SPENCER'S ORGANICISM

The theory of organicism, which was highly influential during the nineteenth century, provided the theoretical foundation for later systems models. Most importantly, modern functional theory in sociology and anthropology has been strongly influenced by organicism. In order to understand later systems models, it is first necessary, therefore, to discuss the basic principles of sociological organicism.

Organicism asserts the theoretical similarity between the organic principles of biology and the social principles of social organization. Society is treated as analogous to an organism. Frequently, the human body is the organism used as a referent. The organic analogy is in turn based on the assumption that there are certain basic laws or organizing principles which encompass both the biological and social sciences. This is in keeping with nineteenth century beliefs in the unity of science.

Organicism has a long philosophical history, tracing back to earliest writings. Even primitive tribes with no written records often believed strongly in the identity of organic and social life. The early Christian church was compared to a body by the Apostle Paul (1 Corinthians 12:12-30). Auguste Comte, the founder of modern sociology, adhered to the organicist orientation. Perhaps the most significant development of organicism in the early history of sociology, however, is found in the works of Herbert Spencer. It is to his writings that we now turn.

Spencer wrote during the full last half of the
nineteenth century. Following the lead of Auguste
Comte in France, sociology as a scientific discipline
was becoming established. Spencer's task was to
facilitate the establishment of sociology in England by
defining its particular subject matter. Spencer's
definition of society and the relationship of society
to the individual forms the basis for his theory of
organicism.

Spencer accepted the normal philosophical position
of his day that a society was a collection of
individuals. (Spencer's notion of individualism was
discussed in Chapter 11). However, he did not accept
the nominalist or reductionist positions implied by
this statement. Spencer believed that society is
"real" in that it has a separate reality apart from the
nature of its individual members.[1] Permanence is the
particular characteristic of a society which sets it
apart from its constituent elements and gives it a real
character. Spencer considered society to be an entity
in that it was persistent over time.

Spencer likewise followed the philosophy of his
day in asserting that the "reality" of social phenomena
was of a different order than the reality of physical
phenomena. One could not point objectively to a
society in the same sense that one could point to an
individual, an animal or other physical entity. He
argued that society "cannot be manifest to perception,
but can be discerned only by reason."[2] In order to
analyze society, therefore, it is necessary to discover
similarities between social phenomena and biological
phenomena.

> Between a society and anything else, the only
> conceivable resemblance must be one due to
> parallelism of principles in the arrangement
> of components.[3]

Spencer, therefore, sought to discover what kinds
of physical phenomena were comparable to social
phenomena. He distinguished what he called "two great
classes of aggregates:" (1) the inorganic and (2) the
organic.[4] He then sought to discover whether social
phenomena exhibited a greater degree of similarity with
inorganic or with organic phenomena. As one would
imagine, he discovered greater similarities between
social phenomena and organic matter than with inorganic
phenomena. Spencer assumed that there was a similarity

of natural law which tied together social and biological phenomena. Other sociologists have not accepted his assertion that it is necessary to establish a parallelism or degree of similarity between social phenomena and physical phenomena. However, Spencer's whole theoretical system was based on the assertion of an innate or fundamental similarity between social phenomena and other natural, especially biological, phenomena.

SIMILARITIES BETWEEN SOCIETY AND THE HUMAN BODY

Spencer described six essential ways in which society is like an organism. This does not mean that Spencer fully believed that society is in every respect like an organism. He sought rather to abstract out those particular characteristics of society which demonstrate the greatest similarity to an organism. He recognized, however, that this is a process of abstraction and that in many respects society is unlike an organism. We shall first summarize Spencer's discussion of the similarities between society and an organism and then turn to the dissimilarities which he observed.

GROWTH

Both an organism and a society exhibit growth, or what Spencer called "augmentation of mass."[5] Spencer recognized that an organism may grow only at certain points during its lifetime, whereas, a society is more likely to grow continuously. However, growth is a fundamental characteristic of both society and an organism.

STRUCTURE

Just as both a society and an organism increase in size, they also increase in organization or structure. This is one of the fundamental principles of evolution. The increase in size necessitates a resultant increase in social organization. As the number of units increases or multiplies, the units necessarily begin to divide or differentiate, and each unit gradually becomes more specialized. As differentiation increases, however, the organism or the society experiences a need to organize or integrate these differentiated parts into a single whole. Therefore, increase of size leads to differentiation, which leads in turn to a more complex social organization.

345

Evolution proceeds from homogeneity to heterogeneity. In a simple organism or a simple society all of the units resemble each other--that is, the organism or the society is homogeneous. However, with increasing growth and complexity, the parts differentiate and become unlike each other. The society and the organism become heterogeneous.

The formation of social structure provides coordination of these various parts. Spencer asserted that:

> . . .organization consists in such a construction of the whole that its parts can carry on mutually-dependent actions. . . .There must (be) a dependence of each part upon the rest so great that separation is fatal.[6]

Social organization is simply another name for social integration or social cohesion. Organization involves the tying together of differentiated parts into a whole.

Perhaps the main feature of developing social organization is the development of a ruling head or ruling agency.[7] The necessity for regulation and coordination leads to the development of some kind of political system which performs the function of regulation and coordination. In an organism this function is usually performed by the brain, while in a society, it is performed by the government, whether democratic or authoritarian in nature.

FUNCTIONS

Spencer believed that "progressive differentiation of structures is accompanied by progressive differentiation of functions."[8] His definition of function seemed to involve duties or actions which are performed. Each structure which has been differentiated from other structures tends to become differentiated in terms of function. Each separate structure, therefore, performs a separate duty which is not performed by any other structure. In an organism each separate organ of the body performs a specific physiological function. In a society different functions are performed by different occupational or status groups. Each separate function is correlated or associated with a particular structure which is

346

specialized to perform that function. In a primitive organism or a primitive society each unit is like all other units, and each unit is able to perform all physiological or social functions. However, as evolution proceeds, each unit becomes specialized to perform only one function. This means that any particular unit is able to perform only one small part of all the functions necessary to be accomplished in order for the larger aggregate or body to exist.

MUTUAL DEPENDENCE

The preceding similarities lead logically to a fourth similarity, that of mutual dependence. As evolution proceeds, each part becomes progressively differentiated and, therefore, progressively more dependent on other units. In a highly evolved organism or society where each unit can perform only a narrowly specialized function, each unit is dependent upon other units for the fulfilling of other functions. There is a division of labor created among the units in the system such that each part fulfills a highly specialized function and is totally dependent upon other units for fulfilling other functions which allow the total aggregate to remain alive.

The total aggregate, therefore, was conceptualized by Spencer as a system in which each part is mutually dependent on each other part and in which each unit contributes to the total functioning of the whole system. Spencer did not give a definition of his concept "system," but it seems to be derived directly from the usage of the term in the biological sciences. Spencer noted a close parallelism between the mutual dependence of all of the organs of a human body and the mutual dependence of all of the institutions in a society. Each person, each occupation, each institution is dependent upon other persons, occupations, and institutions, in order that the total society may continue to function properly and exist in its environment.

Spencer discussed three separate types of systems which are found in both biological organism and a society. The first is what he called "the sustaining system." The function of this system is to produce the materials necessary for survival. The sustaining system in the biological organism is the digestive system; whereas, in the social system it is the economy. Every system whether biological or social

347

needs to produce the materials for its sustenance. The second system is the "distributing system." This is the system which distributes sustenance to all parts of the body. In a society distribution is accomplished through transportation and communication while in the body the circulatory system performs this function. The third system is called "the regulating system" by Spencer. Every system needs a specialized regulatory agency which will coordinate all of the various parts within the system. In the human body this is accomplished by the brain while in society it is accomplished by the government.

Spencer recognized many similarities in specific organs in the human body and specific institutions in society. This does not mean one can find an analogous institution for every differentiated organ in the physical body. However, there are similarities in the functions which need to be performed and, therefore, in the kind of structure which are developed in both the body and society.

TOTAL COMPOSED OF SMALLER UNITS

Both an organism and a society are wholes which are composed of smaller units. The organism is composed of cells, whereas the society is composed of individual human beings. These individual units are, of course, differentiated and specialized. There are marked differences between some cells and other cells in a body and between the individuals in a society. Spencer, therefore, spoke of a living organism as a nation composed of separate units.

As a biologist does not find it necessary to predict the actions of each individual cell, likewise a sociologist does not find it necessary to predict the actions of each individual person. For both scientists it is enough to study the general effects or characteristics of the total aggregate without the necessity to study the total workings of each individual unit.

AFFECT OF CATASTROPHE

The sixth and last characteristic which Spencer described as demonstrating the similarities between an organism and a society is the reaction of each to a catastrophe. Both a biological organism and a society can be destroyed by a large scale catastrophe.

348

Conversely, if no catastrophe occurs, the life of the organism or society continues indefinitely and has a longer duration than that of each of the individual units.

> By catastrophe the life of the aggregate may be destroyed without immediately destroying the lives of all its units; while, on the other hand, if no catastrophe abridges it, the life of the aggregate is far longer than the lives of its units.[9]

If no great catastrophe such as defeat in war occurs, a society continues to exist indefinitely. Individual members are born, grow to maturity, and die and are successfully replaced by other individual members. However, the aggregate or total society maintains a continuity even though its individual members are replaced.

It is also possible that the total life of the large aggregate can be destroyed without the resulting destruction of the individual units. If a society is invaded and conquered by another society, the individual members will continue to live and function within their occupational and other activities. A new order is created, and the former units are incorporated into the new aggregate. Likewise in a biological organism, the total body can die without the necessary or immediate death of the individual cells. In the case of an organism ingested by a larger organism, the cells may continue to live and function within the larger body in which they are incorporated.

Spencer asserted, therefore, that the life of the total aggregate and the life of the individual units are separable. Each may continue if the other ceases to exist. This separability of the life of the units and the life of the total aggregate is another argument against reducing the society to its individual units. Individual units may die, may come and go, yet the total society continues to exist. One cannot fully explain the life of a larger aggregate by reference solely to the individual characteristics of the individual units which make it up.

DISSIMILARITIES BETWEEN SOCIETY AND AN ORGANISM

Spencer noted two major ways in which a society is unlike an organism. The first dissimilarity he found important, but not enough to reject the organic analogy which he had heretofore developed. Spencer asserted that all of the units of a biological organism form a concrete whole, whereas the units of society are more dispersed or discrete. In a biological organism there is close physical contact of all of the units with all other units. However, a society is not a physically coherent body in the same sense as is an organism.

Spencer argued that physical proximity is necessary in order for biological organisms to function. Each unit must be in physical contact with each other unit in order for the units to influence each other. Mutually dependent functions could not be carried on without physical contact. Social aggregates do not have the same need for physical contact. Coordination of their functions is achieved through language rather than through physical proximity. Therefore, the units of a society, that is, the interacting individuals, may be more widely dispersed or diffused than the units of an organism. Language as a means of communication enables the dispersed individuals to coordinate their activities.

A second contrast or difference between an organism and society had different implications for Spencer. Spencer argued that in an organism each of the units contributes to the proper functioning of the total aggregate. In an organism, therefore, each of the individual units exists for the benefit of the whole. Spencer, however, as the major advocate of individualism in the nineteenth century, asserted that a society has far different characteristics. In a society the individual units have greater importance than the total aggregate or society. The society exists for the good or benefit of the individual units rather than vice versa.

> . . .the welfare of the aggregate, considered apart from that of the units, is not an end to be sought. The society exists for the benefit of its members: not its members for the benefit of the society.[10]

This assertion had important political implications for Spencer, who was an advocate of laissez faire individualism. Spencer asserted that each individual should be left totally free to develop to the fullest his own particular capabilities. The process of evolution should not be hindered by social

350

structures such as a government. Government should keep its hands off the development of the individual. The role of the government is solely to protect the individual and to facilitate his proper evolution and specialization. The benefit of the individual is always the first consideration, and the benefit to the society always a secondary consideration.

Spencer strongly believed in the unity of all sciences. He believed there were natural laws which governed all aspects of life. Arbitrary distinctions between scientific disciplines were man made. Natural laws had wider application than the narrow disciplines defined by scientists. Spencer believed that one of his major tasks was to discover the natural principles governing all life. He believed that he had discovered one of the most basic laws of nature in the law of organicism. Together with evolutionary theory, which is clearly related to organicism, Spencer felt that he had the keys to the understanding not only of social life but to all phenomena subject to human investigation.

SYSTEMS AND EQUILIBRIUM

Later systems theorists have placed great emphasis upon the concept of mutual dependence, which plays an extremely important place in Spencer's organicism, as we have attempted to show. Spencer also foreshadowed the development of modern systems theory in his discussion of the concept of equilibrium and its central importance in the organism. In Spencer's First Principles is found one of the earliest and best discussions of the system concept and "moving equilibrium" found in sociological literature.

Spencer first argued that all phenomena tend to progress toward a state of equilibrium.[11] A rolling stone bounces down the mountainside but eventually comes to rest on the valley floor. The drop of rain falls from a cloud, joins a stream and then a river, and finally comes to rest in the ocean. A harpstring plucked by the harpist vibrates rapidly, but gradually moves toward a state of rest. A charge of electricity may run in a current, but tends eventually to be discharged and diffused. In each of these cases, however, only one movement of the object has ceased. The rock comes to rest vis-a-vis the earth, but still travels at great speed around the earth's axis.

351

When any physical object is in motion, according to Spencer, it continually comes into contact with other objects. Upon striking these objects, its motion is transferred to some extent to them, and it tends to lose or dissipate some of its own motion. Eventually the object comes to a state of rest. However, since its motion has been transmitted to other objects, and from them to still other objects, the motion itself is not lost. Rather it is dissipated. Motion still occurs, but it has been so distributed that it cannot be readily observed. Spencer wrote of this as a tendency toward equilibrium or a balance of forces.

A system is composed of a number of units. Each unit is subject to change or to forces which tend to move it vis-a-vis other units. The system is said to be in a state of equilibrium when each movement in one unit is counterbalanced or compensated for by movements in all the other units. All of the units of the system are in a state of mutual dependence, such that any change or force that affects any unit affects all units. No single unit of the system is independent, but all are dependent upon each other.

Spencer was quick to point that this kind of condition had previously been called <u>equilibrium mobile</u> by French mathematicians[12] (and is commonly called "dynamic equilibrium" by contemporary sociologists). A static equilibrium is one in which each unit as well as the total system is in a complete state of rest, but in which each unit is integrated or in a defined relationship to all other units. According to Spencer, no such static equilibrium exists, because in any system, of any type, some movement of its molecules or other particles exists. All systems are in a state of dynamic equilibrium, in that some of its units must be in a state of motion.

When we think of a moving equilibrium we think of the total system moving in relation to some external point, according to Spencer. A moving bullet has motion in reference to the ground over which it travels. To Spencer's way of thinking, the bullet is not in a state of equilibrium. However, it eventually comes to a state of dynamic equilibrium when it has transmitted its motion to other objects and has come to rest vis-a-vis the ground. Motion continues in the smaller particles encountered by the bullet, but this motion is eventually compensated for and equilibrated.

Terrestrial bodies, organic bodies, and fully-developed societies are all characterized by dynamic equilibrium according to Spencer. Each society is evolving. The processes of change which it goes through exhibit unbalanced forces. However, eventually these forces will be equilibrated, the society will achieve a state of dynamic equilibrium, and the society will cease to evolve.

No society which is still evolving can be said to be in a state of equilibrium. However, each society moves through a series of approximations to equilibrium, such that it continually approaches the state of equilibrium. In other words, the more advanced the society, the closer it is to a state of equilibrium. The tendency toward equilibrium will eventually result in the end of evolution and the total stability of society. This conclusion, of course, does not appear to fit the facts of social life. Most students of social change argue just the reverse: the rate of social change is constantly increasing.

Spencer's argument, however, is one of the most clearly formulated in all sociological literature on the subject of systems and dynamic equilibrium. His assertions provide a clear checkpoint for comparison of other theoretical statements of the systems orientation.

PARETO AND THE SOCIAL SYSTEM

Modern systems theorists usually give the most credit for the development of the concept of social systems to Vilfredo Pareto. Pareto's magnum opus Mind and Society[13] had a major influence on Lawrence J. Henderson, a physiologist who taught at Harvard University. Henderson organized a group of individuals, including Talcott Parsons and George C. Homans, for the study of Pareto's works. This group, which met for several years together during the 1930s, became known as the "Pareto Circle."[14] Parsons and Homans both made major contributions to the systems orientation in contemporary sociology. Both wrote major monographs discussing the work of Pareto, as did Henderson.[15]

DEFINITION OF SYSTEM

A system is composed of a number of units which exist in a state of mutual dependence or reciprocity, such that a change in any one of the units produces a responsive change in all of the other units. It is characterized by interdependence, and no unit within the system is autonomous. Each is closely tied to each other unit, as in Figure 18:1.

Figure 18:1

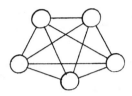

Each unit of the system is an important element in the system. While some units may be larger, more powerful or more influential than other units, each has its place. Each is able to provoke reciprocating reactions throughout the system.

Pareto spoke of cycles of interdependence. If there are four units in a system, A, B, C, D, each will influence the other. "A acts on B, C and D; B acts on A, C and D; C acts on A, B and D; D acts A, B and C."[16] Pareto specifically recognized that one element, for example A, may have a more important effect on the other elements than vice versa. By studying the units of the system and their reciprocating actions, one can determine the magnitude of influence each unit has upon all of the other units.

A system offers "considerable resistance" to change because of the mutual dependence of all its units. Any force tending to move or change a particular unit is resisted by all of the other units of the system. Perhaps the most important defining characteristic of a system is reciprocity. An important effect of reciprocity is stability, or at least relative stability. Stability is achieved when processes within the system, and especially the reciprocal ties binding the units together, operate to bring the system back to some original state. Because of reciprocity, it is not possible to change just one unit of the system. Any force which seeks to change the system must be strong enough to influence all of

354

the units, since all are tied together. Weaker forces have no impact because they are not of sufficient force to change the whole system. Many people make the mistake of trying to change one part of a system, only to find that their attempt has failed because of the reciprocity and equilibrium of the system.

DYNAMIC EQUILIBRIUM

Pareto recognized that every society is subject to social change. Therefore, the concept of stable equilibrium never applies completely to a social system. Most social systems change slowly, but the ties which bind all of the units together tend to persist and maintain the same relationships among the units.

In both mechanics and biology, concepts of dynamic equilibrium have been used to explain the workings of mechanical and organic systems. Pareto was pessimistic about the possibilities of applying these dynamic concepts to social behavior. Instead, he argued in his Cours d'Economie Politique that in sociology one must "consider a series of static equilibria rather than the dynamic equilibrium."[17]

For example, Pareto compared a person descending a hill on a sled to a person walking down the hill and stopping at every step. The former represents dynamic equilibrium. The latter--more appropriate to sociology--represents a series of stable equilibria. In studying a society and in applying the concept of equilibrium to it, it is not necessary to have an exact measurement of every unit at every moment in time. It is sufficient to observe the system at several points in time and measure the relationships among the units at each time. In this way, one can determine the direction and degree of change in the system.

A changing system can still be characterized as being in a state of equilibrium if (1) the state of the system at any moment is determined by the conditions of the system by laws governing the operations of these conditions, and (2) processes within the system operate to maintain a balance or reciprocity among the elements constituting the system. The latter assumes that the system possesses self-regulating mechanisms which tend to maintain the integration of the system. Pareto did not discuss the nature of these self-regulating mechanisms, and may perhaps be criticized for not recognizing their existence. The analysis of these self-regulating mechanisms is one of the most important steps in the study of social systems.

THE SOCIAL SYSTEM

The social system was the major focus of analysis of Pareto's sociological works, principally his <u>Mind and Society (A Treatise on General Sociology)</u>. Pareto recognized the existence of climate, soil and other physical conditions which were external to the social system. Further, there were many social conditions, like the existence of other societies, which were also external to the social system in question. Mutual dependence characterized the relationships of all of the units within the social system. Likewise, all of the factors external to the system were also in a relationship of interdependence with the social system and its elements.[18]

Pareto's model of the social system is therefore an "open" one in contemporary terminology. One can arbitrarily designate the boundaries of a social system and make an analysis of its structure and functions. One should always recognize, however, that the system exists in a broader context. It is continually subject to forces or pressures from outside its boundaries, and is in turn exerting influences outside its boundaries. It is possible, therefore, to treat an individual social system as a unit of a larger system which includes as other units both social and physical conditions.

This furnishes another reason for treating any particular social system as dynamic rather than static. Since it must adjust to a multiplicity of reciprocating forces external to it, it must constantly change to adjust and readjust to these forces. This leads to dynamic readjustments within the system, and therefore continual change.

Pareto developed concepts of "residues" and "derivations" which he used in the analysis of social systems. (These are discussed in Chapter Seven.) He generally regarded these as the main building blocks or units of the social system. However, he was extremely flexible in what he considered fit candidates for units of the system. Patterns of behavior, normative patterns, emotional sentiments, groups with particular

356

characteristics (lions and foxes) and others were all treated as units.[19]

The system concept was a useful tool in the hands of Pareto. With it he was able to examine a variety of historical events and social conditions, and gain new insights thereby. He recognized that any set of facts might be explained in a variety of ways with a variety of theories. Each theory might be equally plausible. Many different lines can be drawn which all may intersect a series of points. Likewise, many different theories can serve to explain a certain set of social facts.[20]

REJECTION OF CAUSATION

Pareto recognized more clearly than early theorists (and most later theorists) that the acceptance of a social system model involved the concomitant rejection of a causal model of social life. If units A, B and C are in a state of mutual dependence, one should not look to discover which is the cause and which are effects. Any change in one unit immediately provokes changes in the other units, which in turn produce a reciprocal effect on the first unit. A series of adjustments takes place in the system until equilibrium is restored.[21] In such a case, any discussion of causation is beside the point. No one unit may be considered a cause of the other, since all are in a state of reciprocity.

Pareto warned repeatedly against the error of attributing a cause-and-effect relationship to units which are in a state of interdependence.[22] For example, he felt the major error of Marxian economic determinism was in attributing causal priority to economic variables and treating other variables as effects. Mutual dependence rather than causation characterizes the relationships among the various institutions of any society. Further, he argued that most social theorists treat behavior as an effect of a prior idea or motive. In reality, behavior and belief are mutually dependent.[23]

Pareto's theory of systems was therefore clearly distinguished from a theory of causation. In Pareto's mind, these are two alternative models by which social reality may be represented. Clearly, Pareto chose reciprocity over causation.

357

Frequently, however, Pareto used the language of causation. He did not deny that certain relationships among variables may be causal. He argued explicitly, however, that one must be careful in attributing causal significance to a particular variable without extensive research. It is natural for people to think in terms of causation, and in terms of <u>simple</u> causation. In reality, causal relationships are extremely complex.[24] The common tendency is to choose from among the multiplicity of causes (or mutually dependent variables) of an event some one or a few for accentuation and analysis. The others are most often totally ignored. This tendency leads to a simplistic notion of the nature of causation, and to a ready acceptance of a causal model rather than a systems model. In his <u>Manuel d'Economie Politique</u>, Pareto noted the variety of ways in which simplistic and even imaginary causes are substituted for a realistic explanation of social relationships.[25]

Pareto observed that most people, especially social scientists, frequently recognize the reciprocity of social variables. Rarely, however, do they go beyond this simple recognition to a study of the nature and direction of the reciprocal relationship. He argued that what is necessary for adequate sociological explanation of reciprocity is a proper use of mathematics, especially differential equations, which will allow the sociologist "not only to know the direction of these variations, but even to calculate exactly their extent and intensity."[26] Pareto himself was a well-trained mathematician. Throughout his works, he utilized mathematics and mathematical expressions to assist in his analysis and presentation of facts.

Both the systems model and the causal model are useful in sociological research. Pareto did not advocate eliminating the causal model in favor of the systems model. One should try to determine by induction which of these models fits a particular case. The systems model appears to be a more sophisticated model which allows a closer fit to social reality in complex cases. However, its use requires an accompanying sophistication in the use of mathematics, particularly differential equations. Few sociologists are well enough trained in mathematics to use these properly. In social research, it is much easier to choose one variable and show its relationship to several other variables, rather than dealing with all

358

relevant variables and showing all of the complex relationships among them.

Henderson, in his excellent short analysis of Pareto's Trattato, considered some of the difficulties in applying the systems model in social research.[27] First, a systems model may not be found to apply adequately in particular cases. Second, social systems are probably more "open" and less isolated than physical and chemical systems. Third, it probably is more difficult to determine the boundaries of social systems than physical and chemical systems. Fourth, "the experimental formation of social systems is very difficult."[28] Fifth, social variables which compose the units of the social system are more difficult to define, characterize and measure than physical variables. Sixth, and probably most important according to Henderson, rigorous mathematical formulations are extremely difficult to apply to sociological phenomena.

SUMMARY

A social system is characterized by interdependence, reciprocity, and dynamic equilibrium. A social system, according to Pareto, comes closer to expressing social reality than does a causal model. The causal model is not to be rejected in sociology; however, a systems model is preferable where applicable. Only by moving toward more sophisticated analyses of social phenomena--utilizing the systems model and mathematical expressions of it--can sociology achieve its maximum development. Pareto's contribution to the theoretical development of the systems orientation in sociology is one of the most important in all sociological literature.

RADCLIFFE-BROWN ON THE CONCEPT OF SYSTEM

Classical functionalists consistently use the systems orientation as their major theoretical perspective. Perhaps better than any other functionalists, A. R. Radcliffe-Brown analyzed and described the conceptual and theoretical framework of this approach. In this final section of the chapter we therefore turn to an analysis of this famous anthropologist's discussion of the concept of system, contained largely in his major theoretical work, A Natural Science of Society.[29] Radcliffe-Brown's definition of a system made several important points.

359

First, any system must be distinguished from its environment. That is, the units which compose the system must be distinguished from the units which belong to other systems and, from the point of view of the first system, are part of its environment. Establishing the boundaries of a social system is one of the important problems confronted in the use of this theoretical model.

Second, a system is composed of units--also referred to as items, entities or components. Radcliffe-Brown noted that in order to define a system for purposes of analysis, one must first begin with a definition or characterization of the nature of the units of which it is composed. These two features of a system are not different from those found in any theoretical analysis. A social scientist using a causal model of social reality must also distinguish the units of analysis and separate them from their environment for analysis.

The third characteristic of a system--the one characteristic which separates it from other theoretical models--is that of interdependence. We may say, therefore, that the essential property of a system is that it is characterized by a state of reciprocity and interdependence of its units such that it forms a functional unity.

INTERDEPENDENCE

Radcliffe-Brown made much of this essential property of a system. He argued that his main orientation in the investigation of social phenomena is to determine the internal nature of the social system--that is, "the relations between its unit constituents."[30] The relation among units which is found in empirical reality, in all types of phenomena, is that of interdependence. Radcliffe-Brown said simply: "The relations within a natural system are relations of interdependence. . . ."[31]

In a section entitled "The Functional Consistency of the Social System," Radcliffe-Brown discussed the nature of this interdependence.[32] In every social system there are a number of usages or norms. One can analyze and describe each usage separately. However, a system underlies these usages. The culture of a society possesses a unity. The norms form a system, in that they all tend to be consistent with each other.

360

It is extremely important to Radcliffe-Brown that the nature of this consistency be explained.

The consistency found in the normative system of a society is not just that of logical consistency, existing in the mind of the observer. Rather, it is a "real" consistency existing in the relations among the units which compose the normative system. There are two "levels" or "orders" to this consistency.

The first order of consistency is simply an absence of conflict. The second order involves reciprocal ties among units such that each contributes to the other. This latter or "higher" order of consistency is "functional" in that the parts of the structure "work closely together to reinforce each other and maintain the structure."[33] Each unit contributes to the survival of the whole system, and therefore of every unit of the whole system, by fulfilling the conditions of existence of the system.

A social system is characterized by interdependence and normative consistency. This does not mean, however, that Radcliffe-Brown assumed that every society is perfectly integrated. Merton's interpretation of Radcliffe-Brown[34] was inaccurate and misleading. For Radcliffe-Brown, the functional unity of a social system is a variable and not a constant. One of the important aspects of empirical research is to analyze the degree of interdependence of the constituent units of a system.

Conflict theorists are on more firm ground when they criticize functionalists for ignoring conflict. Radcliffe-Brown's discussion of social consistency clearly implied that conflict is dysfunctional and that the social system of every society tends to operate in such a way as to reduce or eliminate conflict.[35] In this regard, Radcliffe-Brown took a more extreme position than does Malinowski.

TYPES OF SYSTEMS

Radcliffe-Brown distinguished two different types of systems. The first he called "mechanical" and the second "persistent." A mechanical system is found commonly among physical phenomena. Radcliffe-Brown wrote of this type of system as temporary, in that it involves units in motion which tend to move toward a state of rest. A falling body is a mechanical system, with relations of interdependence among the unit entities--primarily the mass of the falling body and the positions of the mass at various times.[36] A persistent system is characterized by continuity or persistence. The relations among its units tend to persist. Such systems are dynamic; they maintain a continuity over time. An atom, a chemical substance and a living organism are instances of persistent systems.

A social system is a type of persistent system. Its units are "human beings regarded as sets of behavioral events."[37] The relations among the units are social relations. Whenever he discussed the nature of the units of a social system, Radcliffe-Brown argued that they are individual people. However, when he moved from the general and abstract level to the analysis of particular systems, he was much more likely to conceptualize the units as institutions, social roles, constellations of norms, etc. Perhaps this is what he meant when he said that human beings must be regarded as behavioral events. The tendency for individuals to play social roles, to conform to social norms, or to engage in certain patterned forms of behavior, are the real data of social science. It is to these behavioral events that the social scientist must refer for observable data.[38]

We should also note that Radcliffe-Brown made no teleological assumptions about the nature of social systems. In his clear and simple style, he stated: "A social system is not purposive."[39]

SYSTEM AND CAUSATION

Radcliffe-Brown firmly took a position against causation and in favor of reciprocity and covariation. His argument against the use of a causal theoretical model of social life is one of the strongest in sociological literature. First, he notes that for practical scientific purposes, the notion of causation is useful and even essential. If a person is ill, the doctor who treats him must have a notion of causation in order to do something about his illness. If a theft is committed, a lawyer or a judge must determine who is the cause of the crime.

In modern science, Radcliffe-Brown argued, the model of causation is being replaced by a systems model.[40] He rejects a single-causal model of society as totally at odds with the facts of social life. In attributing causation, we almost always have some special purpose in mind which allows us to focus on certain events rather than others. For example, the cause of suicide may variously be attributed to social integration (on the social level), an individual's frustration with a financial disaster (on the psychological level), the firing of a bullet in the head of a victim (on the historical level), or the cessation of neural and motor functions (on the biological level).

If we take a multiple-causal view of the nature of causation, then the attribution of causation becomes so complex that no satisfactory results may ever be achieved. If we attempt to take into account every condition, even every social condition, which may have had some causal influence, our analysis will be so extensive and complicated as to be useless.

Perhaps of most importance, such a view of causation would still neglect the interdependence of the multiplicity of phenomena which may have had a causal influence in determining a given effect. Radcliffe-Brown therefore argued that a causal model of social life is never accurate. A systems model is always more accurate in depicting the nature of social life as well as the determination of a given event. The whole system as a collection of interdependent units acts to produce a given effect. Any model of social life which does not accurately depict the reciprocity of component units of a social system cannot be used for any more than simplistic and superficial analysis and explanation.

Radcliffe-Brown and many other social scientists who have utilized a functionalist orientation have rejected a causal model of social life in favor of a systems model. The systems model has the virtue of recognizing the great complexity of social life as well as the reciprocity and interdependence which characterize it. Functionalists believe that the systems model represents social life more accurately than does a causal model.

We now turn to a discussion of the development of this issue in contemporary sociology and to some of the implications of this issue for contemporary American society.

FOOTNOTES

[1]Herbert Spencer, The Principles of Sociology (New York: Appleton), 1898, Volume 1, p. 447.

[2]Ibid., p. 448.

[3]Loc. cit.

[4]Loc. cit.

[5]Ibid., p. 449.

[6]Ibid., p. 485.

[7]Ibid., p. 472.

[8]Ibid., p. 450.

[9]Ibid., p. 455.

[10]Ibid., pp. 461-462.

[11]Herbert Spencer, First Principles (New York: De Witt Revolving Fund, Inc.), 1958, p. 479.

[12]Ibid., pp. 482-484.

[13]Vilfredo Pareto, The Mind and Society: A Treatise on General Sociology, Four Volumes (New York: Harcourt, Brace and Company), 1935.

[14]Alvin W. Gouldner, The Coming Crisis of Western Sociology (New York: Basic Books), 1970, p. 149, and Barbara S. Heyl, "The Harvard 'Pareto Circle,'" Journal of the History of Behavioral Sciences, 4 (October, 1968), pp. 316-334.

[15]Talcott Parsons, The Structure of Social Action (Glencoe: Free Press), 1949, pp. 178-300; George C. Homans and Charles P. Curtis, Jr., An Introduction to Pareto (New York: Harcourt), 1934; Lawrence J. Henderson, Pareto's General Sociology: A Physiologist's Interpretation (Cambridge: Harvard University Press), 1937.

[16]Vilfredo Pareto, Sociological Writings, try. by Derick Mirfin (New York: Praeger), 1966, p. 260. For ease of expression, I have substituted capital letters for Pareto's lower case letters surrounded by parentheses.

[17]Ibid., p. 104.

[18]Ibid., p. 215.

[19]Ibid., p. 251.

[20]Ibid., p. 145.

[21]See Henderson's excellent discussion on this point. Lawrence J. Henderson, Pareto's General Sociology: A Physiologist's Interpretation (New York: Russell and Russell), 1935, pp. 12-13.

[22]Sociological Writings, pp. 105, 160, 195, 213, 221.

[23]Ibid., pp. 213, 219-221.

[24]Ibid., p. 127.

[25]Ibid., pp. 146-148.

[26]Ibid., p. 104.

[27]Henderson, op. cit., pp. 94-95.

[28]Ibid., p. 95.

[29]A. R. Radcliffe-Brown, A Natural Science of Society (Glencoe: Free Press), 1957.

[30]Ibid., p. 19.

[31]Ibid., p. 20. Italics Radcliffe-Brown's. See also pp. 21-22, 54, 57, 154.

[32]Ibid., pp. 124-128.

[33]Ibid., p. 128.

[34]Robert K. Merton, Social Theory and Social Structure, Revised Edition (Glencoe: Free Press), 1957, esp. pp. 25-26.

[35]_Natural Science of Society_, pp. 44, 125.

[36]_Ibid._, p. 24.

[37]_Ibid._, p. 26.

[38]_Ibid._, pp. 45, 54.

[39]_Ibid._, p. 155.

[40]_Ibid._, pp. 41-42.

CHAPTER NINETEEN

DEVELOPMENTS IN THE CAUSATION VS. SYSTEM ISSUE

Having discussed the classical arguments in favor of both a causal and systems approach, we shall turn in this chapter to a brief discussion of some of the ways this argument has developed since the time of the Old Masters. While we can touch on only some of the high points in the debate over this issue, we shall try to point to significant contributions by noted sociological theorists. Specifically, we shall discuss the contributions of Robert MacIver and modern neo-positivists to the causal approach, and Pitirim Sorokin, Talcott Parsons, George Homans, and Walter Buckley to the systems approach.

SOCIAL CAUSATION: MACIVER

Robert M. MacIver's book, <u>Social Causation</u>,[1] published in 1942, was one of the important landmarks in the causal orientation, and asserted that only through a more sophisticated attempt to "dynamically assess" causal relations in social phenomena can sociology progress. MacIver, a strong advocate of a subjectivist orientation, concluded that the essential element of social causation is the subjective orientation of the members who compose the social group.

When something happens which gains the attention of an individual, he usually asks the question "why?" The answer is given in the form "because," and involves the attempt to specify the causes which produced the observed results. The questioner seeks a connection between some antecedent conditions and the event he has observed. MacIver showed that there are many forms and meanings of the question "why?" And because the questions which people ask differ in their meaning, the causal connections which are identified have different meanings. MacIver distinguished between three types of causes: (1) cause as precipitant, (2) cause as incentive or motive, and (3) cause as responsible agent. Our answer to the question "why?" will differ according as we seek to identify a precipitant, an incentive, or a responsible agent. Yet each of these validly may be considered as causes, and the investigation may seek either to limit its attribution of causation to one of these spheres or pursue an answer on all three levels.

MacIver developed three axioms of causation--primarily derived from the writings of Aristotle and J. S. Mill--which he asserted to be fundamental to all science:

Axiom 1: Whatever happens has a cause.
Axiom 2: Where there is difference in the effect, there is difference in the cause.
Axiom 3: Every cause is the effect of a prior cause and every effect is the cause of a posterior effect.[2]

The three axioms fit together neatly. The third axiom, especially, supports the first axiom, since it implies that causation is continuous and never ceasing. Causation operates universally. By definition, it is dynamic, since it is oriented to the explanation of changes and events, rather than being confined only to universals.

MacIver next addressed those who argued against the scientific validity of the notion of causation. According to MacIver, there are three main objections to the causal orientation. First, it derives from anthropomorphic assumptions that someone "makes something happen."[3] MacIver rejected this argument and asserted that scientific causation may assume either a deterministic or probabilistic perspective without the disabilities of assuming that someone made an event happen. The second argument against causation is the "totality" argument. According to MacIver, those who support this argument assert the invalidity of single causation. They argue that it is not possible to identify all the causes of any event, or describe the "total antecedent situation" which produced a given effect. This "amounts to saying that the whole is the cause of the whole,"[4] which according to MacIver is an unfruitful position. He argued that it is necessary to establish a causal connection between a single effect and one or more causes. For practical purposes, this is both useful and valid, and does not involve the investigator in fruitless searches of the total complexity of social causation.

The third difficulty in the notion of causation concerns the time interval. The causal orientation assumes that the cause precedes the effect, and that the effect follows at an appropriate interval. Questions have arisen, however, as to (1) whether the effect may precede the cause, (2) whether the effect may follow at such an extended interval that no causal attribution can be made, and (3) whether during the time interval between the cause and effect some intervening event may disturb the influence which the cause might have otherwise had upon the effect. MacIver argued that the notion of continuity between cause and effect is basic to science, and that any rejection of the assertion that cause and effect are linked in close proximity in point of time destroys all assumptions of the necessary relationships between variables. According to MacIver, causation is derived from the common-sense impressions of experience, and finds practical application in science. The orderly nature of the universe upon which science is dependent forces the acceptance of the causal orientation in science.[5]

MacIver's polemic was carried on largely with the positivistic researchers of his day who were oriented more to statistical analysis than to subjective attribution of causation. MacIver argued that establishing statistical correlations between two variables is an important first step in causal analysis. Without such a correlation, no causal attribution could be made. But statistical correlation is not sufficient. In addition, the investigator must make a "dynamic assessment,"[6] primarily subjective in nature, of the mechanism by which the effect is produced by the cause. This involves an analysis--through case studies, observation and introspection--of the behavior of individuals in producing the social event in question.

Such dynamic assessment is never certain or complete. Therefore, no causal assessment can ever be considered totally proved and unquestionable. Since social life is dynamic, causal attribution must be too. MacIver believed that his orientation to causation would involve some major shifts in perspective for most sociologists. However, it would result in a more realistic if less rigorous definition of causal relations among variables. It should be noted in conclusion that MacIver's arguments fell on deaf ears. The retreat from causation, which MacIver described, continued consistently after the publication of his book.

369

THE EXPERIMENTAL METHOD IN SOCIOLOGY

The experimental method[7] has long been recognized in science as the most important single method by which causation may be attributed. Of course, some sciences like astronomy are not able to use such a method. However, it has proved its significance in a wide variety of scientific disciplines over many years. Generally it may be said that those disciplines which have been able to use the experimental method have made the most significant advances and are generally regarded as the "most scientific" or most rigorous.

In the social sciences, the most appropriate area for the use of experimental methods is probably social psychology. What has become known as "small group" research has made extensive use of experimental technique, with notable success. Frequently such studies are done under laboratory conditions in which the researcher is able to control extraneous variables. Such experiments necessarily deal with only a small number of subjects, which limits the questions which may be investigated using this method. Generally, perceptual, attitudinal and learning behavior have been the subjects of investigation, although a great many different problems have been attacked with this method. Rarely is it possible to make conclusions about the workings of societal institutions and other large-scale structures. However, the formation of group norms, the effectiveness of institutionalized styles of leadership, the productivity of workers under varying conditions, and many other subjects have been studied fruitfully using the experimental method.

As we saw previously, it is debatable to what extent findings from small-group research may be generalized to larger structures. However, the ability of small-group research to use the experimental technique has given it widespread support. If anything, the utilization of experimental method in social psychology has increased in recent years. It is increasingly being used on a wider variety of problems, and is being used with more sophistication than ever before. Some of the most competent and rigorous studies in the social sciences have been made in this area. The widespread use of the technique has contributed to causal assessment, and experimentalists are some of the most ardent advocates of the causal model.

370

CAUSAL IMPLICATIONS OF SURVEY RESEARCH

Much survey research includes the implicit assumption that causal relations operate in social life. When sociological researchers have established a correlation between two variables, they frequently make assumptions as to the causal connection between these two. Almost invariably this is done without accompanying attempts to rigorously isolate causal connections or presumed causes from other possible causes. It may, therefore, be concluded that survey researchers almost invariably take a causal orientation.

Causal implications in survey research are by no means invalid. Most frequently, especially in modern public opinion polling, the attitudes or behavior to be studied are correlated with so-called "social background" or "face-sheet" variables. These include age, sex, socioeconomic status, urban-rural residence, race, religion, nationality, and many others. As we noted previously, a cause by definition precedes the effect in point of time, and produces the effect rather than vice versa. The "time" and "manipulability" criteria are thus crucial to establishing causal connections.[8] In the case of social background variables, it is relatively easy to demonstrate that they occur in point of time prior to the particular attitudes or behavior being investigated. In addition, they are less manipulable than these attitudes and behaviors. If age and political conservatism are correlated, it is relatively easy to argue that age may be a cause of conservatism, whereas the argument that political conservatism causes a person to become aged is absurd. Social background variables generally include ascribed statuses which are not subject to influence by changes of attitude or behavior. It therefore makes sense to survey researchers to assume that these social background variables operate as causes of the attitudes and behaviors being investigated.

The conspicuous weakness of pollsters is in investigating the mechanisms by which social background variables may produce a given effect. How, for example, does increasing age produce political conservatism? It does not seem sufficient to make such an attribution without more investigation than the typical correlational study. Questionnaires and interviews seldom include the kinds of data which allow

371

extensive investigations of causal connections. Causation is attributed by default, in a sense. This perhaps explains why survey researchers so frequently imply causation and so infrequently utilize the language of causation. Words like "independent" and "dependent" variable, "determines," "produces," and "brings about" replace the more rigorous language of causation. One of the major weaknesses of survey research is its inability to face squarely the issue of causation. Since survey research is the dominant methodology of sociology, this weakness pervades much of sociology. It may be concluded, therefore, that most of sociological research carries implicit assumptions of causation while explicitly avoiding both the language of causation and the much more difficult research processes which would enable causal connections to be studied more directly.

STATISTICAL METHODS FOR STUDYING CAUSATION

The notable exception to the above conclusions was Hubert M. Blalock's monograph <u>Causal Inferences in Nonexperimental Research</u>,[9] which went a long way toward bringing the causal implications of survey research to the fore. Blalock assumed the causal orientation was valid, and sought to explicate the statistical and methodological implications of causation in order to enable survey researchers to more clearly study causal relations. He argued that causation is assumed by the very notion of science. However, causal assertions are theoretical in nature. Empirical research never "proves" causation, but only establishes "covariations and temporal sequences."[10] Blalock did not believe it necessary to make the assumption that causal relations are found "in reality." Rather, causal assumptions enable the theorist to explain and predict events in social life. Causation should be judged by its fruitfulness rather than by any standards of "reality." Blalock asserted that causal language is more restrictive than mathematical language. The investigator must go beyond the conclusions which can be made on the basis of mathematical inferences. After making a number of simplifying assumptions, Blalock discussed the methodological and statistical operations which are necessary to make causal inferences from survey data. These involve the kinds of statistical comparisons which may be made, the nature of the statistical considerations to be taken into account (e.g., looking at the slope of regression rather than at the correlation coefficient), eliminating measurement errors, statistically sorting out various confounding influences that may disturb the causal connection, and many more.

The methodology which Blalock advocates is rigorous and therefore very difficult to put into practice. There is no doubt, however, that it increased the interest of survey researches in the causal implications of their data. It forced many to face more squarely the problems of making causal attributions from survey data, and provided a notable advance in the statistical techniques available for establishing causal connections.

In this regard, we should mention briefly the development of path analysis in sociological statistics. Path analysis seeks to demonstrate through correlational analysis the causal conjunctions among a set of interrelated variables. It traces the path of causation from one variable to another. The initial use of this type of analysis was found in Blau and Dunca's study of occupational mobility in the United States. Their book, The American Occupational Structure,[11] traced the causal connections which lead from Father's occupation and education to Respondent's education and first job to the final effect--Respondent's current occupation. The significance of this research monograph lies both in its obvious and significant contributions to statistical methodology and in its substantive contributions to the analysis of social stratification in the United States.

To sum up this section, we may say that the causal orientation in sociology, after a period of neglect, seems to be making a comeback. With the continuing work of the experimentalists and survey researchers, and with more sophisticated techniques available to make judgments about causal connections from data, the causal orientation in sociological research is receiving renewed interest and vigor. It should be noted, however, that sociologists still have a long way to go before specific causal connections can be empirically verified with a high degree of confidence and acceptability to the profession. The causal orientation remains a plausible orientation with much future promise. There is not yet agreement, however, on specific causal connections among sociological data which would allow one to conclude that this promise has been fulfilled.

THE DEVELOPMENT OF THE SYSTEMS ORIENTATION
IN CONTEMPORARY SOCIOLOGY

We now turn to a discussion of the development of the systems orientation as an alternative orientation in sociological theory. As we have alluded previously, the systems orientation, especially the functionalist orientation, was predominant during the 1940s and 1950s in sociology. Pitirim Sorokin and Talcott Parsons, the preeminent theorists of that period, were both proponents of this orientation. Other prominent theorists, including Robert Merton and George Homans, also were identified as systems theorists, although they did not follow this orientation as consistently as the former two.

MEANINGFUL-CAUSAL SYSTEMS: SOROKIN

Sorokin's influence upon sociological theory was significant for a time, but declined rapidly. Like Parsons, the most significant aspect of Sorokin's theoretical orientation was his combination of subjectivism and the systems orientation. Sorokin's perspective was complicated, however, by his use of both the terms "causal" and "systems" in a given conceptual phrase.

Sorokin distinguished between "congeries" and "systems." Congeries are composed of numerous components or elements which have some physical adjacency but no definite unity or relationship. If all the parts of an automobile were piled up in an unassembled form, they would represent a congeries. A system, in contrast, is composed of a number of components which have a definite causal unity. The components are related to each other. Mutual dependence characterizes these relationships. The distinguishing characteristic of a system, according to Sorokin, is interdependence.

Sorokin took pains to distinguish a cultural system from the physical systems studied by the natural scientists. Cultural systems are characterized by the influence of subjective "meaning" upon the relationships among the parts. Taking as an example Harvard University, Sorokin argued that it is meaning which ties together the books, buildings, brooms, fossils, and scalpels into a system which has cultural relevance.[12]

374

Because of this fact, sociocultural systems are not characterized by the "pure" causal relations among physical objects described by the physical sciences. Cultural systems exhibit "meaningful-causal" relations. That is, it is subjective meaning which exerts causal significance in tying the units of cultural system together "in a meaningful way." If one seeks for causes among sociocultural phenomena, he must become acquainted with the influence of ideas upon people's actions.

Sorokin was not clear, however, on his meaning of "cause." He used the term frequently, but almost always in conjunction with the term "system." Further, he specifically argued in favor of an interdependent model of social reality and against a multiple- or single-causal model.[13] This is even more confusing since at the time Sorokin was writing, the cause vs. systems issue was being heatedly debated at Harvard University by the Pareto circle, and the two were thought of as alternative theoretical orientations. One can only surmise that Sorokin's intent was to show that the issue is a false one, and that both the causal and systems orientations can validly be included in the same theory. Without addressing himself directly to this subject, however, Sorokin has bequeathed us too many ambiguities to enable us to gain a clear perspective on his intentions. We can only note that Sorokin himself did not make a clear distinction between cause and system, but implied that both orientations can be synthesized into a single theory. Perhaps this legacy is the most important of Sorokin's contributions to this issue.

THE SOCIAL SYSTEM: PARSONS

Certainly the most important systems theorist in recent sociology was Talcott Parsons. Parsons's functional and systems orientation, closely related to each other, dominated sociological theory in the United States from the 1930s to the 1970s. It was only partially due to pomposity that in several articles summarizing the current state of sociological theory, Parsons chose to discuss only his own thinking on a variety of subjects, ignoring theoretical works by other authors.

In Parsons's early work, especially The Structure of Social Action,[14] the systems orientation was almost totally undeveloped. Even in his discussion of Pareto,

Parsons focused primarily on Pareto's subjectivist orientation rather than on his systems orientation. Parsons's systems orientation came to the fore in his major writings of the 1950s, especially The Social System and Toward a General Theory of Action.[15] Even in these works, however, Parsons took the concepts of system and equilibrium for granted, rather than detailing the meaning which these concepts had for him and their implications for the development of sociological theory.

In those few passages in which Parsons explicitly addressed himself to the meaning of "system," the essence of the concept for Parsons seemed to be interdependence. Interdependence in a social system is brought about chiefly by interaction of the individual members of the group. Interdependence also necessitates integration for Parsons, since he believed that the parts of the system must be brought into compatibility with each other.[16]

Parsons nowhere defined the term "equilibrium" although throughout his works there was an assumption that equilibrating tendencies operate in all social systems. According to him, if changes are introduced externally to the system, the system operates to either (1) restore the previous state, or (2) make adjustments in the units of the system until a new equilibrium is reached.[17] One of the important functional requirements of every social system, according to Parsons, is "boundary maintenance." Boundaries are maintained partly through control of changes within the system and partly through adjustment to the external environment.[18]

Parsons never came to grips in his writings with the causation vs. systems issue. In his article "Cause and Effect in Sociology,"[19] certainly one of the landmarks of obscurantism in sociological theory, he drew attention in one sentence to the issue, then addressed himself to a discussion of a variety of subjects having almost no relationships to causation. In the published question and answers which followed his lecture on this subject, Parsons admitted that causation was not a part of his vocabulary.[20] He eluded the question of why his own systems approach was more fruitful than a causal orientation.

Parsons's major contribution to the systems orientation was the description, often exceedingly

insightful, or the mutual relationships among a great
variety of social phenomena. The relationship of role
definitions to socialization, of socialization to
deviant behavior, of deviant behavior to social change,
etc., are only examples of the subjects he addressed.
He generally drew upon only his own insight and
observation rather than upon empirical sociological
research. Yet his analyses have significance precisely
because of Parsons's attempts (often successful) to
synthesize many different observations in a variety of
subject matter areas within a single theoretical
system.

INTERNAL AND EXTERNAL SYSTEMS: HOMANS

Another significant contribution to the
development of the contemporary systems orientation was
George C. Homans's book, The Human Group,[21] published
in 1950. Homans's writing style was remarkably facile
for a sociologist. This and the significance of
Homans's ideas made the book one of the most
influential in its time. It is important to note,
here, that Homans later abandoned his systems approach
for a positivist and causal orientation. Let us first
discuss his contributions to systems theory, then turn
to the later changes in theoretical orientation.

In The Human Group, Homans developed a theory of
social behavior applicable primarily to small-scale
groups. He utilized five empirical studies, including
the Roethlisberger and Dickson Western Electric studies
and Whyte's Street Corner Society, as the basis for
inductive development of theoretical propositions.
Being critical of attempts to develop general theories
with no grounding on facts, Homans carefully built his
own theory on the empirical generalizations derived
from these five studies. This is one of the notable
features of Homans's work, in contrast to such
theorists as Parsons.

Homans defined three variables--sentiment,
activity and interaction--which form the core concepts
of his analysis.[22] In addition, he added a number of
others, including norms, rank conflict, etc. The
essence of Homans's method was to develop empirically
grounded propositions which state the mutually
dependent relations among his important variables.
Throughout, Homans asserted that his propositions are
"reversible." For example, as the interaction between
two people increases, they tend to develop more

377

positive sentiments toward each other. Conversely, if the frequency of interaction decreases, positive sentiments will also be reduced. A change in sentiment, however, will also introduce a change in interaction: if there is an increase in positive sentiment between two people, they will tend to interact more frequently. The variables which comprise the system, according to Homans, are mutually dependent. They vary together, so that any change in one provokes a change in all others, and vice versa. Homans expressed his frustration in the inability to express all relationships among all variables in a system at the same time.[23] Lacking a system of differential equations which would accomplish this, Homans said that one must discuss in turn each relationship among components in the system, finally arriving at a comprehensive statement of the nature of the system.

A major element of Homans's book was his distinction between what he called the "external" system and the "internal" system. The external system of a social group includes those elements which are most directly related to the external environment, and which allow the group to persist in its environment.[24] The system possesses a boundary--an imaginary and arbitrary theoretical designation for the benefit of the analyst--which distinguishes the group from its environment.[25] The concept of external system allowed Homans to study the interchanges between the system and this environment.

The internal system includes those theoretically isolated components of the system which encompass the sentiments of the members of group and the internal relations which are "elaborated" within the group. These are over and above those sentiments, activities and interactions necessary in order for the group to adapt to its external environment. Homans recognized that this distinction was not altogether satisfactory, and did not hold consistently to the distinction between the two.

Perhaps one of the distinguishing features of Homans's work was his clear discussion of the concepts of "feedback" and "equilibrium." Using the analogy of an electrical circuit, Homans argued that feedback is a universal feature of social systems. Any changes or forces present in one system--say the external system--are fed back into the other system, as

378

electrical power may be fed back to an earlier point in an electrical circuit.[26] The reciprocal development of interaction and positive sentiment outside the job (in the internal system) may increase the efficiency of production on the job (in the external system).

Homans's discussion of equilibrium is found in his chapter on Social Control.[27] He identified the social control mechanisms of a group as the principal means by which equilibrium is attained. Homans avoided the distinction between stable and dynamic equilibrium. He never implies that a system is in such perfect equilibrium that it is always able to return to its original state. Even in the physical sciences, according to Homans, the correct meaning of equilibrium encompasses the notion of change. For Homans, a system is in a state of equilibrium when any change introduced into the system or any of its parts results in a change within the system to minimize the change. That is, the various components of the system react to the intrusive change in such a way that the magnitude of the change is minimized. This assumes that some changes will have to take place in many if not all of the components of the system, but that the system as a whole will remain as closely as possible to its original state.

For equilibrium to be maintained, it is necessary that there be present in the system some mechanisms which will operate to minimize changes within the system. In a social system, the mechanism of equilibrium is social control, according to Homans. Norms and positive sanctions, supported by the processes of socialization and economic distribution, serve to minimize any deviation by any member of the group. If deviation occurs, negative sanctions are applied to bring the deviant back to conformity again.

One of Homans's important contributions was in identifying this equilibrium-maintaining mechanism, whereas many systems theorists assume that such a mechanism exists without clearly identifying it. For Homans, there was nothing "naturalistic" or "deterministic" in the concept of equilibrium. A system does not "seek" equilibrium.[28] The degree to which the equilibrium-maintaining mechanism operates is different in each group. But no group can long exist without some minimum level of social control. Just as each group must develop some degree of interdependence among its component parts in order to survive in its environment, so it must also maintain some degree of equilibrium.

Homans's clearly worked out systems orientation is one of the most important in all sociological literature. It is therefore all the more notable that in his later work, especially Social Behavior: Its Elementary Forms and The Nature of Social Science,[29] he abandoned the systems orientation for a rigorous experimental and causal orientation grounded on behavioristic psychology. Homans's most recent point of view is that empirical generalizations should be stated in correlational form. These generalizations should be incorporated into an inductively formulated system of propositions which possess hypothetico-deductive form. While the generalizations are stated in correlational form, the causal direction of these generalizations is clearly implied in both the experimental methodology used to arrive at them, and in the theoretical implications of the form of deductive theory utilized. Finally, Homans claimed that all social science is a single broad discipline, and that all separate disciplines are only parts of this unity. Because of this, Homans asserted that the empirical generalizations of sociology are ultimately derivable from the theoretical propositions of behavioristic psychology. This position is rarely found among sociologists, and is more fully discussed in Chapter Fifteen.

The influence of Homans's writings has been extensive and significant, and he must be ranked as one of the foremost sociological theorists in the contemporary period.

CYBERNETICS AND THE FEEDBACK CYCLE

Cybernetics as a separate scientific discipline has had a remarkable development. The term, "cybernetics" was coined by Norbert Wiener, and first appeared in a book by the same title published in 1948.[30] According to Wiener, cybernetics covers the areas of communication and control in both machines and animals. It is based on the assertion that in the physical, biological, and social worlds there exist complex systems which possess feedback mechanisms. This assertion has been utilized on a wide range of applications, especially computers and learning machines, with astounding results.

Many physical mechanisms possess feedback mechanisms which influence their operation. A simple example is the heating system linked to a thermostat. The thermostat acts as a sensor to measure the heat present in the house. In a sense, it measures the actual behavior of the heating system. The thermostat contains an automatic mechanism to shut off the heat when it becomes excessive and turn it on again when it drops again. Effective thermostats also control wide swings in temperatures which might be expected from constantly switching on and off of the heating system.

Wiener asserted that many such feedback mechanisms exist in both animals and machines. He did extensive clinical research on the neuro-muscular system of the cat to demonstrate the existence of a complicated "proprioceptive" system by which the brain of the cat was notified of the position and tension of numerous muscles within the leg. Such feedback systems are extensively found in all kinds of organisms. Likewise, Wiener's research on antiaircraft guns during the Second World War gave him much insight and understanding of feedback systems in machines, especially those involving radar sensing devices and electronic computing devices.

Since this pioneering monograph by Wiener, the field of cybernetics has grown to encompass investigations in many areas.[31] Its most important contemporary applications have been in computers, learning machines, and military applications. Extremely complex feedback mechanisms have been built into such machines, allowing a machine to perform many activities previously performed only by human beings. This has led Wiener and many others to the assertion that the human brain operates much like an extremely sophisticated computer, and that the human operations of the brain can be "simulated" on a computer.

Cybernetics has had a significant influence upon "information theory." Indeed, some believe the two terms to be identical. Clinical research on a variety of psychological and physiological problems of humans has been fostered by cybernetics. Much of this research is so new that is has not yet been properly evaluated. But many possess the belief that the behavior of individuals follows the principles of information and feedback developed by cybernetics. Further research into the feedback mechanisms of the human brain, therefore, may bring important breakthroughs in the understanding of human behavior.

Cybernetics provides an important theoretical and empirical foundation for modern systems theory in sociology. It was an essential prerequisite to the development of the non-Parsonian systems theory most frequently identified with the name of Walter Buckley.

"MODERN" SYSTEMS THEORY: BUCKLEY

Walter Buckley became the chief champion of a "modern" systems theory in sociology based on cybernetics and the "general systems" orientation. His book, Sociology and Modern Systems Theory,[32] published in 1967, had wide influence, but this influence has quickly waned.[33] Buckley argued that sociology has tended to incorporate some of the terminology of cybernetics while being almost unaffected by the theoretical ideas behind this terminology.[34]

Sociological theory, according to Buckley, is still dependent upon the older mechanistic and organismic theories of Sorokin, Parsons, and Homans. The mechanical model of a system assumes that the system has definite boundaries and stable relations among components of the system.[35] Further, it possesses a mechanism to restore the system to its initial state if change is extruded into the system. It is accompanied by the assumption that the relationships among components can "be measured and expressed in terms of laws" like those of mechanics.[36] Equilibrium involves the assumptions (1) that the system will return to the original state whenever disturbed, (2) change always originates external to the system, and (3) there are limits, to equilibrium such that if the change introduced is of too great a magnitude, the system is destroyed.[37]

The organic model of a system also stresses the importance of mutual dependence of parts. The system, however, is characterized by orderly change, as in the growth of the organism. Homeostasis (the term coined by Cannon) replaces equilibrium as the term to describe the process by which stability and adaptability of the system is maintained.[38] Buckley notes that organisms are "open" in that they are frequently subject to external changes, and "adaptive" in that they are constantly making internal changes to adjust to external conditions. Organic systems are

382

self-regulating. For example, the human body possesses processes by which the blood sugar level is stabilized. The most notable feature of organisms is their ability to maintain homeostasis in the face of instability of the environment and of the components of the system itself.

Buckley rejected both of these models for a more modern systems model based upon cybernetics. How does this model differ from the mechanical and organic models? Buckley specified a number of different ways. First, a social system (and therefore the cybernetic system developed to explain it) is subject to a greater degree of change than mechanical or organic systems. Further, this change is not necessarily in a given direction, as is the maturation of the human body. Second, change can be endogenous as well as exogenous.[39] Buckley wrote of the "morphogenetic process"[40] by which changes originate within the system. Third, social systems are able to undergo internal restructuring to a much greater degree than organic systems.[41] This involves the assertion that emergent properties are much more likely to be found in social than in organic systems.[42] Fourth, change is assumed to be normal and beneficial, rather than abnormal and harmful.[43] Fifth, modern systems theory places emphasis upon "relations" rather than "entities."[44] The dynamic properties of the system, the processes contained therein, and the relations among units are more important than the components themselves. Sixth, the social system is assumed to be self-directing rather than self-maintaining.[45] In organic systems, homeostasis is accomplished through the workings of autonomous mechanisms not subject to conscious direction. Social systems to which modern systems theory is applicable are goal-directed--subject to conscious change in directions prescribed by those in the "control center." In sum, modern social systems are characterized by "emergence, purpose or goal-seeking, self-regulation, adaptation, and the like."[46]

Perhaps the most questionable aspect of Buckley's argument was his dismissal of the need to define his use of the term system as merely a "sport."[47] It is unclear why the term system has been maintained by the cyberneticists and general systems theorists in the face of the major changes they have introduced in its use. It seems obvious that communication would be improved if the term were kept for the older connotations encompassing the notions of equilibrium and homeostasis, and that a new term be utilized to describe the kinds of conditions and relations found in social life. Obviously one purpose in keeping the term system is to enable a theoretical comparison of many kinds of phenomena across the lines of scientific disciplines, as the general systems theorists hope to do.

According to Buckley, the links between units of a social system are "information links" by which communication is achieved. The social system is generally goal-directed.[48] Elaborate feedback mechanisms are found in society to measure the degree to which goals are being achieved. The regulatory mechanisms of society, to which Buckley gave great attention, utilize power and sanctions to move the social system along the paths toward the goals which those in authority have selected.

Buckley's discussion of causality was especially crucial.[49] He accepted the causal orientation and causal terminology as legitimate for sociological purposes. However, he argued that the simplistic notions of causation assumed by most sociologists, and the inadequate correlational methodology utilized by them, should be replaced. He discussed (1) the possibility of "step-function" rather than incremental relations among variables, (2) the existence of "buffer mechanisms" which prevent causes from producing known effects, and (3) the importance of establishing causal priority among variables rather than assuming complete reciprocity as some of the important questions not yet answered by sociologists. Traditional causal analysis must be replaced by a more sophisticated methodology based on the analysis of "mutual interaction," complex feedback of causes and effects, and emergence. The kind of systems methodology he hoped would be developed would more clearly identify complex causes, possible conditions and consequences, mutual interaction, and emergence.[50]

To his credit, Buckley included an extensive criticism of the cybernetic systems model as it applies to social systems. To summarize, these criticisms involve questions as to (1) whether social systems are goal-directed, (2) whether any social system has a "control center," (3) the degree to which the complicated nature of the feedback process in the social system is similar to that of, say, an

384

antiaircraft gun, (4) the implications of the long time-lag between inputs and outputs in a social system, (5) whether the social system makes an "automatic and unfailing transformation of decisions into final actions,"[51] and (6) the degree to which the social system can handle the difficulties of testing, correcting, and over-correcting of feedback information.

Buckley recognized the complexity of the social system and the difficulties in applying any theoretical model to it. Yet he retained his confidence that the cybernetic systems model fits social reality more fully than any other theoretical model. He recognized that many of the theoretical problems of the cybernetic systems model were yet to be explored, and that his work represented only an incomplete first attempt to explore the application of the model to social life.

CONCLUSION

Perhaps it is not time yet to reach closure on the causation vs. system issue. From both a philosophical and sociological perspective, causation is a thorny issue with many difficult theoretical problems. Likewise, the systems approach, especially its simpler manifestations in what Buckley called the mechanical and organic models, have many weaknesses. What shall it be? Are social relations causal or reciprocal?

Our answer must be a tentative one. We do not see the two models as mutually exclusive. Interdependence and causality can both be used within the same theoretical framework. This is especially true if we are more careful in specifying the time dimension in our studies. What appears to be a reciprocal influence in which two variables mutually influence each other may on closer examination be a series of mutual influences over time in which one variable influences the other, and an instant later the second variable influences or "works back on" the first. This reduces reciprocity to a number of relatively small causal influences which may be difficult to measure but certainly can be identified at the abstract level.

We believe most sociologists have not gone far enough in their research to establish causal connections between the variables they are studying. We echo Durkheim's criticism that most sociologists end their work prematurely, after establishing correlations

385

but before the further exploration of the causal connections behind these correlations.

Certainly there is much interdependence in social life, but much of this interdependence can be treated within a causal framework. Causal analysis is difficult and time consuming, but the theoretical payoff is exceedingly valuable. While our conclusion must still be tentative, we believe that the causal model is applicable to more of the data of social life than in the systems model, and that pursuing causal connections more energetically will provide a richer harvest for sociological research and theory.

Many social causes lie within the individual and are the result of human initiative. It is fruitful to recognize that these subjective phenomena tend to become objectified in social structures. It is also fruitful in many cases to approach the study of social phenomena from the group rather than the individual perspective. But ultimately, we believe it is individuals, not groups, who act. Fundamentally and essentially, individual human actions of a causal nature flowing from subjective choices of individual actors are the stuff from which the fabric of social life is woven.

FOOTNOTES

[1]Robert M. MacIver, Social Causation (Boston: Ginn), 1942.

[2]Ibid., pp. 23-34.

[3]Ibid., pp. 57-61.

[4]Ibid., p. 41.

[5]Ibid., pp. 5-10.

[6]Ibid., pp. 291-350.

[7]Samuel A. Stouffer, "Some Observations on Study Design," American Journal of Sociology, 55 (January 1950), pp. 355-361.

[8]Morris Rosenberg, The Logic of Survey Analysis (New York: Basic Books), 1968, p. 11.

[9]Hubert M. Blalock, Jr., Causal Inferences in Nonexperimental Research (Chapel Hill: University of North Carolina Press), 1961.

[10]Ibid., p. 172.

[11]Peter M. Blau and Otis Dudley Duncan, The American Occupational Structure (New York: Wiley), 1967.

[12]Pitirim A. Sorokin, Social and Cultural Dynamics, 4 vols. (New York: American Books), 1937-1941 vol. 4, pp. 3-44; and Pitirim A. Sorokin, Society, Culture and Personality: Their Structure and Dynamics (New York: Cooper Square Publishers), 1962, pp. 537-554.

[13]Pitirim A. Sorokin, Sociocultural Causality, Space, Time (Durham: Duke University Press), 1943, p. 11.

[14]Talcott Parsons, The Structure of Social Action (New York: McGraw-Hill), 1937. See Wsevolod W. Isajiw, Causation and Functionalism in Sociology (London: Routledge & Kegan Paul), 1968 for an excellent discussion of the causal implications of functionalism.

[15]Talcott Parsons, The Social System (Glencoe: Free Press), 1951; and Talcott Parsons and Edward A. Shils, editors, Toward a General Theory of Action (Cambridge: Harvard University Press), 1951.

[16]Toward A General Theory of Action, p. 107.

[17]Ibid., pp. 107-108.

[18]Ibid., p. 108.

[19]Talcott Parsons, "Cause and Effect in Sociology," in Daniel Lerner, editor, Cause and Effect (New York: Free Press), 1965, pp. 51-73.

[20]Ibid., pp. 67-68.

[21]George C. Homans, The Human Group (New York: Harcourt), 1950.

[22]Ibid., pp. 34-40.

[23]Ibid., pp. 9-10.

[24]Ibid., p. 90.

[25]Ibid., p. 86.

[26]Ibid., p. 153.

[27]Ibid., p. 301-308. See especially pp. 302-304.

[28]Ibid., p. 305.

[29]George C. Homans, Social Behavior: Its Elementary Forms (New York: Harcourt), 1961, and The Nature of Social Science (New York: Harcourt), 1967.

[30]Norbert Wiener, Cybernetics: Or Control and Communication in the Animal and the Machine, 2nd Edition, (New York: Wiley), 1961. See also Norbert Wiener, The Human Use of Human Beings: Cybernetics and Society (Boston: Houghton Mifflin), 1950; Magorah Maruyama, "Mutual Causality in General Systems," in John H. Milsum, editor, Positive Feedback: A General Systems Approach to Positive/Negative Feedback and Mutual Causality (Oxford: Pergamon Press), 1968, pp. 80-100; and Robert Lilienfeld, The Rise of Systems Theory (New York: Wiley), 1978.

[31]For a sampling of the literature, see the following: Robert Boguslaw, The New Utopians (Englewood Cliffs, N.J.: Prentice-Hall), 1965; C. West Churchman, The Systems Approach (New York: Delacorte Press), 1968; Robert H. Kupperman, Mathematical Foundations of Systems Analysis (Reading, Mass.: Addison-Wesley), 1969; Oscar R. Lange, Wholes and Parts (New York: Pergamon Press), 1965; David I. Cleland and William R. King, editors, Systems, Organizations, Analysis, Management (New York: McGraw-Hill), 1969; Otto J. M. Smith, Feedback Control Systems (New York: McGraw-Hill), 1958; and American Society for Cybernetics, Purposive Systems (New York: Spartan Books), 1968.

[32]Walter Buckley, Sociology and Modern Systems Theory (Englewood Cliffs, N.J.: Prentice-Hall), 1967.

[33]George Ritzer, Sociological Theory (New York: Knopf), 1983, pp. 397-401.

[34]Ibid., pp. 8-36.

[35]Ibid., pp. 8-11.

[36]Ibid., p. 8.

[37]Ibid., p. 56.

[38]Ibid., pp. 11-17, and Walter B. Cannon, The Wisdom of the Body (New York: Norton), 1932.

[39]Buckley, Op. cit., p. 10.

[40]Ibid., p. 58.

[41]Ibid., pp. 14-15.

[42]Ibid., p. 42.

[43]Ibid., p. 10.

[44]Ibid., p. 39.

[45]Ibid., p. 163.

[46]Ibid., p. 79.

[47]Ibid., p. 41.

[48]Ibid., p. 69.

[49]Ibid., pp. 66-80.

[50]Ibid., p. 80.

[51]Ibid., p. 175.

SUBJECT INDEX

Abstraction, 261, 264, 324
Alienation, 221
Alternative Perspectives, 4
Anomie (see also Anomic Suicide), 195
Asceticism, 106

Behaviorism, 69-72, 79, 167, 293, 380
Bureaucracy, 111

Capitalism, 19, 97, 102
Catastrophe, 358
Causation, 303-342, 358, 362, 367-373, 384
    Axioms of, 368
    Cause vs. System Issue, 8
    Definition of, 307
    Interactive, 337
    Meaning of, 304
    Multiple, 247, 264, 311, 328, 339, 363
    Rejection of, 357
    Single, 309-316
    Social, 315
    Types of, 367
Change, 262, 266
Child-Rearing Practices, 186
Choice, 276, 279
Collective Conscience, 31-32
Collective Representations, 31-32
Communism, 19
Concomitant Variation, 317
Conflict Theory, 176
Culture Lag, 36
Cybernetics, 380

Definition of the Situation, 79, 155
Determinism, 8-9, 206, 219, 252, 263, 278, 296
Divide Et Impera, 62
Division of Labor, 36-39, 204
Dyad, 55-57
Dynamic Assessment, 369
Dynamic Equilibrium, 352, 355

Economic Determinism, 17, 357
Emergence 59, 63
Empathic Understanding, 90
Equilibrium, 351, 376, 378
Ethnocentrism, 127
Ethnomethodology, 176, 178, 252
Evolution, 229, 268

391

393

NAME INDEX

Abel, Theodore, 254
Almond, Gabriel, 27
Alpert, Harry, 209
Aron, Raymond, 235
Ayer, A.J., 84

Bales, Robert F., 293, 301
Bandura, Albert, 72
Barnes, Harry E., 114
Bendix, Reinhard, 11, 181
Berelson, Bernard, 28, 81, 86
Berger, Bennett, 176, 181
Bergmann, Gustav, 84
Blalock, Hubert M. Jr., 176, 372, 387
Blau, Peter M., 176, 178, 180, 301, 373, 387
Bloch, Joseph, 22, 27
Blumer, Herbert, 176, 246, 252
Bogardus, Emory, 81
Boguslaw, Robert, 388
Boskoff, Alvin, 11
Buckley, Walter, 382, 388
Burnham, James, 130
Burns, Emile, 27

Calvin, John, 104
Campbell, Donald T., 86, 255
Cannon, Walter B., 389
Caplow, Theodore, 67
Chomsky, Noam, 176, 178
Churchman, C. West, 388
Cicourel, Aaron, 177, 178, 180
Cleland, David I., 388
Coleman, James S., 27
Collins, Randall, 176, 302
Comte, Auguste, 29, 30, 47, 176, 211-218, 234, 239, 343
Cooley, Charles Horton, 133, 170, 176, 273, 284, 288
Coser, Lewis A., 11, 67, 176
Curtis, Charles P. Jr., 364

Dahendorf, Ralf, 176
De Coulanges, Fustel, 38
De George, Fenande M., 180
De George, Richard T., 180
Deutsch, Morton, 301
Duke, James T., 11, 12, 26, 28, 48, 67, 181
Duncan, Otis Dudley, 11, 373, 387
Dupre, Louis, 26

Durkheim, Emile, 29-48, 46, 114, 116, 176, 177,
    183-210, 208, 239, 259, 284, 288, 291, 292, 297,
    303-320, 321

Emerson, Richard M., 301
Engels, Friedrich, 13-28, 26, 176, 177, 218-225, 235

Feuerbach, Ludwig, 14, 26, 219
Finch, Henry A., 271, 341
Foote, Nelson J., 12
Freedman, Robert, 26
Freud, Sigmund, 2, 292

Garfinkel, Harold, 176, 177, 246, 252
Gaudet, Hazel, 28, 81, 86
Gerth, Hans, 117
Giddens, Anthony, 46, 177, 180
Giddings, Franklin, 199
Goffman, Erving, 176, 246
Goode, William J., 11
Gouldner, Alvin W., 26, 364
Gross, Llewellyn, 5, 11, 181

Habermas, Jurgen, 176
Hatt, Paul K., 11
Hegel, Georg, 14
Heisenberg, Werner, 251
Henderson, A. M., 271, 300
Henderson, Lawrence J., 353, 359, 364
Hollingshead, August B., 28
Homans, George C., 176, 291, 293, 301, 353, 364, 377,
    382, 387
Hook, Sidney, 235
Horowitz, Irving Louis, 11

Isajiw, Wsevolold W., 387

Janowitz, Morris, 172, 288
Jennings, Herbert S., 172
Jones, Robert Alun, 114

Kaplan, Abraham, 84
Kaufman, Arnold S., 84
Keller, Albert G., 131
Kelley, Harold H., 301
King, William R., 388
Kraft, Victor, 84
Kronus, Sidney, 114
Kupperman, Robert H., 388

Lachs, John, 235
Lange, Oscar R., 388
Lanternari, Vittorio, 28
Lazarsfeld, Paul F., 28, 81, 86
Lefebvre, Henri, 27
Lenin, V. I., 22, 27
Lerner, Daniel, 320
Levy-Strauss, Claude, 176, 178
Lilienfield, Robert, 388
Lippett, Ronald, 27
Lipset, Seymour Martin, 12, 27
Luckmann, Thomas, 176
Lukes, Steven, 46
Lundberg, George A., 72-80, 85, 176, 239, 254
Luther, Martin, 104

MacIver, Robert M., 176, 367-369, 386
Malinowski, Bronislaw, 2, 11, 176, 292
Martindale, Don, 115
Martineau, Harriet, 234
Maruyama, Magorah, 388
Marx, Karl, 13-28, 26, 109, 111, 114, 176, 177,
     218-225, 235, 357
Mayhew, Bruce, 298, 302
Mead, George Herbert, 71, 142, 171, 176, 274, 284, 288
Merton, Robert K., 1, 11, 170, 177, 180, 341, 365
Mills, C. Wright, 12, 26, 117, 176, 235
Milsum, John H., 388
Montesquieu, Charles, 306
Morris, Charles W., 142, 288
Mullins, Nicholas C., 180

Nowell-Smith, Patrick H., 320

Ogburn, William F., 36, 47

Pareto, Vilfredo, 123-131, 176, 292, 303-359, 364,
     375-376
Parsons, Talcott, 114, 176, 271, 291, 292, 300, 320,
     364, 374, 375, 382, 387
Payne, Robert, 26
Pearson, Karl, 84
Peck, R. F., 28
Piaget, Jean, 176
Pope, Liston, 28

Radcliffe-Brown, A. R., 176, 359-363, 365
Redlich, Frederick, 28
Rhea, Buford, 11
Rheinstein, Max, 116

Ritzer, George, 177, 180, 388
Rose, Arnold M., 3, 11
Rosenberg, Morris, 86, 386
Roth, Julius, 28
Rousseau, Jean Jacques, 306

Saint-Simon, Henri de, 35-36, 47
Saussure, Ferdinand de, 176
Schnore, Leo F., 11
Schutz, Alfred, 176
Schwartz, Richard D., 86, 255
Scott, John Finley, 180, 293, 301
Sechrest, Lee, 86, 255
Selvin, Hanan C., 47
Sensat, Julius Jr., 181
Shils, Edward A., 271, 300, 341
Simmel, Georg, 33, 46, 49-67, 176, 198
Skinner, B. F., 72, 176
Smelser, Neil, 12
Smith, Otto J. M., 388
Sorokin, Pitirim A., 176, 374, 382, 387
Spencer, Herbert, 30, 176, 199, 225-233, 236, 331-333,
    341, 343-353, 364
Steiner, Gary A., 28
Stouffer, Samuel A., 86, 386
Stryker, Sheldon, 176, 177, 180
Sumner, William Graham, 123-129, 130, 176

Thibaut, John W., 301
Thomas, Dorothy Swaine, 172, 342
Thomas, William Isaac, 85, 153, 172, 176, 281, 288,
    333, 341
Thurstone, L. L., 81
Tiryakian, Edward, 176
Tonnies, Ferdinand, 198
Truzzi, Marcello, 115
Tucker, Robert C., 26
Turner, Ralph, 176

Volkart, Edmund H., 172, 289, 341

Wagner, Helmut R., 12
Wallace, Walter L., 12
Ward, Lester Frank, 131, 176, 198, 268, 272
Watson, John B., 69-72, 84, 143, 176
Webb, Eugene, 86, 255
Weber, Max, 87-131, 176, 239, 257, 271, 291, 300,
    323-331, 341
White, Harrison C., 176, 178, 180
Wiener, Norbert, 380, 388

Williams, Robin, 6, 12
Wolff, Kurt H., 66, 322

Zetterberg, Hans, 254
Znaniecki, Florian, 172, 176, 337, 341